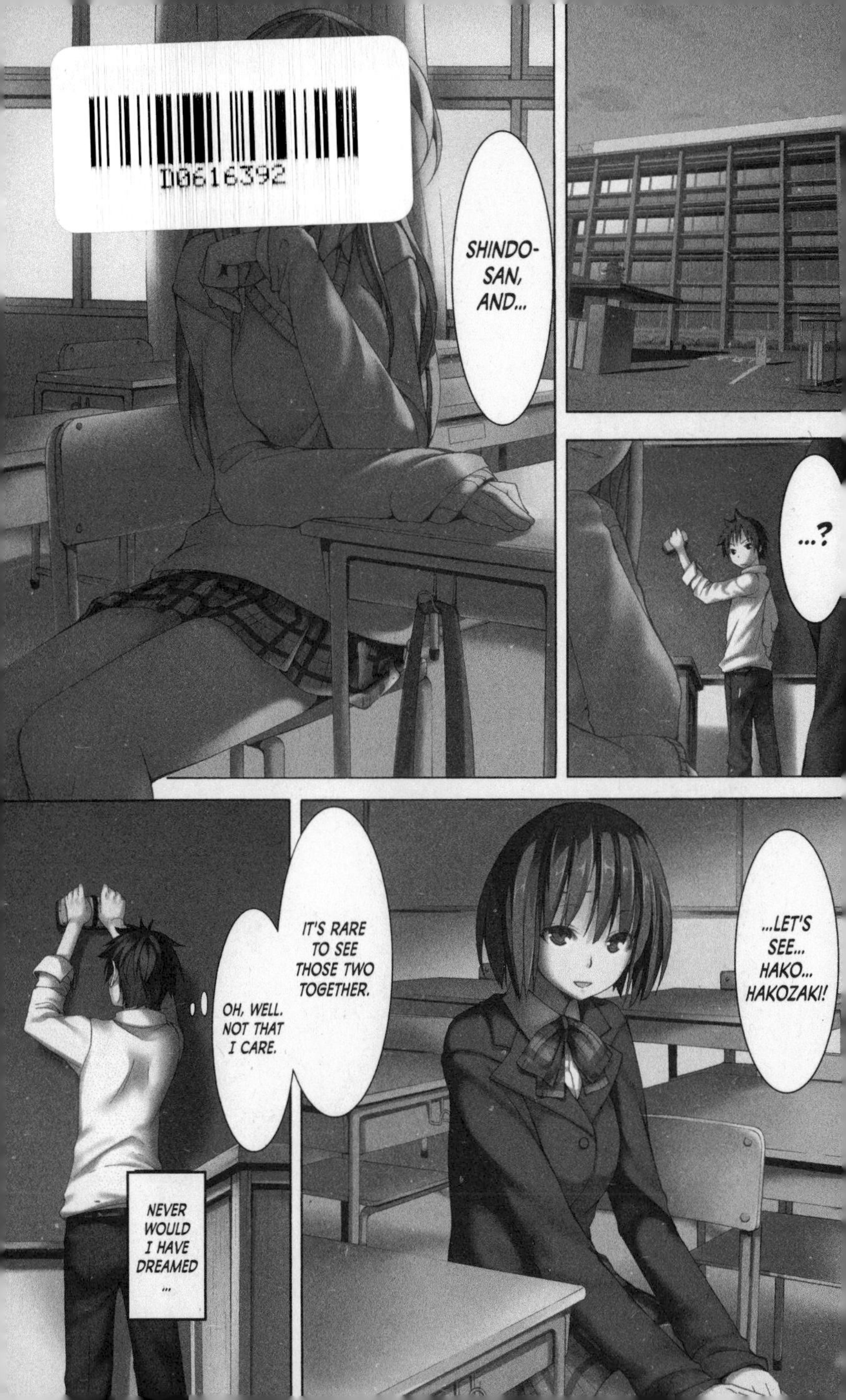
...?
SHINDO-SAN, AND...
...LET'S SEE... HAKO... HAKOZAKI!
IT'S RARE TO SEE THOSE TWO TOGETHER.
OH, WELL. NOT THAT I CARE.
NEVER WOULD I HAVE DREAMED ...

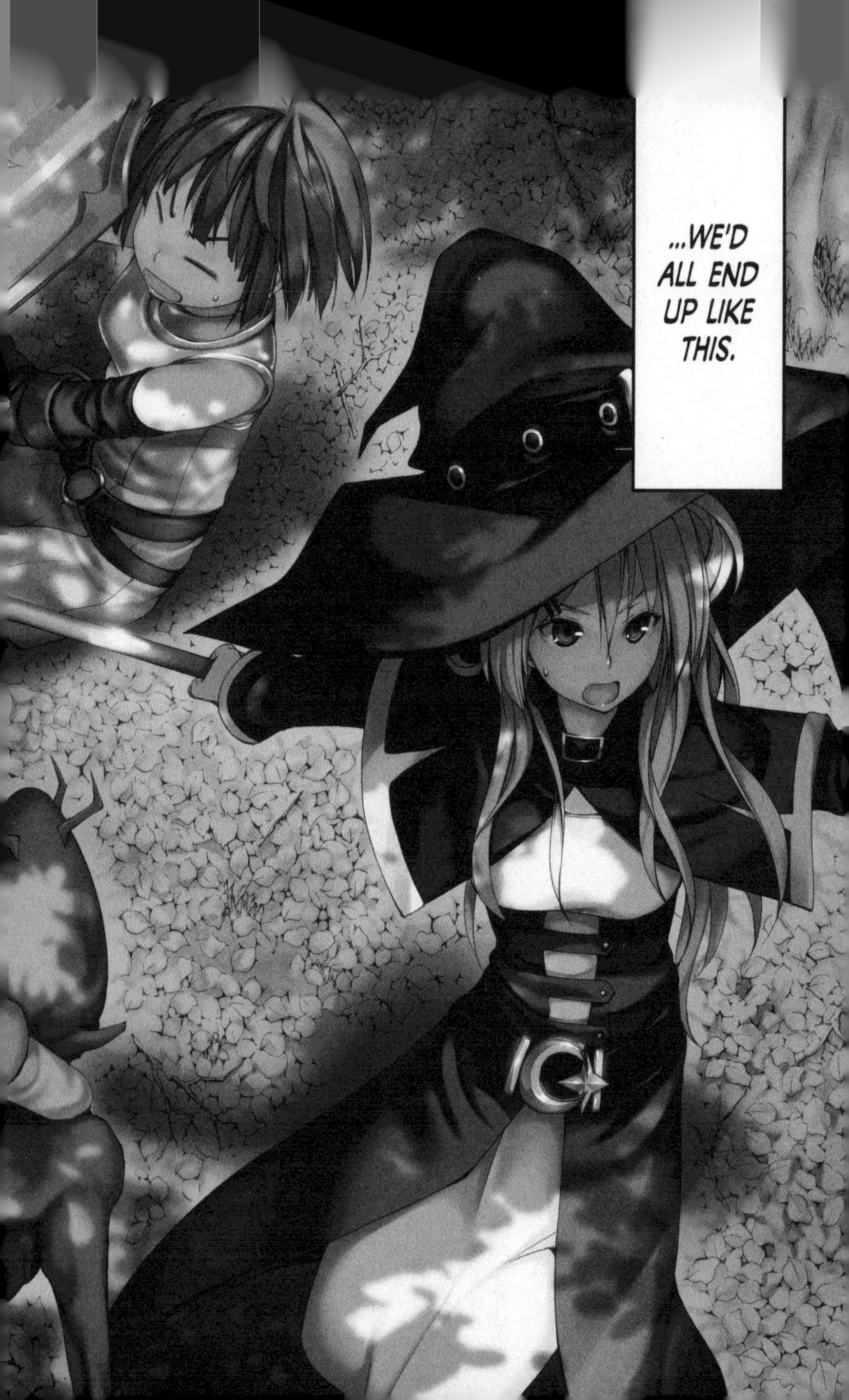
...WE'D ALL END UP LIKE THIS.

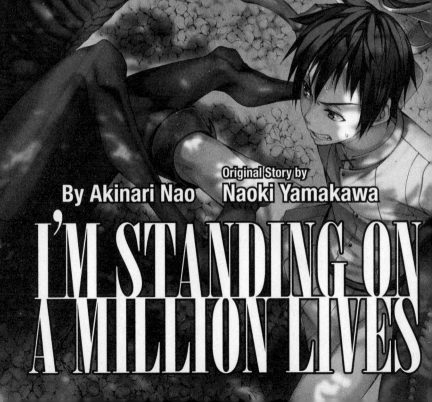

1

By Akinari Nao

Original Story by
Naoki Yamakawa

I'M STANDING ON
A MILLION LIVES

CONTENTS

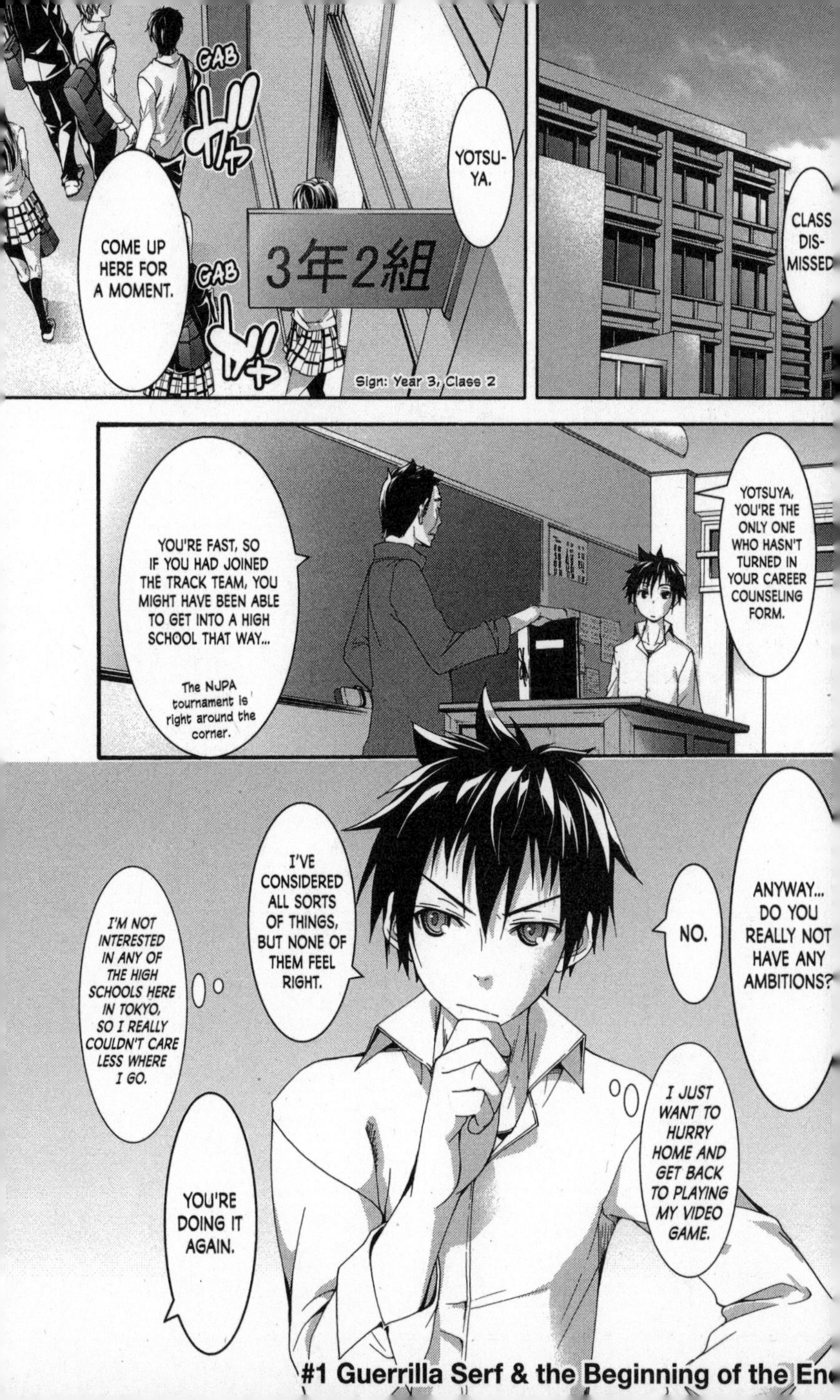
CLASS DIS-MISSED
YOTSU-YA.
GAB
COME UP HERE FOR A MOMENT.
GAB
Sign: Year 3, Class 2
3年2組
YOTSUYA, YOU'RE THE ONLY ONE WHO HASN'T TURNED IN YOUR CAREER COUNSELING FORM.
YOU'RE FAST, SO IF YOU HAD JOINED THE TRACK TEAM, YOU MIGHT HAVE BEEN ABLE TO GET INTO A HIGH SCHOOL THAT WAY...
The NJPA tournament is right around the corner.
ANYWAY... DO YOU REALLY NOT HAVE ANY AMBITIONS?
NO.
I'VE CONSIDERED ALL SORTS OF THINGS, BUT NONE OF THEM FEEL RIGHT.
I'M NOT INTERESTED IN ANY OF THE HIGH SCHOOLS HERE IN TOKYO, SO I REALLY COULDN'T CARE LESS WHERE I GO.
I JUST WANT TO HURRY HOME AND GET BACK TO PLAYING MY VIDEO GAME.
YOU'RE DOING IT AGAIN.
#1 Guerrilla Serf & the Beginning of the Ene

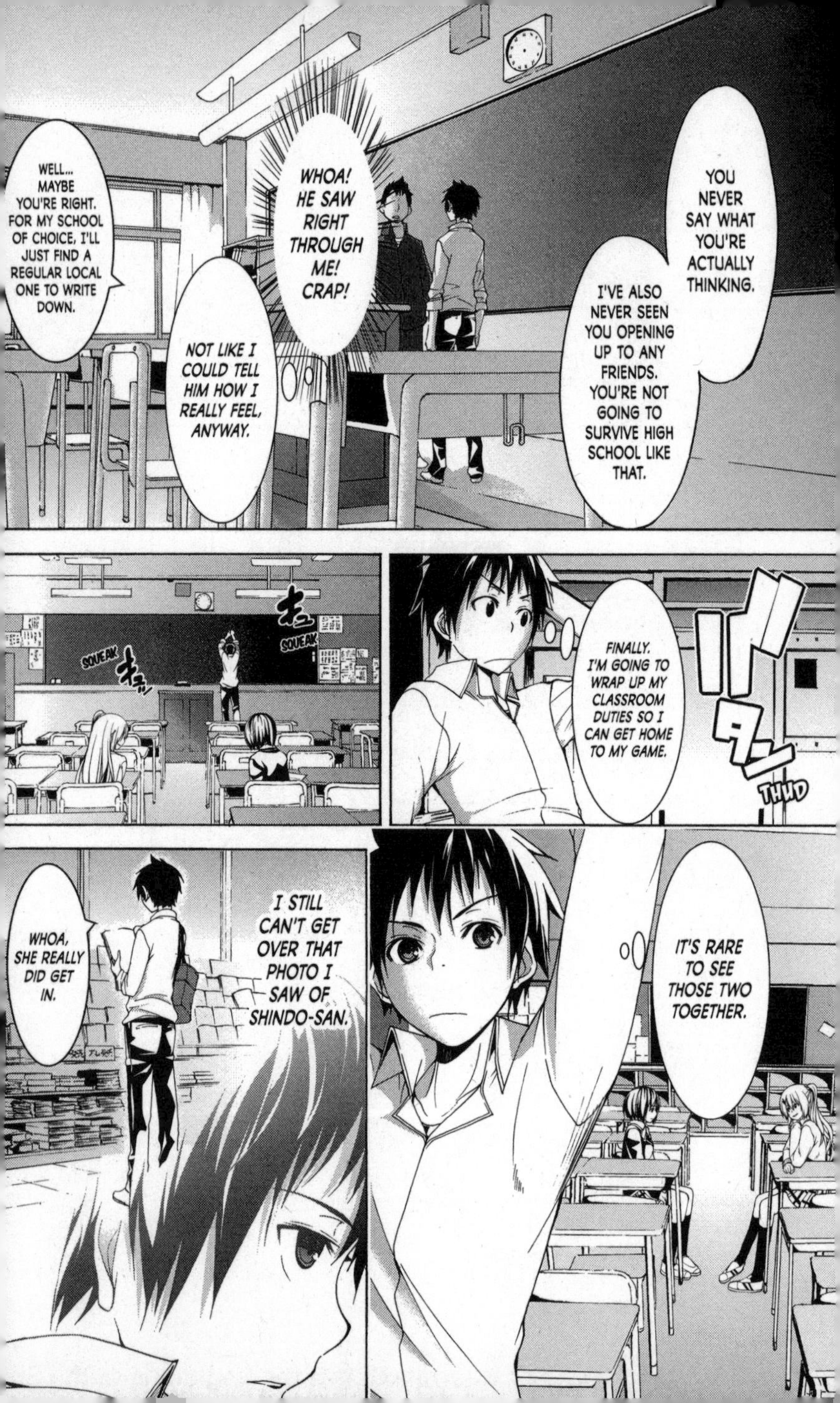
YOU NEVER SAY WHAT YOU'RE ACTUALLY THINKING.
I'VE ALSO NEVER SEEN YOU OPENING UP TO ANY FRIENDS. YOU'RE NOT GOING TO SURVIVE HIGH SCHOOL LIKE THAT.
WHOA! HE SAW RIGHT THROUGH ME! CRAP!
NOT LIKE I COULD TELL HIM HOW I REALLY FEEL, ANYWAY.
WELL... MAYBE YOU'RE RIGHT. FOR MY SCHOOL OF CHOICE, I'LL JUST FIND A REGULAR LOCAL ONE TO WRITE DOWN.
THUD
FINALLY. I'M GOING TO WRAP UP MY CLASSROOM DUTIES SO I CAN GET HOME TO MY GAME.
SQUEAK
SQUEAK
IT'S RARE TO SEE THOSE TWO TOGETHER.
I STILL CAN'T GET OVER THAT PHOTO I SAW OF SHINDO-SAN.
WHOA, SHE REALLY DID GET IN.

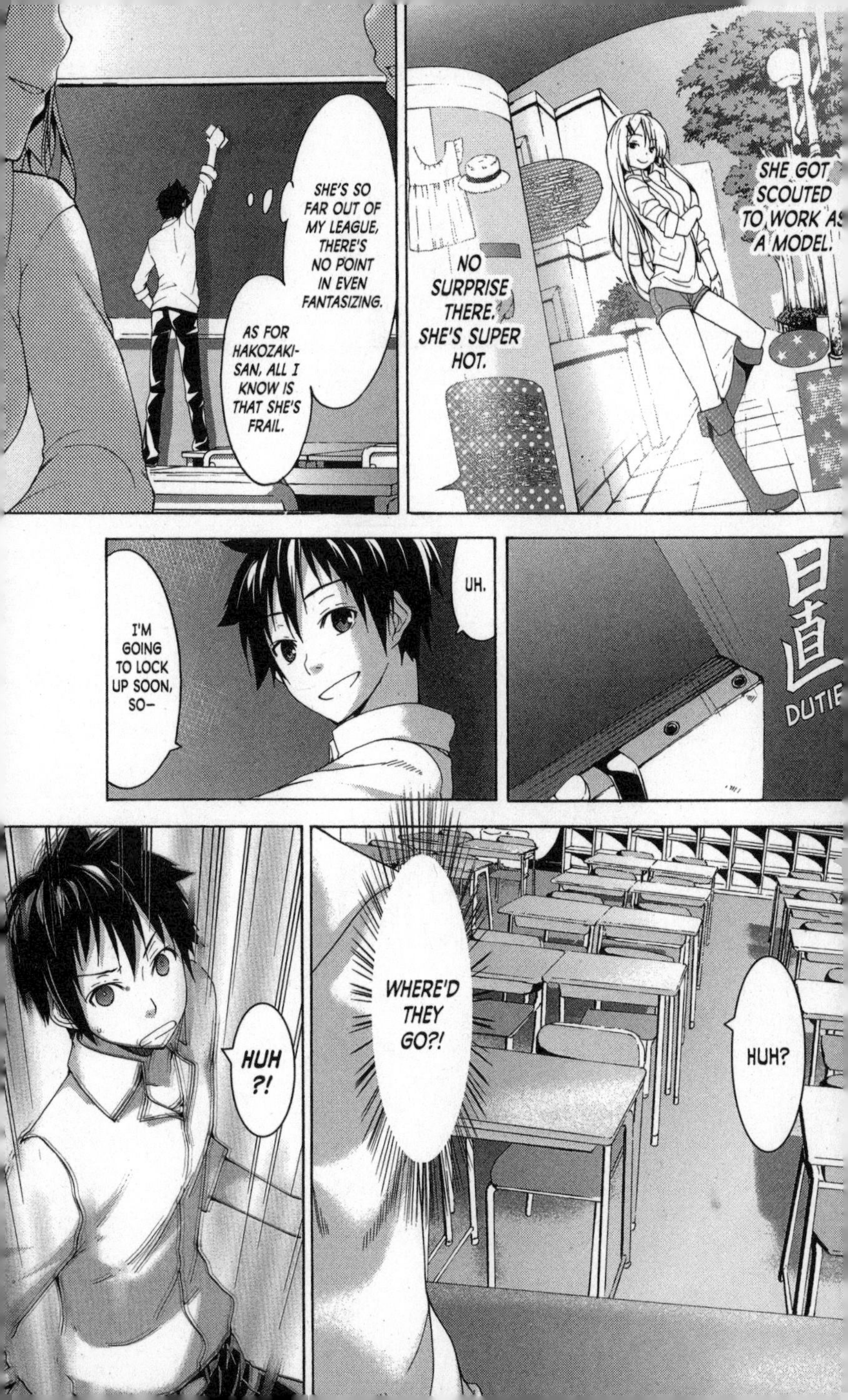
SHE GOT SCOUTED TO WORK AS A MODEL.
NO SURPRISE THERE. SHE'S SUPER HOT.
SHE'S SO FAR OUT OF MY LEAGUE, THERE'S NO POINT IN EVEN FANTASIZING.
AS FOR HAKOZAKI-SAN, ALL I KNOW IS THAT SHE'S FRAIL.
日直
DUTIE
UH.
I'M GOING TO LOCK UP SOON, SO—
HUH?
WHERE'D THEY GO?!
HUH ?!

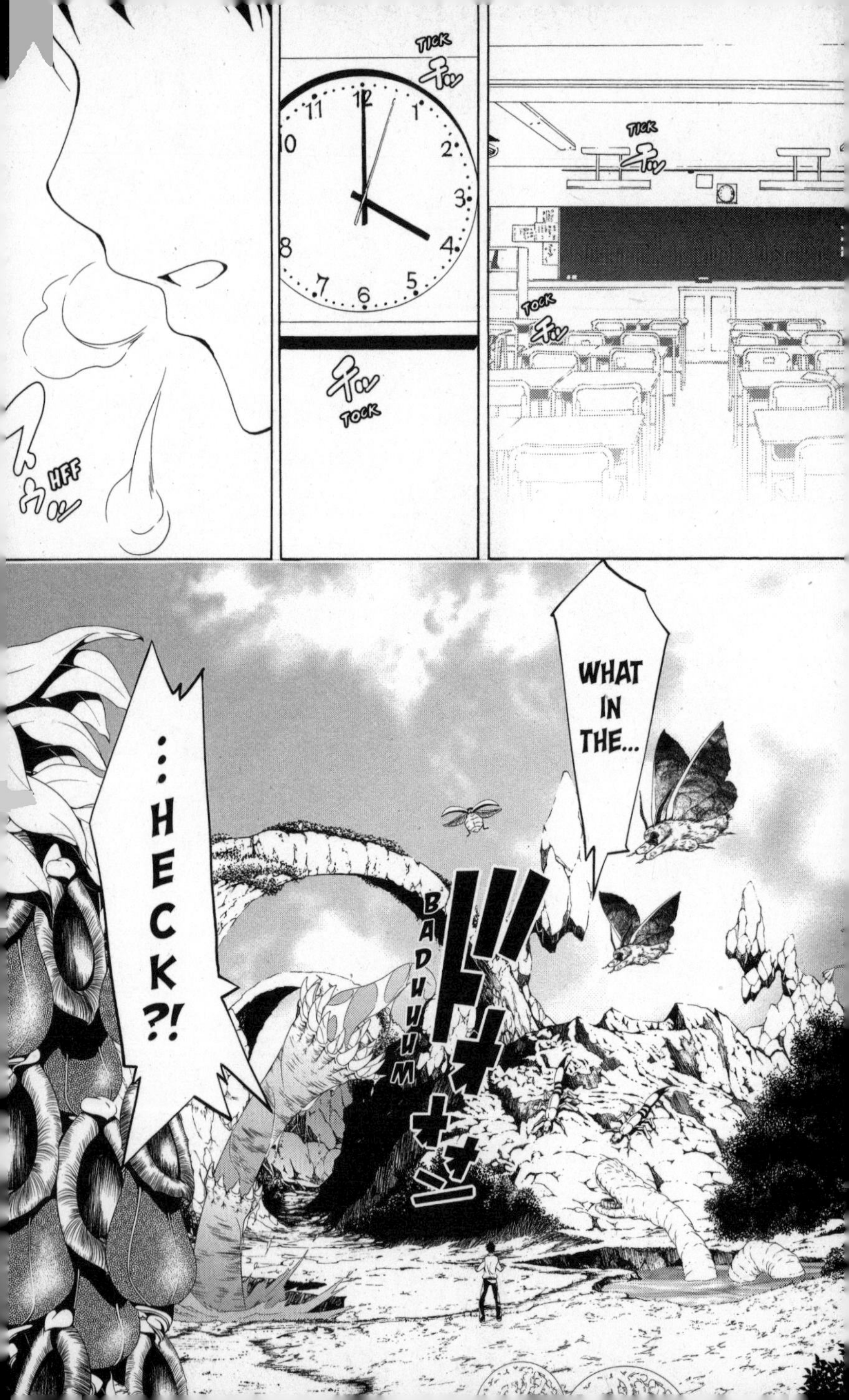
TICK
TICK
TOCK
TOCK
HFF
WHAT IN THE...
...HECK?!
BADUUUM

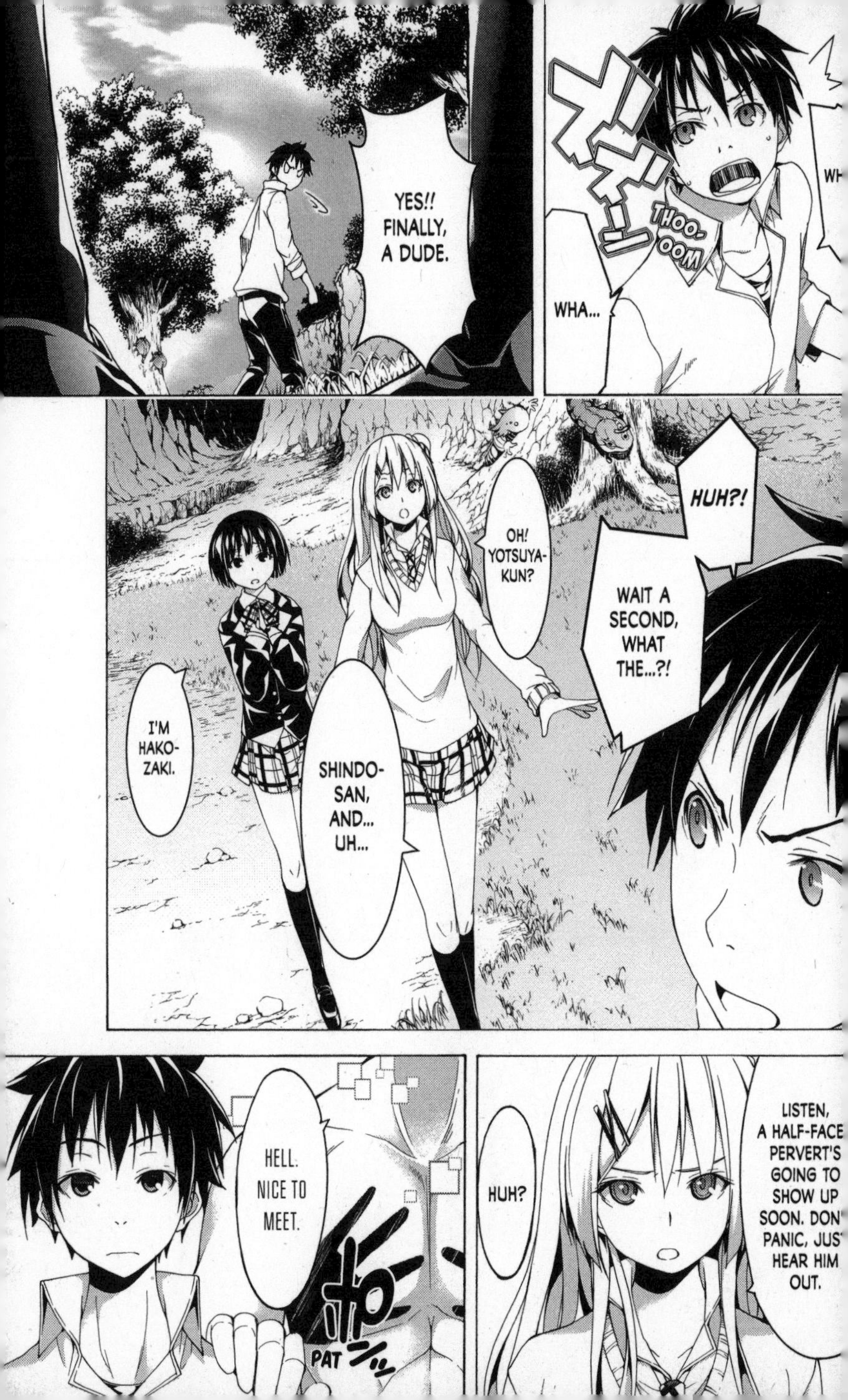
WH
WHA...
THOO-OOM
YES!! FINALLY, A DUDE.
HUH?!
WAIT A SECOND, WHAT THE...?!
OH! YOTSUYA-KUN?
SHINDO-SAN, AND... UH...
I'M HAKO-ZAKI.
LISTEN, A HALF-FACE PERVERT'S GOING TO SHOW UP SOON. DON' PANIC, JUS HEAR HIM OUT.
HUH?
HELL. NICE TO MEET.
PAT

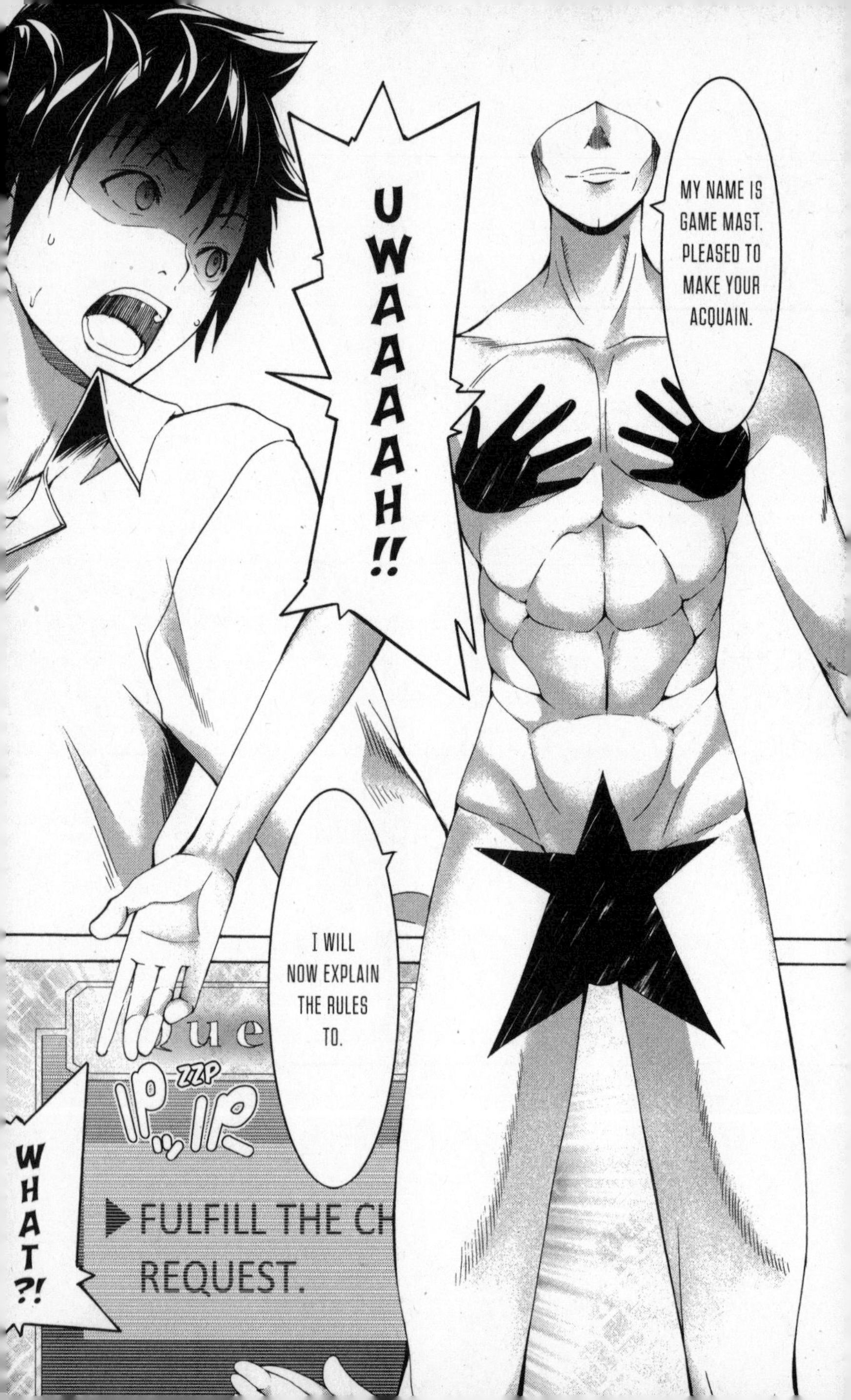
MY NAME IS GAME MAST. PLEASED TO MAKE YOUR ACQUAIN.
UWAAAAAH!!
I WILL NOW EXPLAIN THE RULES TO.
Que
ZZP
▶FULFILL THE CH
REQUEST.
WHAT?!

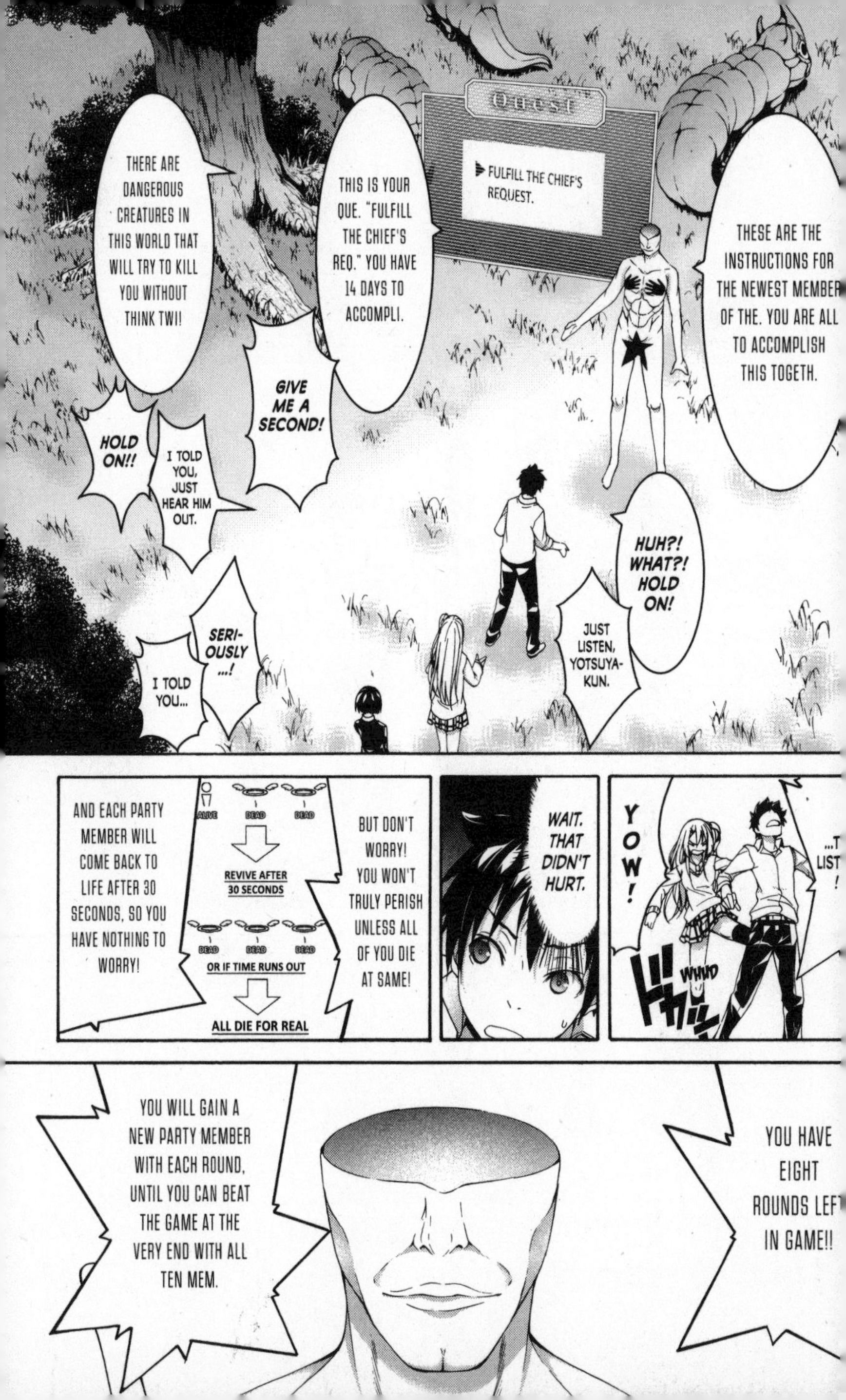
Quest
FULFILL THE CHIEF'S REQUEST.
THESE ARE THE INSTRUCTIONS FOR THE NEWEST MEMBER OF THE. YOU ARE ALL TO ACCOMPLISH THIS TOGETH.
THIS IS YOUR QUE. "FULFILL THE CHIEF'S REQ." YOU HAVE 14 DAYS TO ACCOMPLI.
THERE ARE DANGEROUS CREATURES IN THIS WORLD THAT WILL TRY TO KILL YOU WITHOUT THINK TWI!
HUH?! WHAT?! HOLD ON!
JUST LISTEN, YOTSUYA-KUN.
GIVE ME A SECOND!
I TOLD YOU, JUST HEAR HIM OUT.
HOLD ON!!
SERI-OUSLY ...!
I TOLD YOU...
...T LIST !
YOW!
WHUD
WAIT. THAT DIDN'T HURT.
BUT DON'T WORRY! YOU WON'T TRULY PERISH UNLESS ALL OF YOU DIE AT SAME!
ALIVE
DEAD
DEAD
REVIVE AFTER 30 SECONDS
DEAD
DEAD
DEAD
OR IF TIME RUNS OUT
ALL DIE FOR REAL
AND EACH PARTY MEMBER WILL COME BACK TO LIFE AFTER 30 SECONDS, SO YOU HAVE NOTHING TO WORRY!
YOU HAVE EIGHT ROUNDS LEF IN GAME!!
YOU WILL GAIN A NEW PARTY MEMBER WITH EACH ROUND, UNTIL YOU CAN BEAT THE GAME AT THE VERY END WITH ALL TEN MEM.

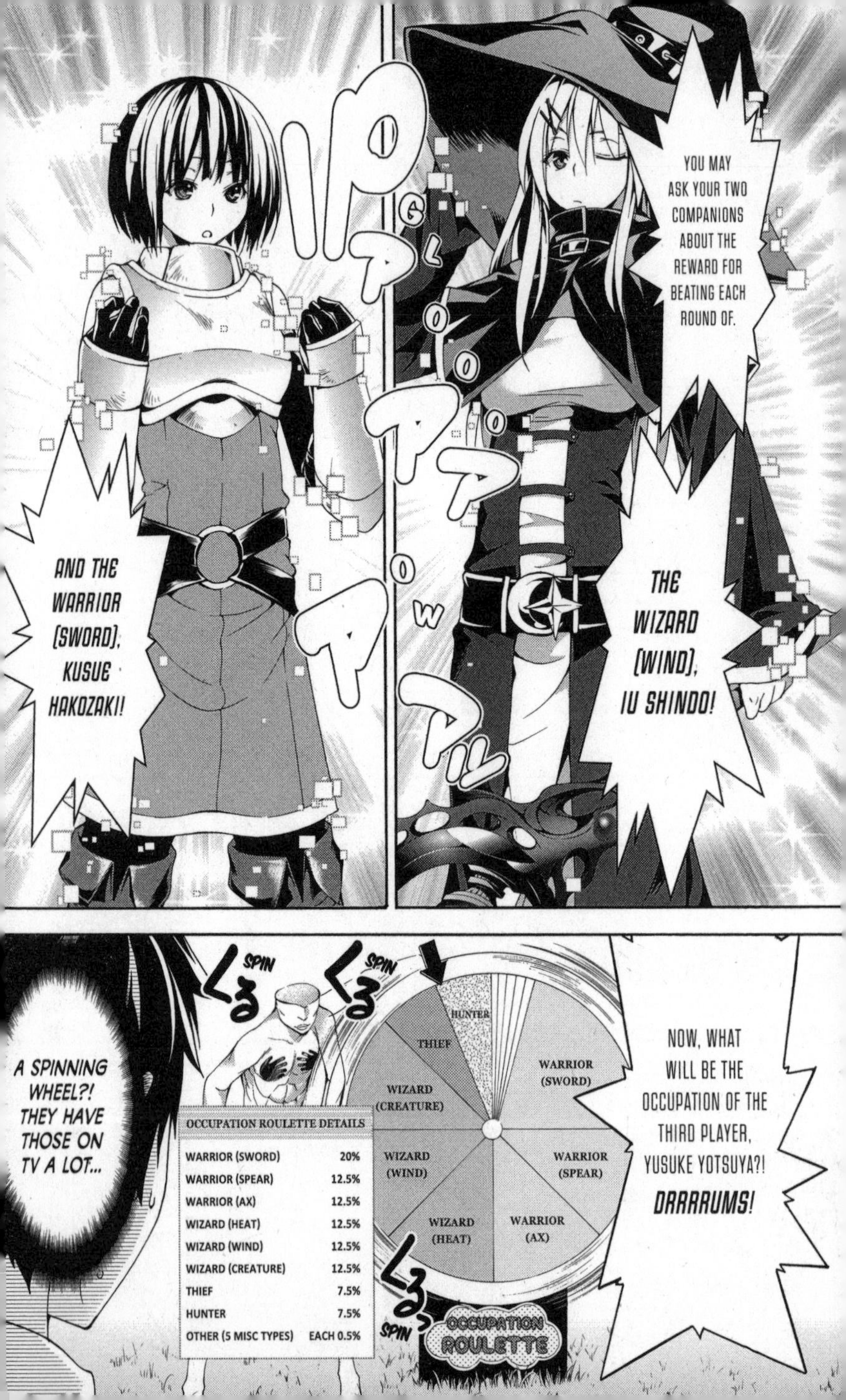

YOU MAY ASK YOUR TWO COMPANIONS ABOUT THE REWARD FOR BEATING EACH ROUND OF.
THE WIZARD (WIND), IU SHINDO!
GLOOOOOW
AND THE WARRIOR (SWORD), KUSUE HAKOZAKI!
NOW, WHAT WILL BE THE OCCUPATION OF THE THIRD PLAYER, YUSUKE YOTSUYA?! DRRRRUMS!
SPIN
SPIN
SPIN
HUNTER
THIEF
WARRIOR (SWORD)
WIZARD (CREATURE)
WIZARD (WIND)
WARRIOR (SPEAR)
WIZARD (HEAT)
WARRIOR (AX)
OCCUPATION ROULETTE
A SPINNING WHEEL?! THEY HAVE THOSE ON TV A LOT...
OCCUPATION ROULETTE DETAILS
WARRIOR (SWORD) 20%
WARRIOR (SPEAR) 12.5%
WARRIOR (AX) 12.5%
WIZARD (HEAT) 12.5%
WIZARD (WIND) 12.5%
WIZARD (CREATURE) 12.5%
THIEF 7.5%
HUNTER 7.5%
OTHER (5 MISC TYPES) EACH 0.5%

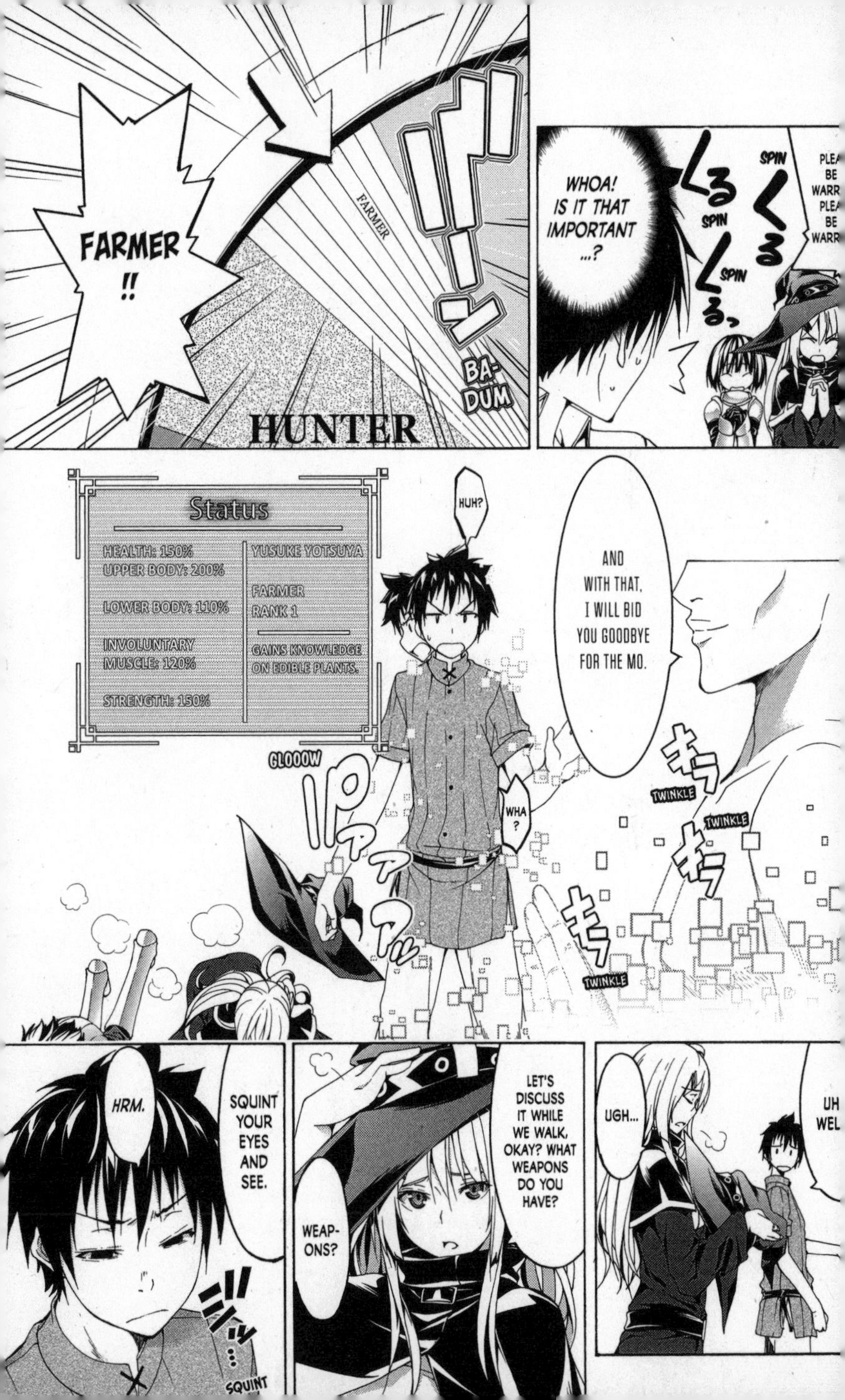
PLEA BE WARR PLEA BE WARR
SPIN
くる
くる
SPIN
くる
SPIN
くるっ
WHOA! IS IT THAT IMPORTANT ...?
BA-DUM
FARMER
HUNTER
FARMER !!
AND WITH THAT, I WILL BID YOU GOODBYE FOR THE MO.
TWINKLE
TWINKLE
TWINKLE
HUH?
WHA ?
GLOOOW
Status
HEALTH: 150%
UPPER BODY: 200%
LOWER BODY: 110%
INVOLUNTARY MUSCLE: 120%
STRENGTH: 150%
YUSUKE YOTSUYA
FARMER
RANK 1
GAINS KNOWLEDGE ON EDIBLE PLANTS.
UH WEL
UGH...
LET'S DISCUSS IT WHILE WE WALK, OKAY? WHAT WEAPONS DO YOU HAVE?
WEAP- ONS?
SQUINT YOUR EYES AND SEE.
HRM.
SQUINT

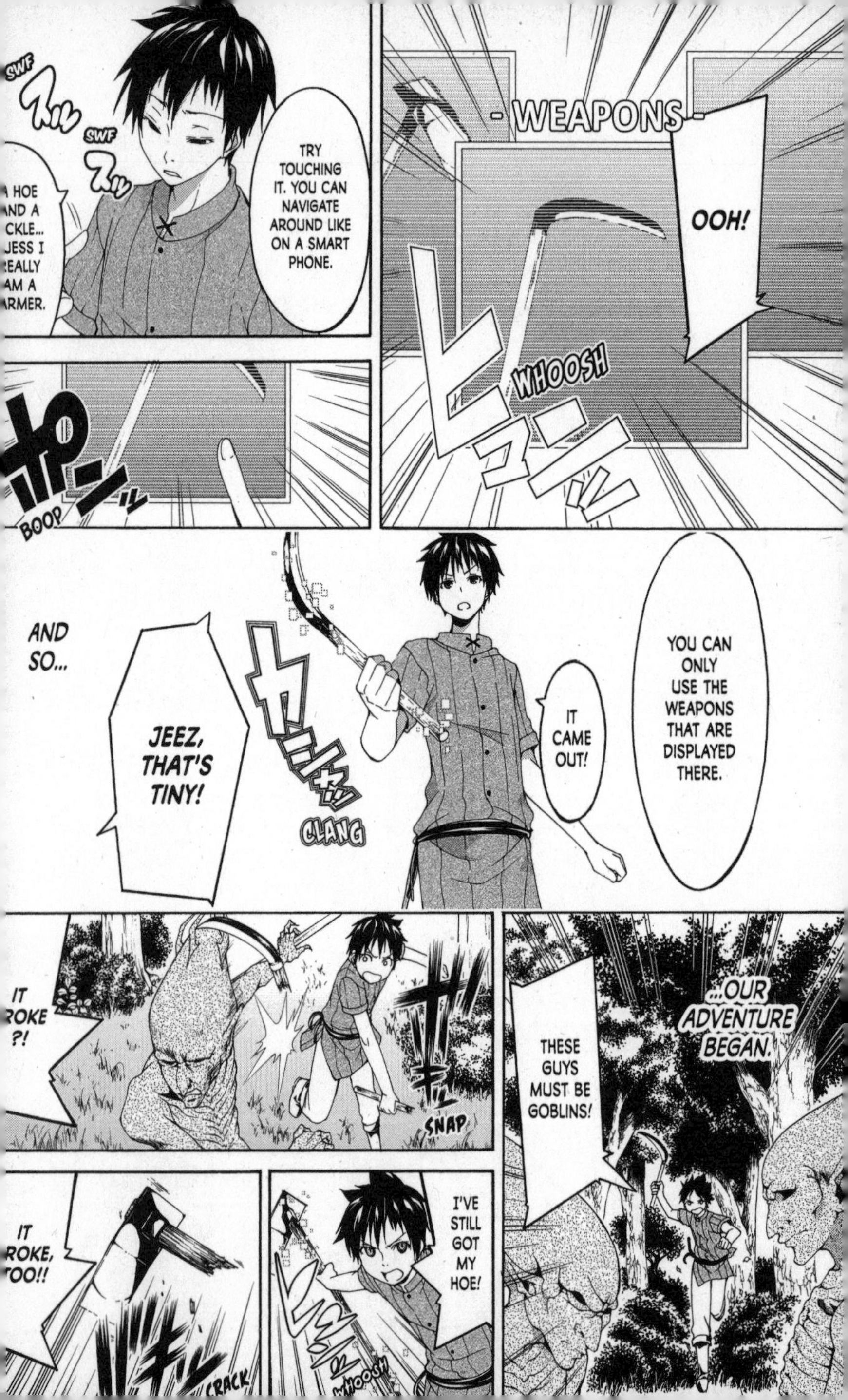

- WEAPONS -
OOH!
WHOOSH
SWF
SWF
TRY TOUCHING IT. YOU CAN NAVIGATE AROUND LIKE ON A SMART PHONE.
A HOE AND A CKLE... JESS I EALLY AM A RMER.
BOOP
YOU CAN ONLY USE THE WEAPONS THAT ARE DISPLAYED THERE.
IT CAME OUT!
CLANG
JEEZ, THAT'S TINY!
AND SO...
...OUR ADVENTURE BEGAN.
THESE GUYS MUST BE GOBLINS!
SNAP
IT ROKE?!
I'VE STILL GOT MY HOE!
WHOOSH
IT ROKE, TOO!!
CRACK

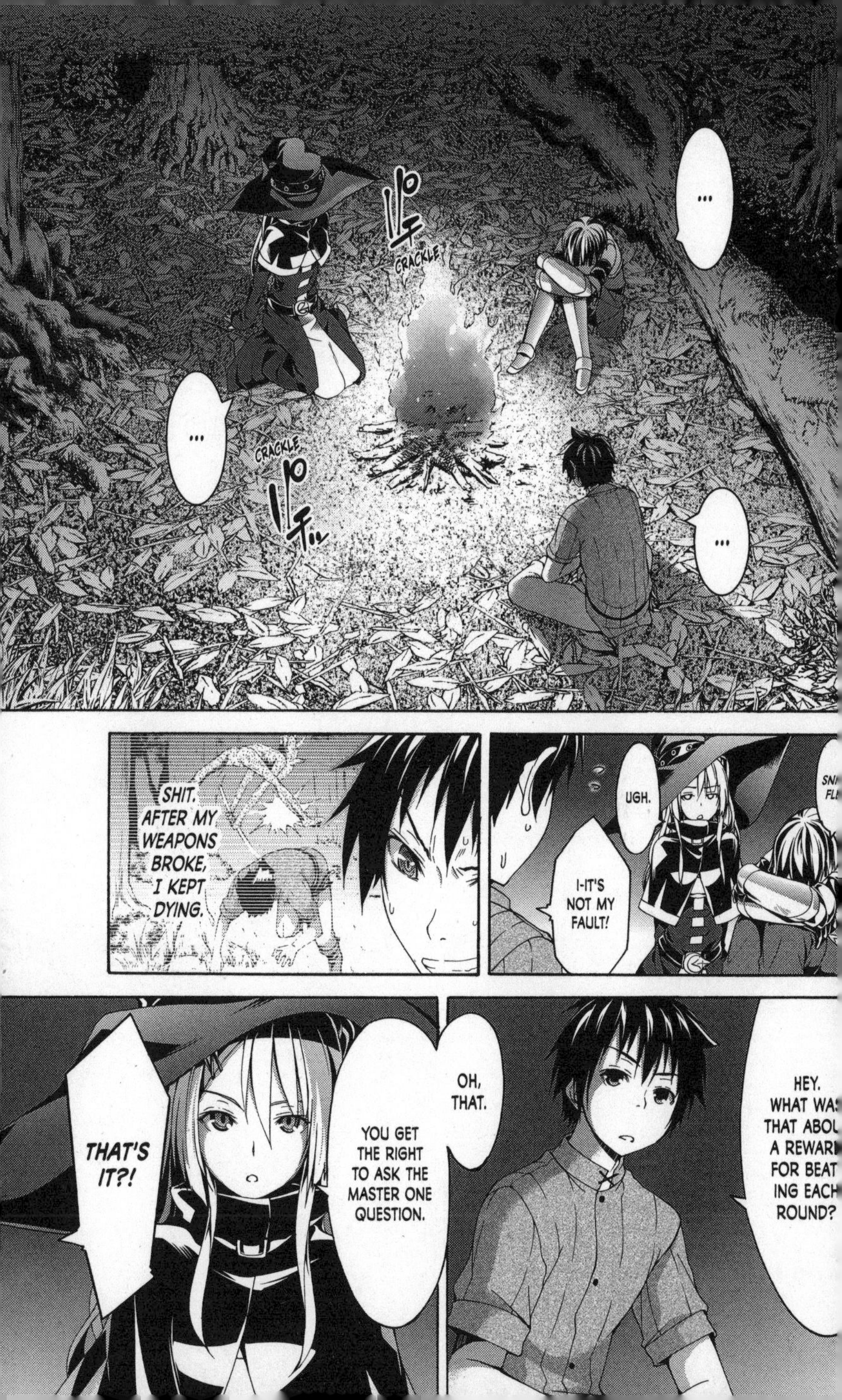
...
CRACKLE
...
CRACKLE
...
UGH.
I-IT'S NOT MY FAULT!
SHIT. AFTER MY WEAPONS BROKE, I KEPT DYING.
HEY. WHAT WAS THAT ABOU A REWARI FOR BEAT ING EACH ROUND?
OH, THAT.
YOU GET THE RIGHT TO ASK THE MASTER ONE QUESTION.
THAT'S IT?!

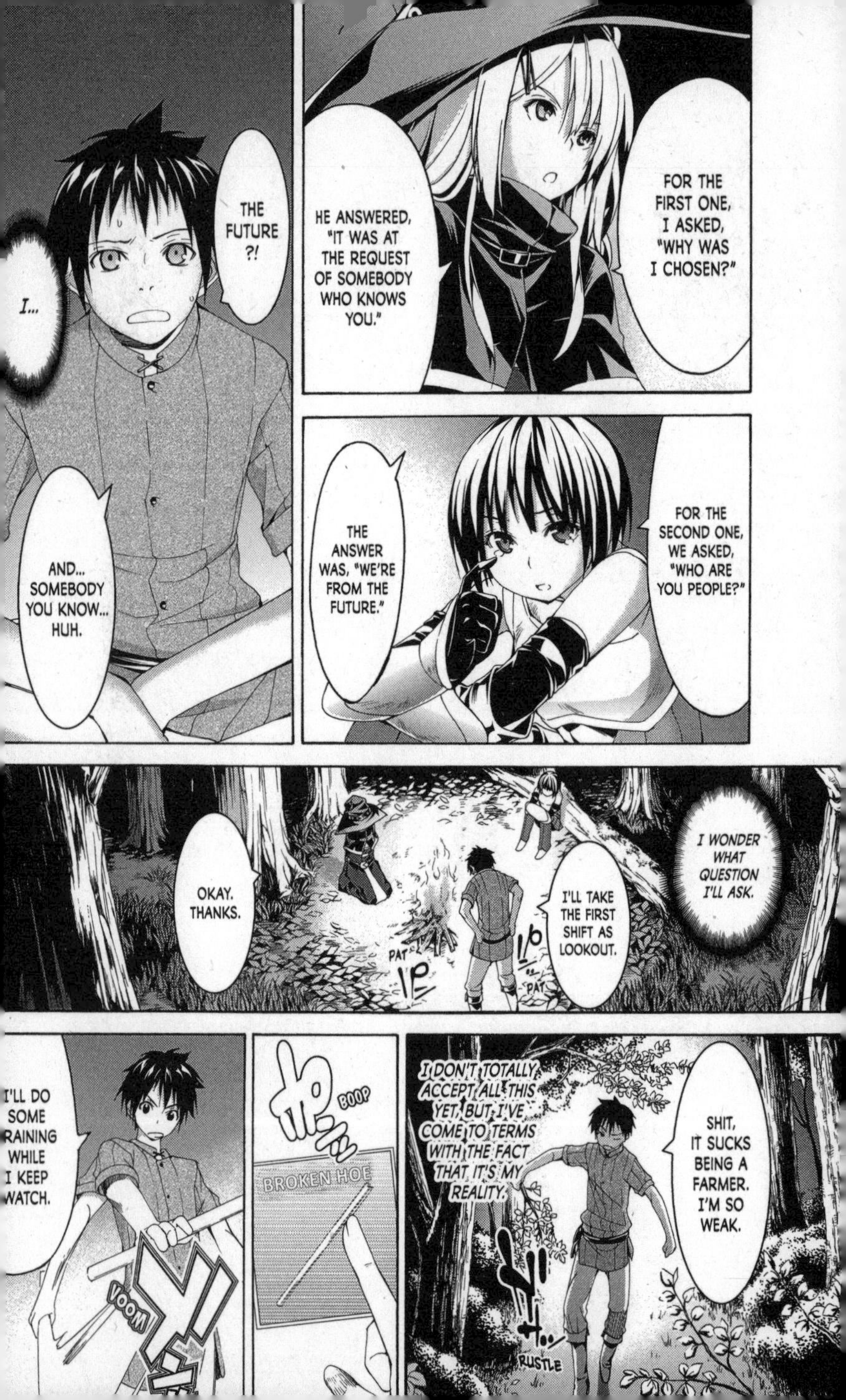
FOR THE FIRST ONE, I ASKED, "WHY WAS I CHOSEN?"
HE ANSWERED, "IT WAS AT THE REQUEST OF SOMEBODY WHO KNOWS YOU."
FOR THE SECOND ONE, WE ASKED, "WHO ARE YOU PEOPLE?"
THE ANSWER WAS, "WE'RE FROM THE FUTURE."
THE FUTURE ?!
I...
AND... SOMEBODY YOU KNOW... HUH.
I WONDER WHAT QUESTION I'LL ASK.
I'LL TAKE THE FIRST SHIFT AS LOOKOUT.
PAT
PAT
OKAY. THANKS.
SHIT, IT SUCKS BEING A FARMER. I'M SO WEAK.
I DON'T TOTALLY ACCEPT ALL THIS YET, BUT I'VE COME TO TERMS WITH THE FACT THAT IT'S MY REALITY.
RUSTLE
BOOP
BROKEN HOE
I'LL DO SOME RAINING WHILE I KEEP WATCH.
VOOM

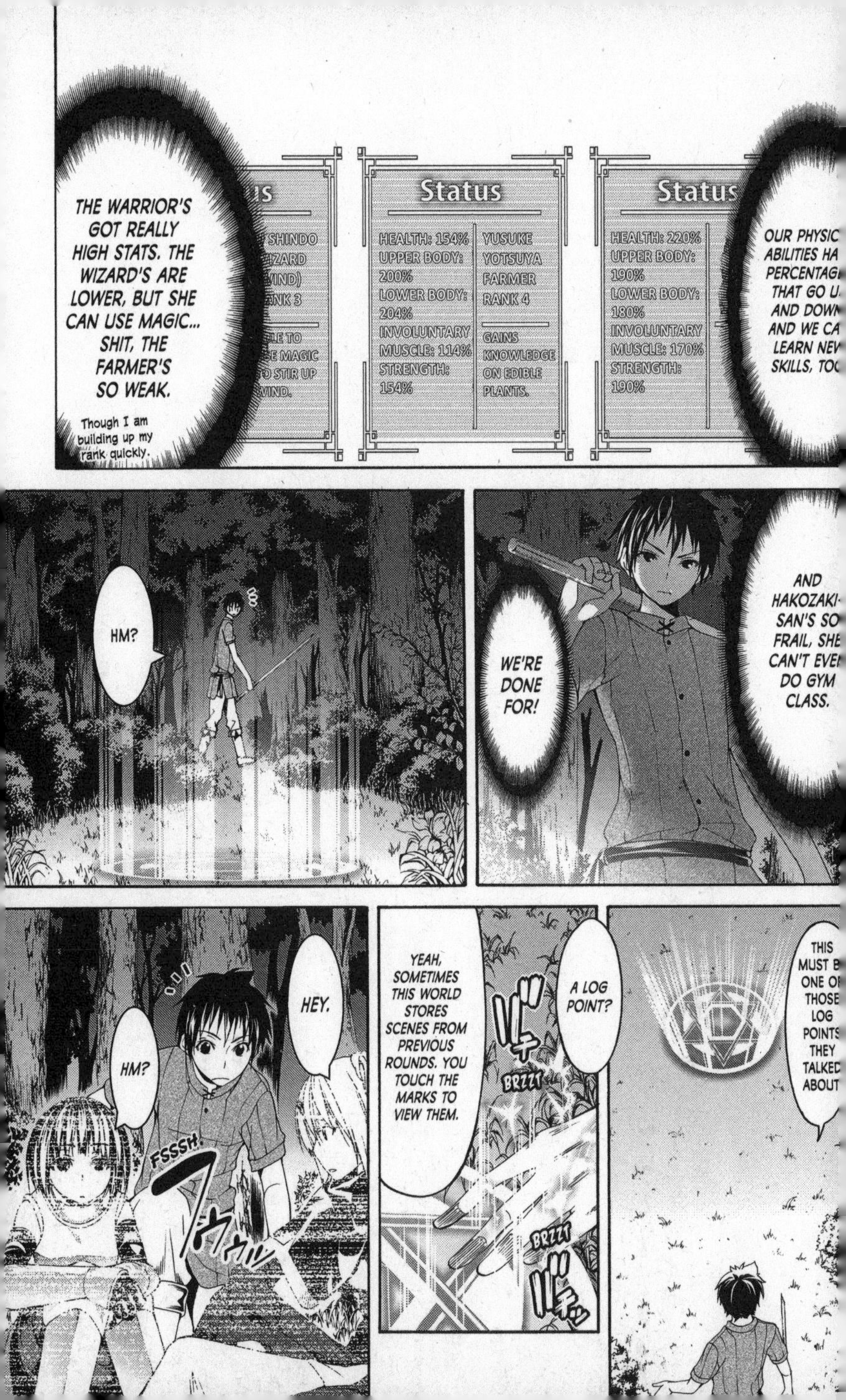
OUR PHYSIC ABILITIES HA PERCENTAG THAT GO U AND DOWN AND WE CA LEARN NEV SKILLS, TO
Status
HEALTH: 220%
UPPER BODY: 190%
LOWER BODY: 180%
INVOLUNTARY MUSCLE: 170%
STRENGTH: 190%
Status
HEALTH: 154%
UPPER BODY: 200%
LOWER BODY: 204%
INVOLUNTARY MUSCLE: 114%
STRENGTH: 154%
YUSUKE YOTSUYA
FARMER
RANK 4
GAINS KNOWLEDGE ON EDIBLE PLANTS.
US
SHINDO
ZARD
WIND)
ANK 3
LE TO
E MAGIC
O STIR UP
WIND.
THE WARRIOR'S GOT REALLY HIGH STATS. THE WIZARD'S ARE LOWER, BUT SHE CAN USE MAGIC... SHIT, THE FARMER'S SO WEAK.
Though I am building up my rank quickly.
AND HAKOZAKI-SAN'S SO FRAIL, SHE CAN'T EVEN DO GYM CLASS.
WE'RE DONE FOR!
HM?
THIS MUST B ONE OF THOSE LOG POINTS THEY TALKED ABOUT
A LOG POINT?
BRZZT
YEAH, SOMETIMES THIS WORLD STORES SCENES FROM PREVIOUS ROUNDS. YOU TOUCH THE MARKS TO VIEW THEM.
BRZZT
HEY.
HM?
FSSSH.

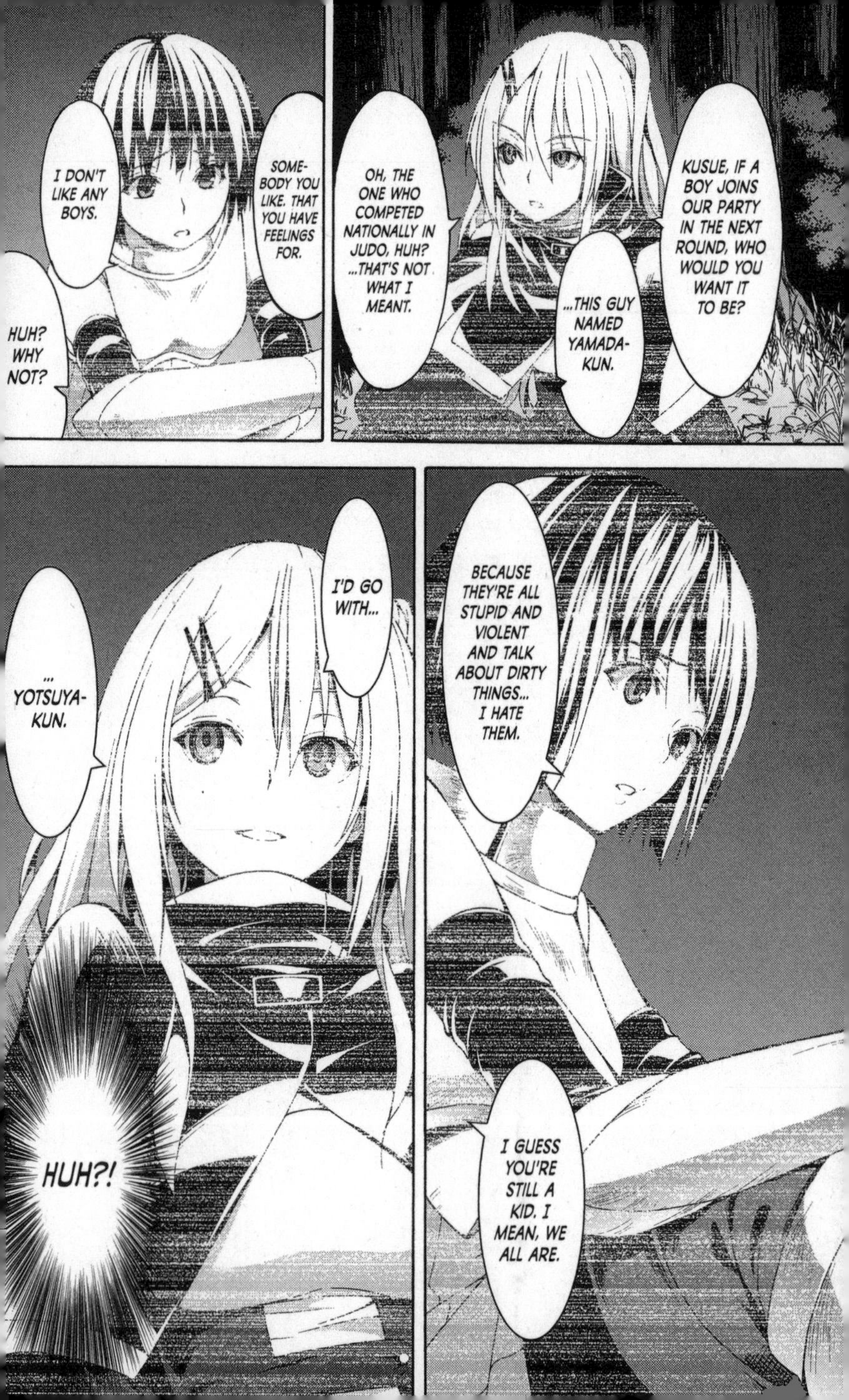
KUSUE, IF A BOY JOINS OUR PARTY IN THE NEXT ROUND, WHO WOULD YOU WANT IT TO BE?
...THIS GUY NAMED YAMADA-KUN.
OH, THE ONE WHO COMPETED NATIONALLY IN JUDO, HUH? ...THAT'S NOT WHAT I MEANT.
SOME-BODY YOU LIKE. THAT YOU HAVE FEELINGS FOR.
I DON'T LIKE ANY BOYS.
HUH? WHY NOT?
BECAUSE THEY'RE ALL STUPID AND VIOLENT AND TALK ABOUT DIRTY THINGS... I HATE THEM.
I GUESS YOU'RE STILL A KID. I MEAN, WE ALL ARE.
I'D GO WITH...
... YOTSUYA-KUN.
HUH?!

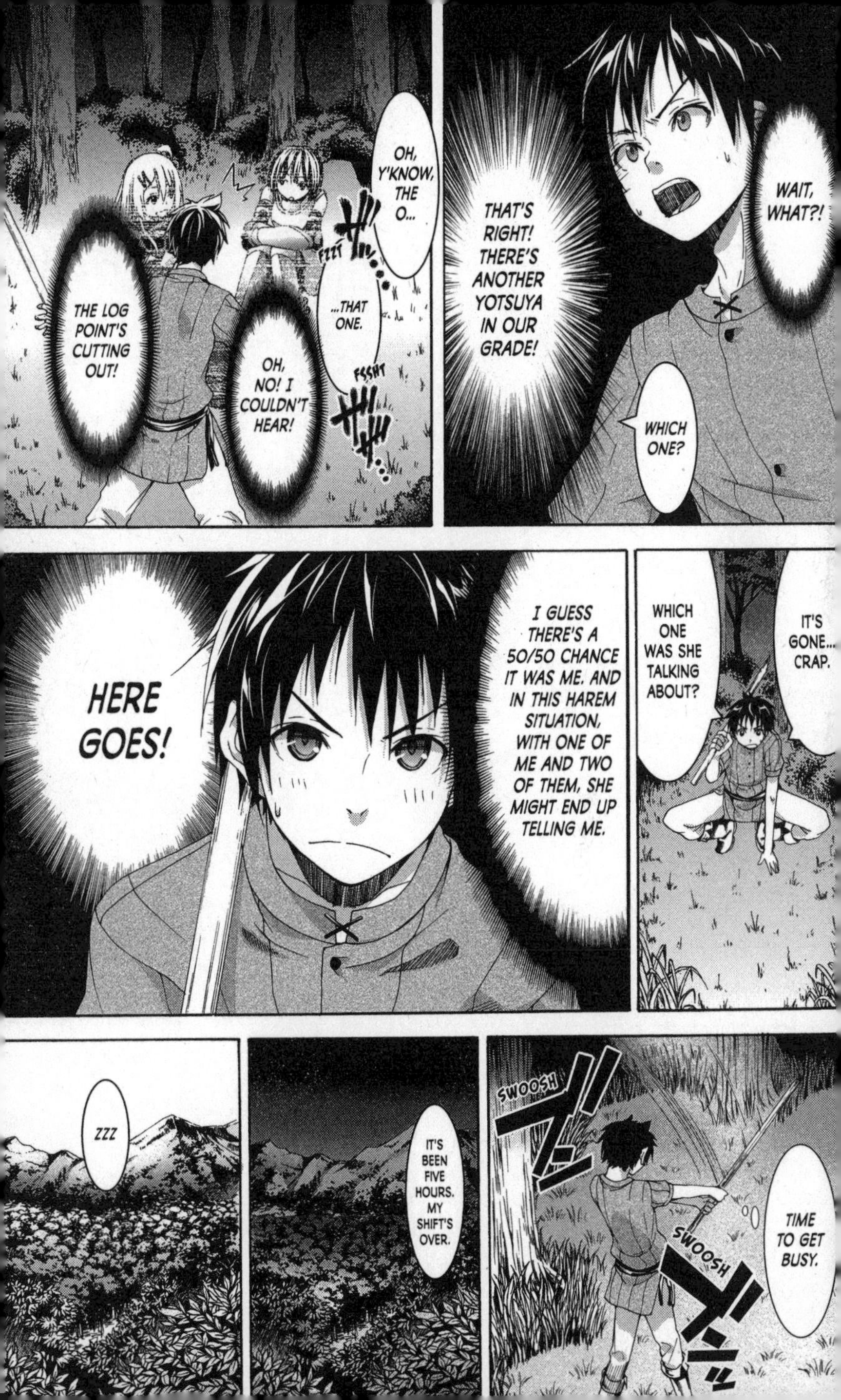
WAIT, WHAT?!
THAT'S RIGHT! THERE'S ANOTHER YOTSUYA IN OUR GRADE!
WHICH ONE?
OH, Y'KNOW, THE O...
FZZT
...THAT ONE.
FSSHT
OH, NO! I COULDN'T HEAR!
THE LOG POINT'S CUTTING OUT!
IT'S GONE... CRAP.
WHICH ONE WAS SHE TALKING ABOUT?
I GUESS THERE'S A 50/50 CHANCE IT WAS ME. AND IN THIS HAREM SITUATION, WITH ONE OF ME AND TWO OF THEM, SHE MIGHT END UP TELLING ME.
HERE GOES!
TIME TO GET BUSY.
SWOOSH
SWOOSH
IT'S BEEN FIVE HOURS. MY SHIFT'S OVER.
ZZZ

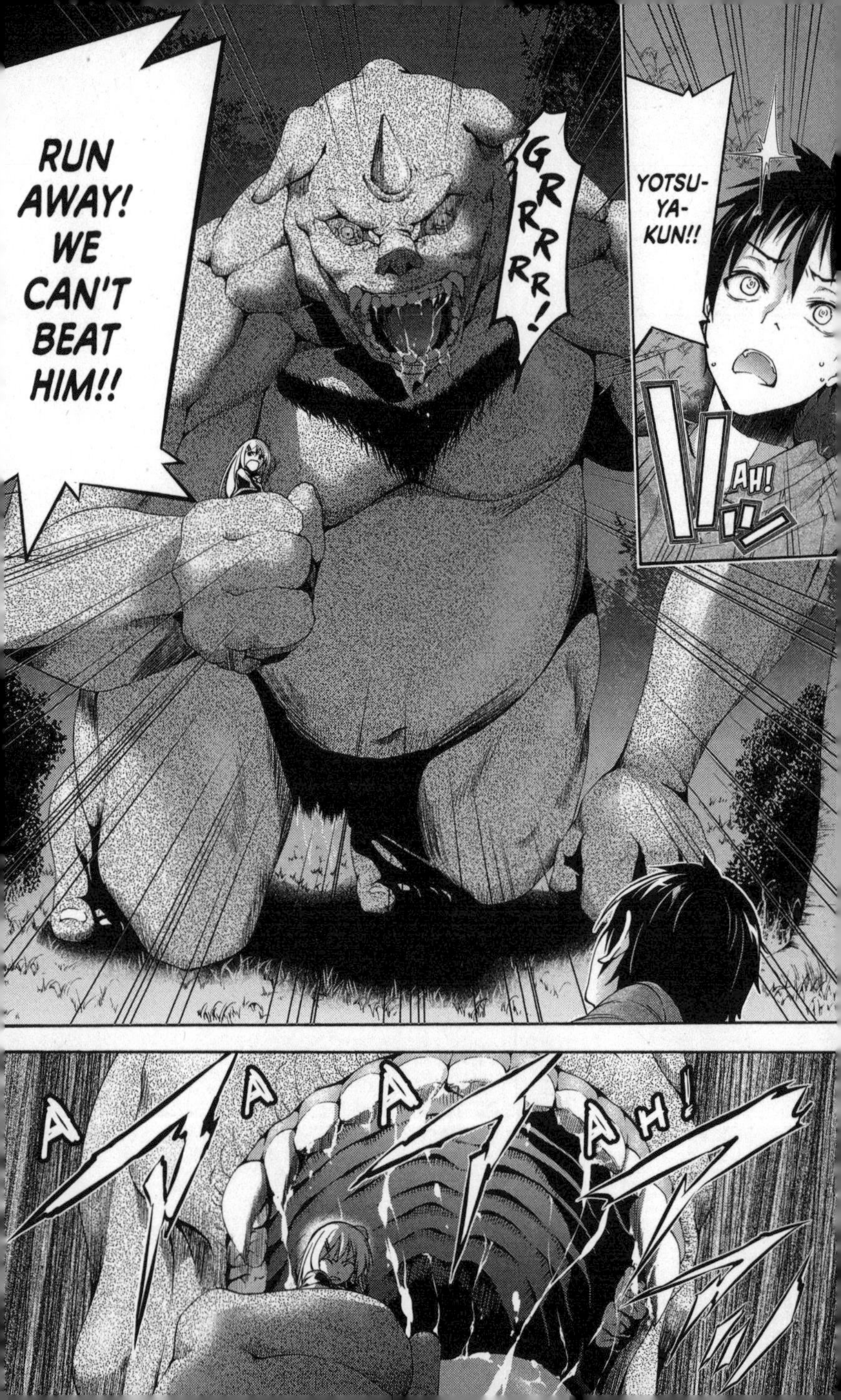
YOTSU-YA-KUN!!
AH!
GRRRRR!
RUN AWAY! WE CAN'T BEAT HIM!!
AAAAH!

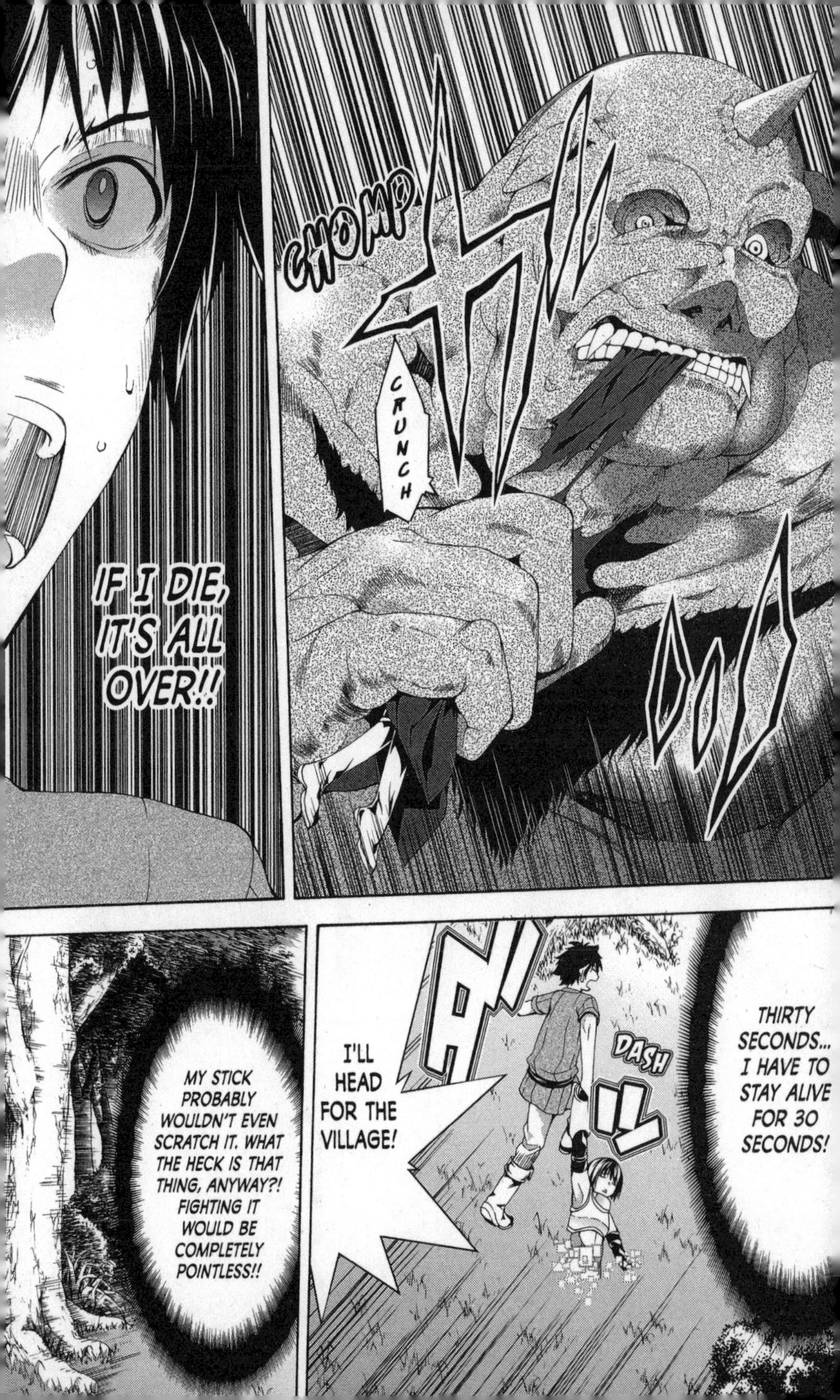
CHOMP
CRUNCH
IF I DIE, IT'S ALL OVER!!
THIRTY SECONDS... I HAVE TO STAY ALIVE FOR 30 SECONDS!
DASH
I'LL HEAD FOR THE VILLAGE!
MY STICK PROBABLY WOULDN'T EVEN SCRATCH IT. WHAT THE HECK IS THAT THING, ANYWAY?! FIGHTING IT WOULD BE COMPLETELY POINTLESS!!

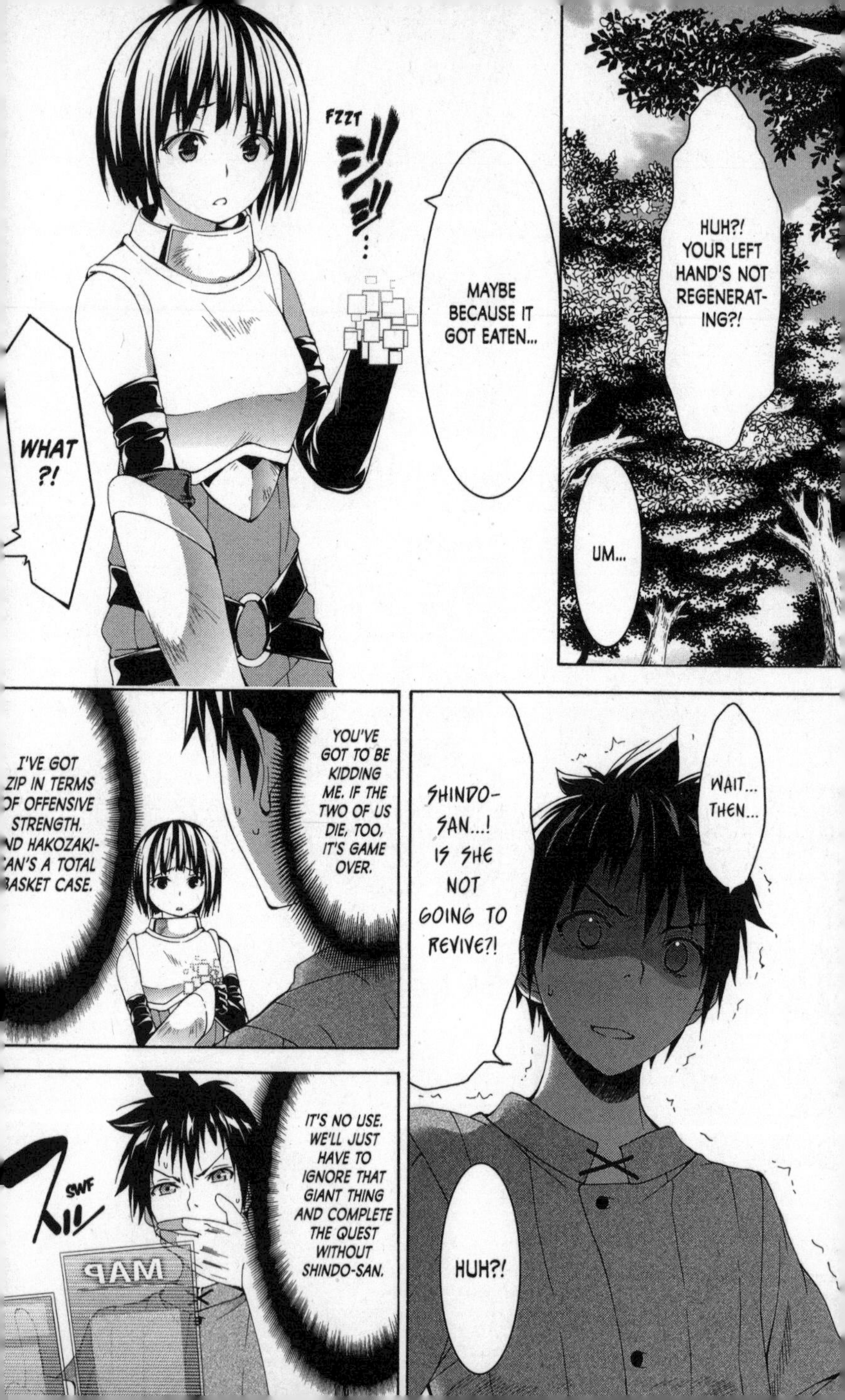
HUH?! YOUR LEFT HAND'S NOT REGENERAT-ING?!
UM...
MAYBE BECAUSE IT GOT EATEN...
FZZT
WHAT?!
WAIT... THEN...
SHINDO-SAN...! IS SHE NOT GOING TO REVIVE?!
HUH?!
YOU'VE GOT TO BE KIDDING ME. IF THE TWO OF US DIE, TOO, IT'S GAME OVER.
I'VE GOT ZIP IN TERMS OF OFFENSIVE STRENGTH. ND HAKOZAKI-AN'S A TOTAL ASKET CASE.
IT'S NO USE. WE'LL JUST HAVE TO IGNORE THAT GIANT THING AND COMPLETE THE QUEST WITHOUT SHINDO-SAN.
SWF
MAP

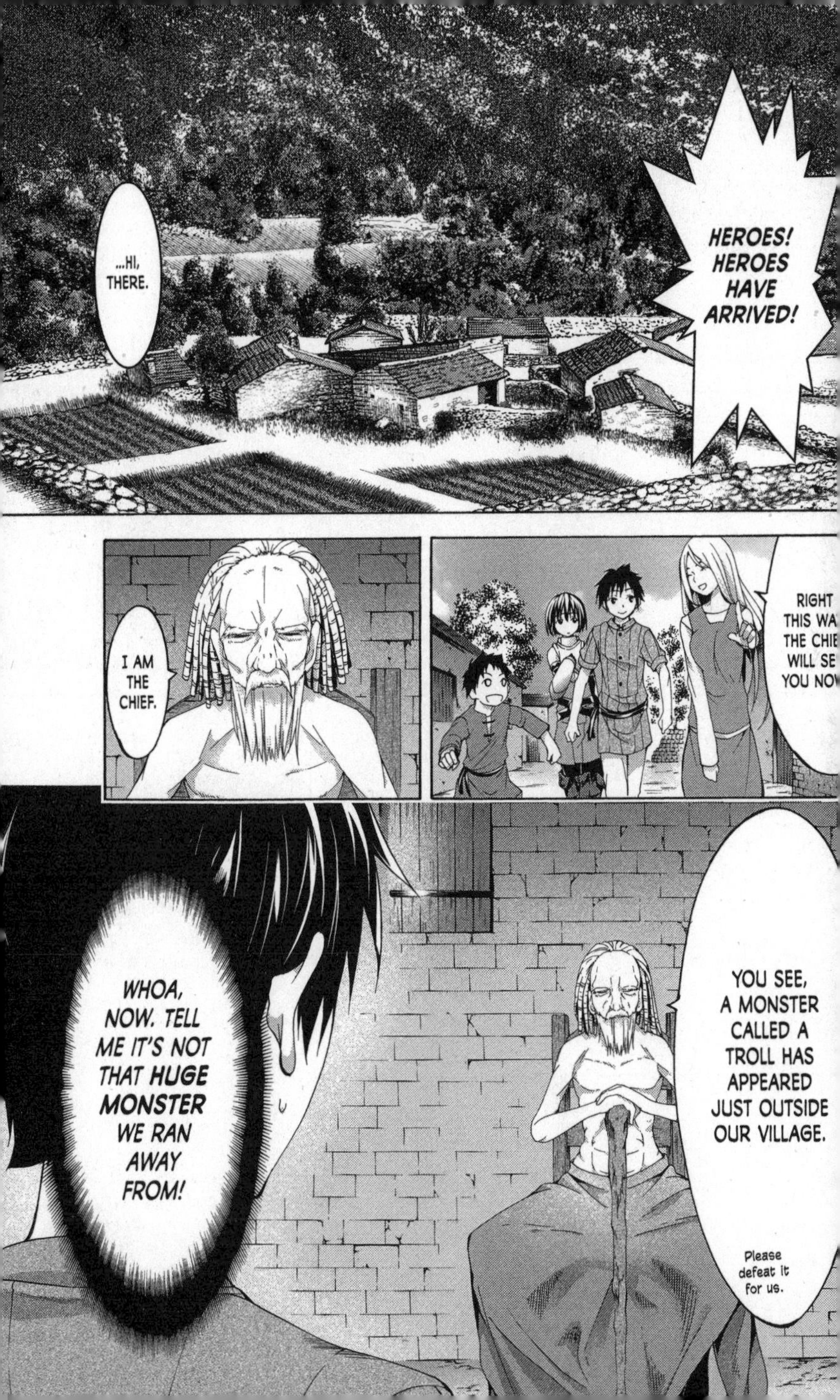
HEROES! HEROES HAVE ARRIVED!
...HI, THERE.
RIGHT THIS WA THE CHIE WILL SE YOU NO
I AM THE CHIEF.
YOU SEE, A MONSTER CALLED A TROLL HAS APPEARED JUST OUTSIDE OUR VILLAGE.
Please defeat it for us.
WHOA, NOW. TELL ME IT'S NOT THAT HUGE MONSTER WE RAN AWAY FROM!

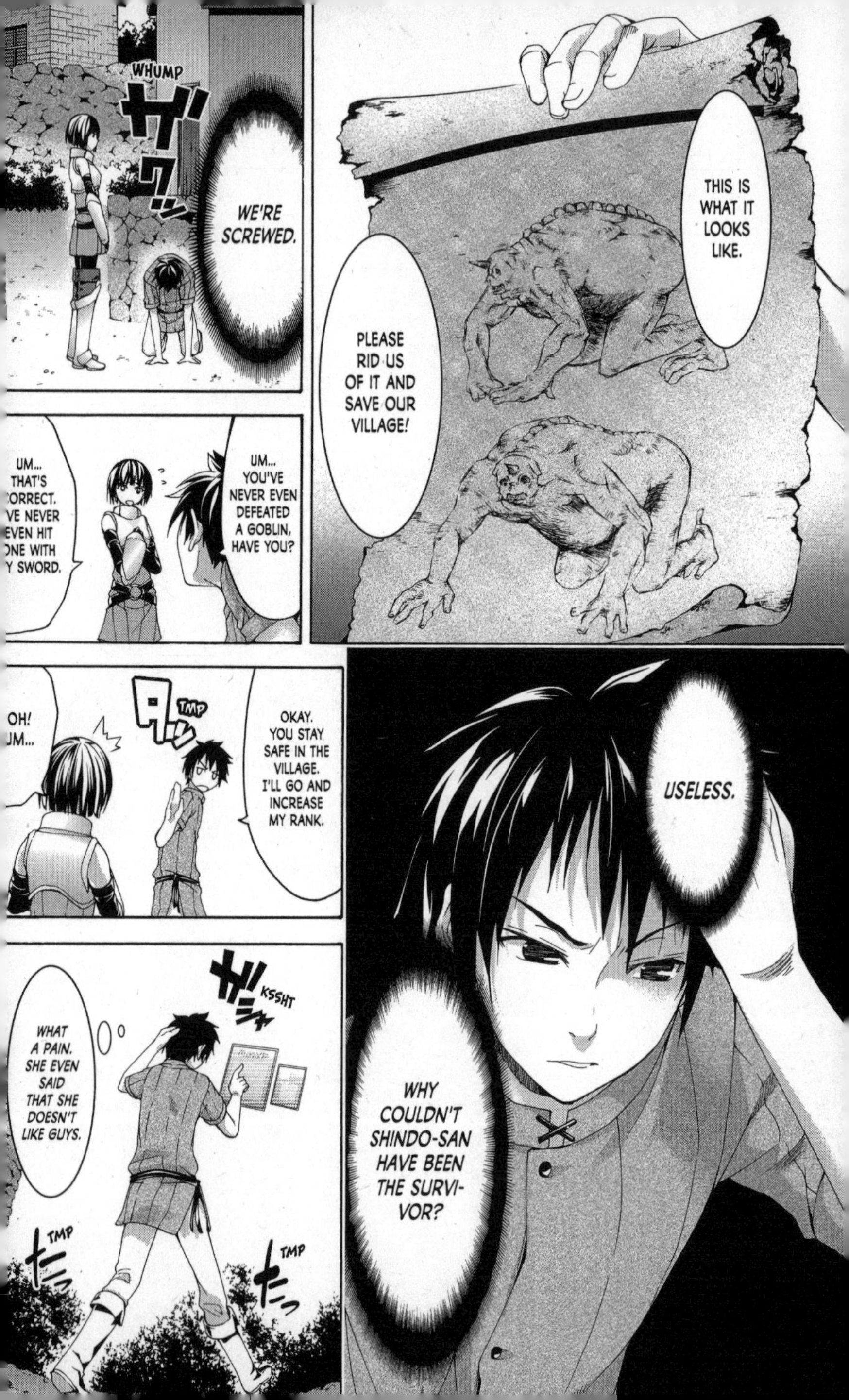
THIS IS WHAT IT LOOKS LIKE.
PLEASE RID US OF IT AND SAVE OUR VILLAGE!
WHUMP
WE'RE SCREWED.
UM... YOU'VE NEVER EVEN DEFEATED A GOBLIN, HAVE YOU?
UM... THAT'S ORRECT. VE NEVER EVEN HIT ONE WITH Y SWORD.
USELESS.
WHY COULDN'T SHINDO-SAN HAVE BEEN THE SURVIVOR?
OKAY. YOU STAY SAFE IN THE VILLAGE. I'LL GO AND INCREASE MY RANK.
TMP
OH! UM...
KSSHT
WHAT A PAIN. SHE EVEN SAID THAT SHE DOESN'T LIKE GUYS.
TMP
TMP

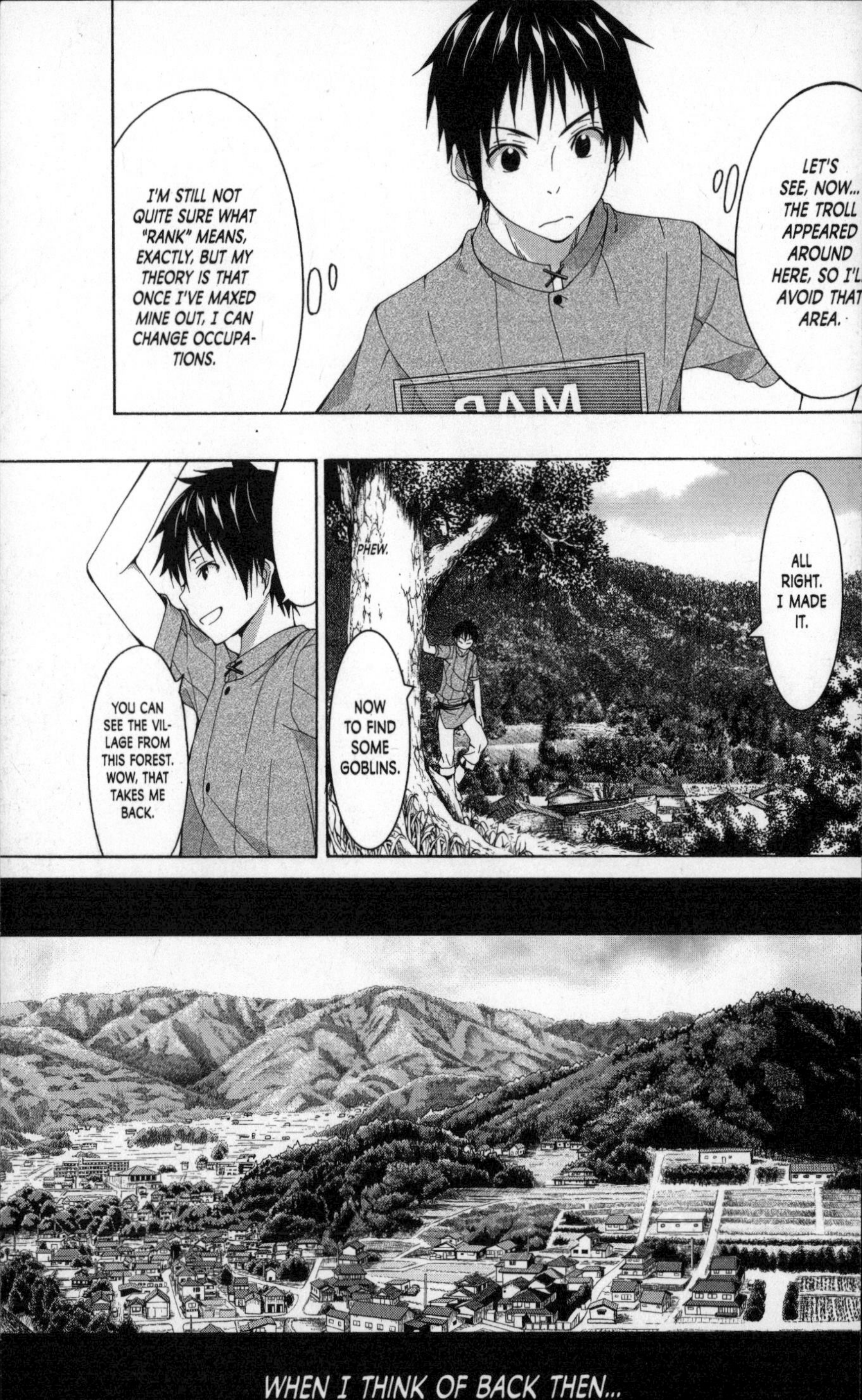

LET'S SEE, NOW... THE TROLL APPEARED AROUND HERE, SO I'L AVOID THAT AREA.
I'M STILL NOT QUITE SURE WHAT "RANK" MEANS, EXACTLY, BUT MY THEORY IS THAT ONCE I'VE MAXED MINE OUT, I CAN CHANGE OCCUPA-TIONS.
ALL RIGHT. I MADE IT.
PHEW.
NOW TO FIND SOME GOBLINS.
YOU CAN SEE THE VIL-LAGE FROM THIS FOREST. WOW, THAT TAKES ME BACK.
WHEN I THINK OF BACK THEN...

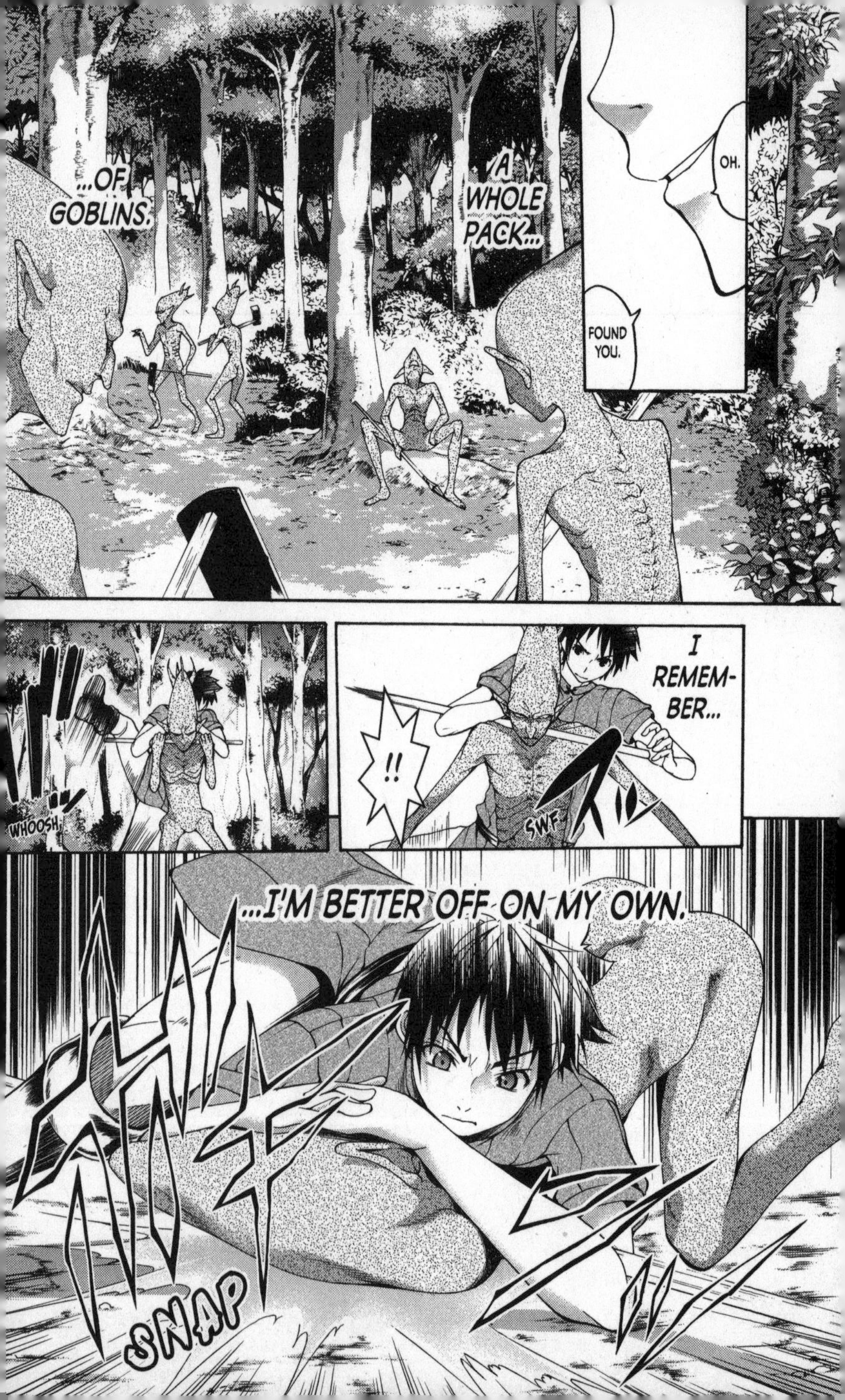
OH.
FOUND YOU.
A WHOLE PACK...
...OF GOBLINS.
I REMEMBER...
!!
SWF
WHOOSH
...I'M BETTER OFF ON MY OWN.
SNAP

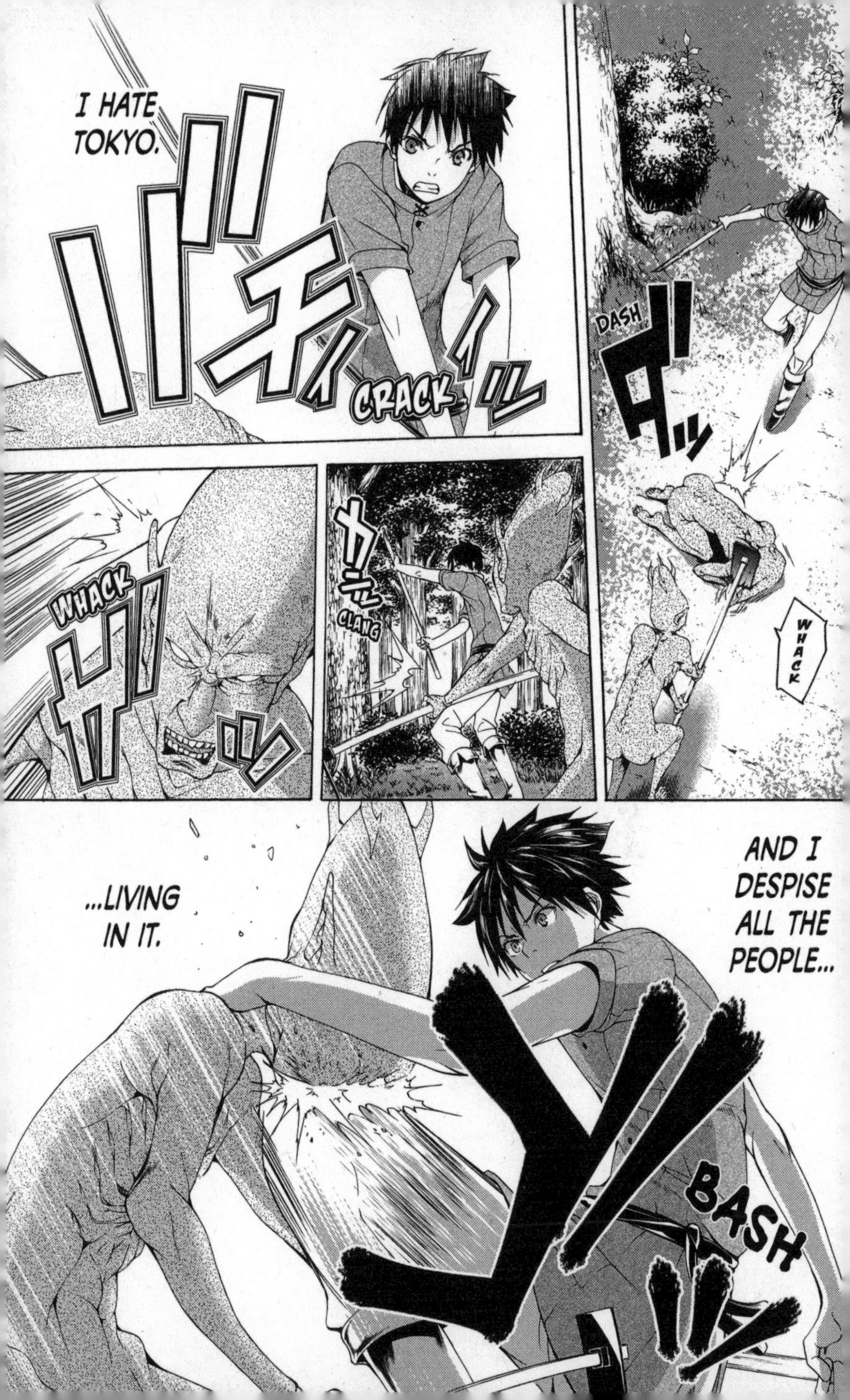
DASH
WHACK
I HATE TOKYO.
CRACK
CLANG
WHACK
AND I DESPISE ALL THE PEOPLE...
...LIVING IN IT.
BASH

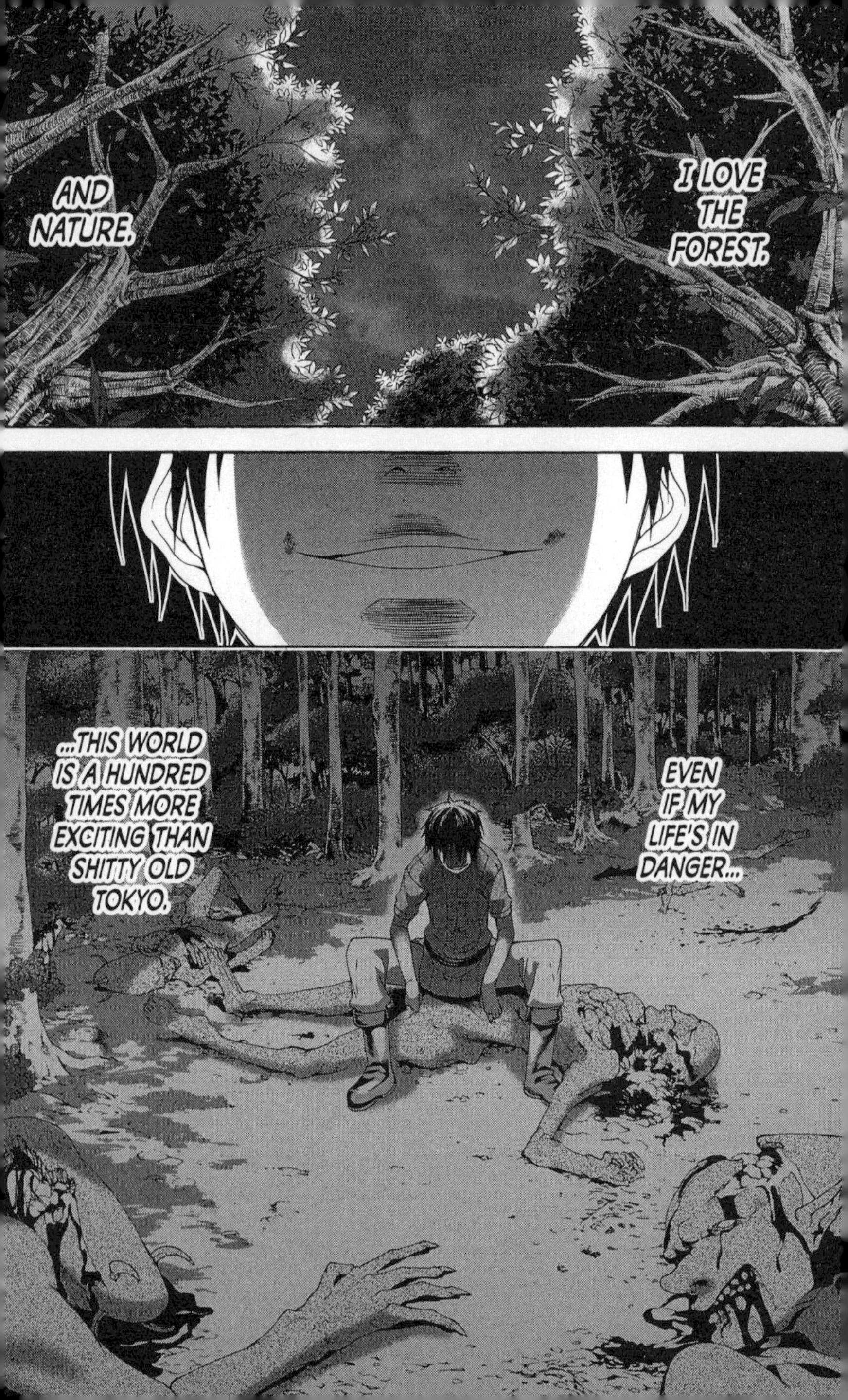
I LOVE THE FOREST.
AND NATURE.
EVEN IF MY LIFE'S IN DANGER...
...THIS WORLD IS A HUNDRED TIMES MORE EXCITING THAN SHITTY OLD TOKYO.

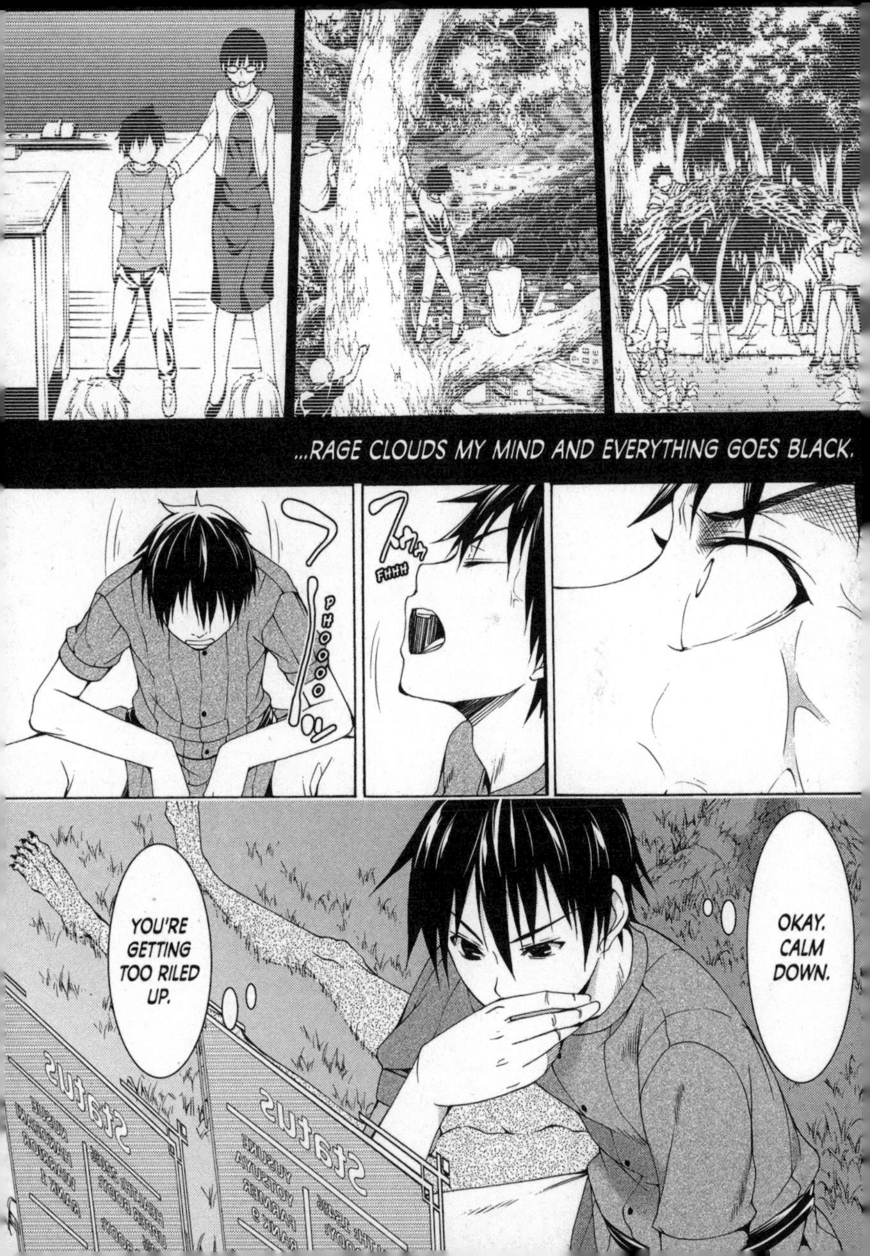
...RAGE CLOUDS MY MIND AND EVERYTHING GOES BLACK.
FHHH
PHOOOOO
OKAY. CALM DOWN.
YOU'RE GETTING TOO RILED UP.

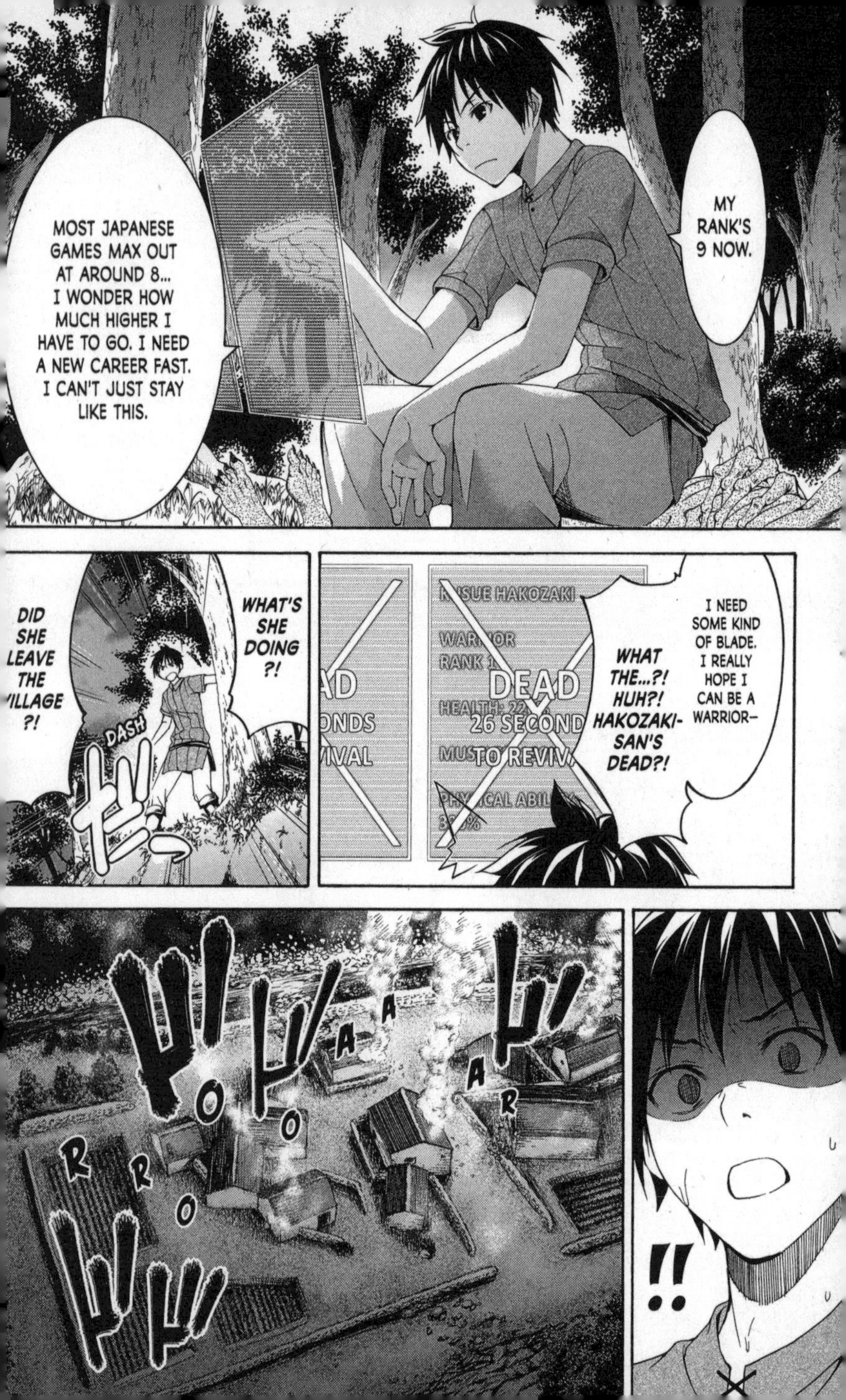
MY RANK'S 9 NOW.
MOST JAPANESE GAMES MAX OUT AT AROUND 8... I WONDER HOW MUCH HIGHER I HAVE TO GO. I NEED A NEW CAREER FAST. I CAN'T JUST STAY LIKE THIS.
I NEED SOME KIND OF BLADE. I REALLY HOPE I CAN BE A WARRIOR—
WHAT THE...?! HUH?! HAKOZAKI-SAN'S DEAD?!
DEAD
WHAT'S SHE DOING?!
DID SHE LEAVE THE VILLAGE?!
DASH
!!
RROOOAAR

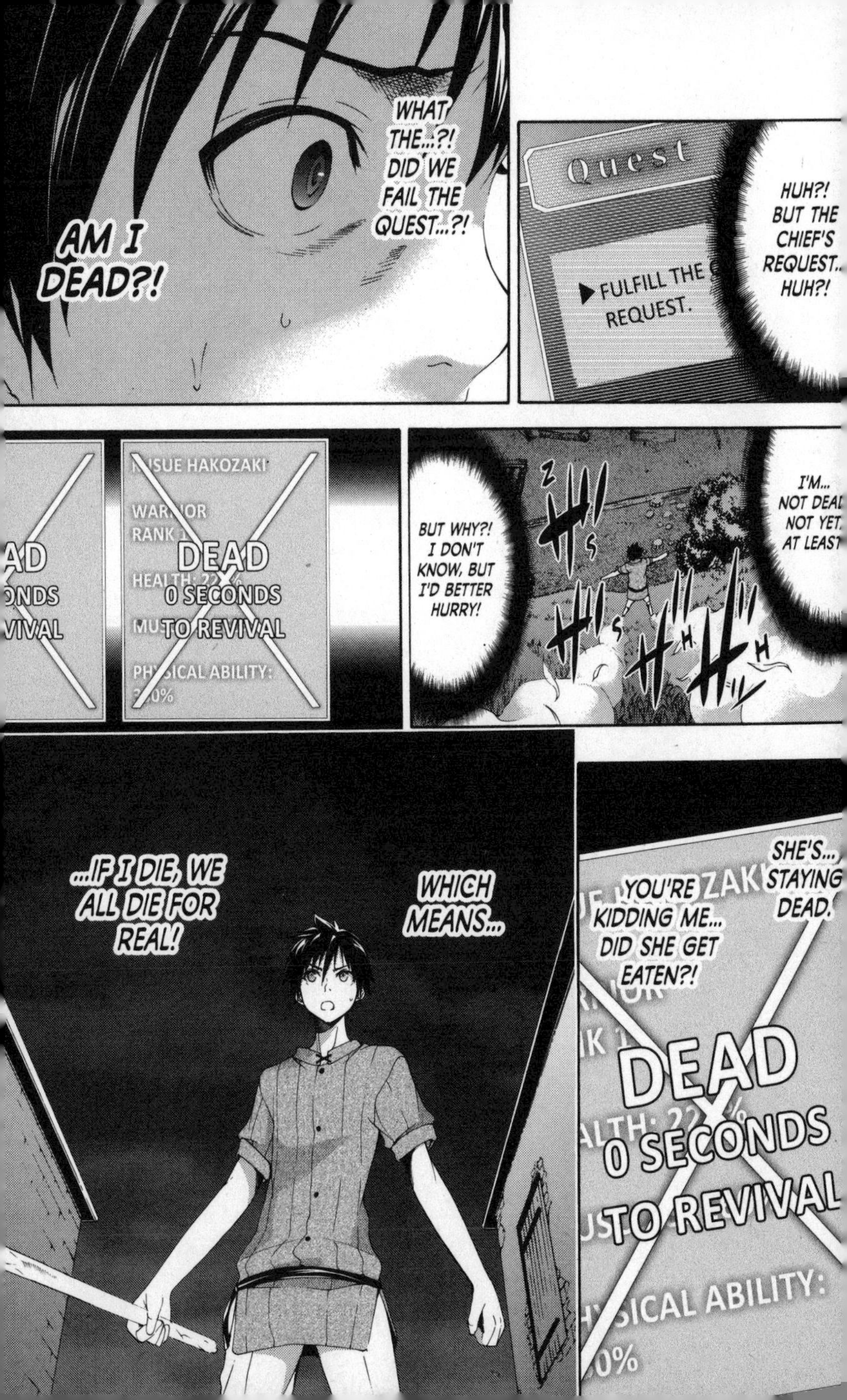
HUH?! BUT THE CHIEF'S REQUEST.. HUH?!
Quest
▶ FULFILL THE
REQUEST.
WHAT THE...?! DID WE FAIL THE QUEST...?!
AM I DEAD?!
I'M... NOT DEAD NOT YET. AT LEAST
BUT WHY?! I DON'T KNOW, BUT I'D BETTER HURRY!
SUE HAKOZAKI
WARRIOR
RANK 1
DEAD
0 SECONDS
TO REVIVAL
PHYSICAL ABILITY:
SHE'S... STAYING DEAD.
YOU'RE KIDDING ME... DID SHE GET EATEN?!
DEAD
0 SECONDS
TO REVIVAL
PHYSICAL ABILITY:
WHICH MEANS...
...IF I DIE, WE ALL DIE FOR REAL!

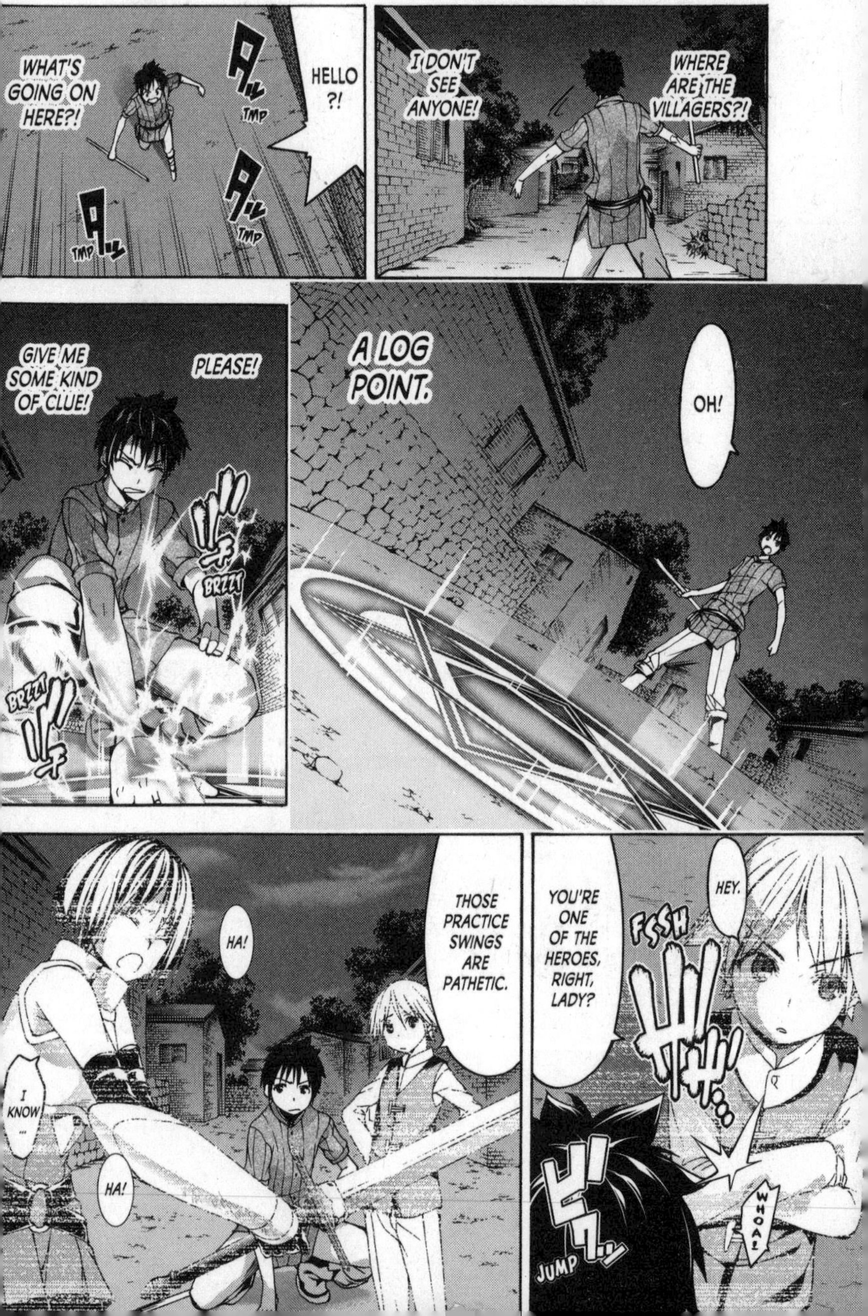
WHERE ARE THE VILLAGERS?!
I DON'T SEE ANYONE!
HELLO ?!
WHAT'S GOING ON HERE?!
TMP
TMP
TMP
OH!
A LOG POINT.
PLEASE!
GIVE ME SOME KIND OF CLUE!
BRZZT
BRZZT
HEY.
FSSH
YOU'RE ONE OF THE HEROES, RIGHT, LADY?
WHOA!
JUMP
THOSE PRACTICE SWINGS ARE PATHETIC.
HA!
I KNOW...
HA!

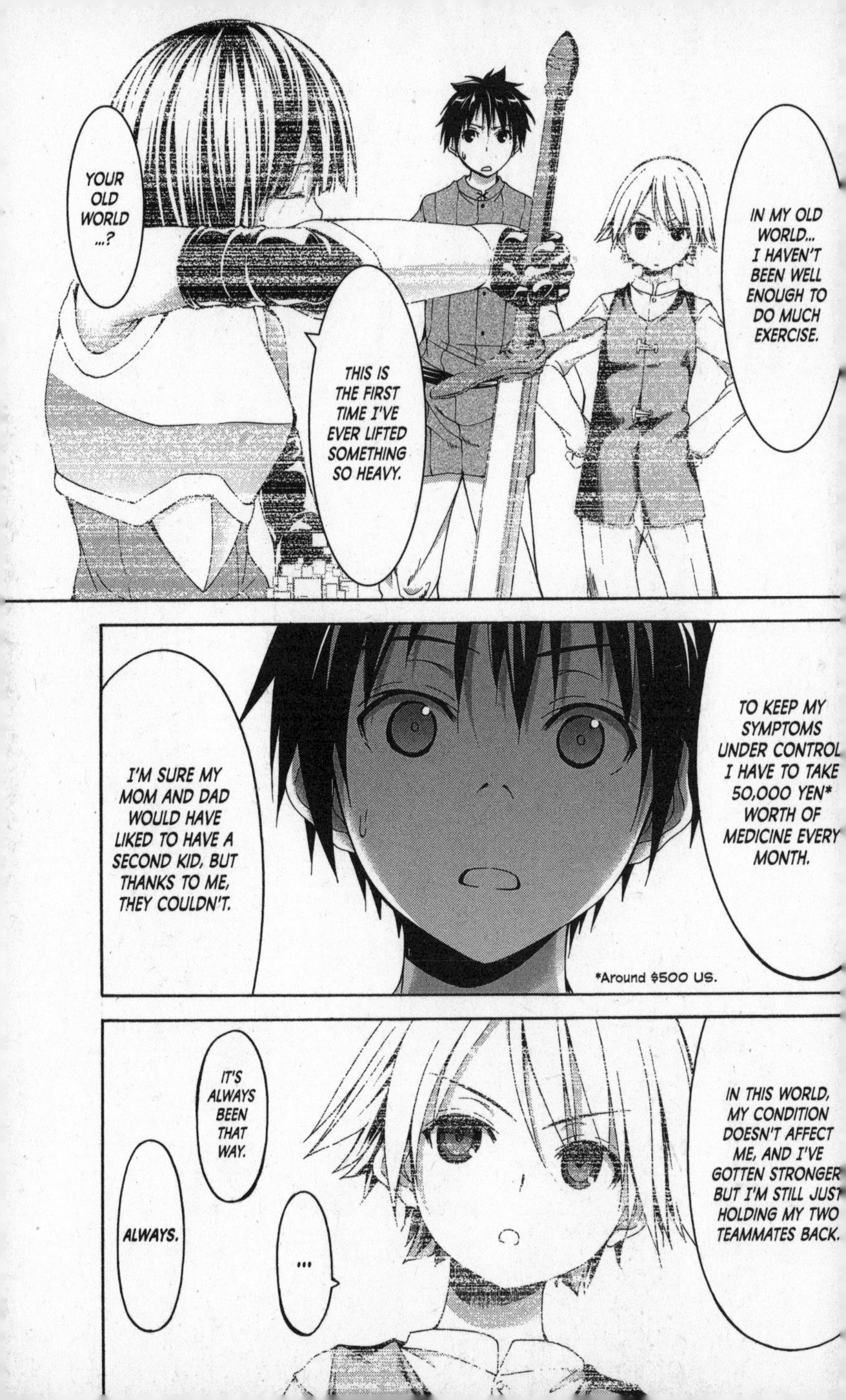
IN MY OLD WORLD... I HAVEN'T BEEN WELL ENOUGH TO DO MUCH EXERCISE.
YOUR OLD WORLD ...?
THIS IS THE FIRST TIME I'VE EVER LIFTED SOMETHING SO HEAVY.
TO KEEP MY SYMPTOMS UNDER CONTROL I HAVE TO TAKE 50,000 YEN* WORTH OF MEDICINE EVERY MONTH.
I'M SURE MY MOM AND DAD WOULD HAVE LIKED TO HAVE A SECOND KID, BUT THANKS TO ME, THEY COULDN'T.
*Around $500 US.
IN THIS WORLD, MY CONDITION DOESN'T AFFECT ME, AND I'VE GOTTEN STRONGER BUT I'M STILL JUST HOLDING MY TWO TEAMMATES BACK.
IT'S ALWAYS BEEN THAT WAY.
...
ALWAYS.

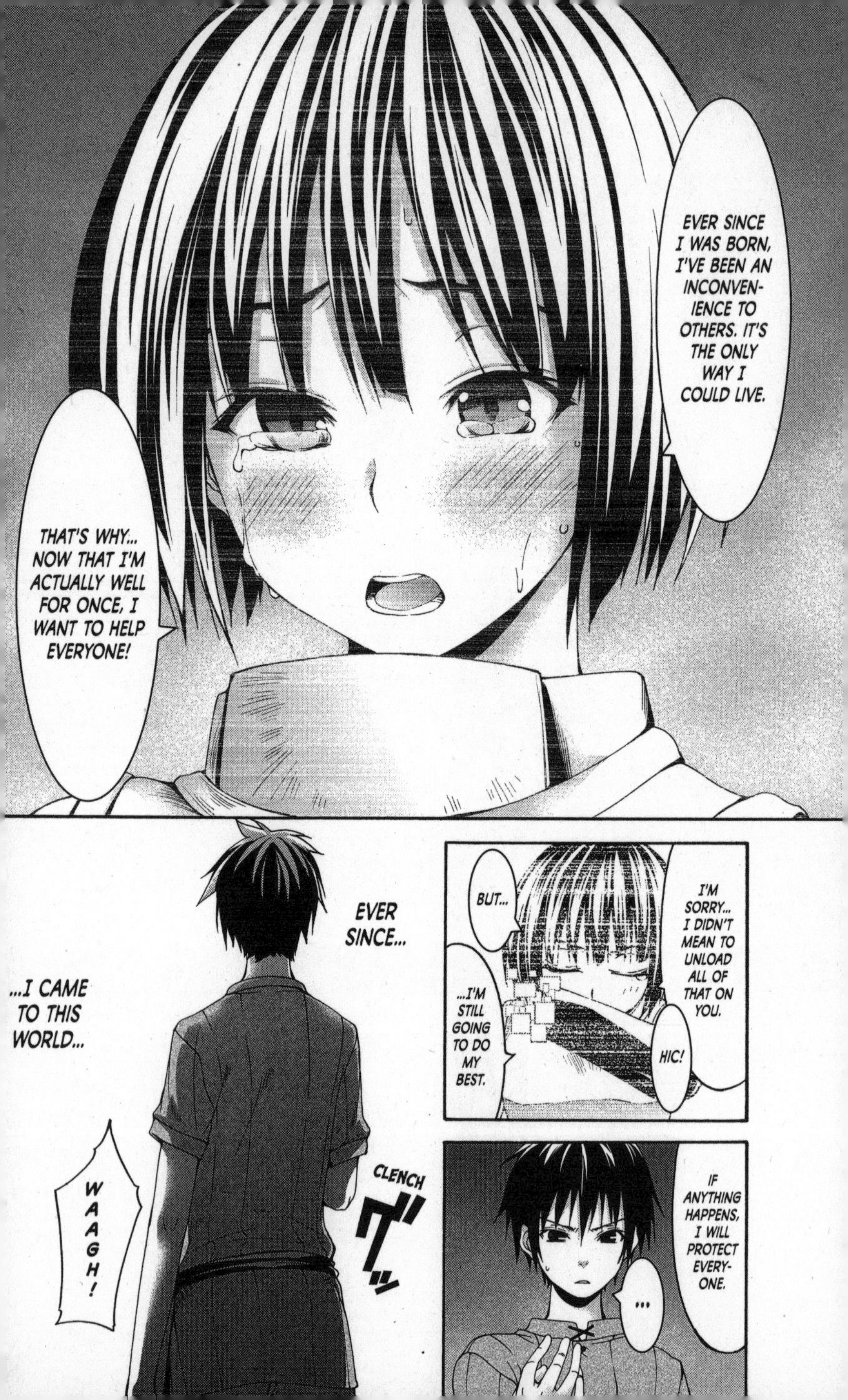
EVER SINCE I WAS BORN, I'VE BEEN AN INCONVEN-IENCE TO OTHERS. IT'S THE ONLY WAY I COULD LIVE.
THAT'S WHY... NOW THAT I'M ACTUALLY WELL FOR ONCE, I WANT TO HELP EVERYONE!
I'M SORRY... I DIDN'T MEAN TO UNLOAD ALL OF THAT ON YOU.
HIC!
BUT...
...I'M STILL GOING TO DO MY BEST.
IF ANYTHING HAPPENS, I WILL PROTECT EVERY-ONE.
...
EVER SINCE...
...I CAME TO THIS WORLD...
CLENCH
WAAGH!

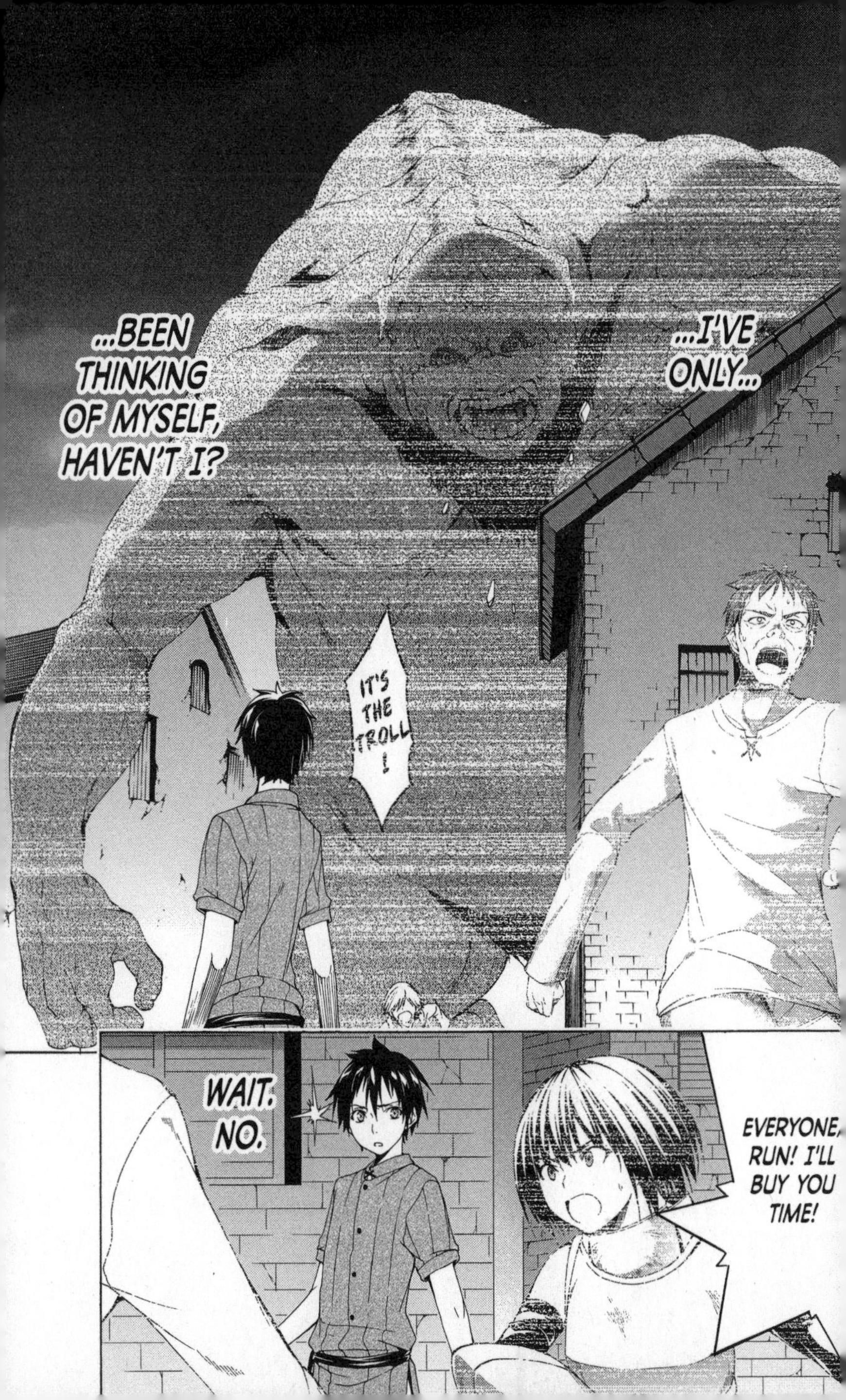
...I'VE ONLY...
...BEEN THINKING OF MYSELF, HAVEN'T I?
IT'S THE TROLL!
EVERYONE, RUN! I'LL BUY YOU TIME!
WAIT. NO.

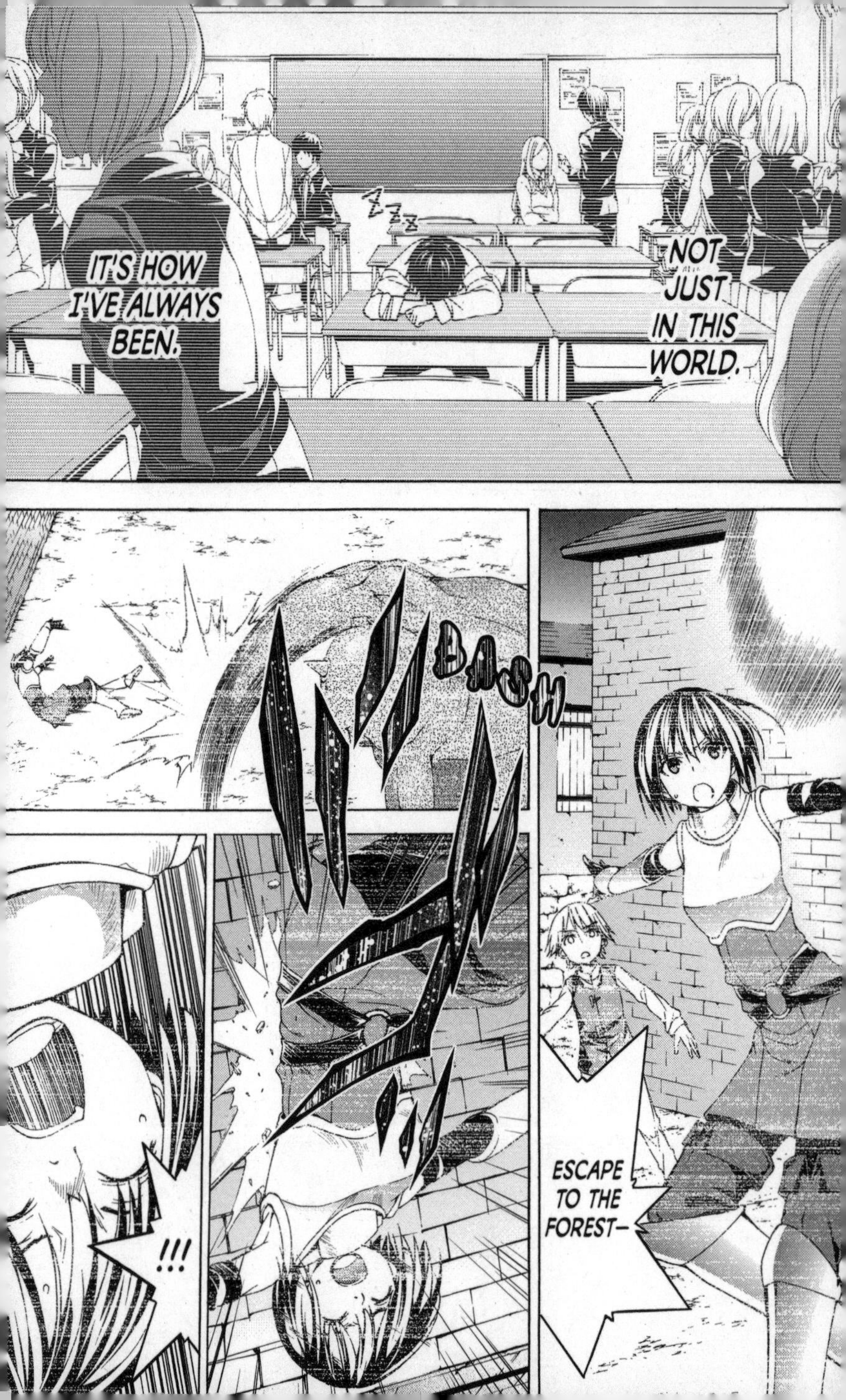
Z Z Z
NOT JUST IN THIS WORLD.
IT'S HOW I'VE ALWAYS BEEN.
ESCAPE TO THE FOREST—
BASH
!!!

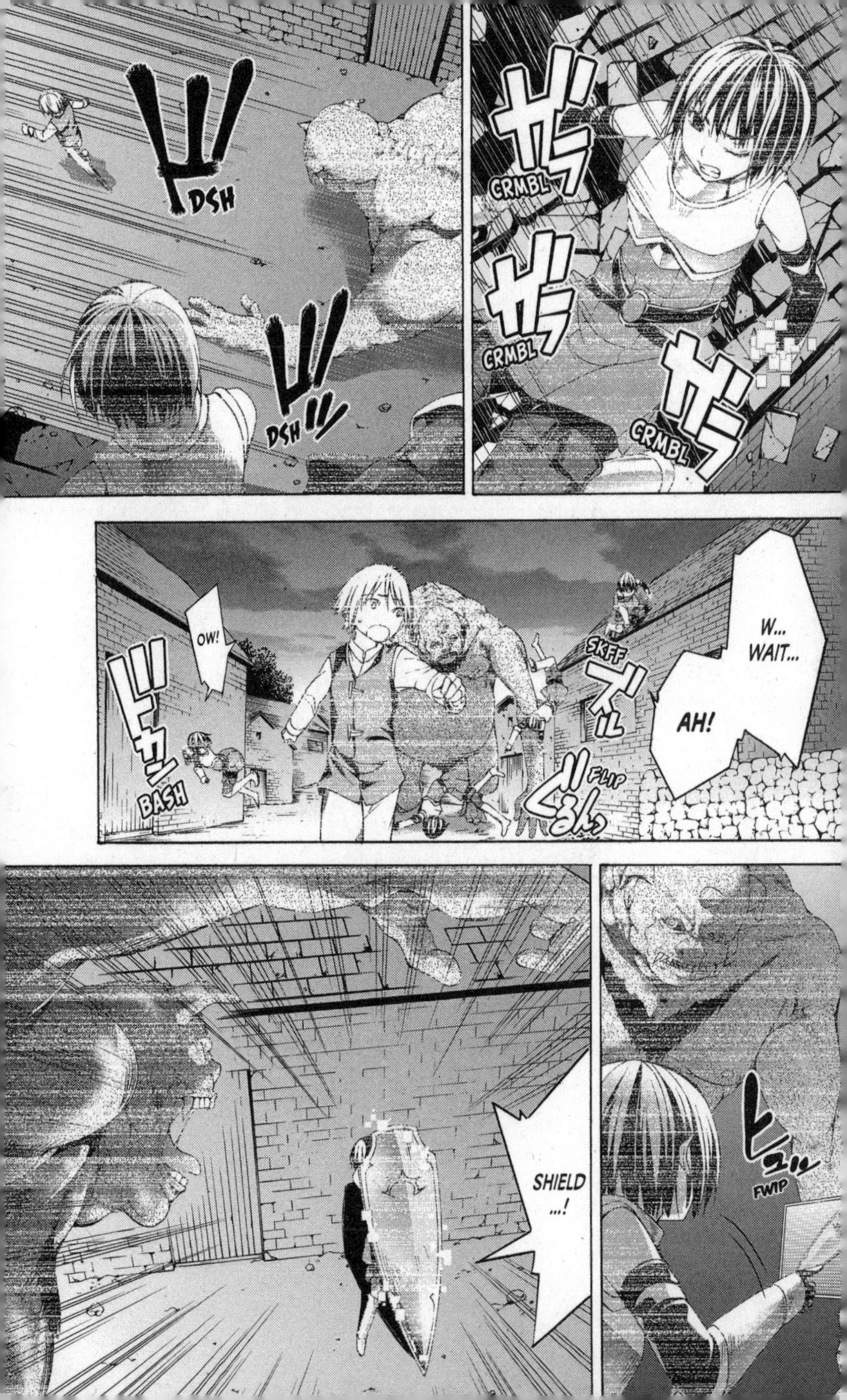
ザラ
CRMBL
ザラ
CRMBL
ザラ
CRMBL
ドッ
DSH
ドッ
DSH
W... WAIT...
AH!
ズル
SKFF
くるんっ
FLIP
OW!
ドカン
BASH
ヒュッ
FWIP
SHIELD ...!

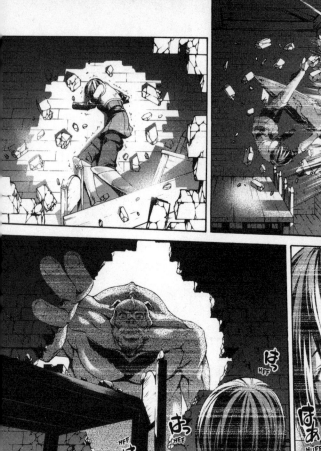

SMASH

HFF

はっ HFF

は HFF

はっ HFF

はあ HUFF

はあ HUFF

はあ HUFF

HELP...

ZRRK

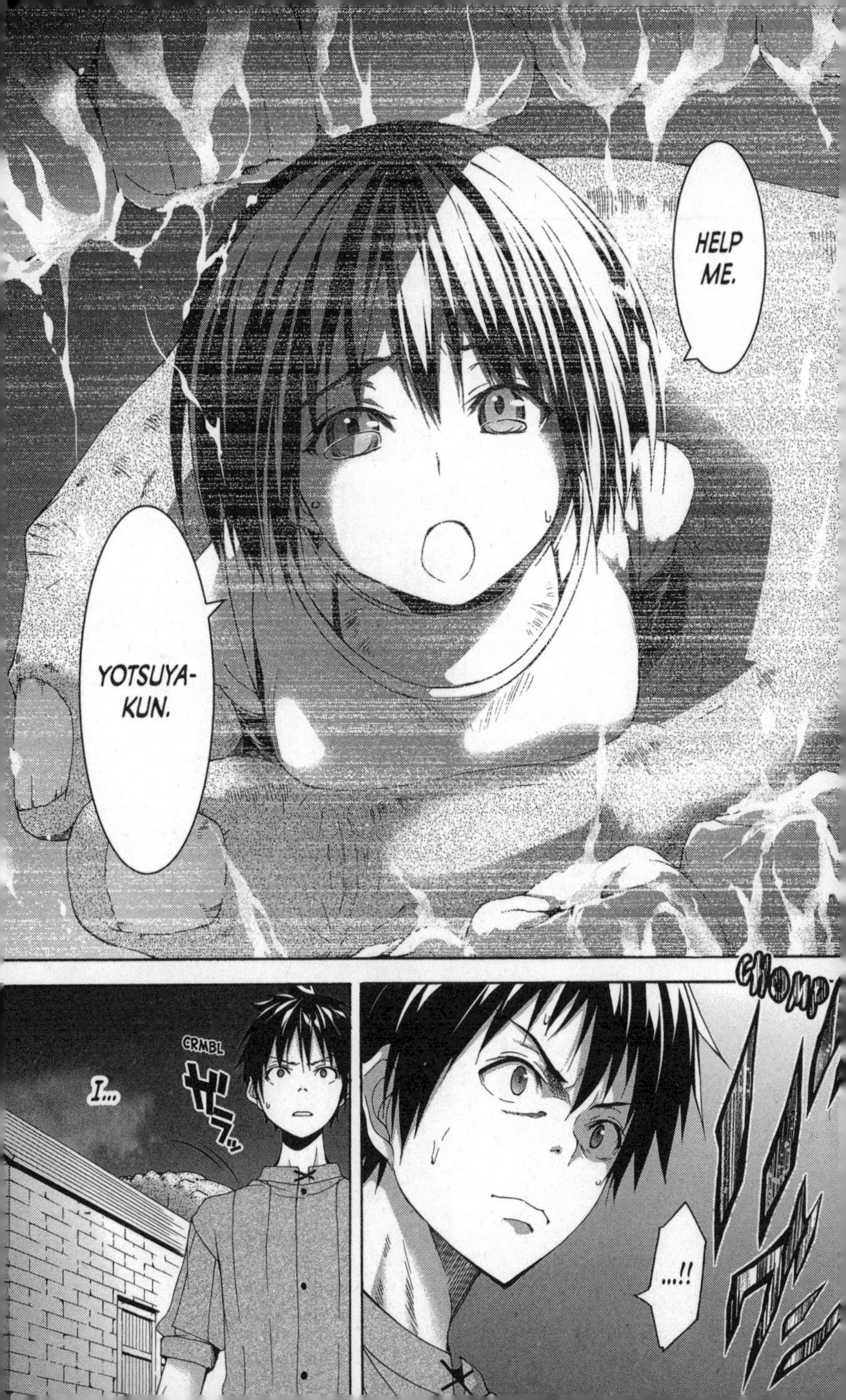
HELP ME.
YOTSUYA-KUN.
CHOMP
...!!
CRMBL
I...

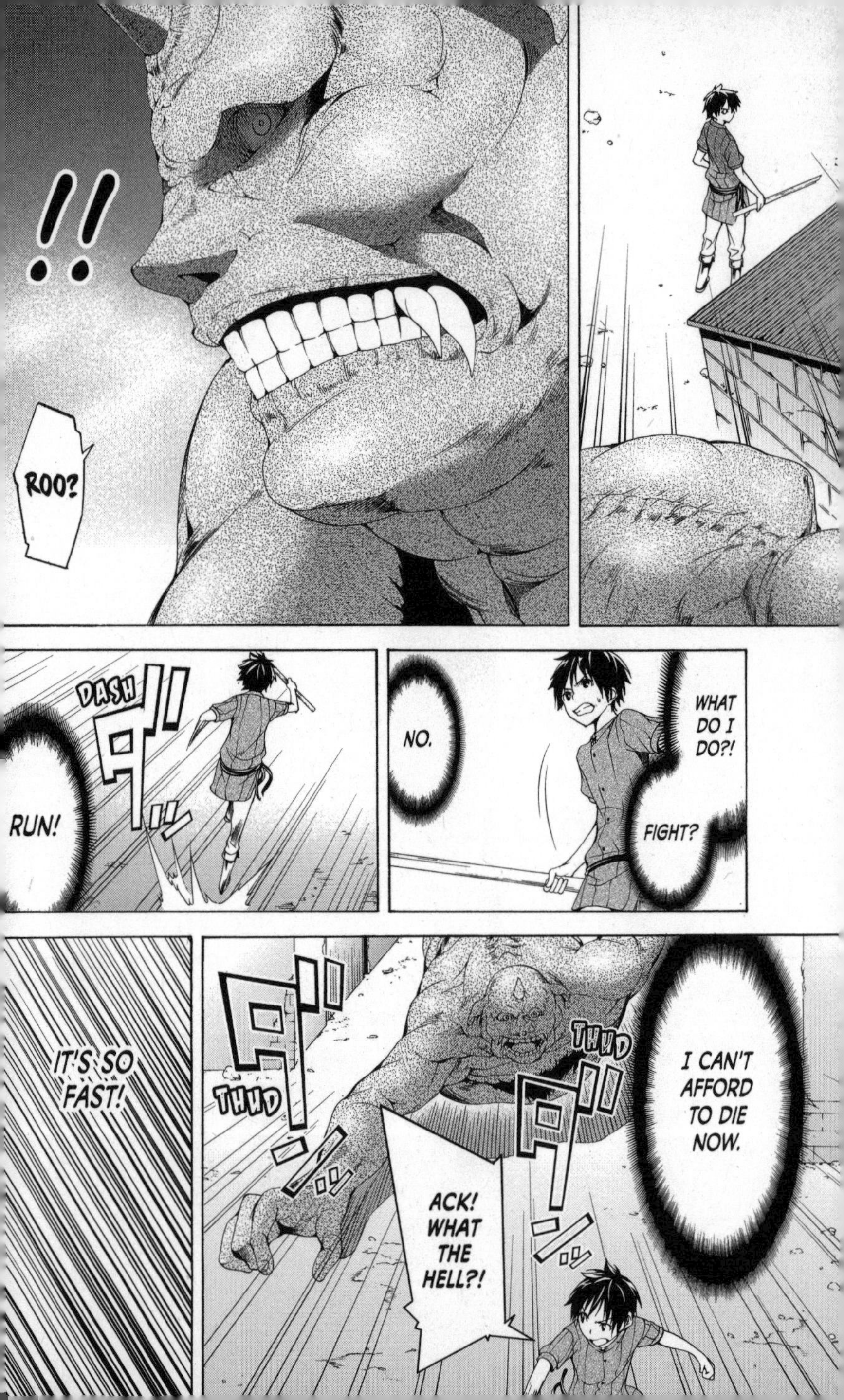
!!
ROO?
WHAT DO I DO?!
FIGHT?
NO.
DASH
RUN!
I CAN'T AFFORD TO DIE NOW.
THUD
ACK! WHAT THE HELL?!
THUD
IT'S SO FAST!

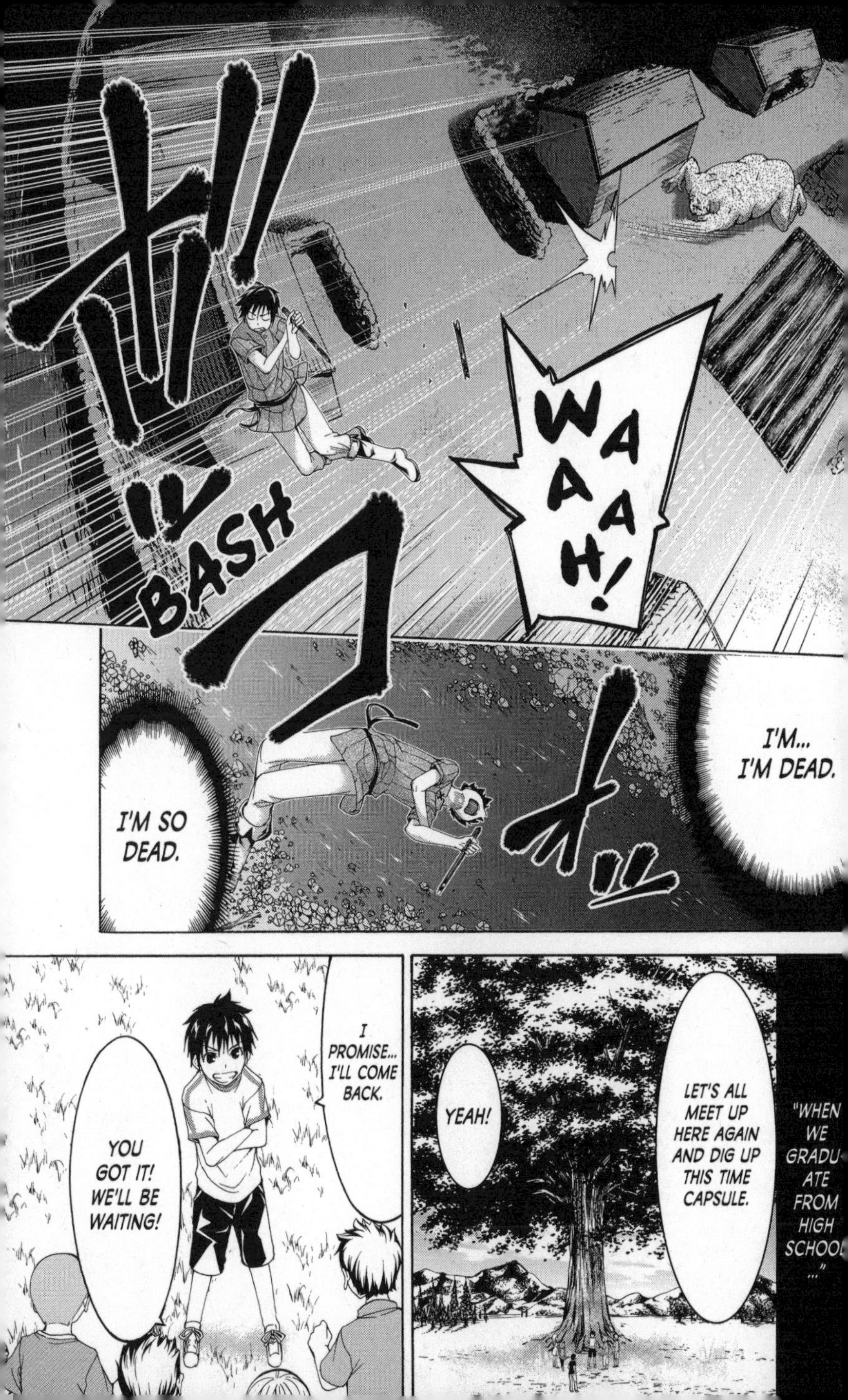
WAAAH!
BASH
I'M... I'M DEAD.
I'M SO DEAD.
"WHEN WE GRADUATE FROM HIGH SCHOOL..."
LET'S ALL MEET UP HERE AGAIN AND DIG UP THIS TIME CAPSULE.
YEAH!
I PROMISE... I'LL COME BACK.
YOU GOT IT! WE'LL BE WAITING!

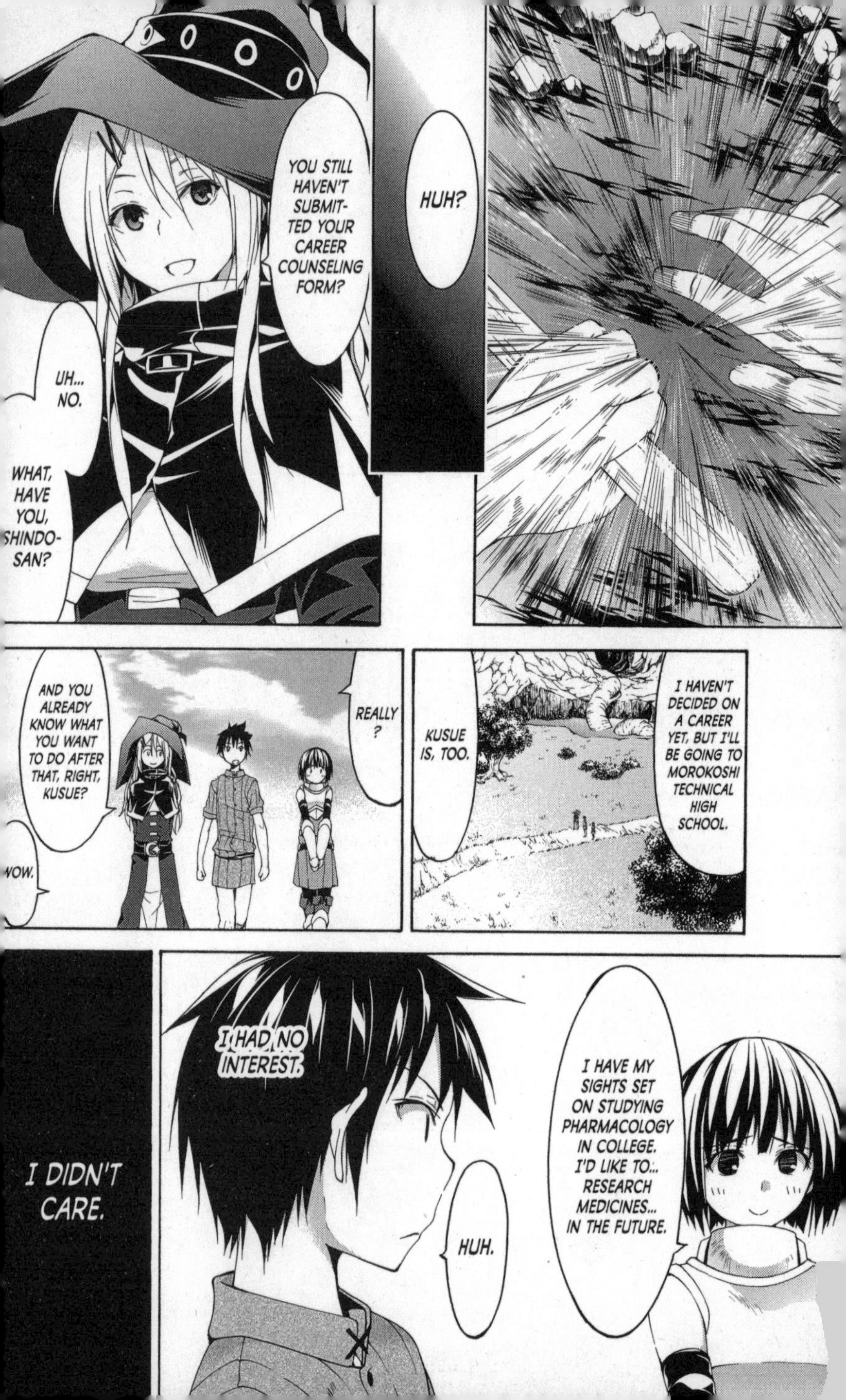
HUH?
YOU STILL HAVEN'T SUBMIT-TED YOUR CAREER COUNSELING FORM?
UH... NO.
WHAT, HAVE YOU, SHINDO-SAN?
I HAVEN'T DECIDED ON A CAREER YET, BUT I'LL BE GOING TO MOROKOSHI TECHNICAL HIGH SCHOOL.
KUSUE IS, TOO.
REALLY?
AND YOU ALREADY KNOW WHAT YOU WANT TO DO AFTER THAT, RIGHT, KUSUE?
NOW.
I HAVE MY SIGHTS SET ON STUDYING PHARMACOLOGY IN COLLEGE. I'D LIKE TO... RESEARCH MEDICINES... IN THE FUTURE.
HUH.
I HAD NO INTEREST.
I DIDN'T CARE.

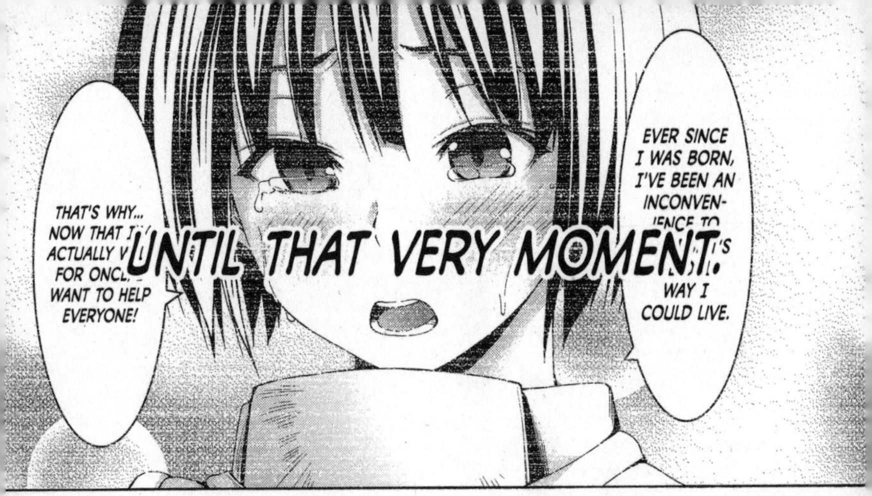
EVER SINCE I WAS BORN, I'VE BEEN AN INCONVEN-IENCE TO
WAY I COULD LIVE.
THAT'S WHY... NOW THAT I
ACTUALLY
FOR ONC
WANT TO HELP EVERYONE!
UNTIL THAT VERY MOMENT.

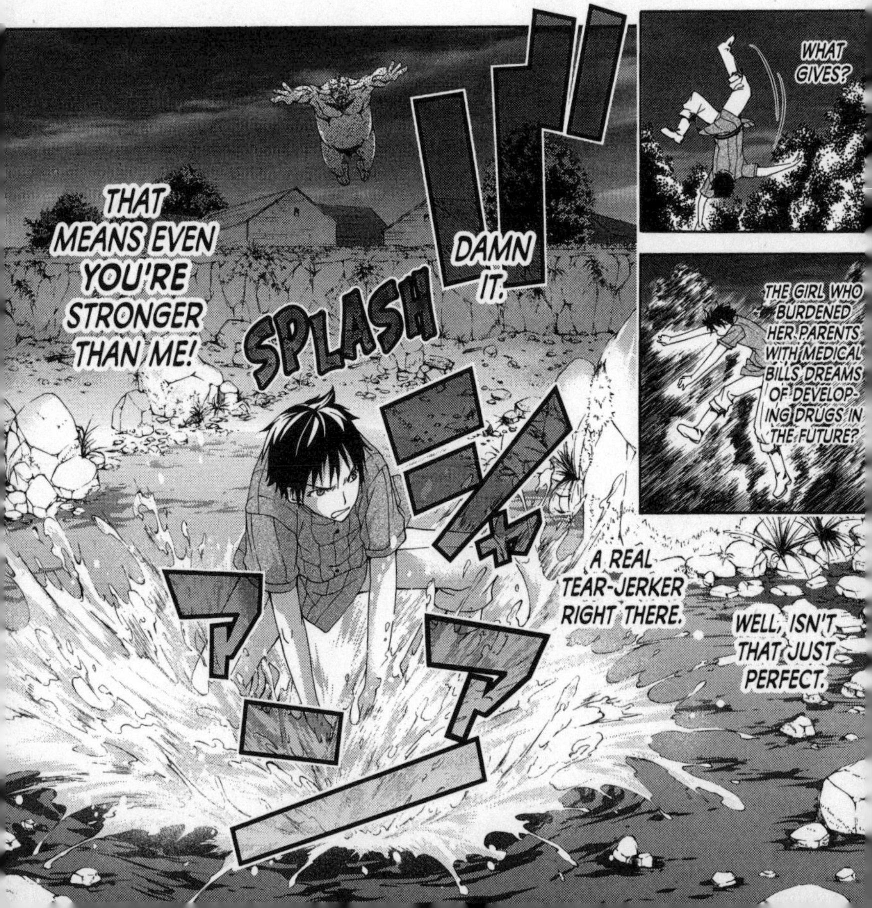
WHAT GIVES?
THE GIRL WHO BURDENED HER PARENTS WITH MEDICAL BILLS DREAMS OF DEVELOP-ING DRUGS IN THE FUTURE?
WELL, ISN'T THAT JUST PERFECT.
A REAL TEAR-JERKER RIGHT THERE.
DAMN IT.
THAT MEANS EVEN YOU'RE STRONGER THAN ME!
SPLASH

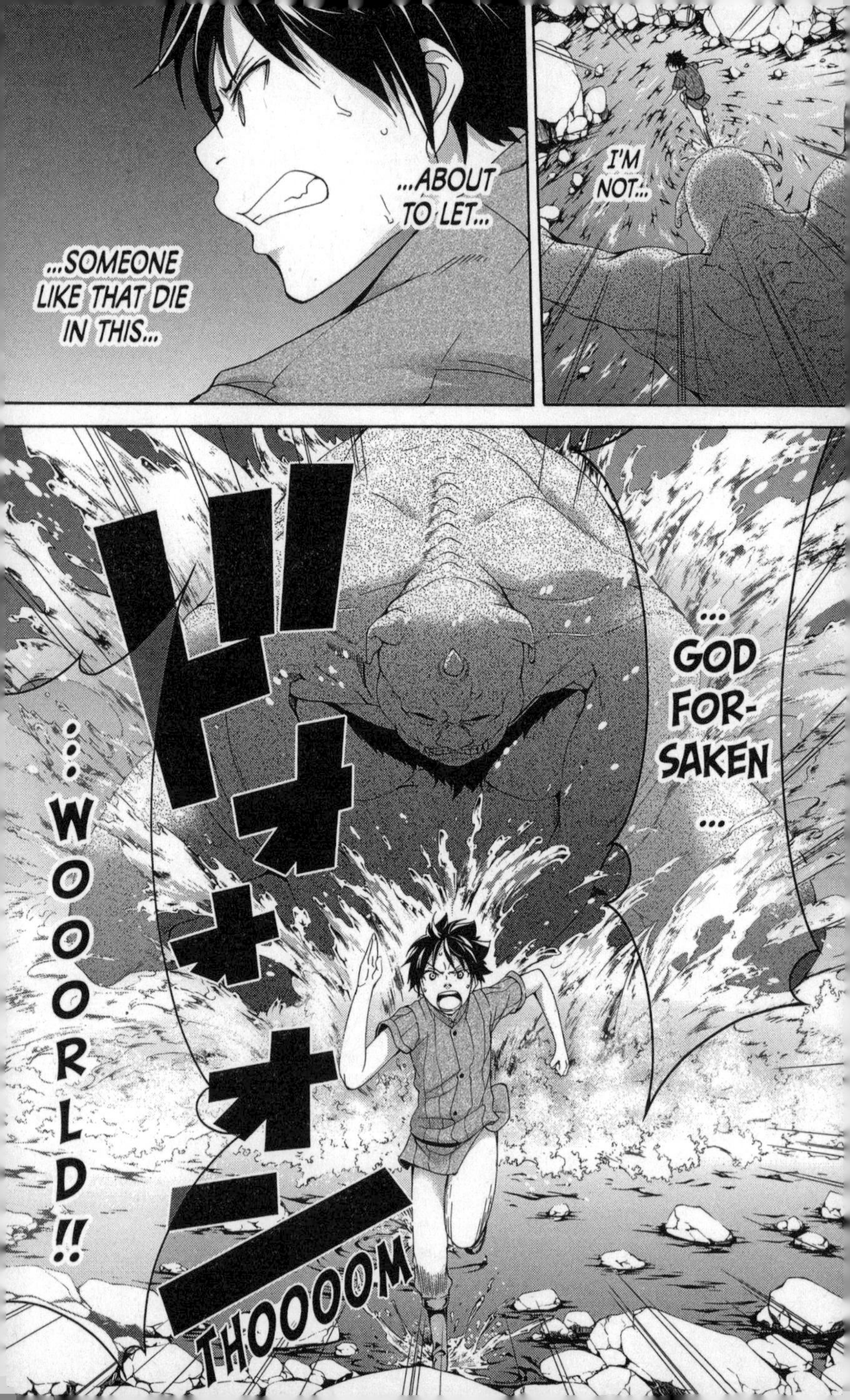
I'M NOT...
...ABOUT TO LET...
...SOMEONE LIKE THAT DIE IN THIS...
...GOD FOR-SAKEN ...
...WOOORLD!!
THOOOOM

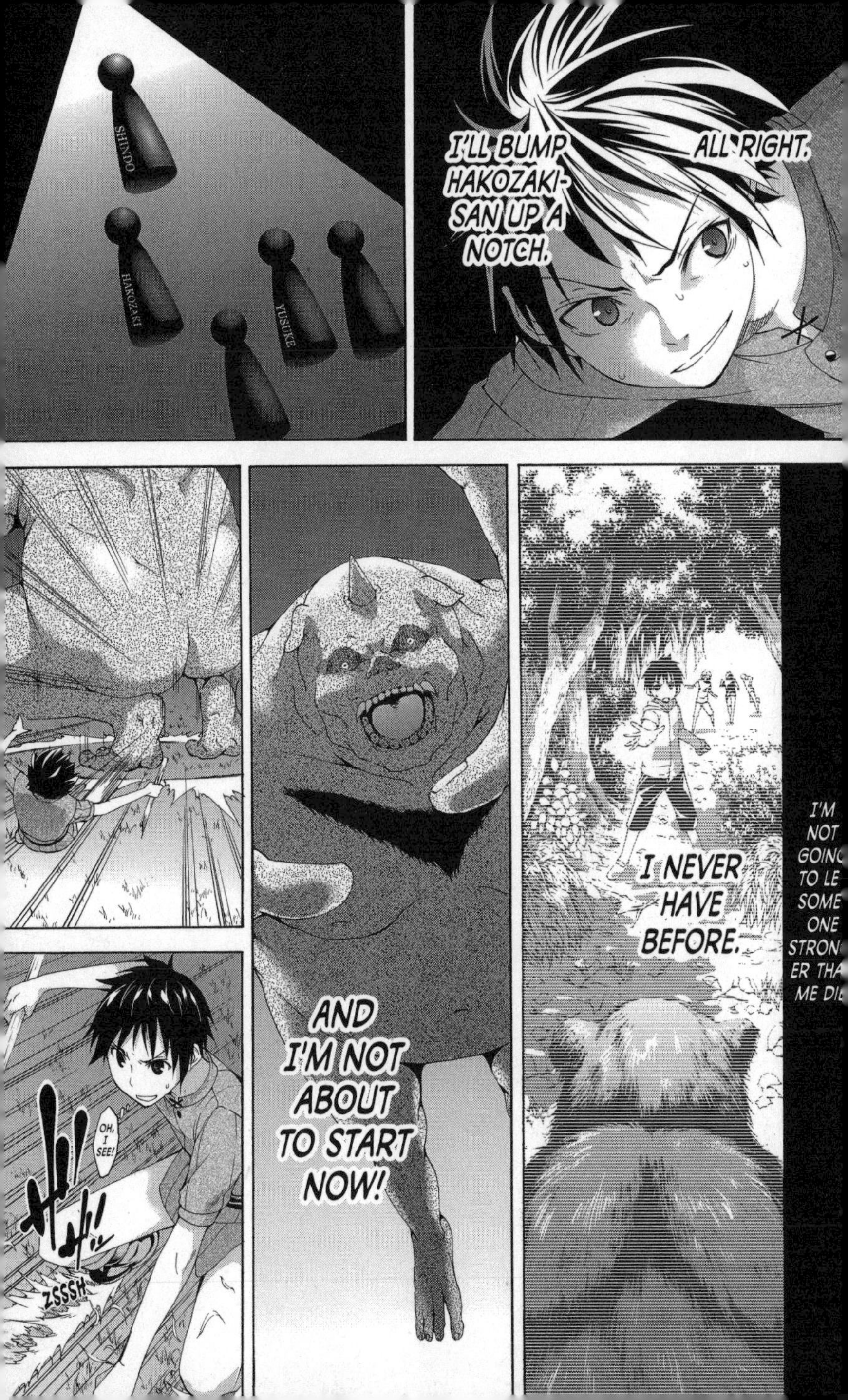

ALL RIGHT.
I'LL BUMP HAKOZAKI-SAN UP A NOTCH.
SHINDO
HAKOZAKI
YUSUKE
I'M NOT GOIN TO LE SOME ONE STRON ER THA ME DI
I NEVER HAVE BEFORE.
AND I'M NOT ABOUT TO START NOW!
OH, I SEE!
ZSSSH

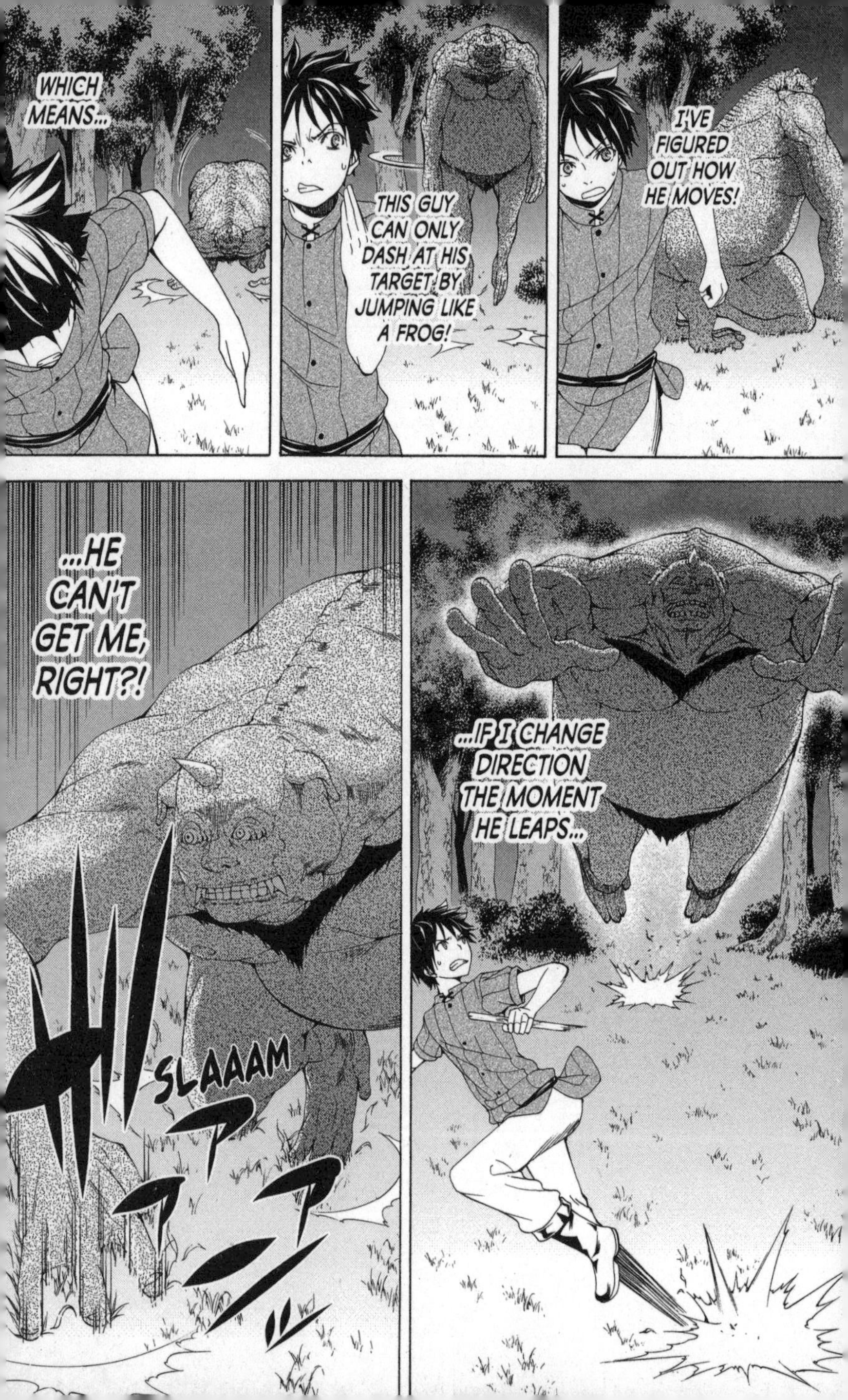
I'VE FIGURED OUT HOW HE MOVES!
THIS GUY CAN ONLY DASH AT HIS TARGET BY JUMPING LIKE A FROG!
WHICH MEANS...
...IF I CHANGE DIRECTION THE MOMENT HE LEAPS...
...HE CAN'T GET ME, RIGHT?!
SLAAAM

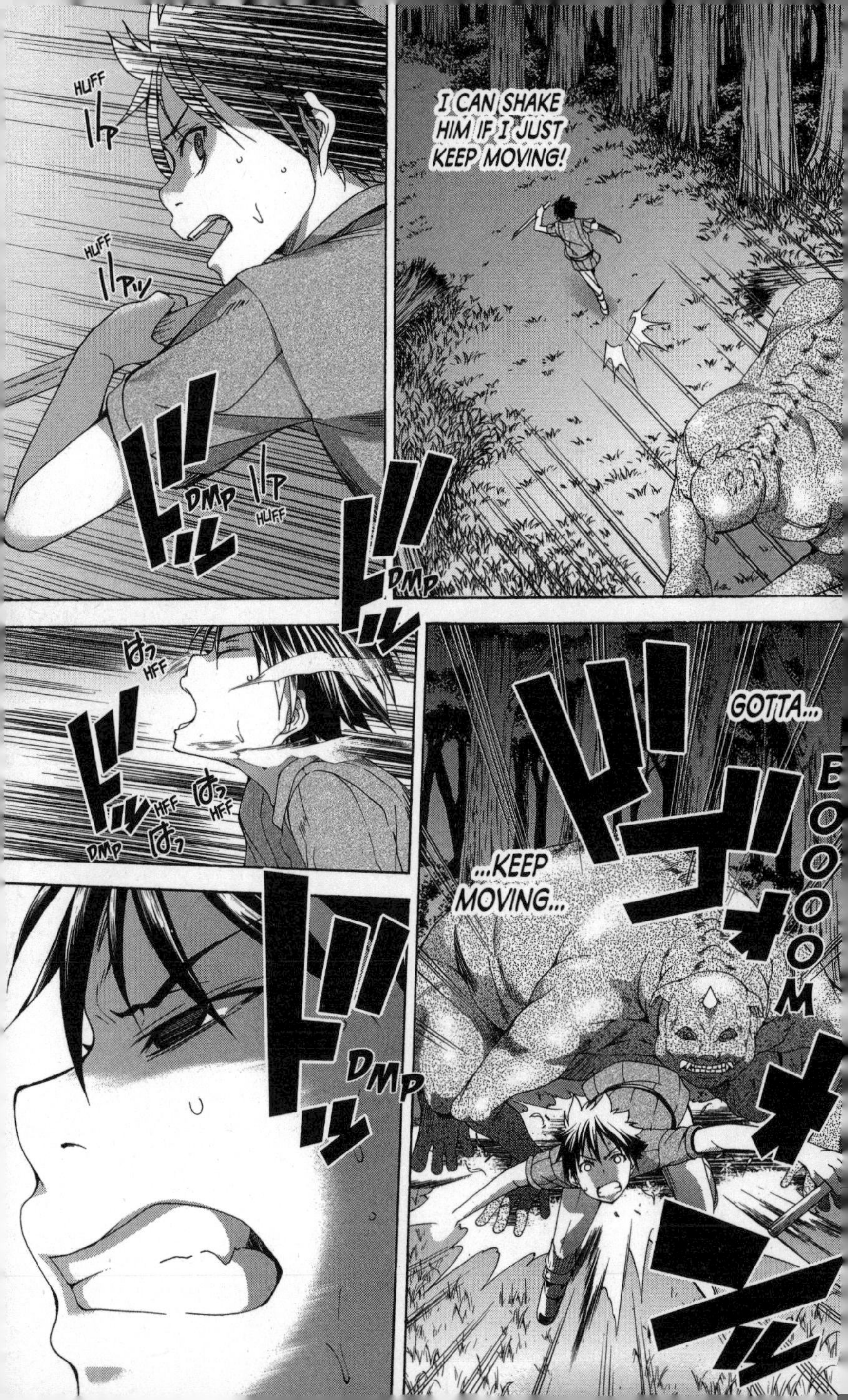
I CAN SHAKE HIM IF I JUST KEEP MOVING!
DMP
HUFF
HUFF
DMP
HUFF
GOTTA...
...KEEP MOVING...
BOOOOOM
はっ
HFF
はっ
HFF
HFF
はっ
DMP
DMP

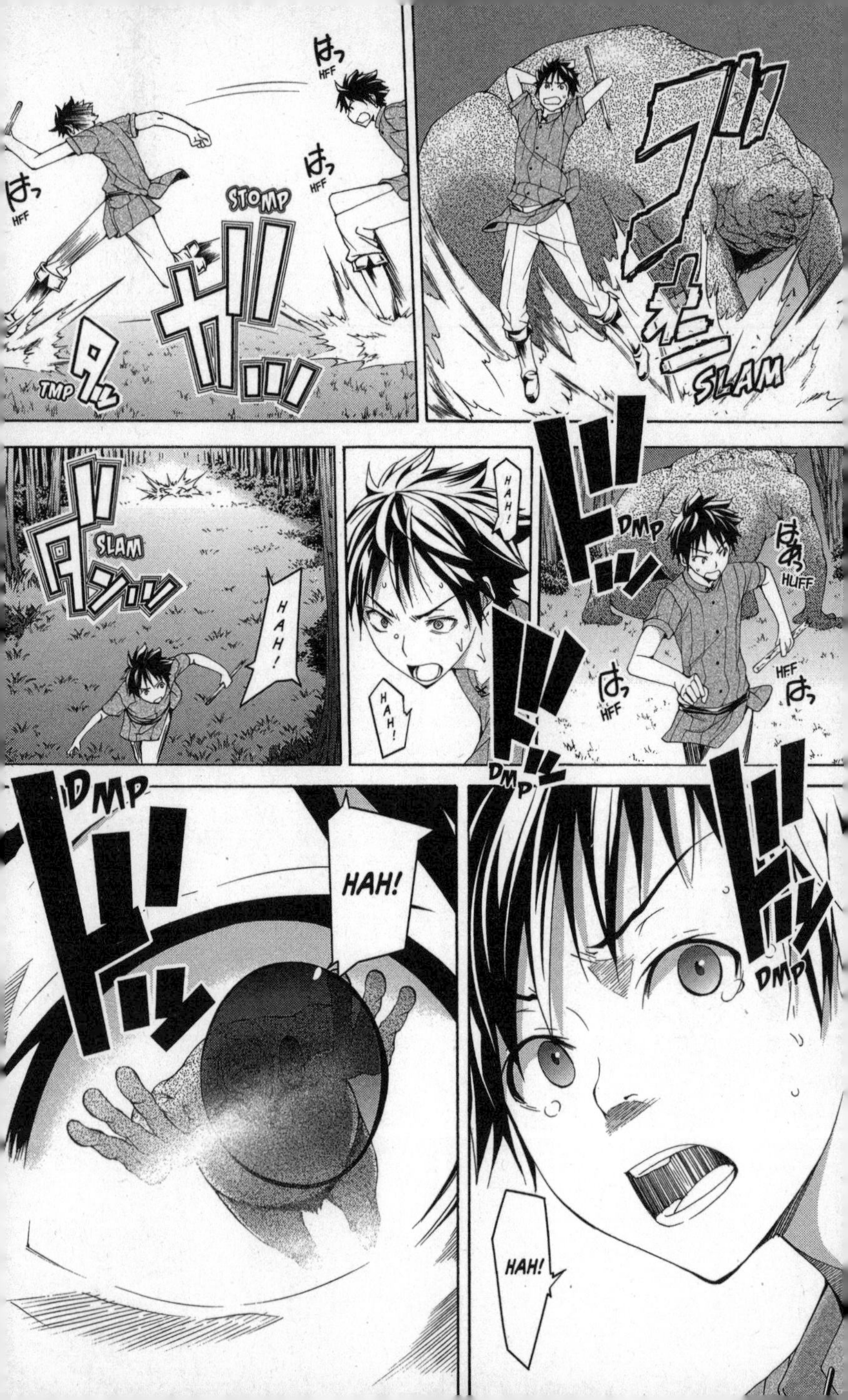

SLAM
はっ
HFF
はっ
HFF
STOMP
ザッ
タッ
TMP
はっ
HFF
ドッ
DMP
はあっ
HUFF
はっ
HFF
はっ
HFF
HAH!
HAH!
ダンッ
SLAM
HAH!
ドッ
DMP
ドッ
DMP
HAH!
ドッ
DMP
HAH!

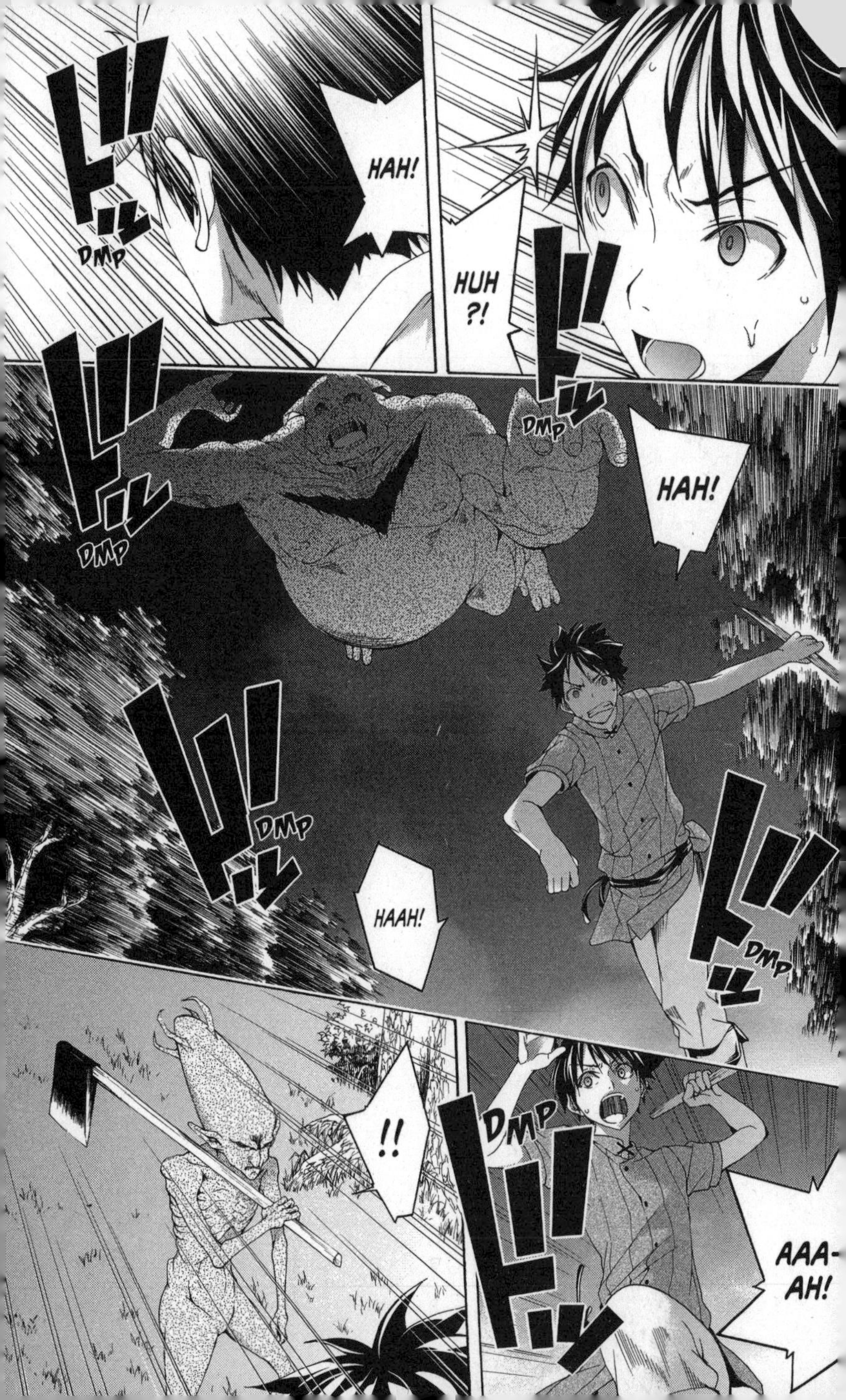

HUH ?!
HAH!
DMP
DMP
HAH!
DMP
DMP
DMP
HAAH!
AAA-AH!
DMP
!!

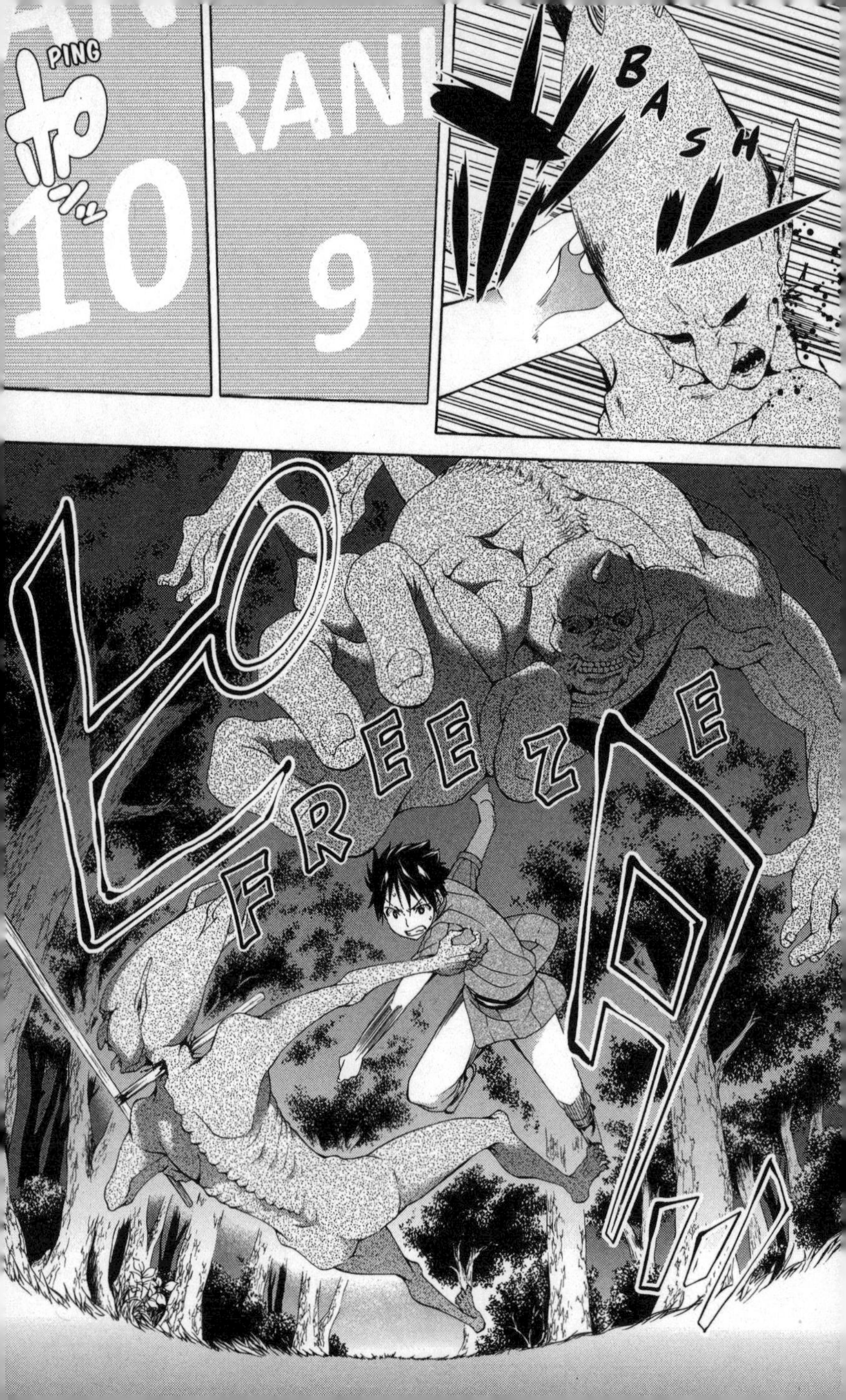
BASH
RAN
9
PING
10
FREEZE

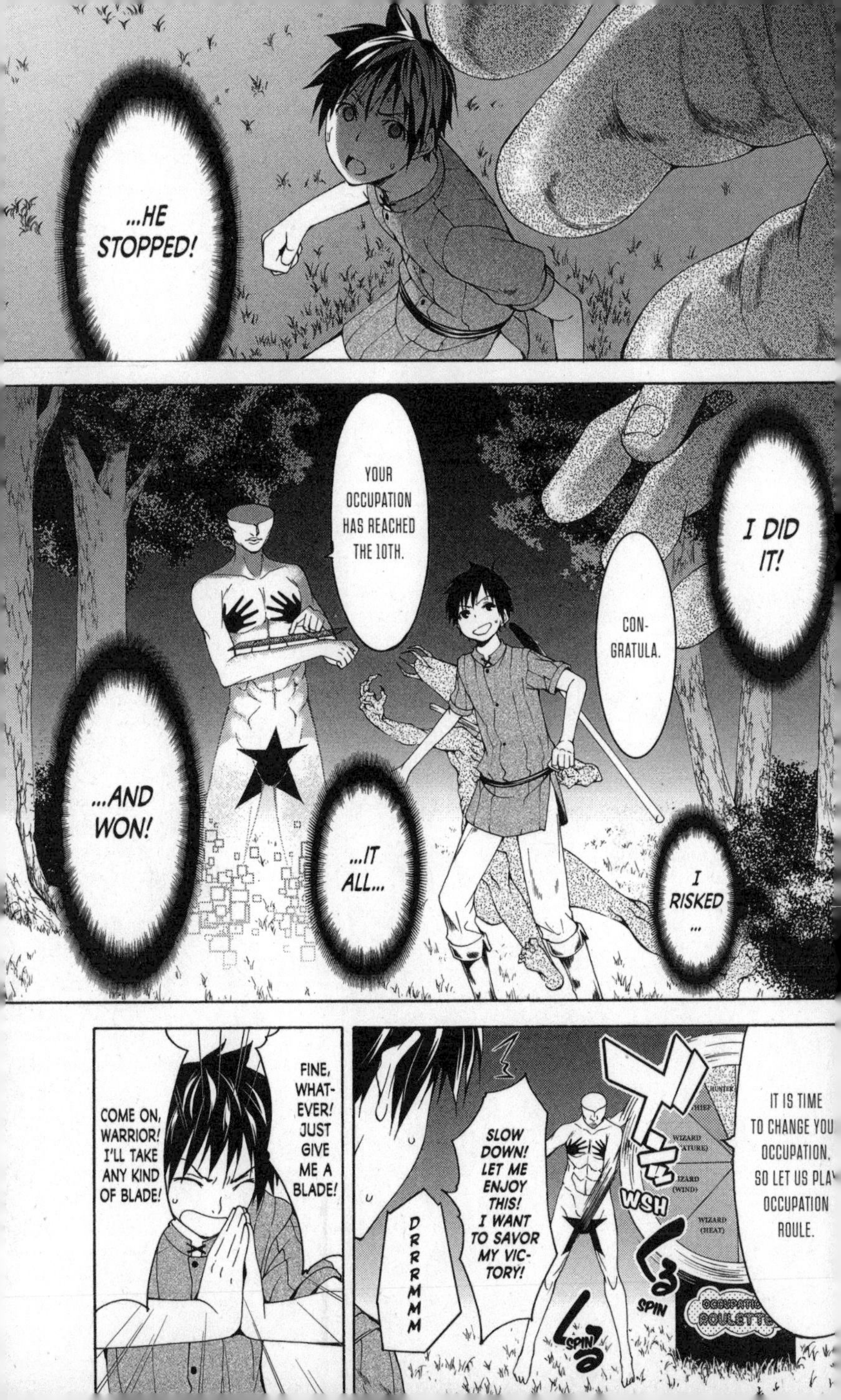
...HE STOPPED!
I DID IT!
CON-GRATULA.
YOUR OCCUPATION HAS REACHED THE 10TH.
I RISKED...
...IT ALL...
...AND WON!
IT IS TIME TO CHANGE YOU OCCUPATION, SO LET US PLA OCCUPATION ROULE.
WSH
SPIN
SPIN
SLOW DOWN! LET ME ENJOY THIS! I WANT TO SAVOR MY VIC-TORY!
DRRRMMM
FINE, WHAT-EVER! JUST GIVE ME A BLADE!
COME ON, WARRIOR! I'LL TAKE ANY KIND OF BLADE!

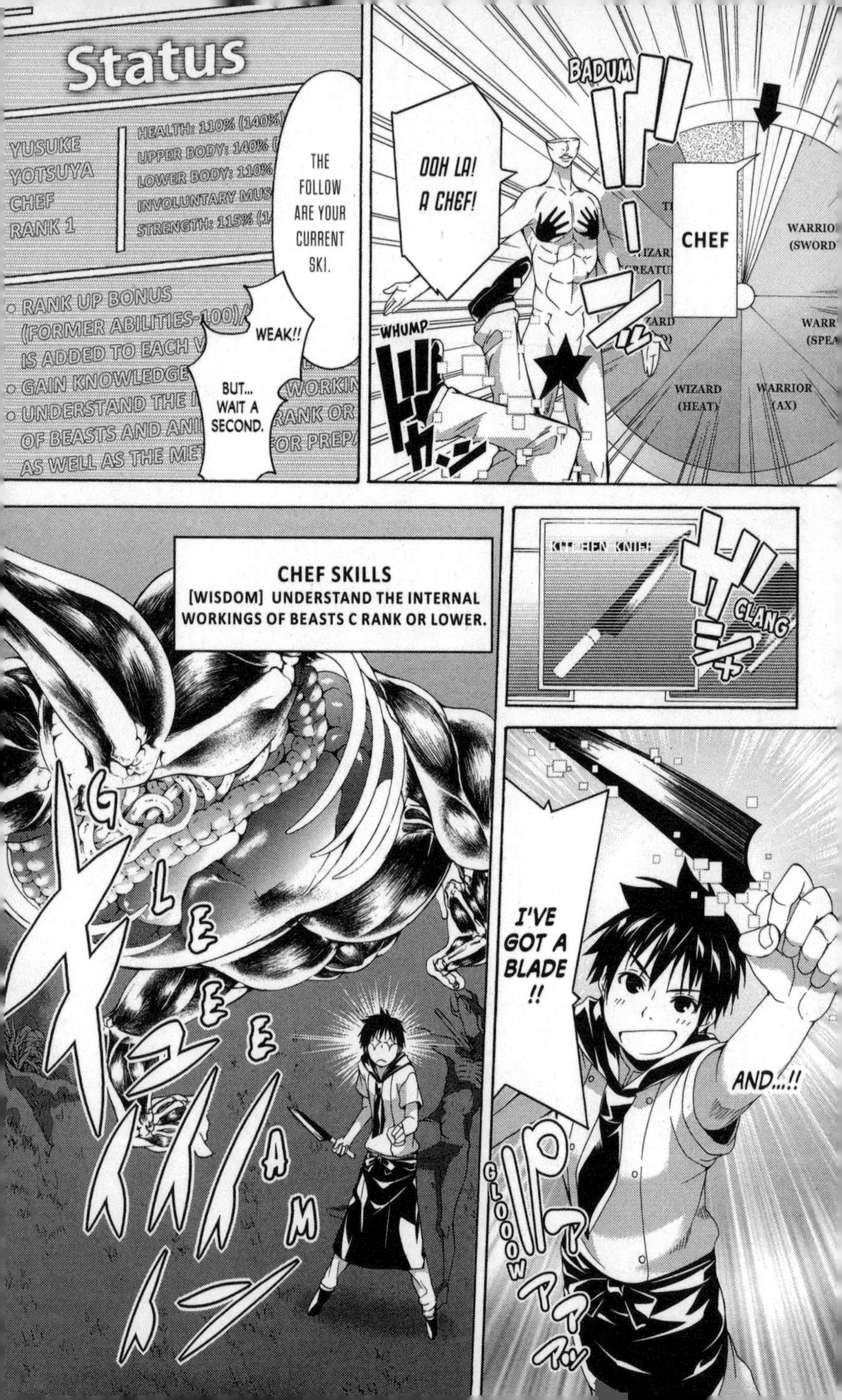
BADUM
OOH LA! A CHEF!
CHEF
WARRIOR (SWORD)
WIZARD
WARRIOR (AX)
WIZARD (HEAT)
WHUMP
Status
YUSUKE YOTSUYA CHEF RANK 1
HEALTH: 110% (140%)
UPPER BODY: 140%
LOWER BODY: 110%
INVOLUNTARY MUS
STRENGTH: 115%
RANK UP BONUS (FORMER ABILITIES-100)/
IS ADDED TO EACH V
GAIN KNOWLEDGE
UNDERSTAND THE
OF BEASTS AND ANI
AS WELL AS THE ME
WORKIN
RANK OR
FOR PREP
THE FOLLOW ARE YOUR CURRENT SKI.
WEAK!!
BUT... WAIT A SECOND.
KITCHEN KNIFE
CLANG
I'VE GOT A BLADE!!
AND...!!
GLOOOW
CHEF SKILLS
[WISDOM] UNDERSTAND THE INTERNAL WORKINGS OF BEASTS C RANK OR LOWER.
GLLEEEAM

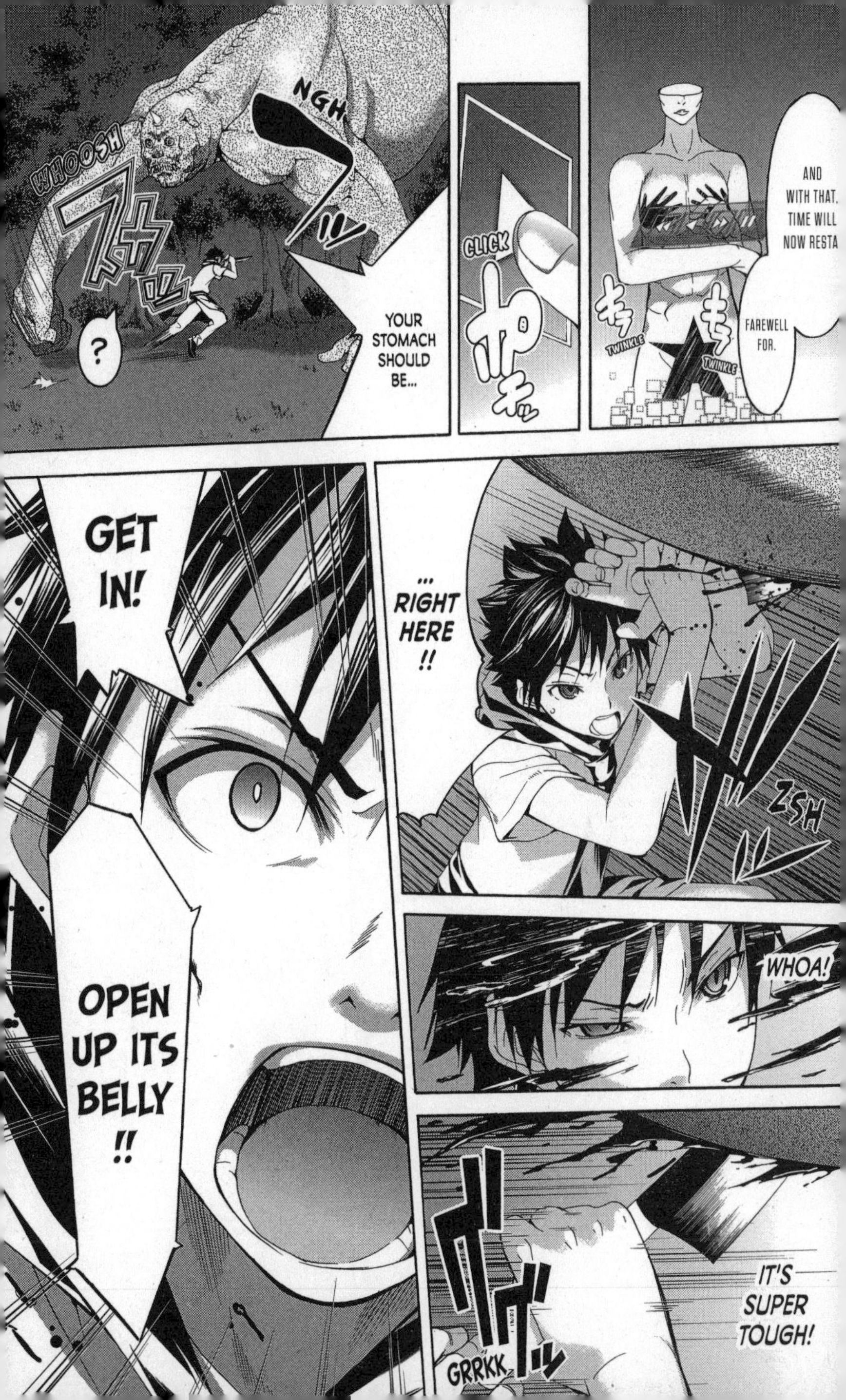
AND WITH THAT, TIME WILL NOW RESTA
FAREWELL FOR.
TWINKLE
TWINKLE
CLICK
NGH
WHOOSH
?
YOUR STOMACH SHOULD BE...
... RIGHT HERE !!
ZSH
WHOA!
IT'S SUPER TOUGH!
GRRKK
GET IN!
OPEN UP ITS BELLY !!

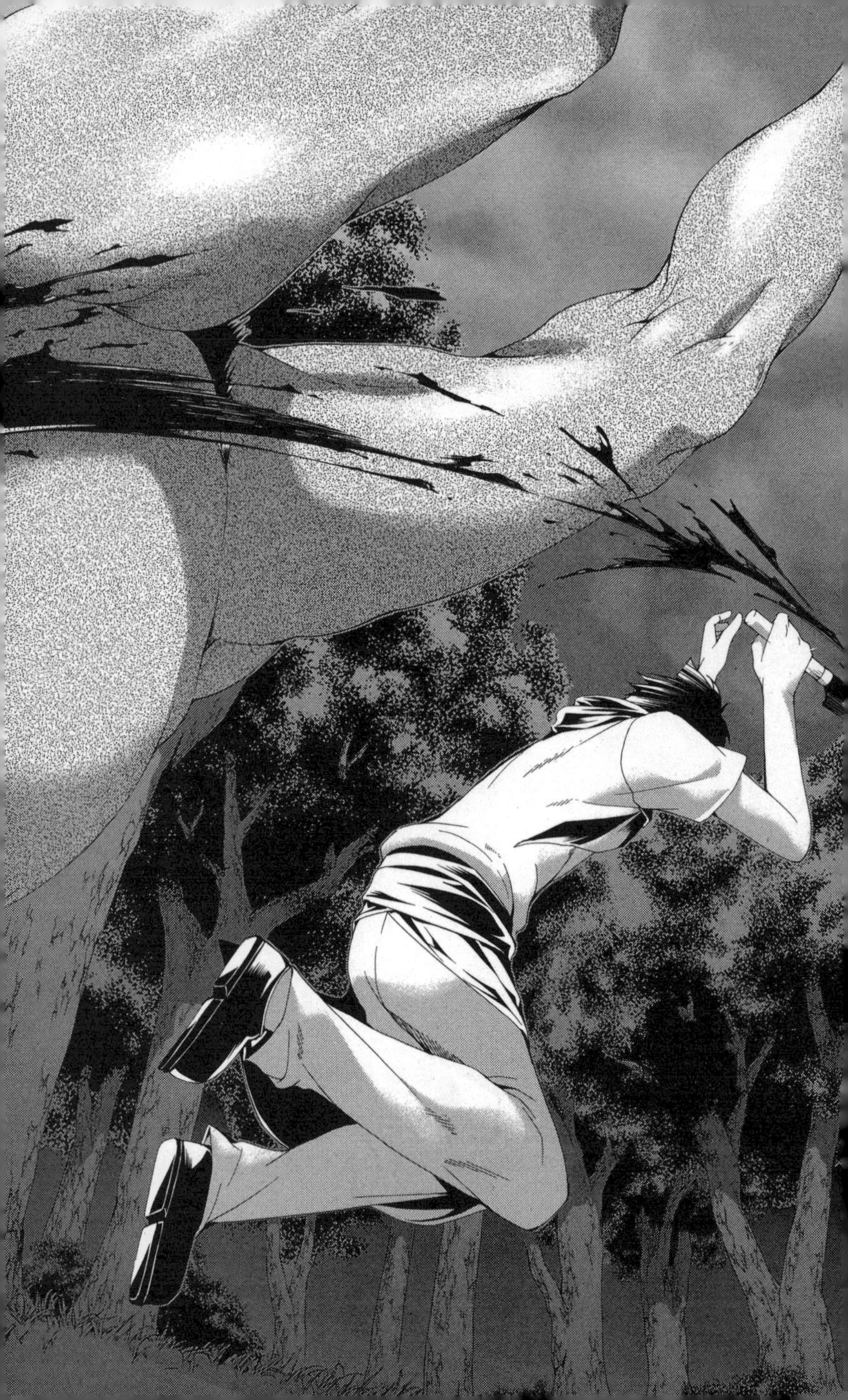

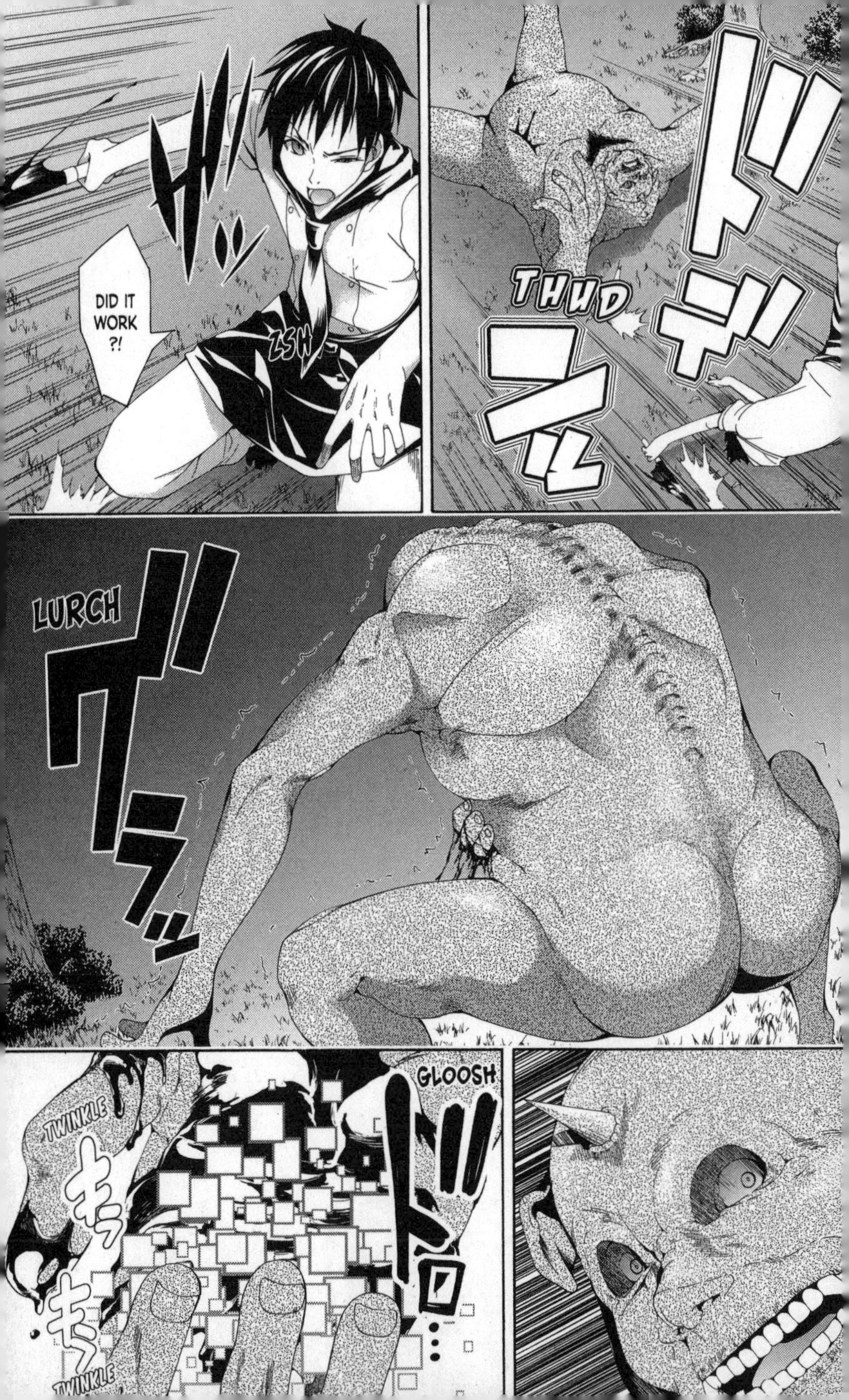
THUD
ZSH
DID IT WORK ?!
ザッ
LURCH
グラッ
GLOOSH
ドロ
TWINKLE
キラ
キラ
TWINKLE

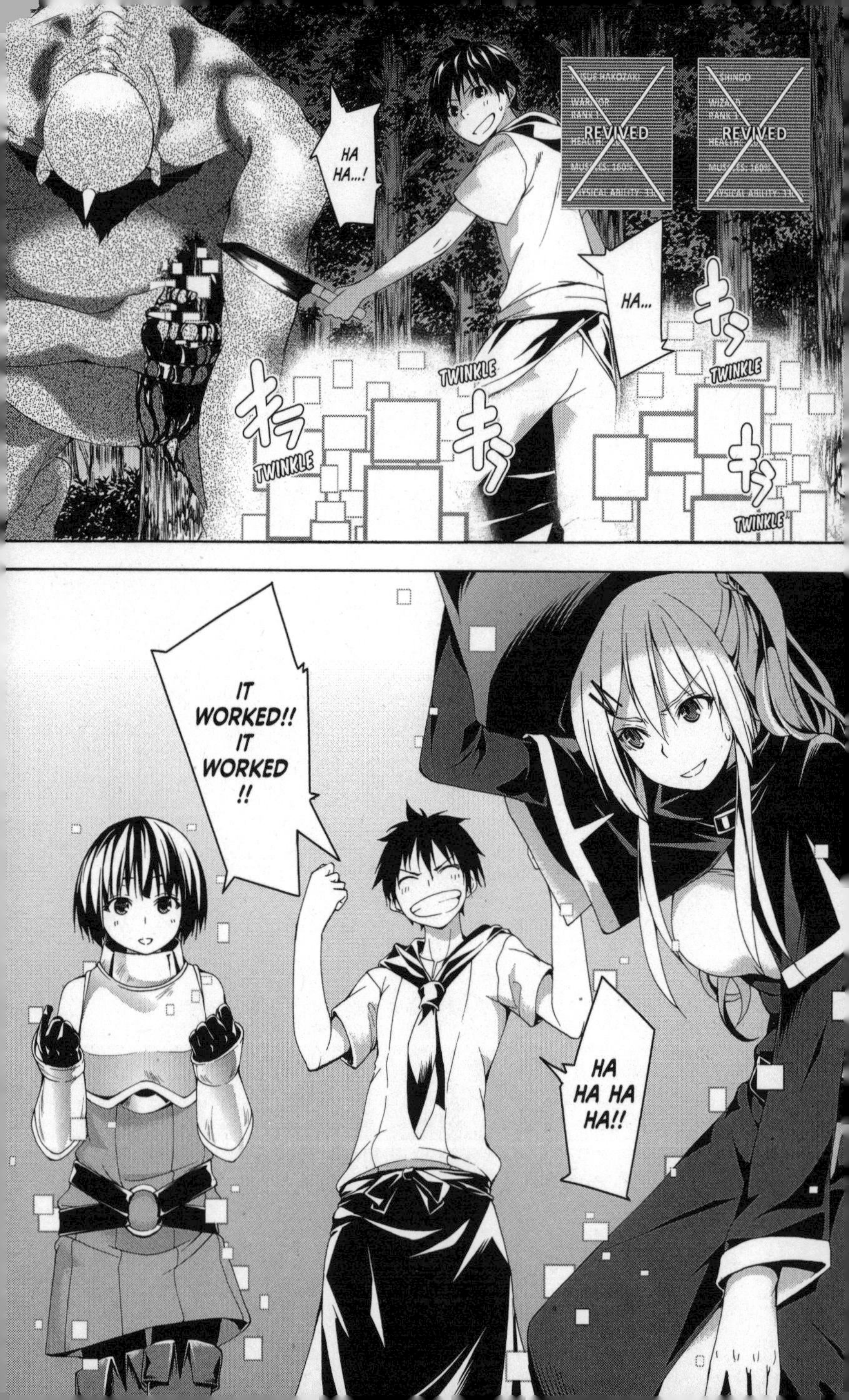
REVIVED
REVIVED
HA...
TWINKLE
TWINKLE
TWINKLE
TWINKLE
HA HA...!
IT WORKED!! IT WORKED!!
HA HA HA HA!!

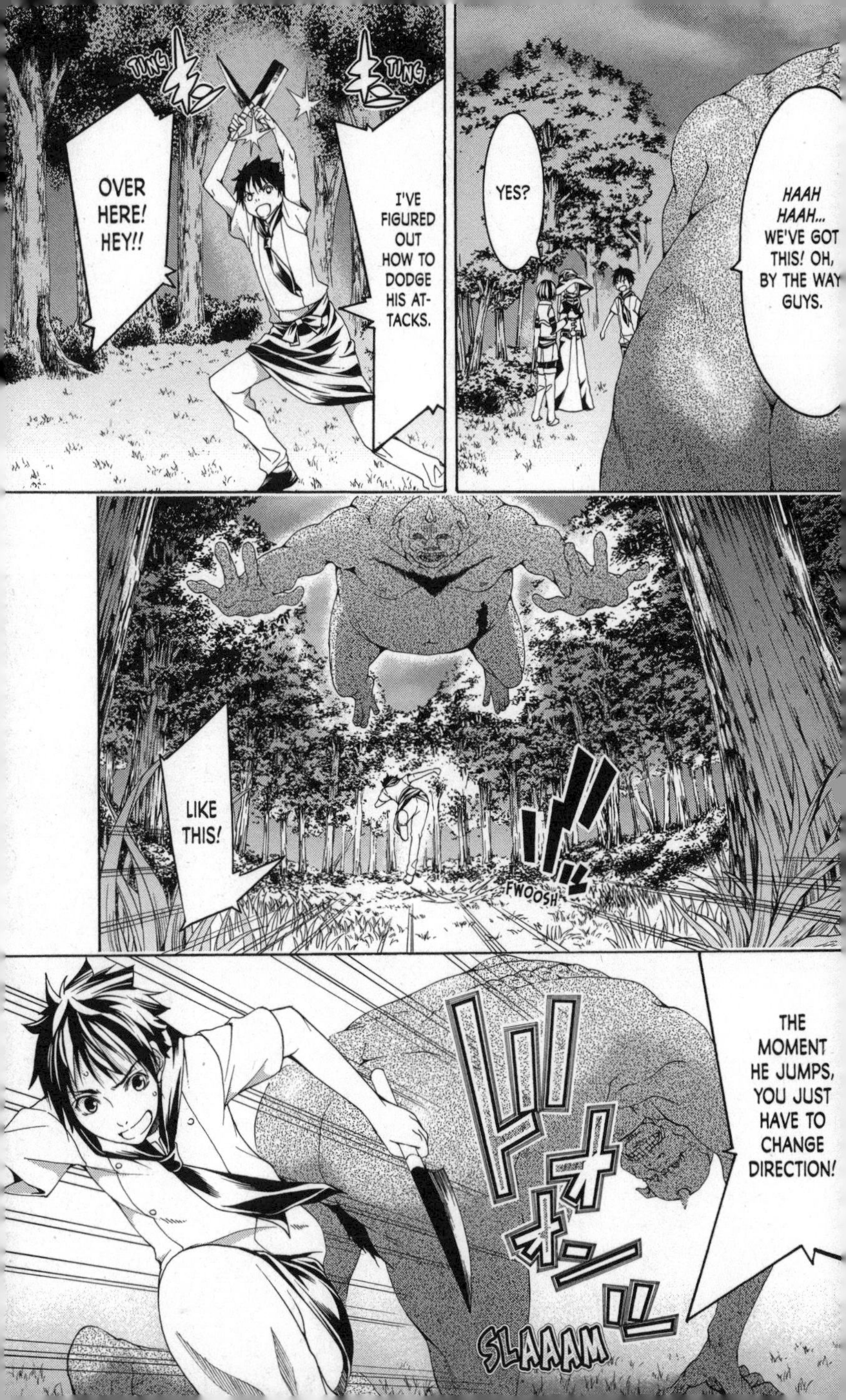
HAAH HAAH... WE'VE GOT THIS! OH, BY THE WAY GUYS.
YES?
TING
TING
I'VE FIGURED OUT HOW TO DODGE HIS AT-TACKS.
OVER HERE! HEY!!
FWOOSH
LIKE THIS!
THE MOMENT HE JUMPS, YOU JUST HAVE TO CHANGE DIRECTION!
SLAAAM

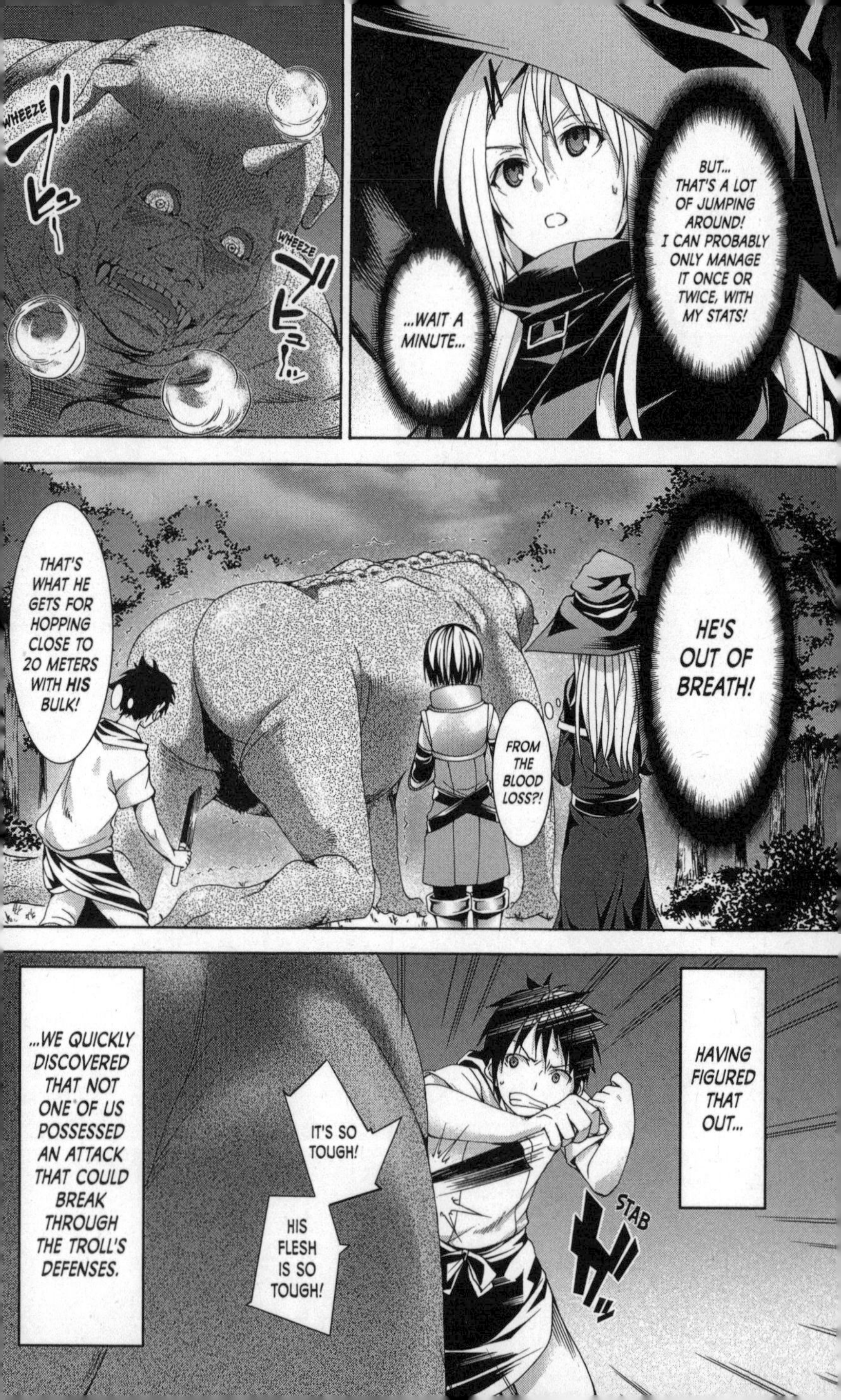
BUT... THAT'S A LOT OF JUMPING AROUND! I CAN PROBABLY ONLY MANAGE IT ONCE OR TWICE, WITH MY STATS!
...WAIT A MINUTE...
WHEEZE
WHEEZE
HE'S OUT OF BREATH!
FROM THE BLOOD LOSS?!
THAT'S WHAT HE GETS FOR HOPPING CLOSE TO 20 METERS WITH HIS BULK!
HAVING FIGURED THAT OUT...
STAB
IT'S SO TOUGH!
HIS FLESH IS SO TOUGH!
...WE QUICKLY DISCOVERED THAT NOT ONE OF US POSSESSED AN ATTACK THAT COULD BREAK THROUGH THE TROLL'S DEFENSES.

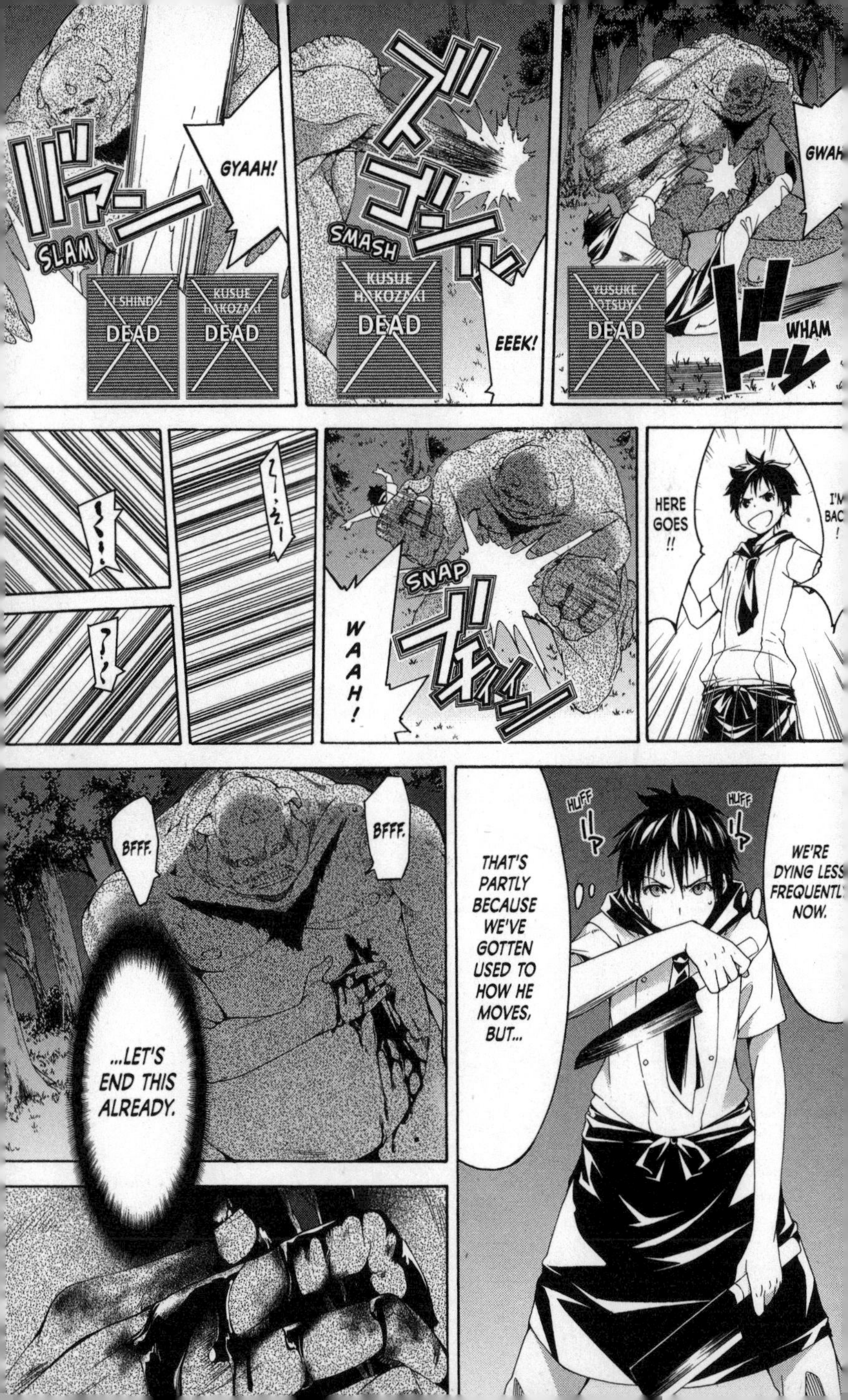
GWAH
YUSUKE
DEAD
WHAM
SMASH
KUSUE HAKOZAKI
DEAD
EEEK!
GYAAH!
SLAM
DEAD
KUSUE HAKOZAKI
DEAD
I'M BAC
HERE GOES!!
SNAP
WAAAH!
HUFF
HUFF
WE'RE DYING LESS FREQUENTL NOW.
THAT'S PARTLY BECAUSE WE'VE GOTTEN USED TO HOW HE MOVES, BUT...
BFFF.
BFFF.
...LET'S END THIS ALREADY.

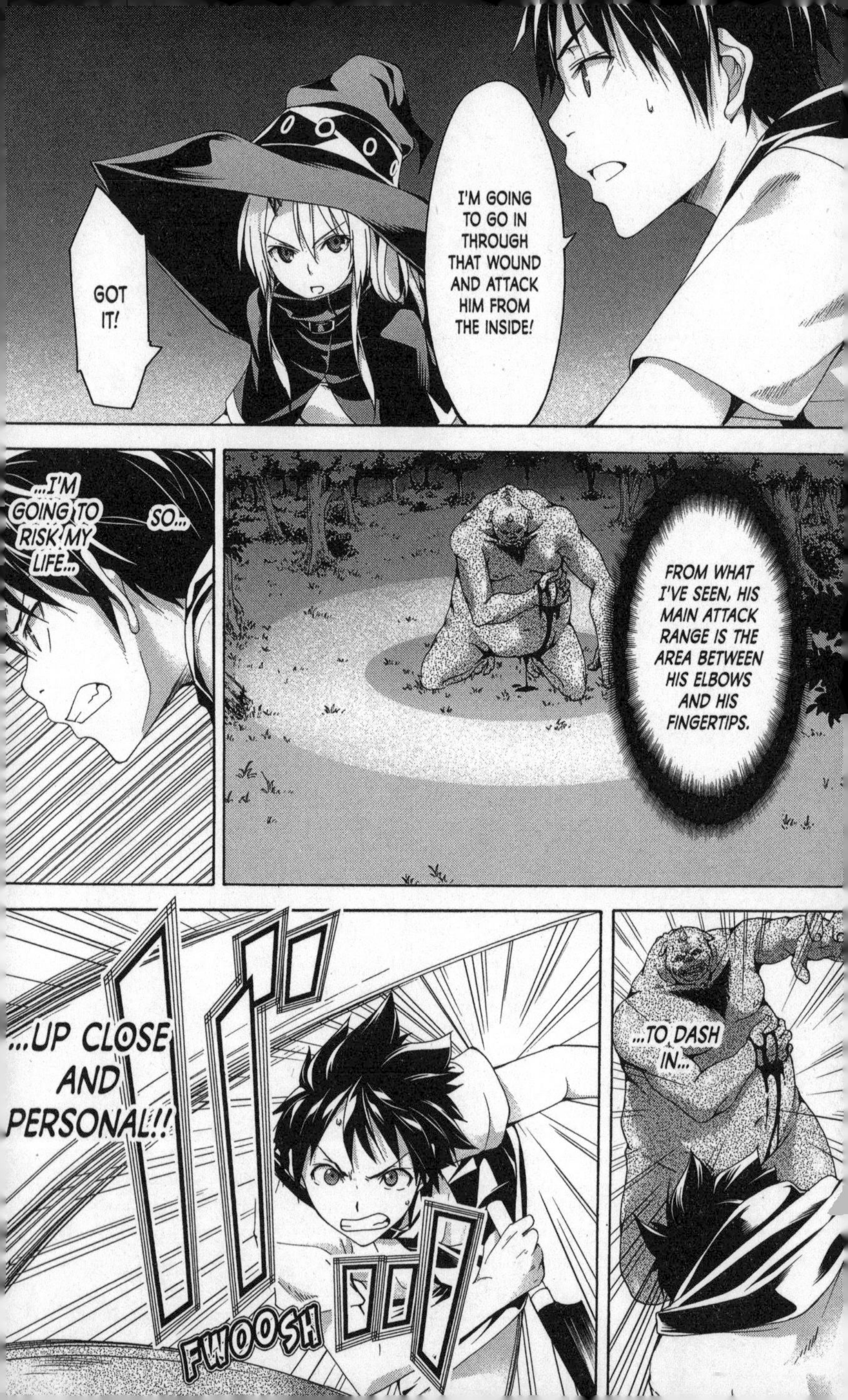
I'M GOING TO GO IN THROUGH THAT WOUND AND ATTACK HIM FROM THE INSIDE!
GOT IT!
FROM WHAT I'VE SEEN, HIS MAIN ATTACK RANGE IS THE AREA BETWEEN HIS ELBOWS AND HIS FINGERTIPS.
SO...
...I'M GOING TO RISK MY LIFE...
...TO DASH IN...
...UP CLOSE AND PERSONAL!!
FWOOSH

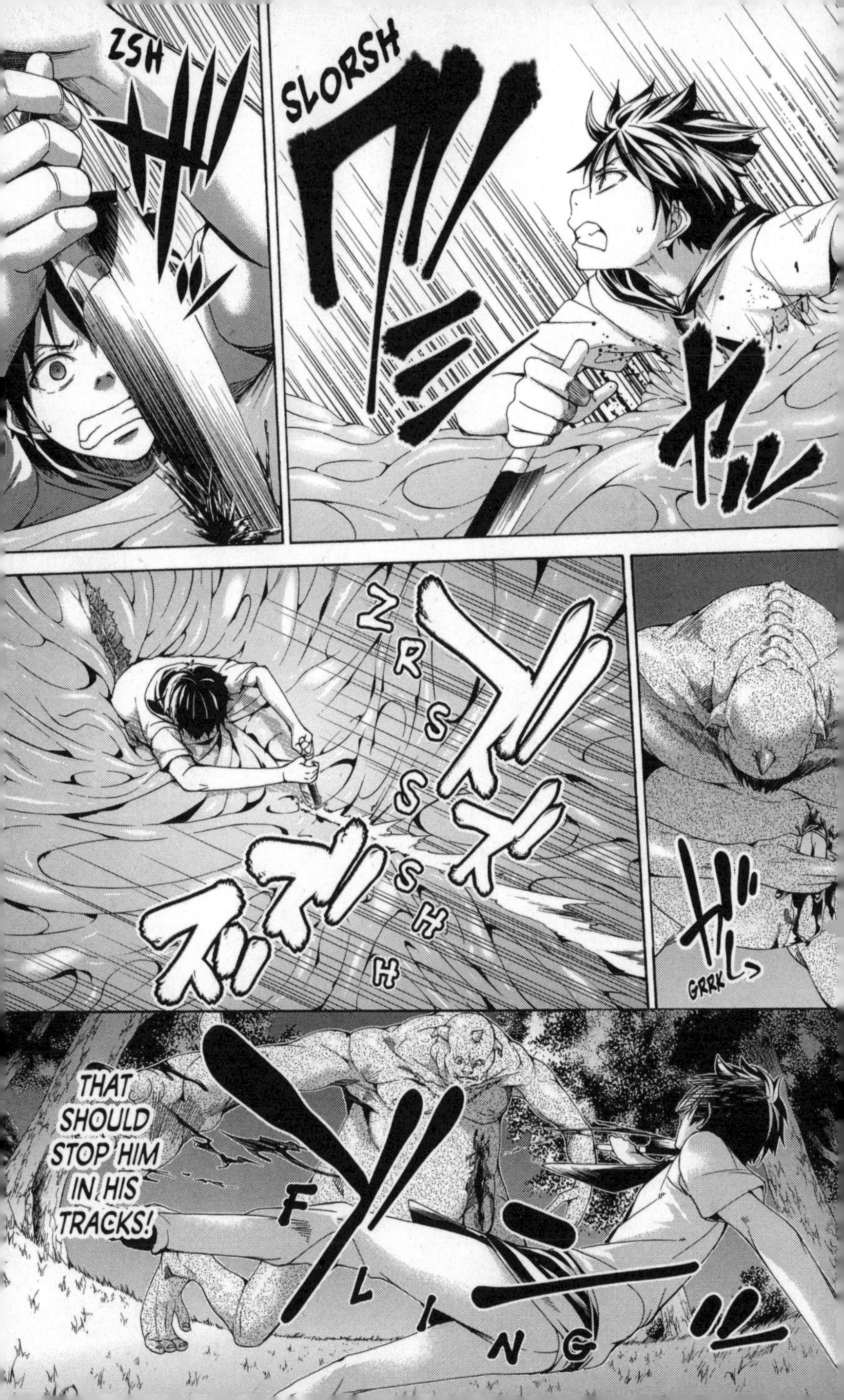
SLORSH
ZSH
GRRK
ZRSSSHH
THAT SHOULD STOP HIM IN HIS TRACKS!
FLING

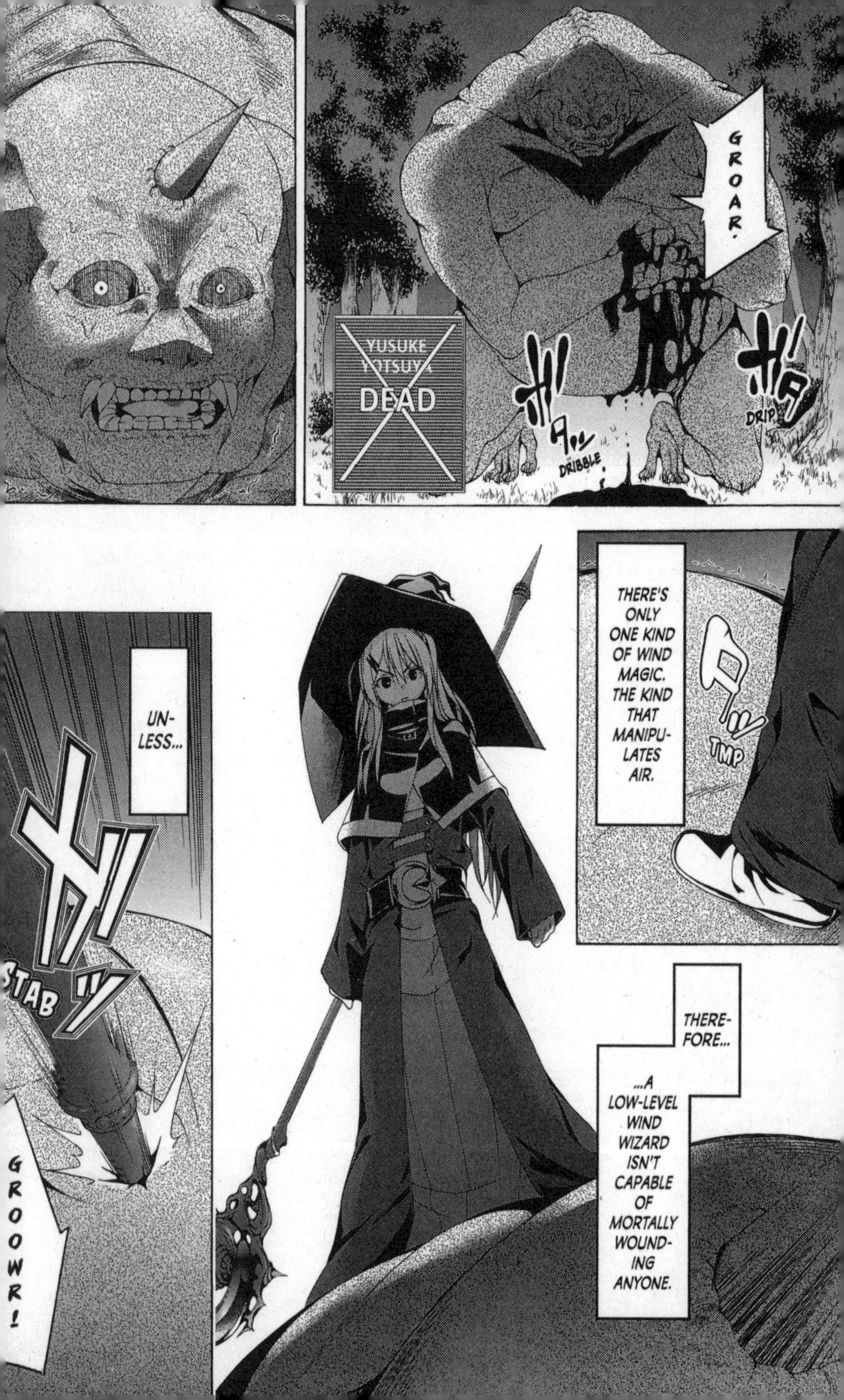
GROAR.
YUSUKE YOTSUYA
DEAD
DRIBBLE
DRIP
THERE'S ONLY ONE KIND OF WIND MAGIC. THE KIND THAT MANIPULATES AIR.
TMP
THEREFORE...
...A LOW-LEVEL WIND WIZARD ISN'T CAPABLE OF MORTALLY WOUNDING ANYONE.
UNLESS...
STAB
GROOOWR!

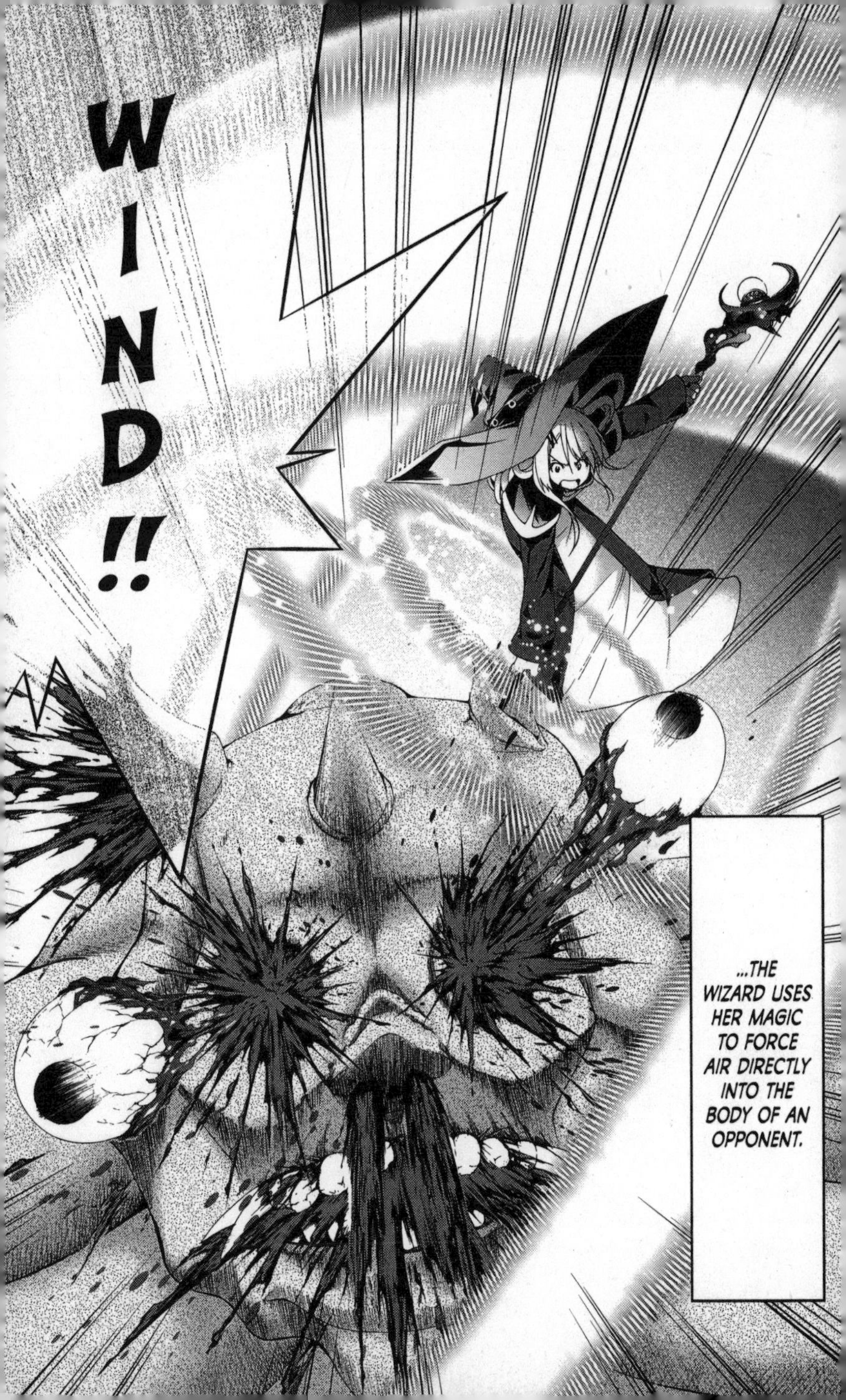
WIND!!
...THE WIZARD USES HER MAGIC TO FORCE AIR DIRECTLY INTO THE BODY OF AN OPPONENT.

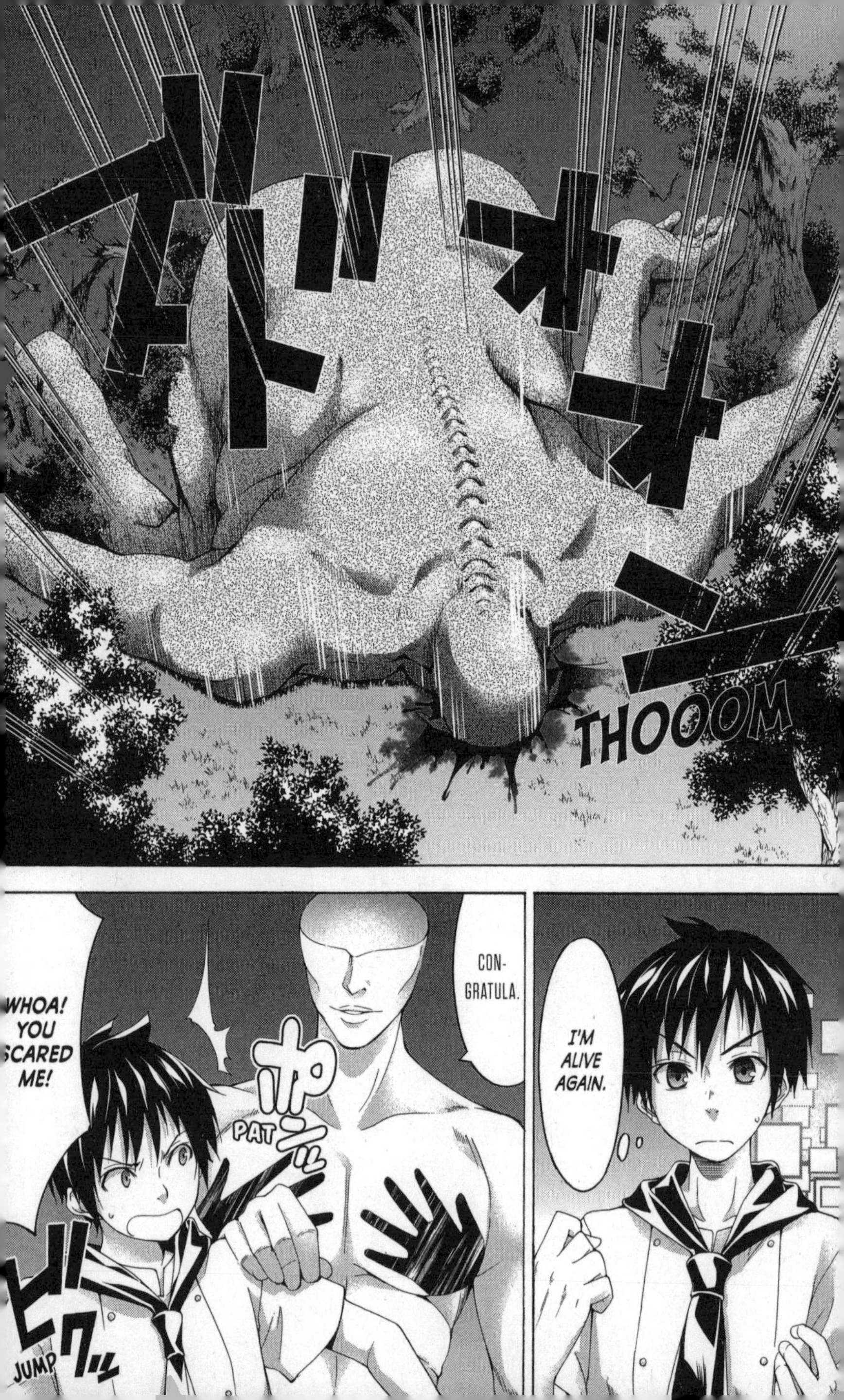
THOOOM
I'M ALIVE AGAIN.
CON-GRATULA.
WHOA! YOU SCARED ME!
PAT
JUMP

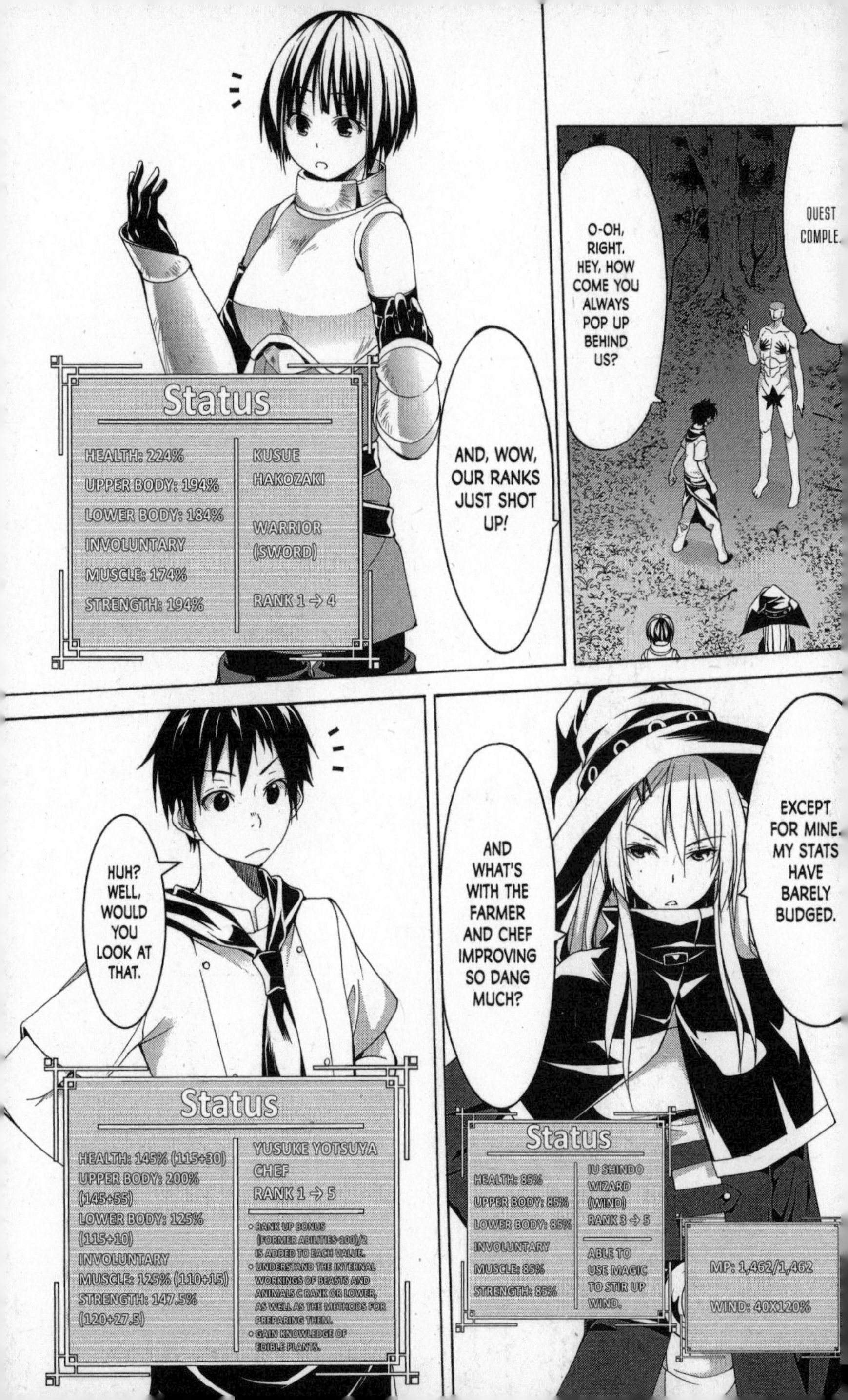
QUEST COMPLE.
O-OH, RIGHT. HEY, HOW COME YOU ALWAYS POP UP BEHIND US?
AND, WOW, OUR RANKS JUST SHOT UP!
Status
HEALTH: 224%
UPPER BODY: 194%
LOWER BODY: 184%
INVOLUNTARY MUSCLE: 174%
STRENGTH: 194%
KUSUE HAKOZAKI
WARRIOR (SWORD)
RANK 1 → 4
EXCEPT FOR MINE. MY STATS HAVE BARELY BUDGED.
AND WHAT'S WITH THE FARMER AND CHEF IMPROVING SO DANG MUCH?
Status
HEALTH: 85%
UPPER BODY: 85%
LOWER BODY: 85%
INVOLUNTARY MUSCLE: 85%
STRENGTH: 85%
IU SHINDO
WIZARD (WIND)
RANK 3 → 5
ABLE TO USE MAGIC TO STIR UP WIND.
MP: 1,462/1,462
WIND: 40X120%
HUH? WELL, WOULD YOU LOOK AT THAT.
Status
HEALTH: 145% (115+30)
UPPER BODY: 200% (145+55)
LOWER BODY: 125% (115+10)
INVOLUNTARY MUSCLE: 125% (110+15)
STRENGTH: 147.5% (120+27.5)
YUSUKE YOTSUYA
CHEF
RANK 1 → 5
• RANK UP BONUS (FORMER ABILITIES-100)/2 IS ADDED TO EACH VALUE.
• UNDERSTAND THE INTERNAL WORKINGS OF BEASTS AND ANIMALS C RANK OR LOWER, AS WELL AS THE METHODS FOR PREPARING THEM.
• GAIN KNOWLEDGE OF EDIBLE PLANTS.

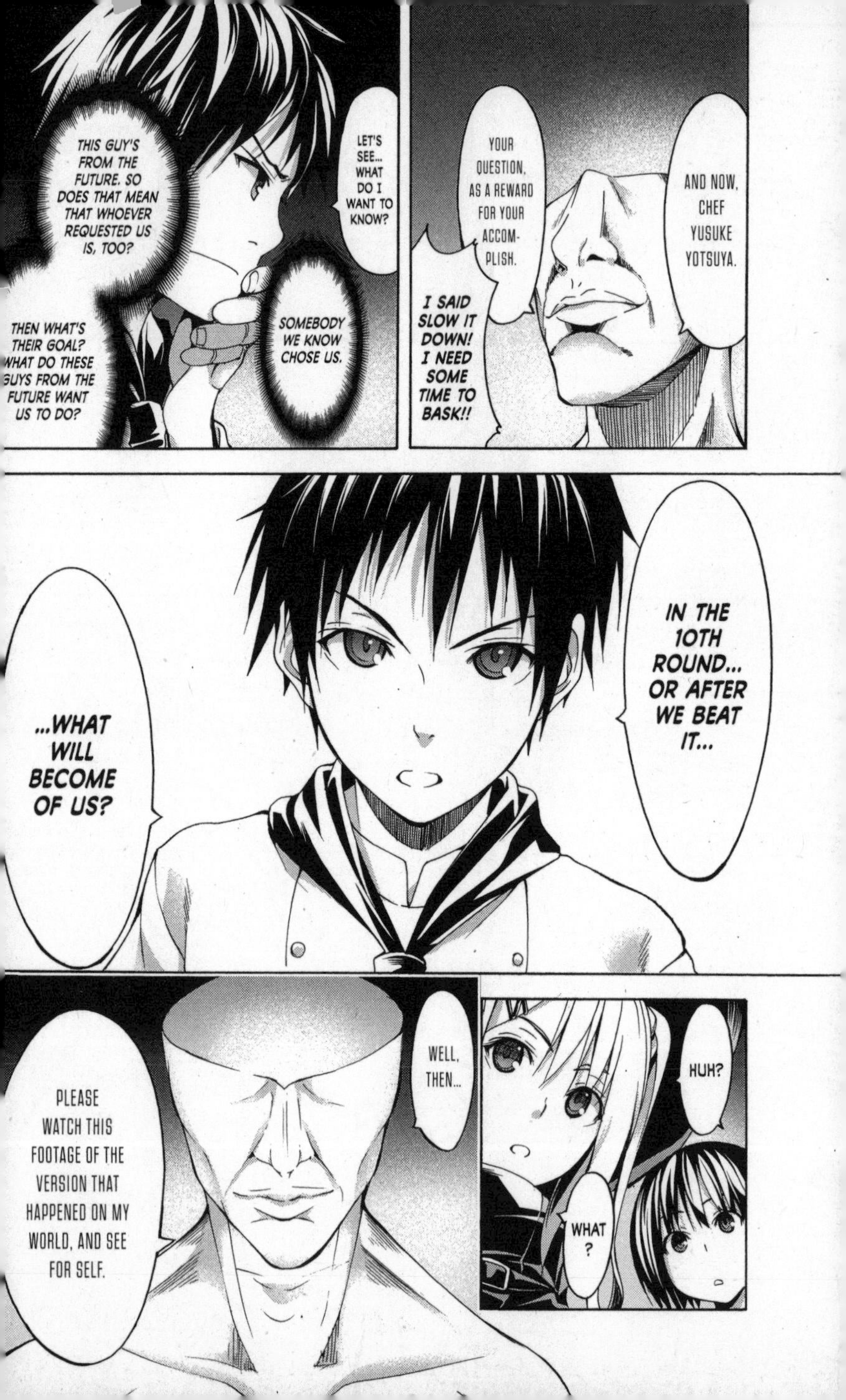
AND NOW, CHEF YUSUKE YOTSUYA.
YOUR QUESTION, AS A REWARD FOR YOUR ACCOMPLISH.
I SAID SLOW IT DOWN! I NEED SOME TIME TO BASK!!
LET'S SEE... WHAT DO I WANT TO KNOW?
THIS GUY'S FROM THE FUTURE. SO DOES THAT MEAN THAT WHOEVER REQUESTED US IS, TOO?
SOMEBODY WE KNOW CHOSE US.
THEN WHAT'S THEIR GOAL? WHAT DO THESE GUYS FROM THE FUTURE WANT US TO DO?
IN THE 10TH ROUND... OR AFTER WE BEAT IT...
...WHAT WILL BECOME OF US?
HUH?
WHAT?
WELL, THEN...
PLEASE WATCH THIS FOOTAGE OF THE VERSION THAT HAPPENED ON MY WORLD, AND SEE FOR SELF.

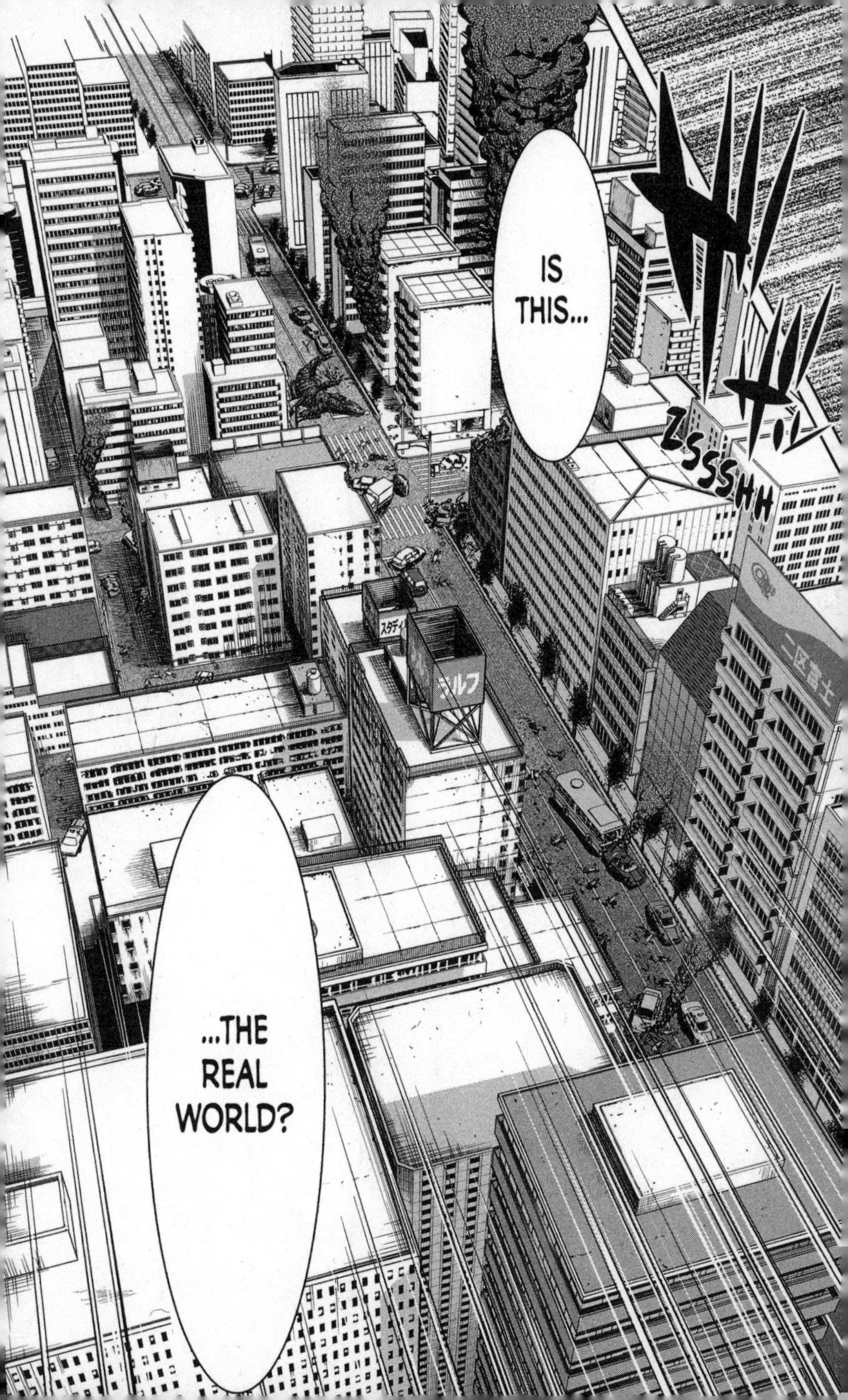
IS THIS...
ZSSSHH
...THE REAL WORLD?

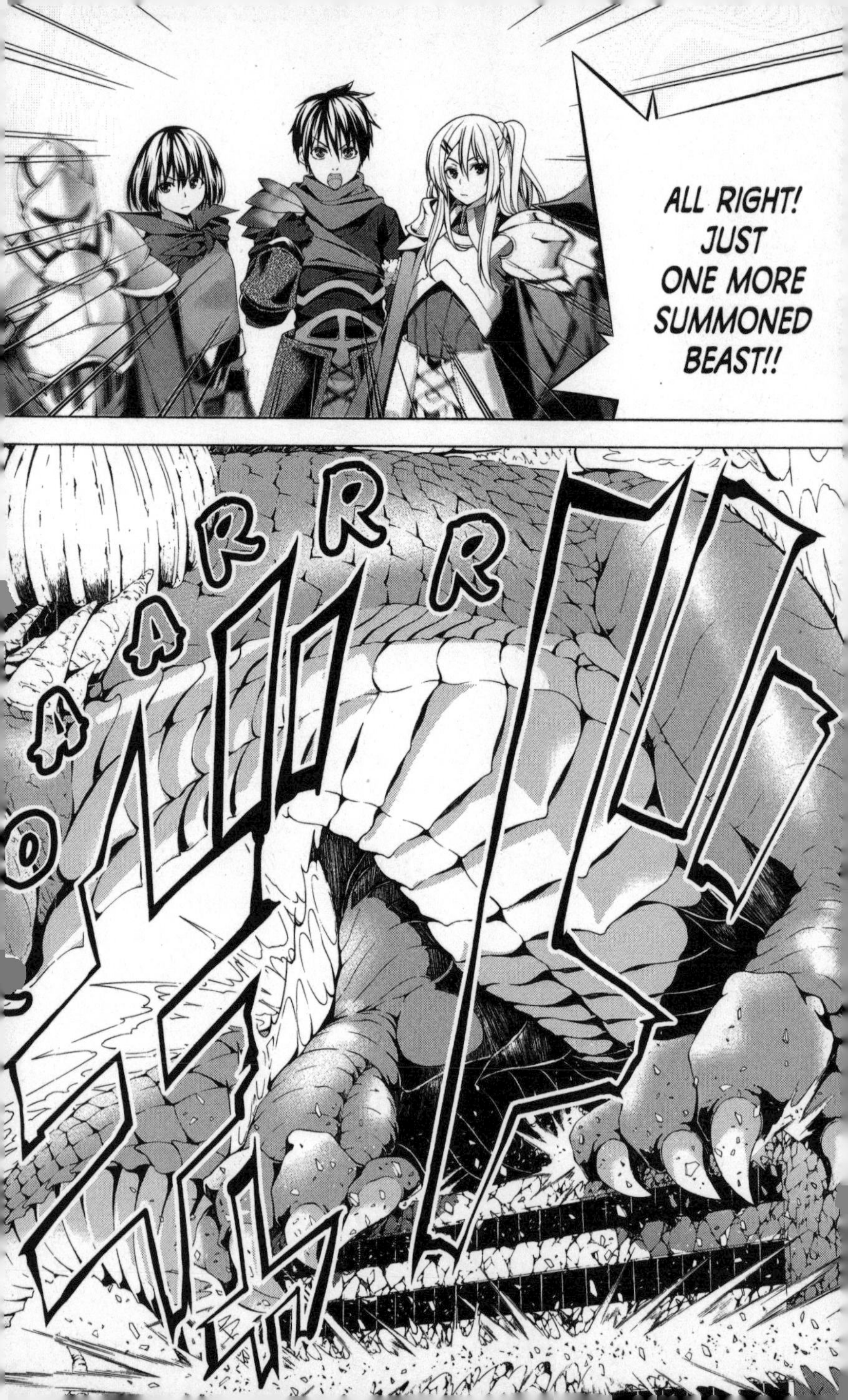
ALL RIGHT! JUST ONE MORE SUMMONED BEAST!!

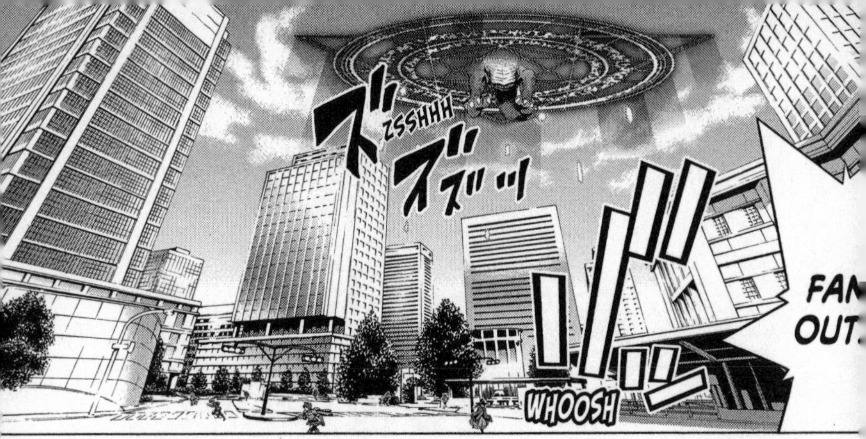
FAN OUT.
WHOOSH
ZSSHHH

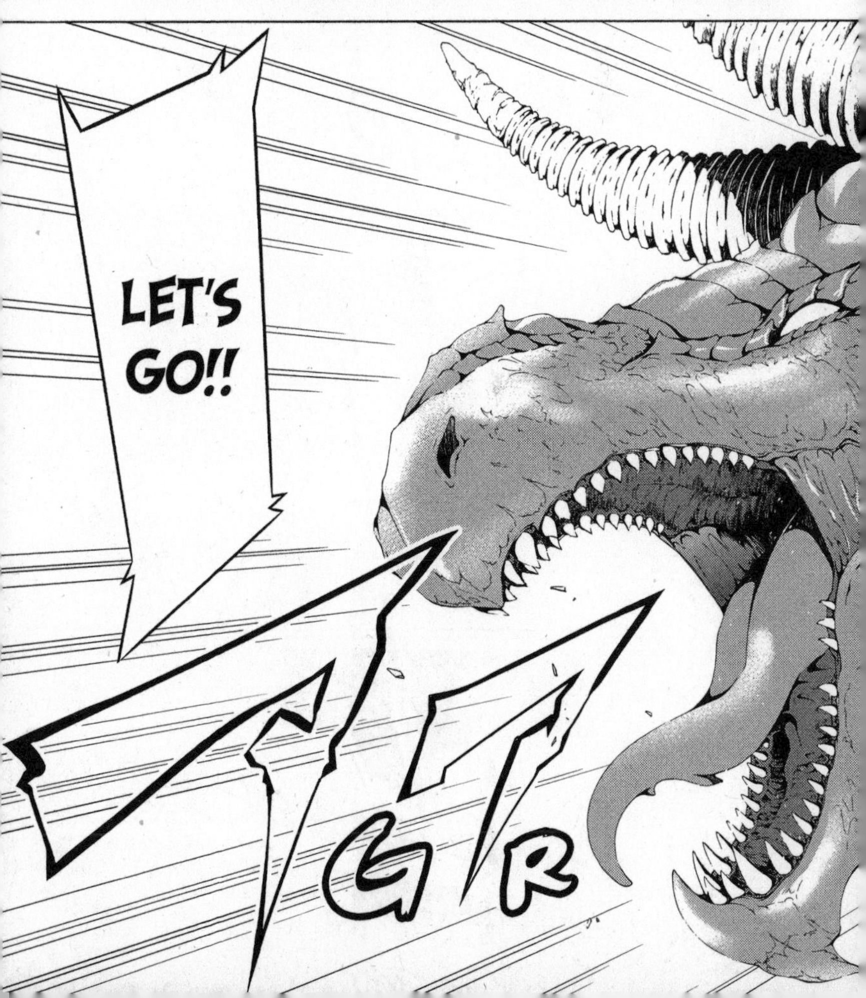
LET'S GO!!
GR

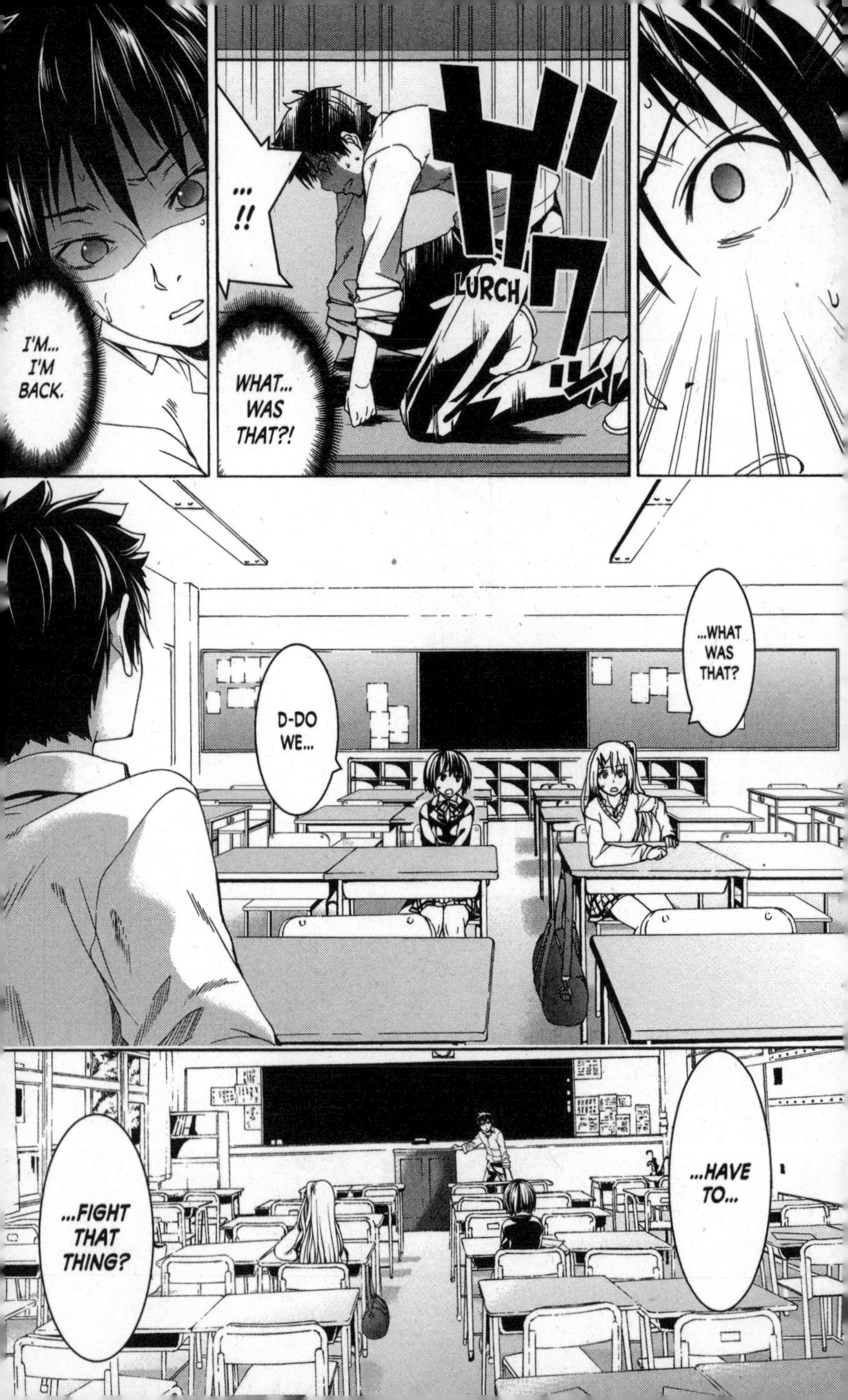

...!!
LURCH
WHAT... WAS THAT?!
I'M... I'M BACK.
...WHAT WAS THAT?
D-DO WE...
...HAVE TO...
...FIGHT THAT THING?

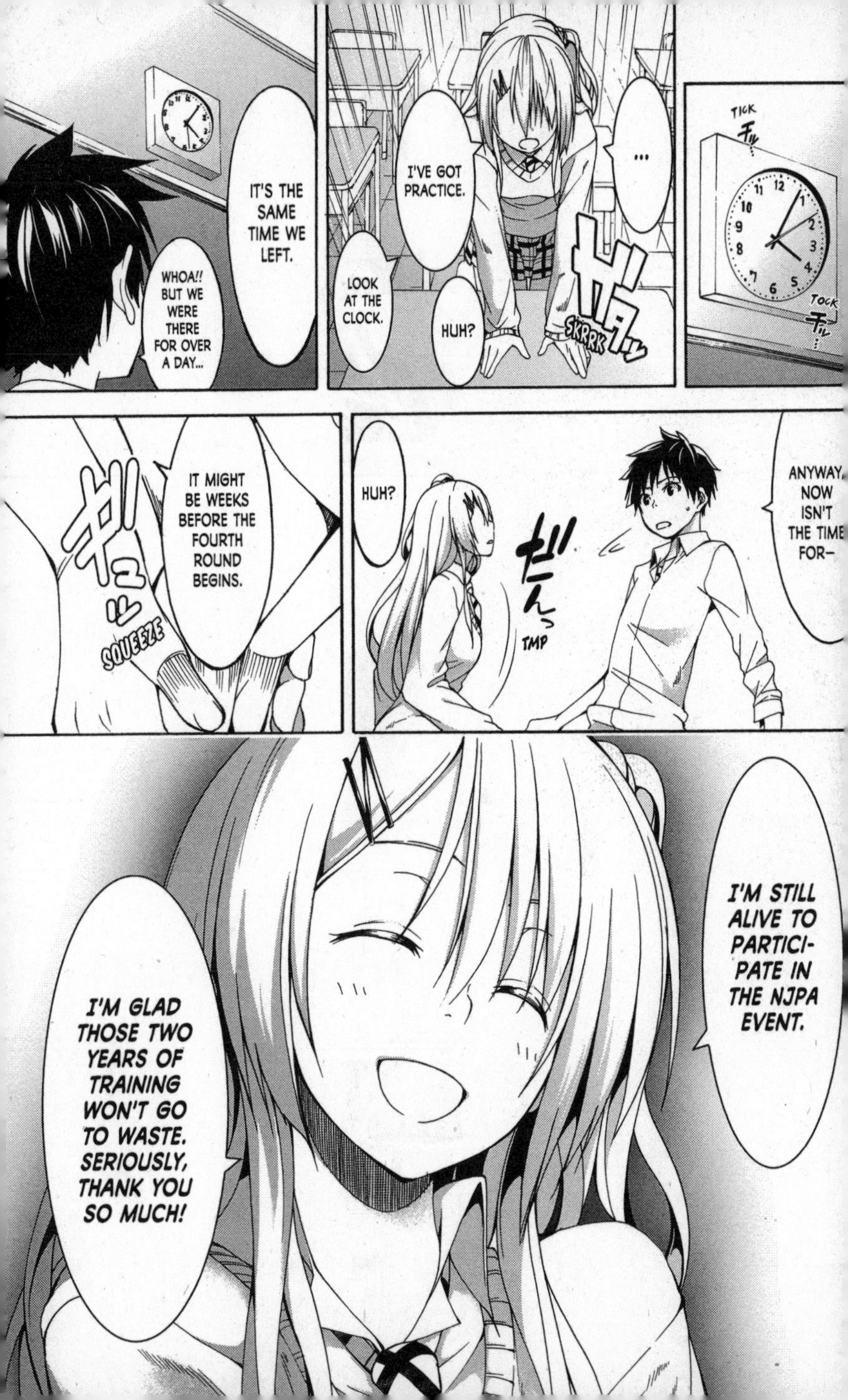
TICK
TOCK
...
SKRRK
I'VE GOT PRACTICE.
HUH?
LOOK AT THE CLOCK.
IT'S THE SAME TIME WE LEFT.
WHOA!! BUT WE WERE THERE FOR OVER A DAY...
ANYWAY, NOW ISN'T THE TIME FOR—
TMP
HUH?
IT MIGHT BE WEEKS BEFORE THE FOURTH ROUND BEGINS.
SQUEEZE
I'M STILL ALIVE TO PARTICIPATE IN THE NJPA EVENT.
I'M GLAD THOSE TWO YEARS OF TRAINING WON'T GO TO WASTE. SERIOUSLY, THANK YOU SO MUCH!

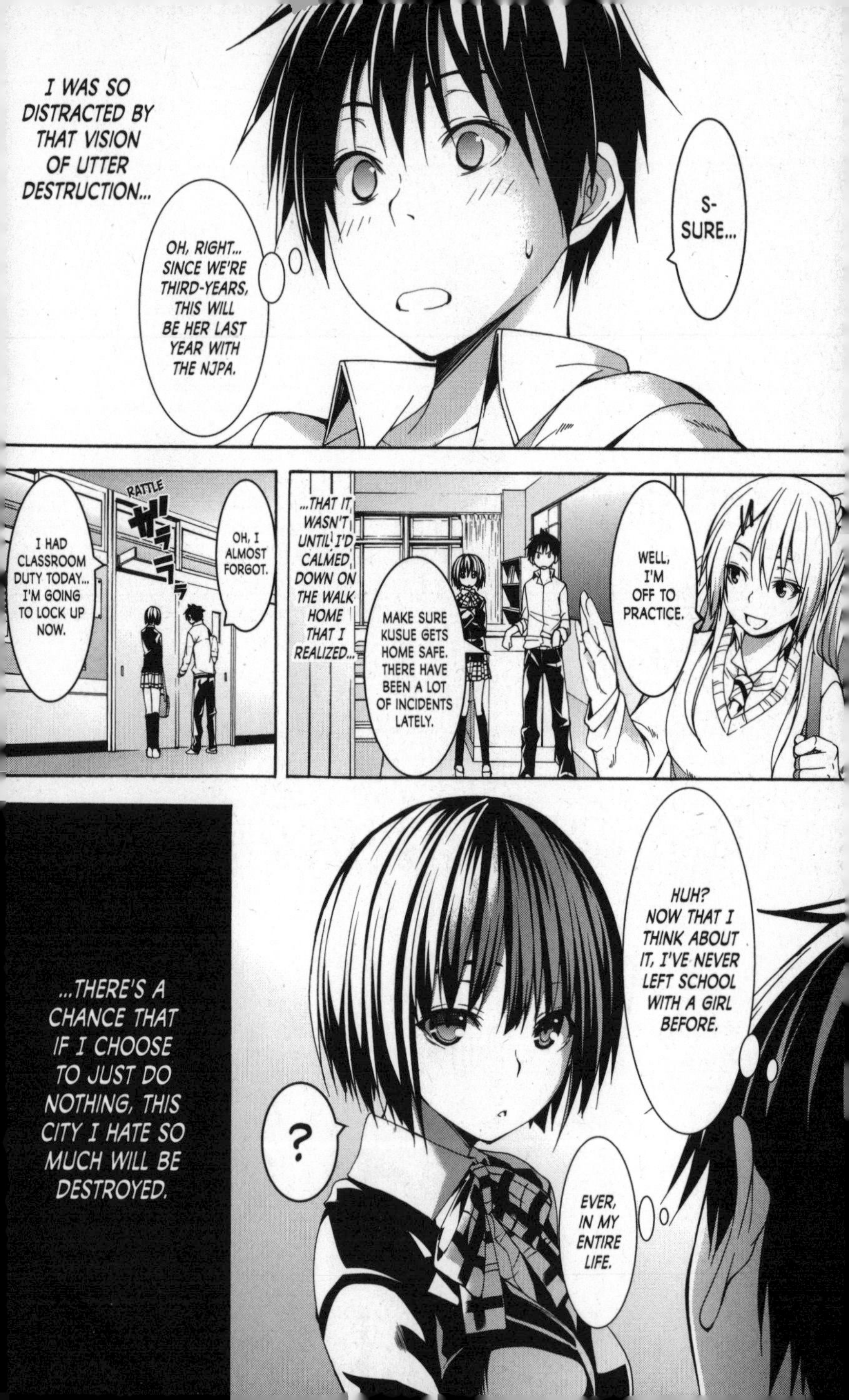
S- SURE...
OH, RIGHT... SINCE WE'RE THIRD-YEARS, THIS WILL BE HER LAST YEAR WITH THE NJPA.
I WAS SO DISTRACTED BY THAT VISION OF UTTER DESTRUCTION...
WELL, I'M OFF TO PRACTICE.
MAKE SURE KUSUE GETS HOME SAFE. THERE HAVE BEEN A LOT OF INCIDENTS LATELY.
...THAT IT WASN'T UNTIL I'D CALMED DOWN ON THE WALK HOME THAT I REALIZED...
RATTLE
OH, I ALMOST FORGOT.
I HAD CLASSROOM DUTY TODAY... I'M GOING TO LOCK UP NOW.
HUH? NOW THAT I THINK ABOUT IT, I'VE NEVER LEFT SCHOOL WITH A GIRL BEFORE.
EVER, IN MY ENTIRE LIFE.
?
...THERE'S A CHANCE THAT IF I CHOOSE TO JUST DO NOTHING, THIS CITY I HATE SO MUCH WILL BE DESTROYED.

I'M STANDING ON A MILLION LIVES

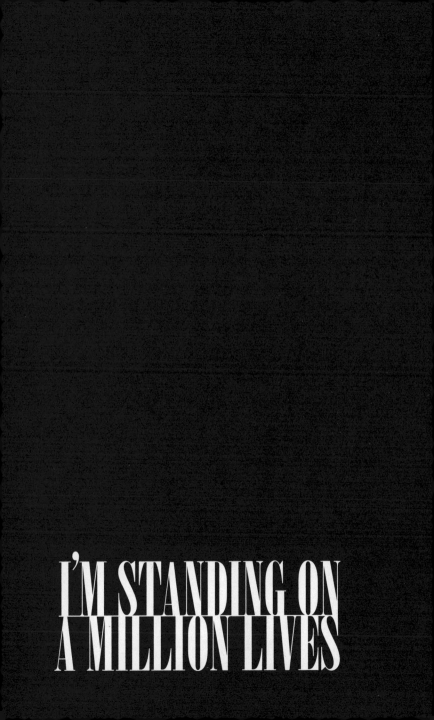

I'M STANDING ON A MILLION LIVES.

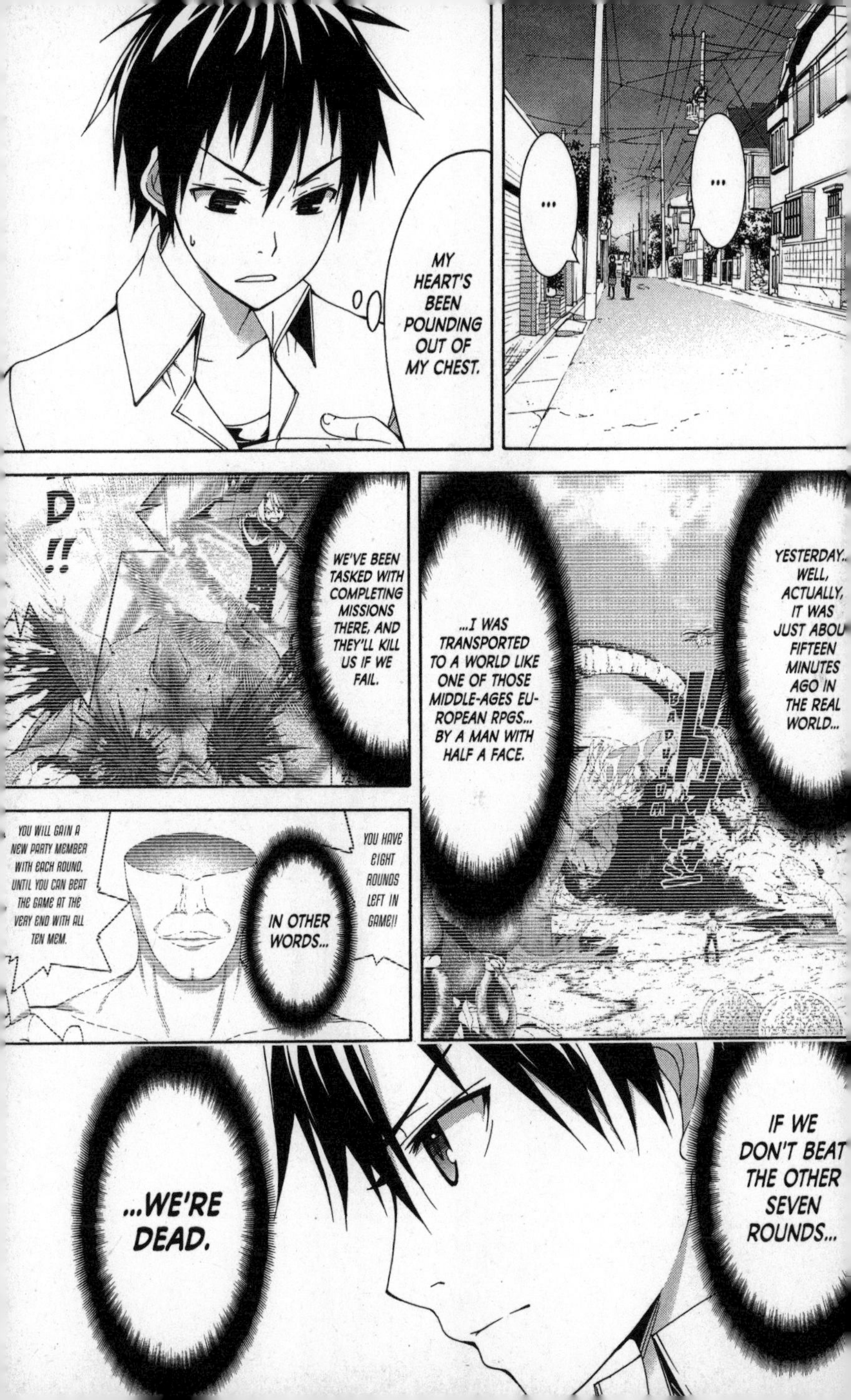
...
...
MY HEART'S BEEN POUNDING OUT OF MY CHEST.
YESTERDAY... WELL, ACTUALLY, IT WAS JUST ABOU FIFTEEN MINUTES AGO IN THE REAL WORLD...
...I WAS TRANSPORTED TO A WORLD LIKE ONE OF THOSE MIDDLE-AGES EU-ROPEAN RPGS... BY A MAN WITH HALF A FACE.
D!!
WE'VE BEEN TASKED WITH COMPLETING MISSIONS THERE, AND THEY'LL KILL US IF WE FAIL.
YOU HAVE EIGHT ROUNDS LEFT IN GAME!!
IN OTHER WORDS...
YOU WILL GAIN A NEW PARTY MEMBER WITH EACH ROUND, UNTIL YOU CAN BEAT THE GAME AT THE VERY END WITH ALL TEN MEM.
IF WE DON'T BEAT THE OTHER SEVEN ROUNDS...
...WE'RE DEAD.

2 Hopeless Nerd & Lecture on Getting Girls

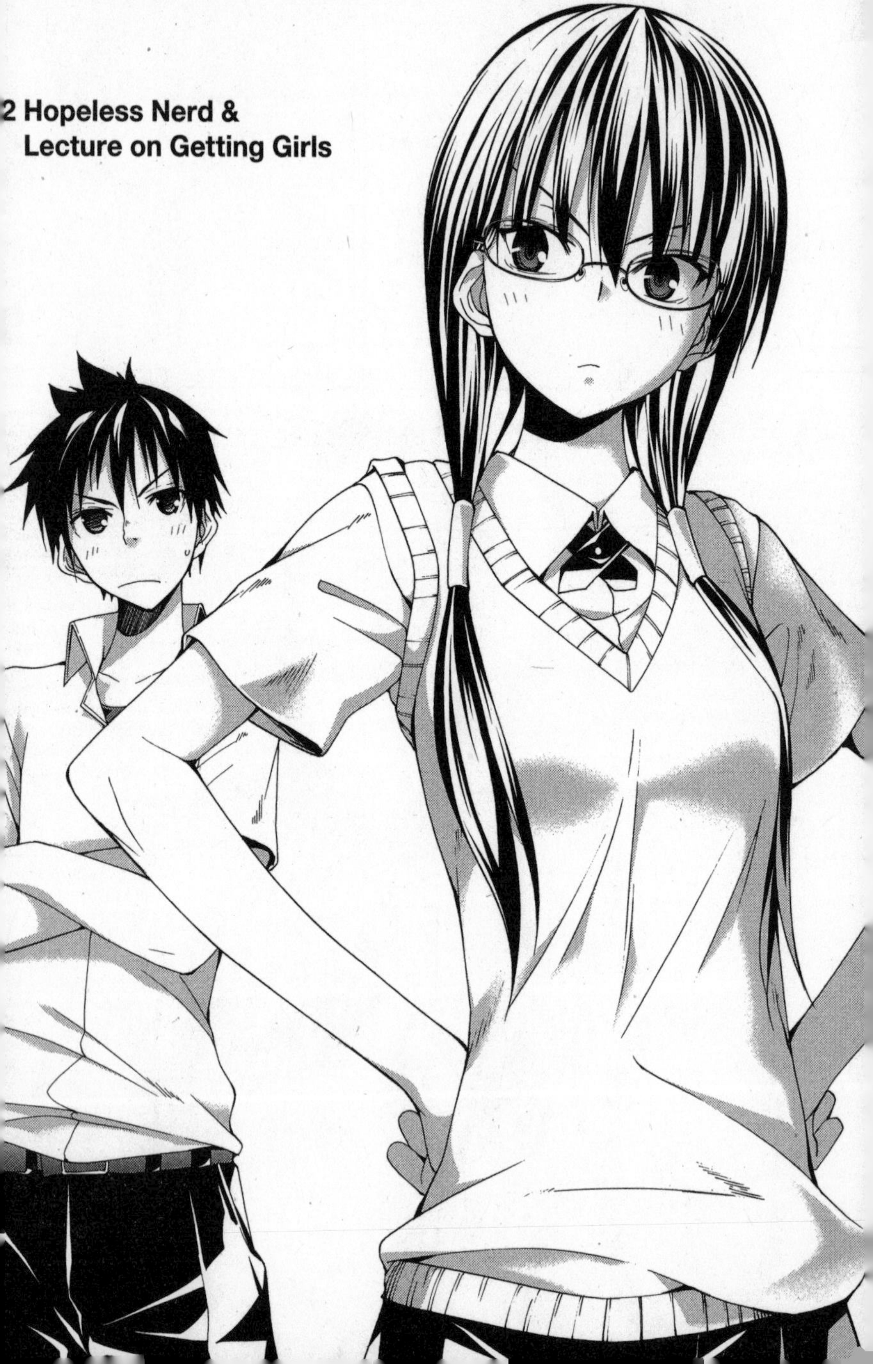

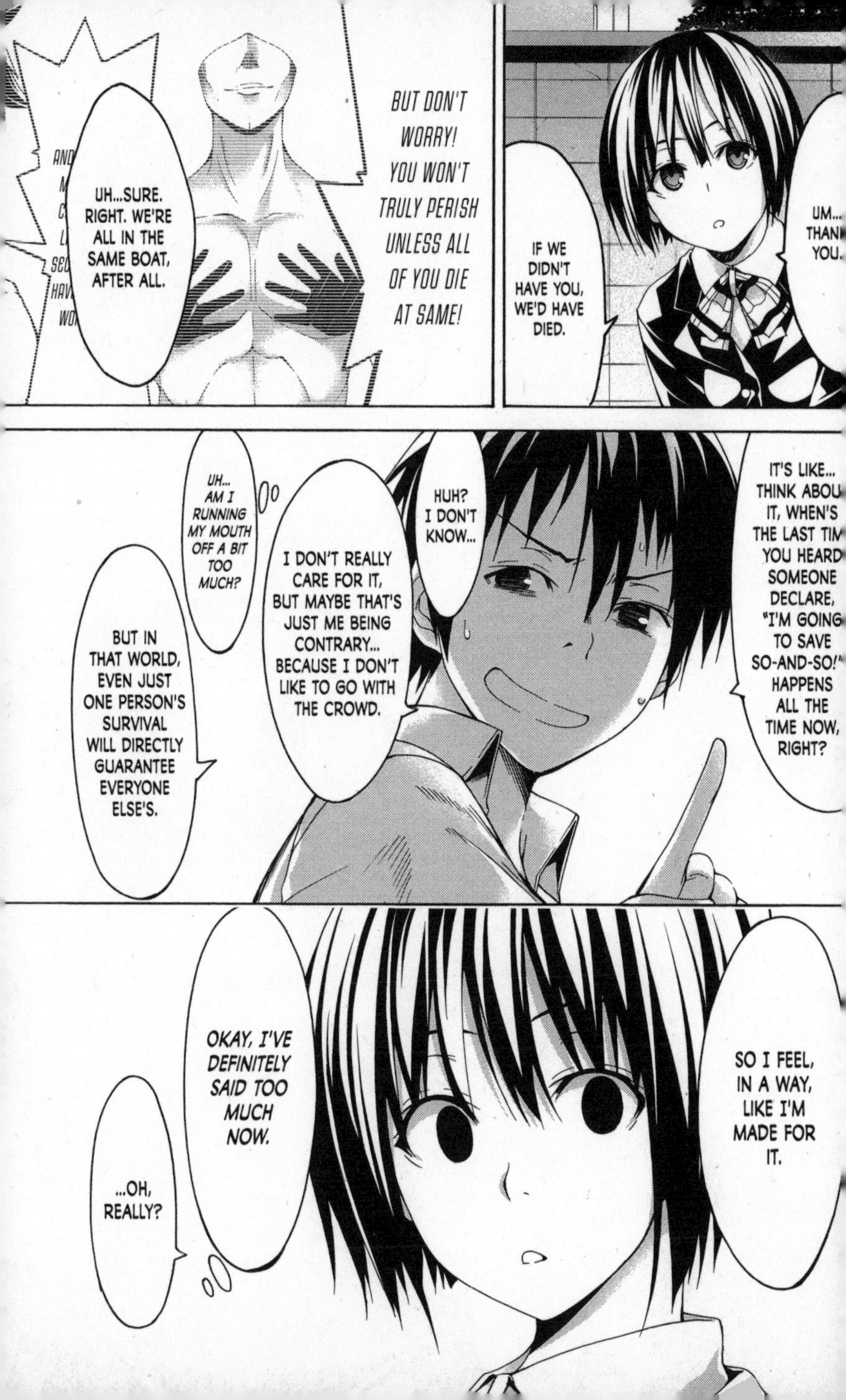
UM... THAN YOU.
IF WE DIDN'T HAVE YOU, WE'D HAVE DIED.
BUT DON'T WORRY! YOU WON'T TRULY PERISH UNLESS ALL OF YOU DIE AT SAME!
UH...SURE. RIGHT. WE'RE ALL IN THE SAME BOAT, AFTER ALL.
IT'S LIKE... THINK ABOU IT, WHEN'S THE LAST TIM YOU HEARD SOMEONE DECLARE, "I'M GOING TO SAVE SO-AND-SO!" HAPPENS ALL THE TIME NOW, RIGHT?
HUH? I DON'T KNOW...
I DON'T REALLY CARE FOR IT, BUT MAYBE THAT'S JUST ME BEING CONTRARY... BECAUSE I DON'T LIKE TO GO WITH THE CROWD.
UH... AM I RUNNING MY MOUTH OFF A BIT TOO MUCH?
BUT IN THAT WORLD, EVEN JUST ONE PERSON'S SURVIVAL WILL DIRECTLY GUARANTEE EVERYONE ELSE'S.
SO I FEEL, IN A WAY, LIKE I'M MADE FOR IT.
OKAY, I'VE DEFINITELY SAID TOO MUCH NOW.
...OH, REALLY?

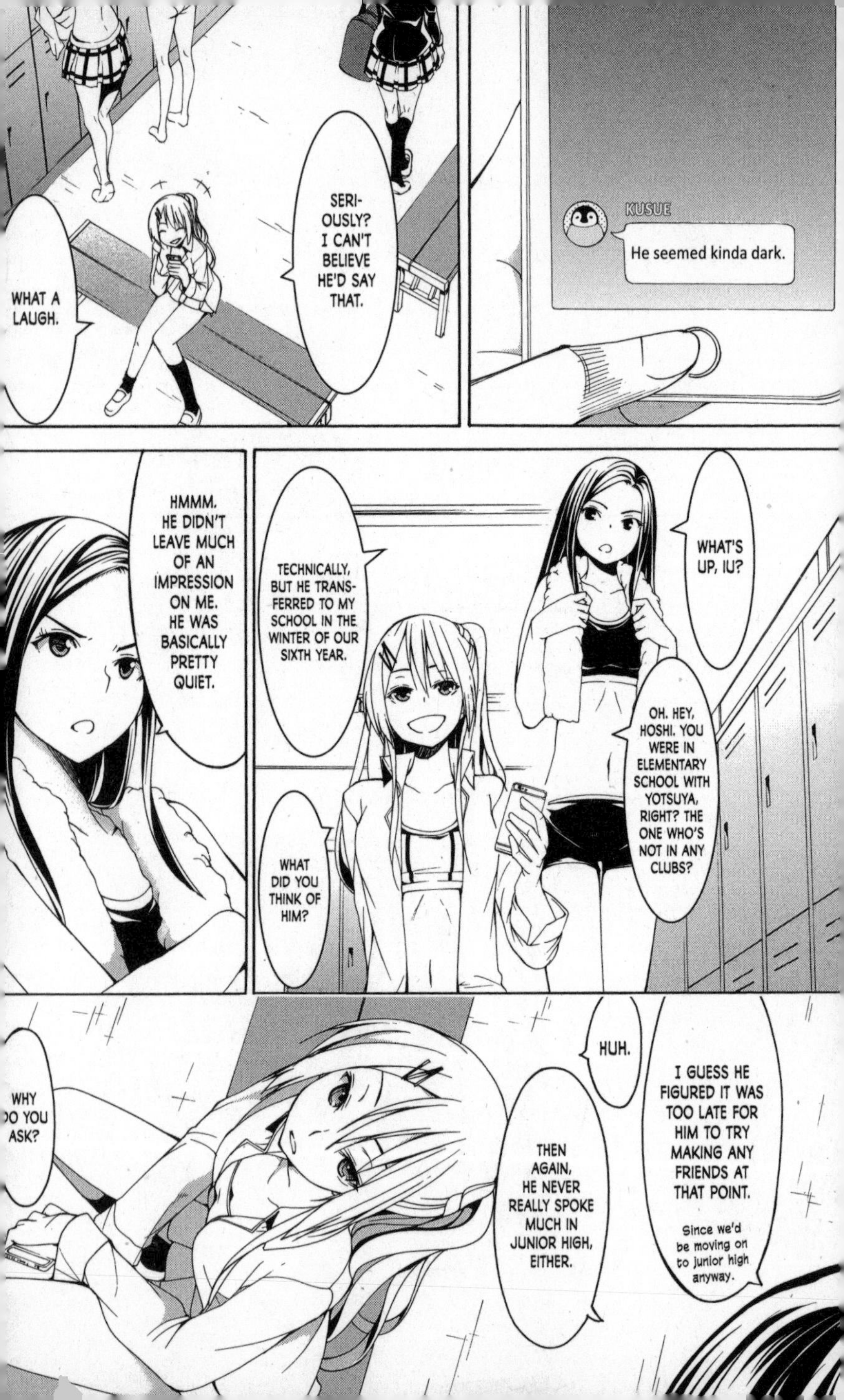
KUSUE
He seemed kinda dark.
SERI-OUSLY? I CAN'T BELIEVE HE'D SAY THAT.
WHAT A LAUGH.
WHAT'S UP, IU?
OH. HEY, HOSHI. YOU WERE IN ELEMENTARY SCHOOL WITH YOTSUYA, RIGHT? THE ONE WHO'S NOT IN ANY CLUBS?
TECHNICALLY, BUT HE TRANS-FERRED TO MY SCHOOL IN THE WINTER OF OUR SIXTH YEAR.
WHAT DID YOU THINK OF HIM?
HMMM. HE DIDN'T LEAVE MUCH OF AN IMPRESSION ON ME. HE WAS BASICALLY PRETTY QUIET.
I GUESS HE FIGURED IT WAS TOO LATE FOR HIM TO TRY MAKING ANY FRIENDS AT THAT POINT.
Since we'd be moving on to junior high anyway.
HUH.
THEN AGAIN, HE NEVER REALLY SPOKE MUCH IN JUNIOR HIGH, EITHER.
WHY DO YOU ASK?

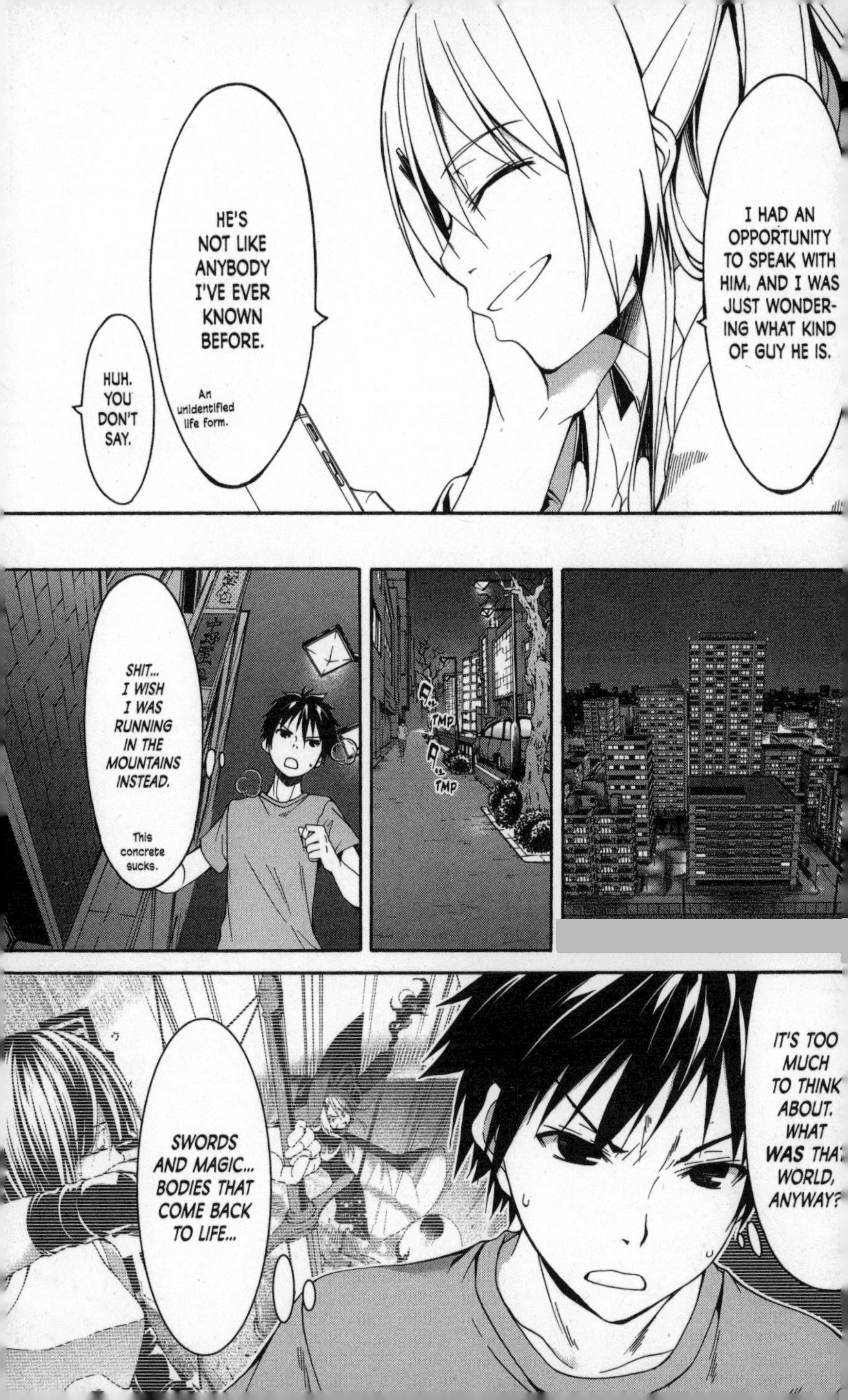
I HAD AN OPPORTUNITY TO SPEAK WITH HIM, AND I WAS JUST WONDERING WHAT KIND OF GUY HE IS.
HE'S NOT LIKE ANYBODY I'VE EVER KNOWN BEFORE.
An unidentified life form.
HUH. YOU DON'T SAY.
TMP
TMP
SHIT... I WISH I WAS RUNNING IN THE MOUNTAINS INSTEAD.
This concrete sucks.
IT'S TOO MUCH TO THINK ABOUT. WHAT WAS THAT WORLD, ANYWAY?
SWORDS AND MAGIC... BODIES THAT COME BACK TO LIFE...

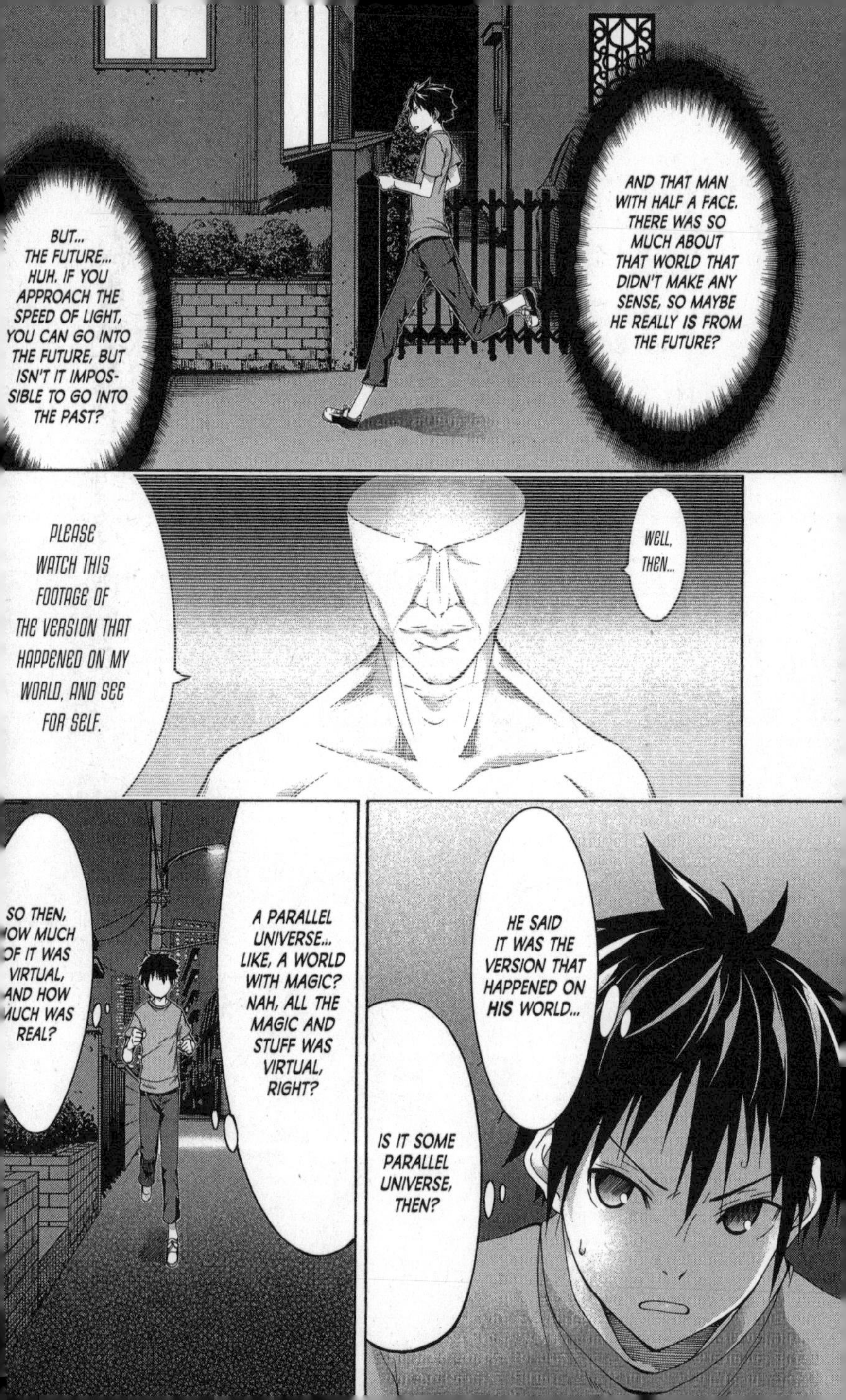
AND THAT MAN WITH HALF A FACE. THERE WAS SO MUCH ABOUT THAT WORLD THAT DIDN'T MAKE ANY SENSE, SO MAYBE HE REALLY IS FROM THE FUTURE?
BUT... THE FUTURE... HUH. IF YOU APPROACH THE SPEED OF LIGHT, YOU CAN GO INTO THE FUTURE, BUT ISN'T IT IMPOS-SIBLE TO GO INTO THE PAST?
WELL, THEN...
PLEASE WATCH THIS FOOTAGE OF THE VERSION THAT HAPPENED ON MY WORLD, AND SEE FOR SELF.
HE SAID IT WAS THE VERSION THAT HAPPENED ON HIS WORLD...
IS IT SOME PARALLEL UNIVERSE, THEN?
A PARALLEL UNIVERSE... LIKE, A WORLD WITH MAGIC? NAH, ALL THE MAGIC AND STUFF WAS VIRTUAL, RIGHT?
SO THEN, HOW MUCH OF IT WAS VIRTUAL, AND HOW MUCH WAS REAL?

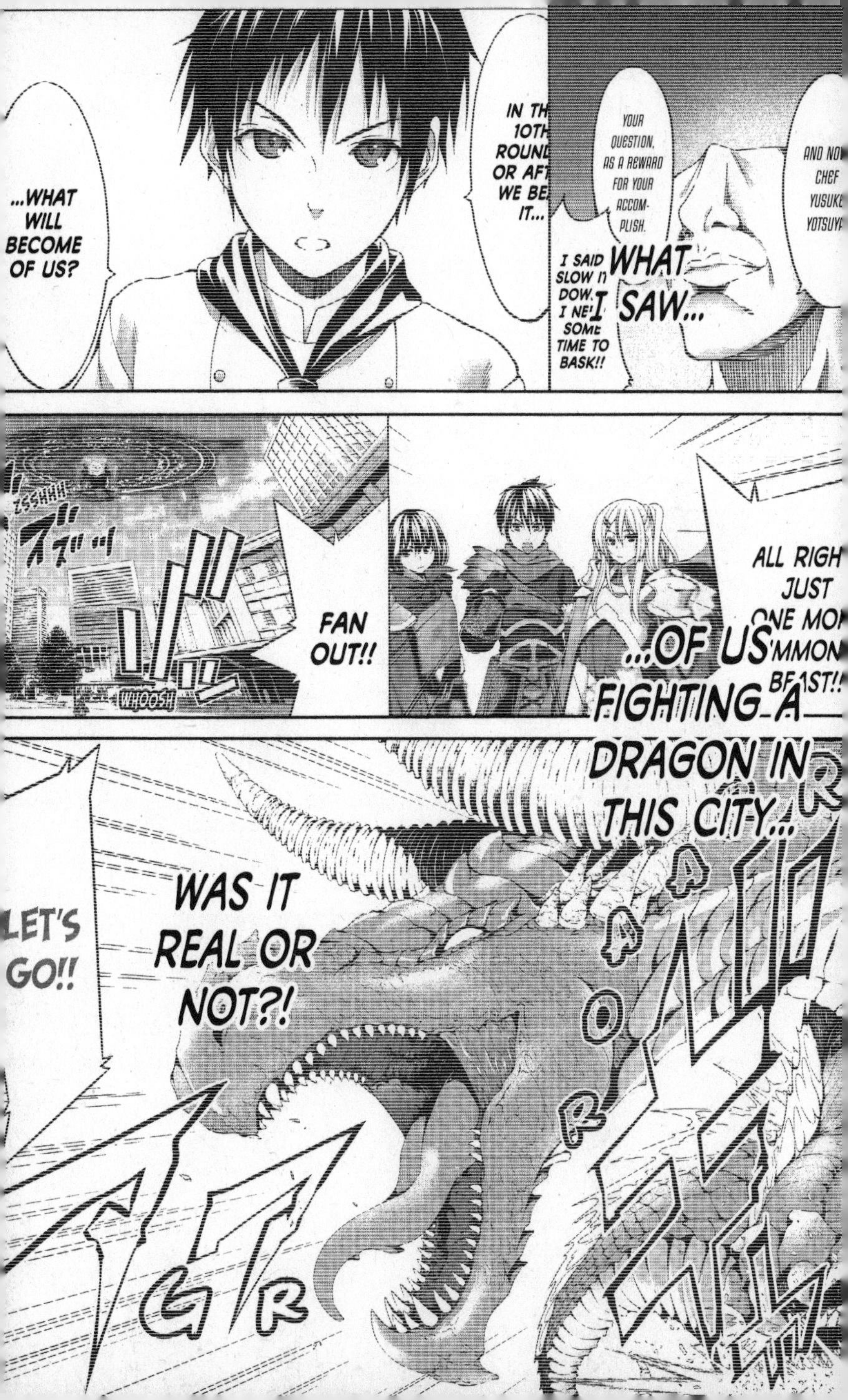
AND NO CHEF YUSUKE YOTSUY
YOUR QUESTION, AS A REWARD FOR YOUR ACCOM-PLISH.
I SAID SLOW I DOW. I NE SOME TIME TO BASK!!
WHAT I SAW...
IN TH 10TH ROUND OR AFT WE BE IT...
...WHAT WILL BECOME OF US?
ALL RIGH JUST ONE MO MMON BEAST!!
...OF US FIGHTING A DRAGON IN THIS CITY...
FAN OUT!!
ZSSHHH
ブブッ
WHOOSH
RAAAOR
WAS IT REAL OR NOT?!
LET'S GO!!
GRR

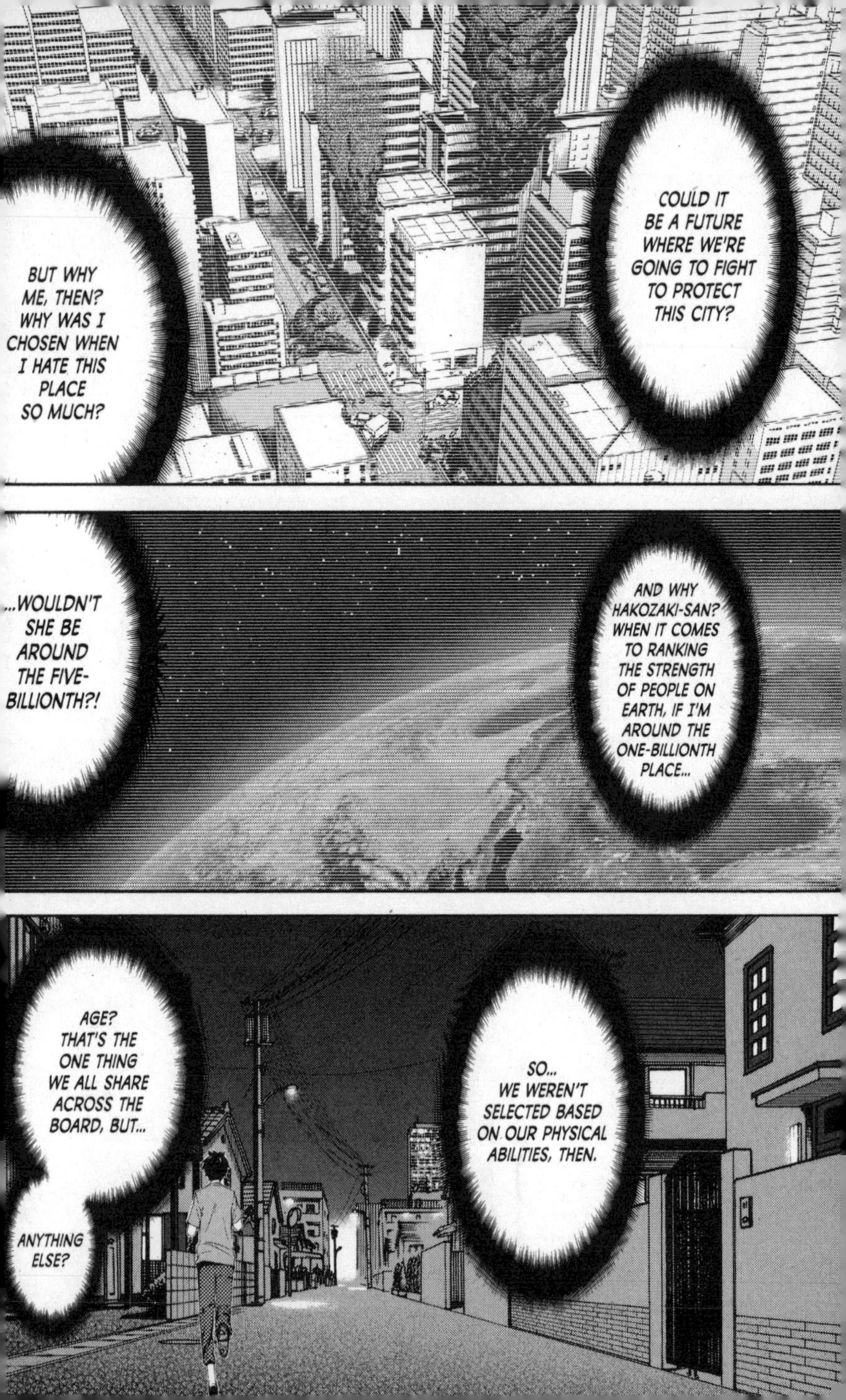
COULD IT BE A FUTURE WHERE WE'RE GOING TO FIGHT TO PROTECT THIS CITY?
BUT WHY ME, THEN? WHY WAS I CHOSEN WHEN I HATE THIS PLACE SO MUCH?
AND WHY HAKOZAKI-SAN? WHEN IT COMES TO RANKING THE STRENGTH OF PEOPLE ON EARTH, IF I'M AROUND THE ONE-BILLIONTH PLACE...
...WOULDN'T SHE BE AROUND THE FIVE-BILLIONTH?!
SO... WE WEREN'T SELECTED BASED ON OUR PHYSICAL ABILITIES, THEN.
AGE? THAT'S THE ONE THING WE ALL SHARE ACROSS THE BOARD, BUT...
ANYTHING ELSE?

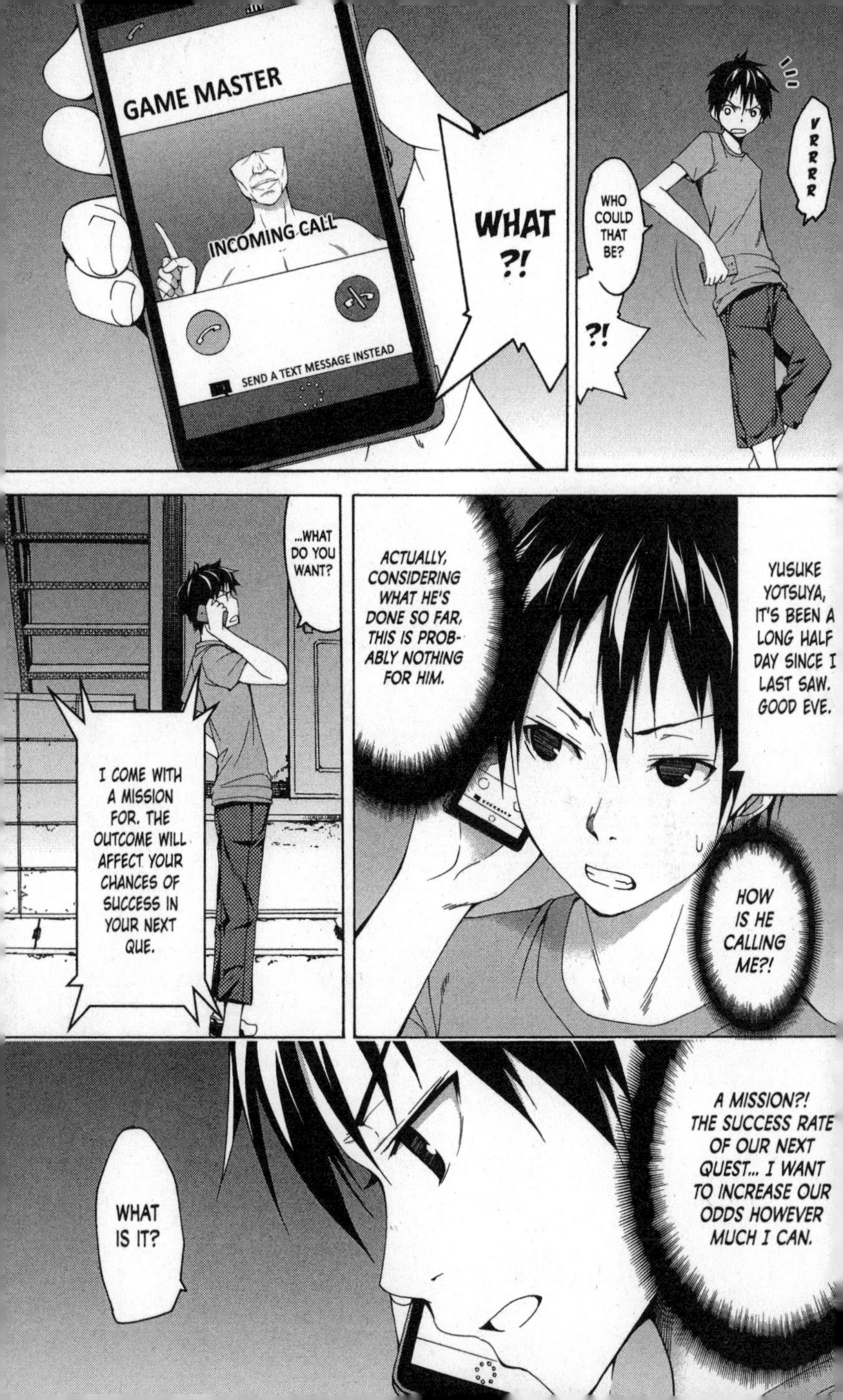
VRRRR
WHO COULD THAT BE?
?!
GAME MASTER
INCOMING CALL
SEND A TEXT MESSAGE INSTEAD
WHAT ?!
YUSUKE YOTSUYA, IT'S BEEN A LONG HALF DAY SINCE I LAST SAW. GOOD EVE.
ACTUALLY, CONSIDERING WHAT HE'S DONE SO FAR, THIS IS PROBABLY NOTHING FOR HIM.
HOW IS HE CALLING ME?!
...WHAT DO YOU WANT?
I COME WITH A MISSION FOR. THE OUTCOME WILL AFFECT YOUR CHANCES OF SUCCESS IN YOUR NEXT QUE.
A MISSION?! THE SUCCESS RATE OF OUR NEXT QUEST... I WANT TO INCREASE OUR ODDS HOWEVER MUCH I CAN.
WHAT IS IT?

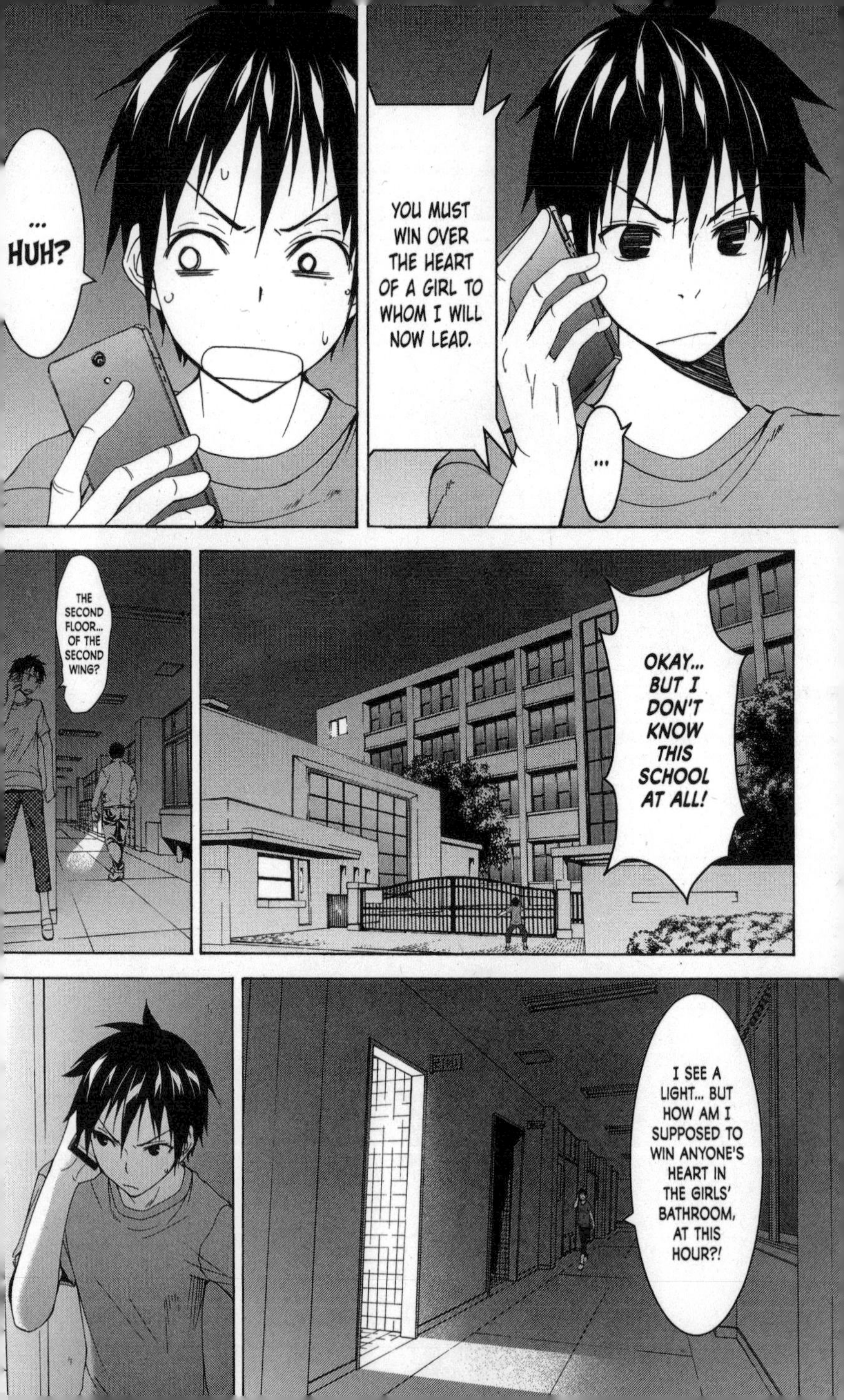
YOU MUST WIN OVER THE HEART OF A GIRL TO WHOM I WILL NOW LEAD.
...
... HUH?
OKAY... BUT I DON'T KNOW THIS SCHOOL AT ALL!
THE SECOND FLOOR... OF THE SECOND WING?
I SEE A LIGHT... BUT HOW AM I SUPPOSED TO WIN ANYONE'S HEART IN THE GIRLS' BATHROOM, AT THIS HOUR?!

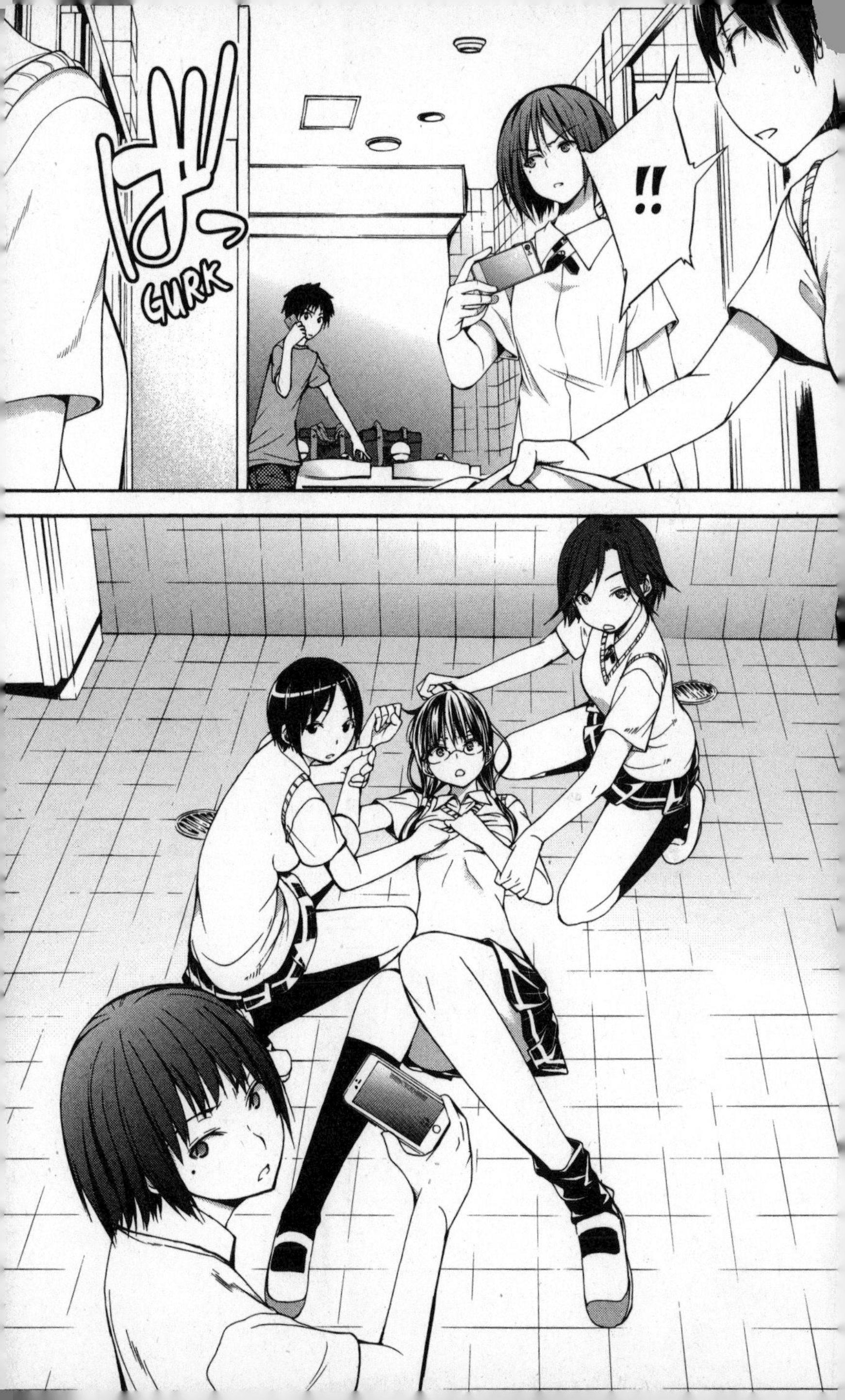

ばっ
GURK
!!

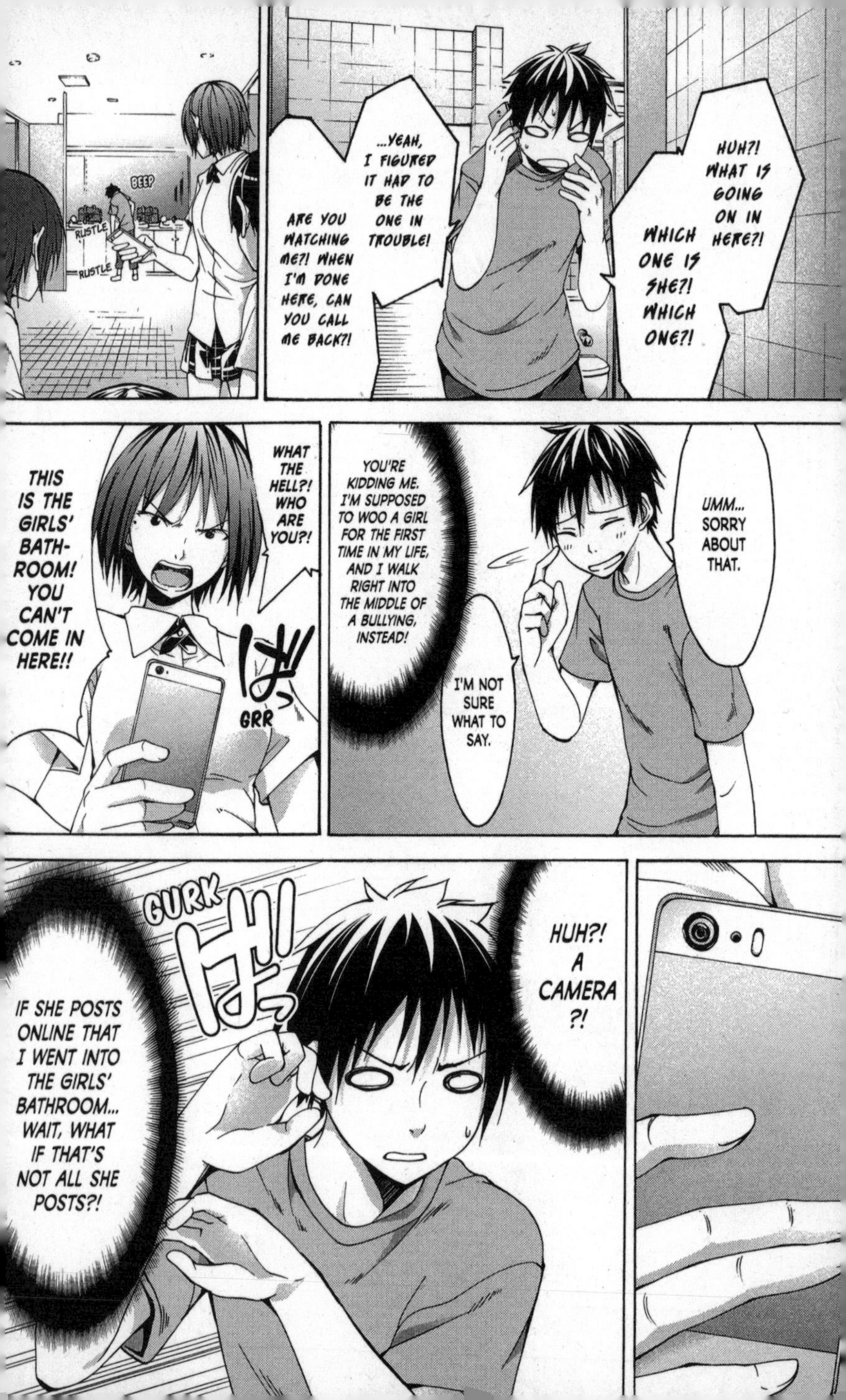
HUH?! WHAT IS GOING ON IN HERE?!
WHICH ONE IS SHE?! WHICH ONE?!
...YEAH, I FIGURED IT HAD TO BE THE ONE IN TROUBLE!
ARE YOU WATCHING ME?! WHEN I'M DONE HERE, CAN YOU CALL ME BACK?!
BEEP
RUSTLE
RUSTLE
UMM... SORRY ABOUT THAT.
YOU'RE KIDDING ME. I'M SUPPOSED TO WOO A GIRL FOR THE FIRST TIME IN MY LIFE, AND I WALK RIGHT INTO THE MIDDLE OF A BULLYING, INSTEAD!
I'M NOT SURE WHAT TO SAY.
WHAT THE HELL?! WHO ARE YOU?!
THIS IS THE GIRLS' BATH-ROOM! YOU CAN'T COME IN HERE!!
GRR
HUH?! A CAMERA ?!
GURK
IF SHE POSTS ONLINE THAT I WENT INTO THE GIRLS' BATHROOM... WAIT, WHAT IF THAT'S NOT ALL SHE POSTS?!

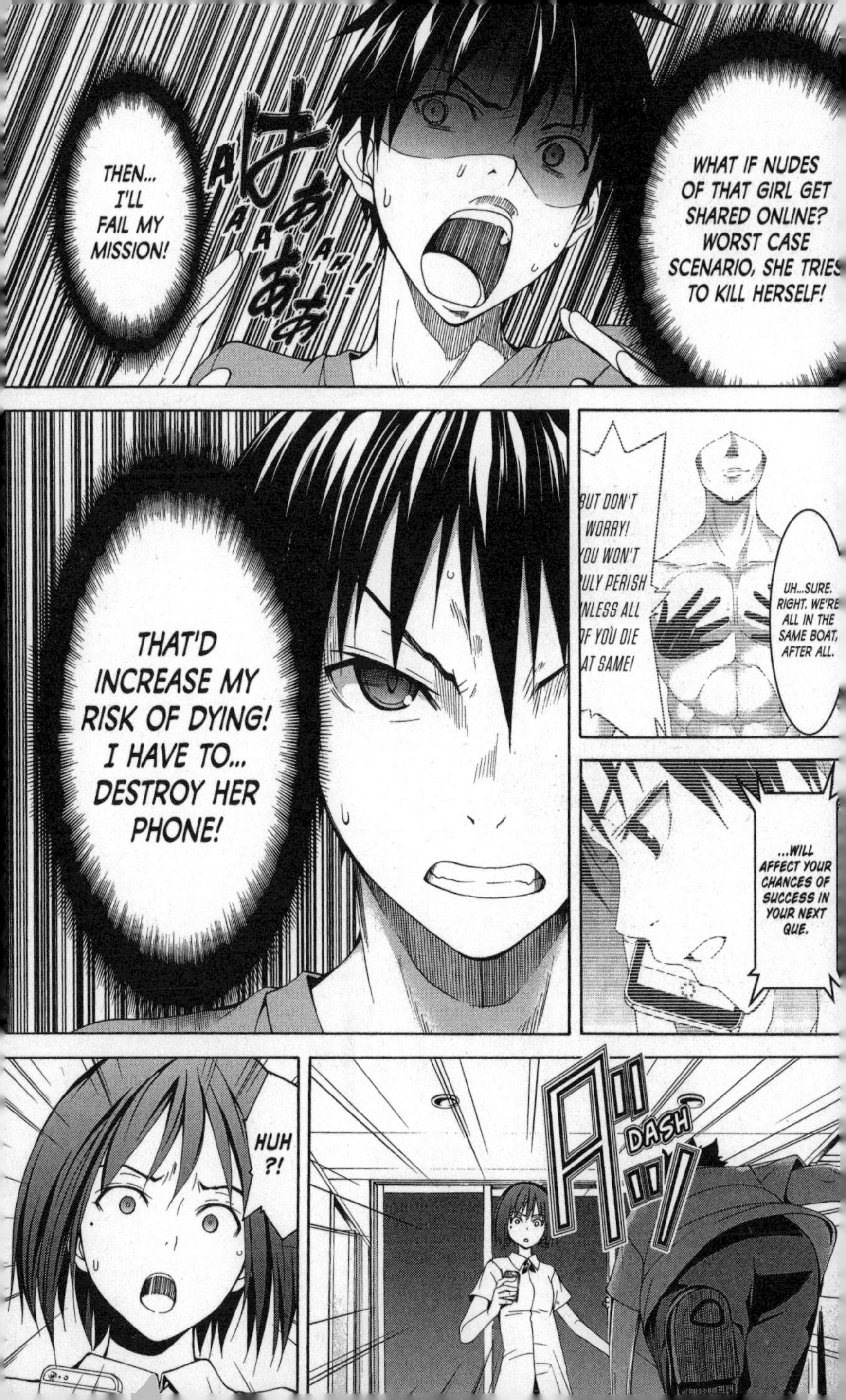
WHAT IF NUDES OF THAT GIRL GET SHARED ONLINE? WORST CASE SCENARIO, SHE TRIES TO KILL HERSELF!
はああああ
AAAAAH!
THEN... I'LL FAIL MY MISSION!
BUT DON'T WORRY! YOU WON'T ULY PERISH NLESS ALL OF YOU DIE AT SAME!
UH...SURE. RIGHT. WE'RE ALL IN THE SAME BOAT, AFTER ALL.
...WILL AFFECT YOUR CHANCES OF SUCCESS IN YOUR NEXT QUE.
THAT'D INCREASE MY RISK OF DYING! I HAVE TO... DESTROY HER PHONE!
ダッ
DASH
HUH ?!

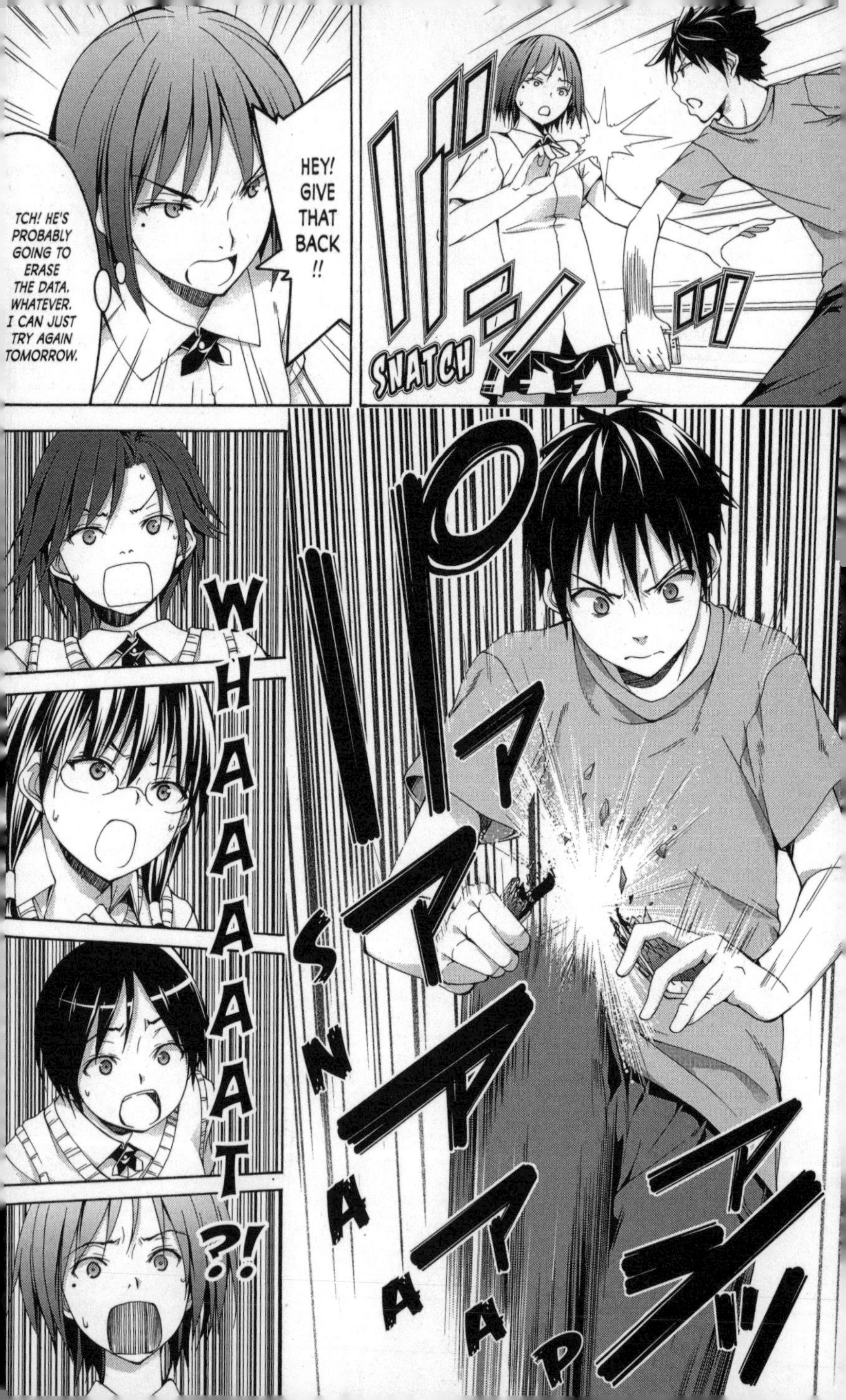
SNATCH
HEY! GIVE THAT BACK!!
TCH! HE'S PROBABLY GOING TO ERASE THE DATA. WHATEVER. I CAN JUST TRY AGAIN TOMORROW.
SNAAAP
WHAAAAAT?!

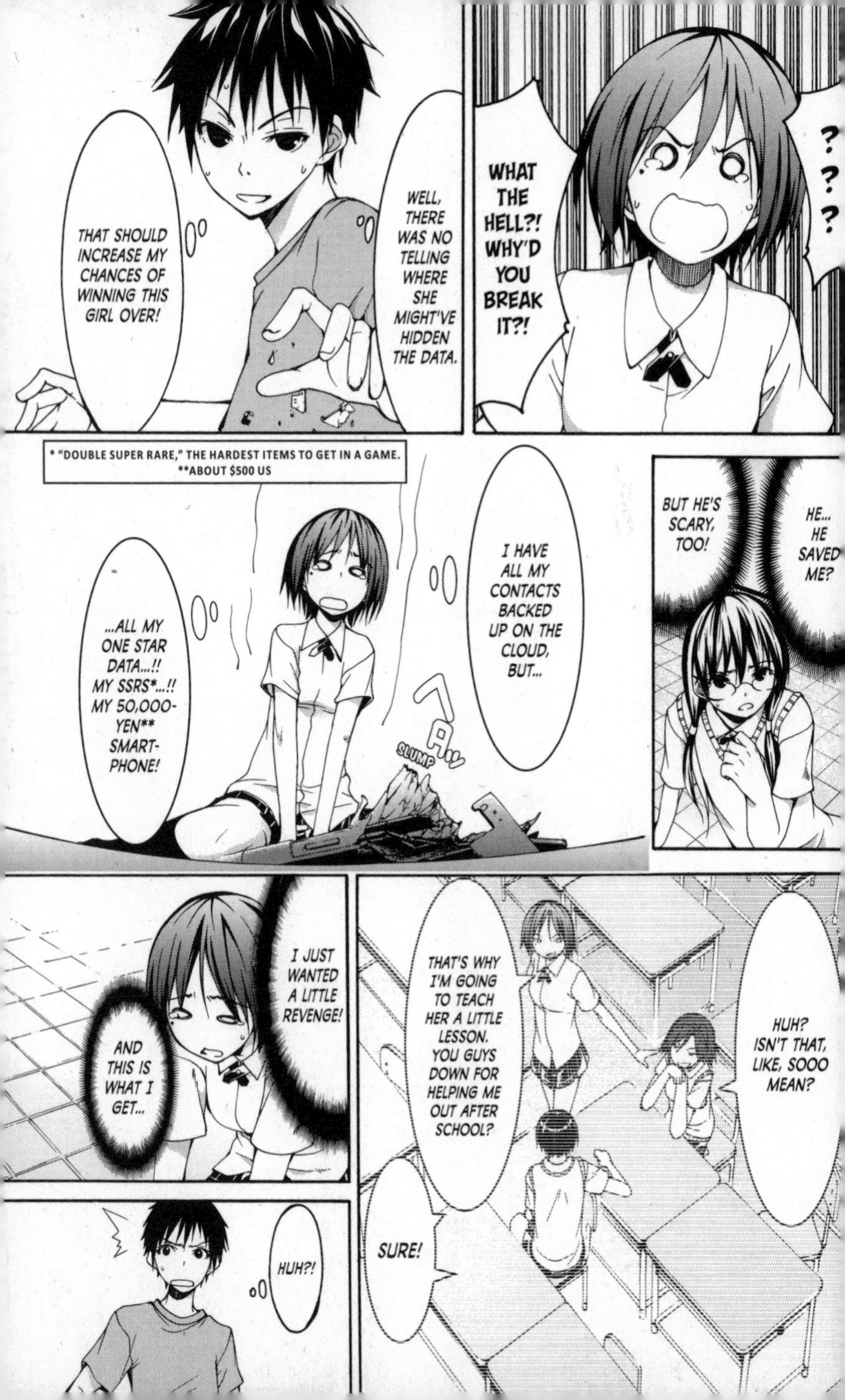
? ? ?
WHAT THE HELL?! WHY'D YOU BREAK IT?!
WELL, THERE WAS NO TELLING WHERE SHE MIGHT'VE HIDDEN THE DATA.
THAT SHOULD INCREASE MY CHANCES OF WINNING THIS GIRL OVER!
HE... HE SAVED ME?
BUT HE'S SCARY, TOO!
I HAVE ALL MY CONTACTS BACKED UP ON THE CLOUD, BUT...
...ALL MY ONE STAR DATA...!! MY SSRS*...!! MY 50,000-YEN** SMARTPHONE!
SLUMP
* "DOUBLE SUPER RARE," THE HARDEST ITEMS TO GET IN A GAME.
**ABOUT $500 US
HUH? ISN'T THAT, LIKE, SOOO MEAN?
THAT'S WHY I'M GOING TO TEACH HER A LITTLE LESSON. YOU GUYS DOWN FOR HELPING ME OUT AFTER SCHOOL?
SURE!
I JUST WANTED A LITTLE REVENGE!
AND THIS IS WHAT I GET...
HUH?!

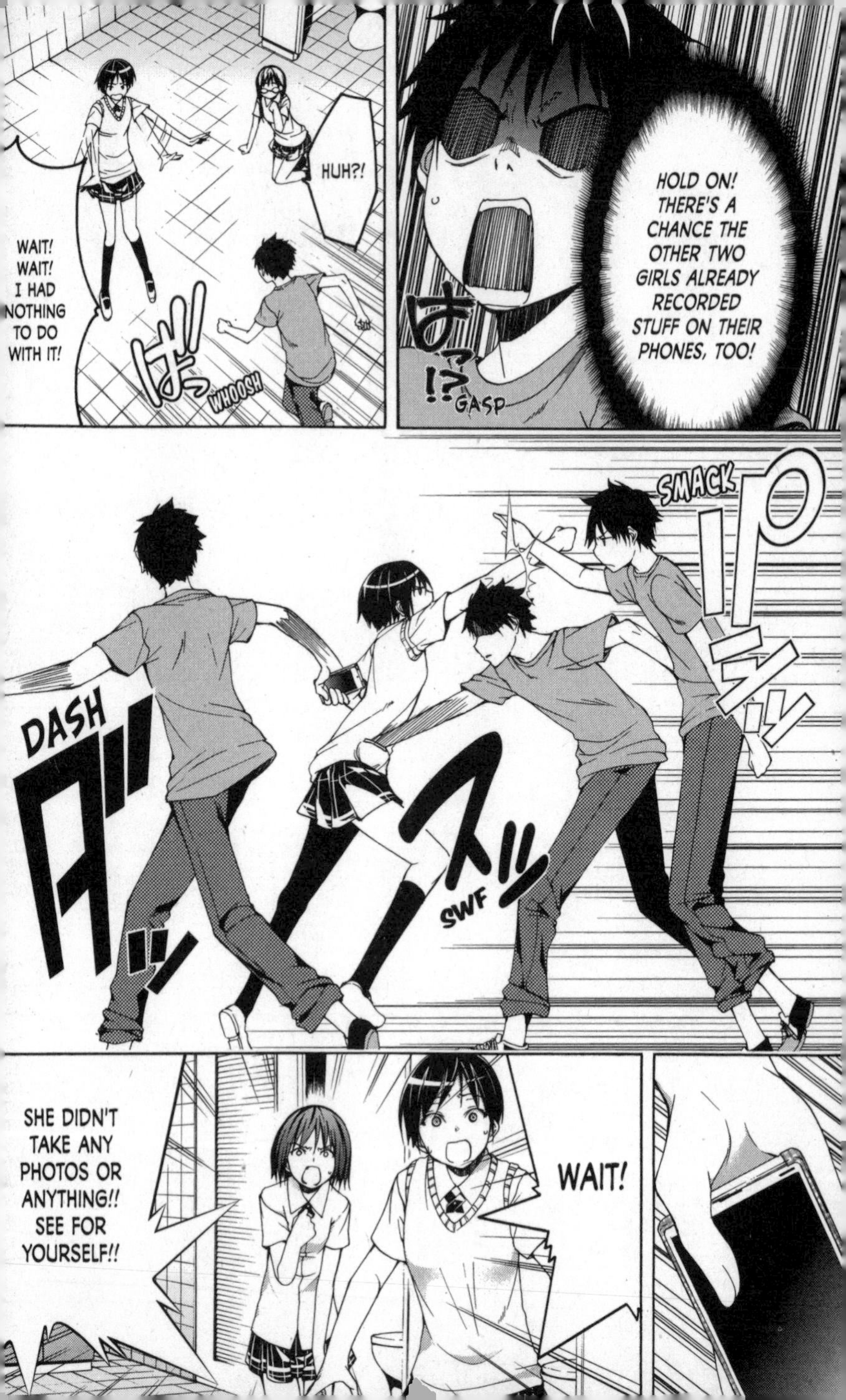
HOLD ON! THERE'S A CHANCE THE OTHER TWO GIRLS ALREADY RECORDED STUFF ON THEIR PHONES, TOO!
GASP
HUH?!
WAIT! WAIT! I HAD NOTHING TO DO WITH IT!
WHOOSH
SMACK
SWF
DASH
WAIT!
SHE DIDN'T TAKE ANY PHOTOS OR ANYTHING!! SEE FOR YOURSELF!!

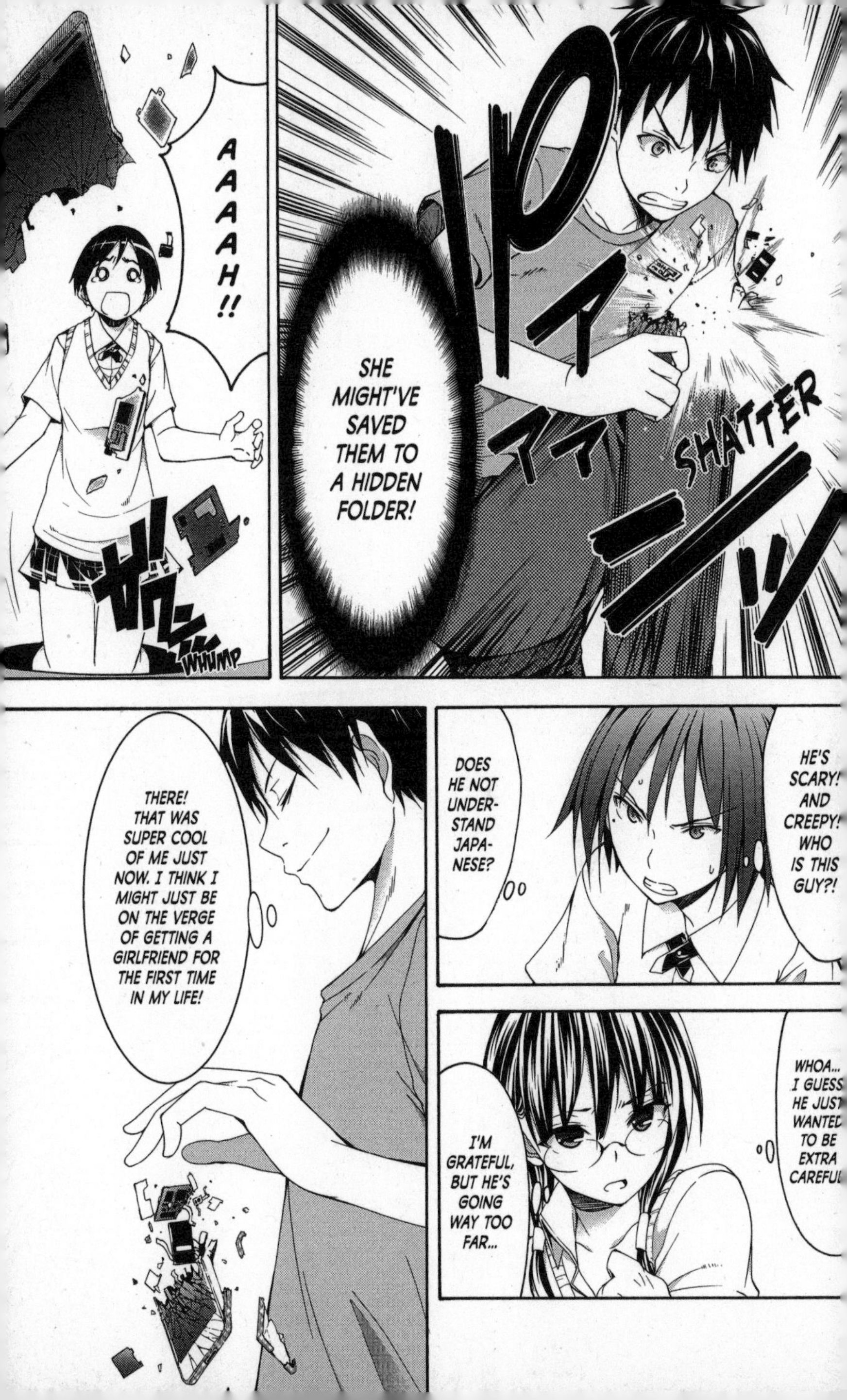
SHE MIGHT'VE SAVED THEM TO A HIDDEN FOLDER!
SHATTER
AAAAAH!!
WHUMP
HE'S SCARY! AND CREEPY! WHO IS THIS GUY?!
DOES HE NOT UNDER-STAND JAPA-NESE?
WHOA... I GUESS HE JUST WANTED TO BE EXTRA CAREFUL
I'M GRATEFUL, BUT HE'S GOING WAY TOO FAR...
THERE! THAT WAS SUPER COOL OF ME JUST NOW. I THINK I MIGHT JUST BE ON THE VERGE OF GETTING A GIRLFRIEND FOR THE FIRST TIME IN MY LIFE!

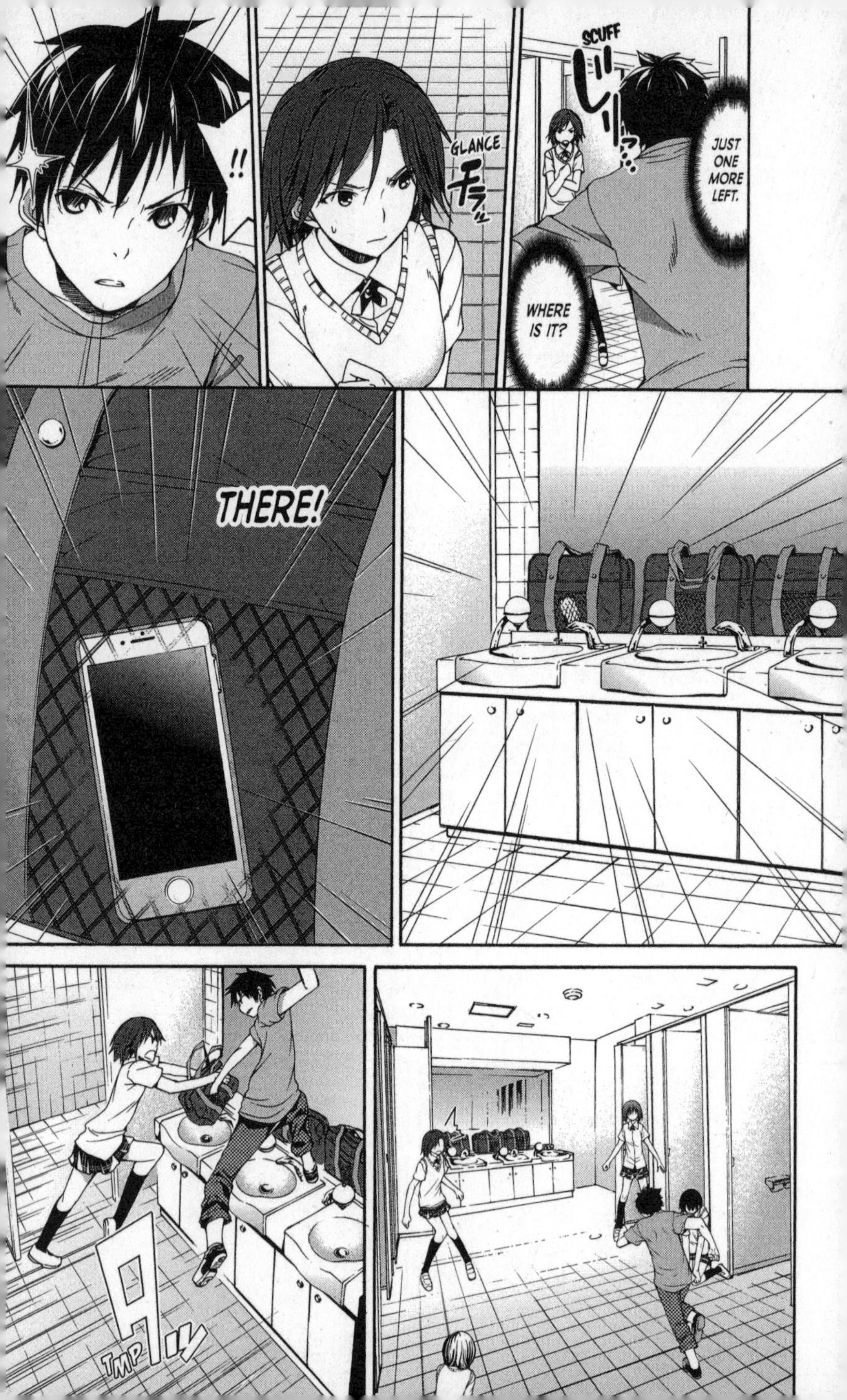
SCUFF
JUST ONE MORE LEFT.
WHERE IS IT?
GLANCE
!!
THERE!
TMP

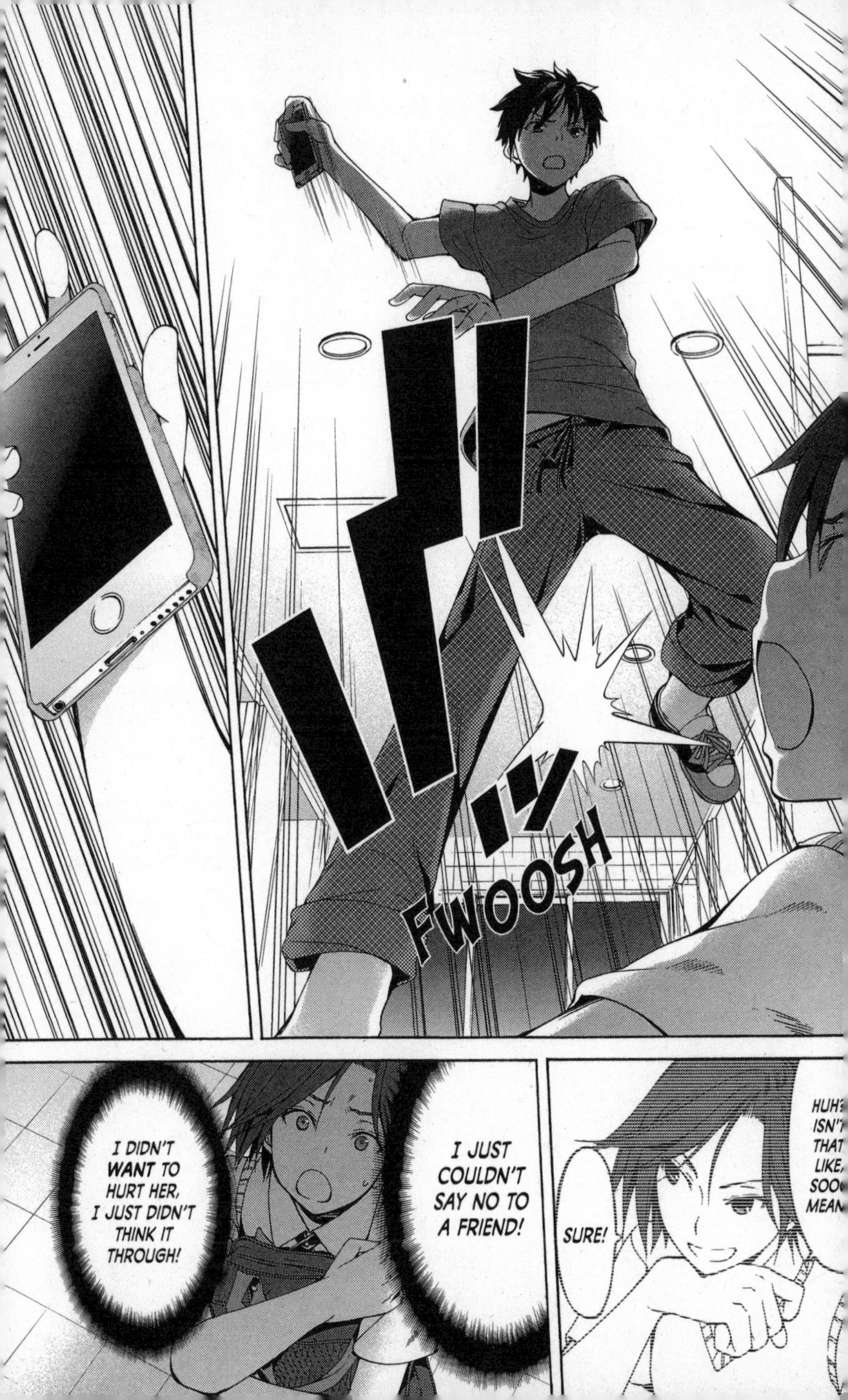
FWOOSH
HUH? ISN' THAT LIKE, SOO MEAN
SURE!
I JUST COULDN'T SAY NO TO A FRIEND!
I DIDN'T WANT TO HURT HER, I JUST DIDN'T THINK IT THROUGH!

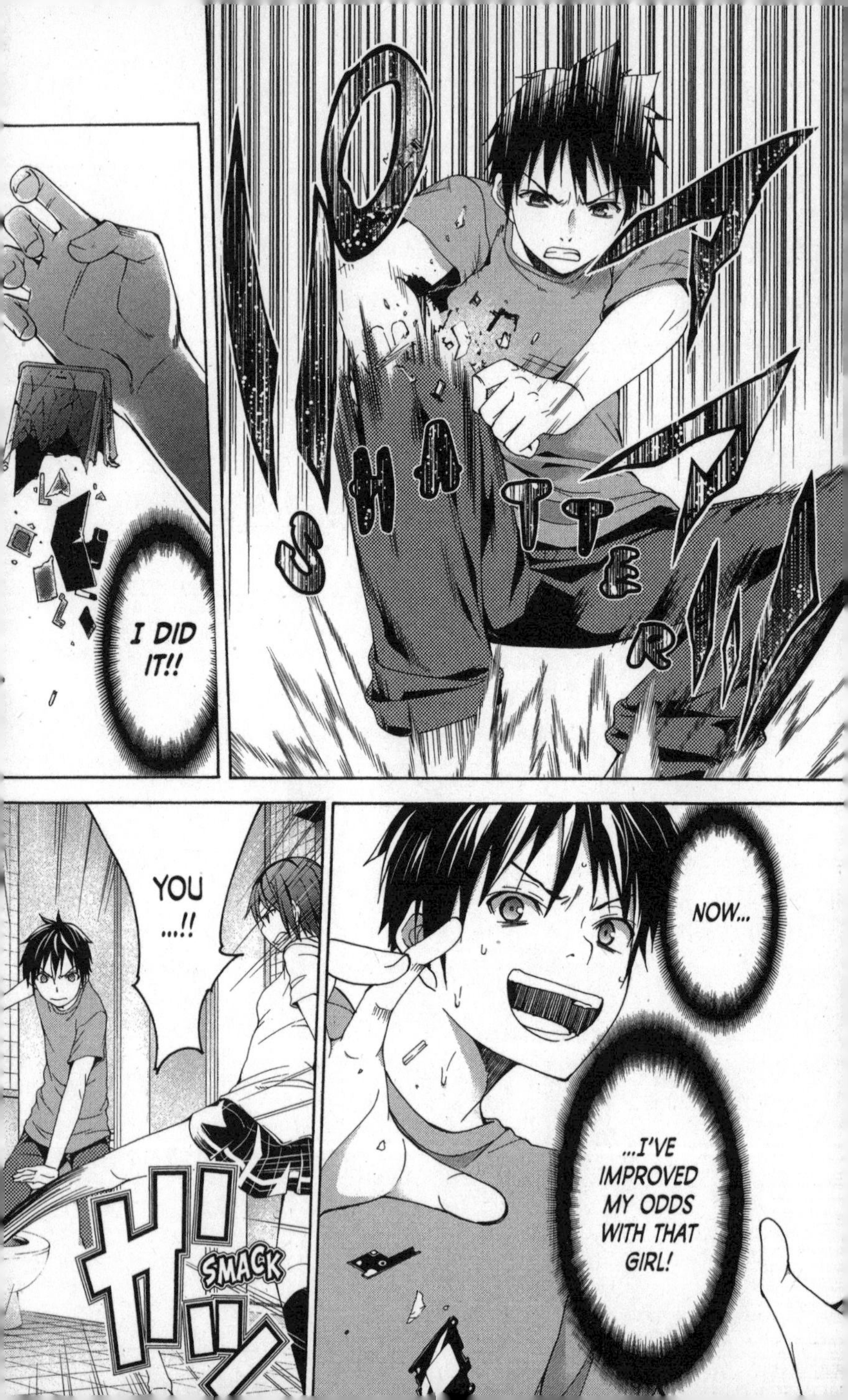
SHATTER
I DID IT!!
NOW...
...I'VE IMPROVED MY ODDS WITH THAT GIRL!
YOU ...!!
SMACK

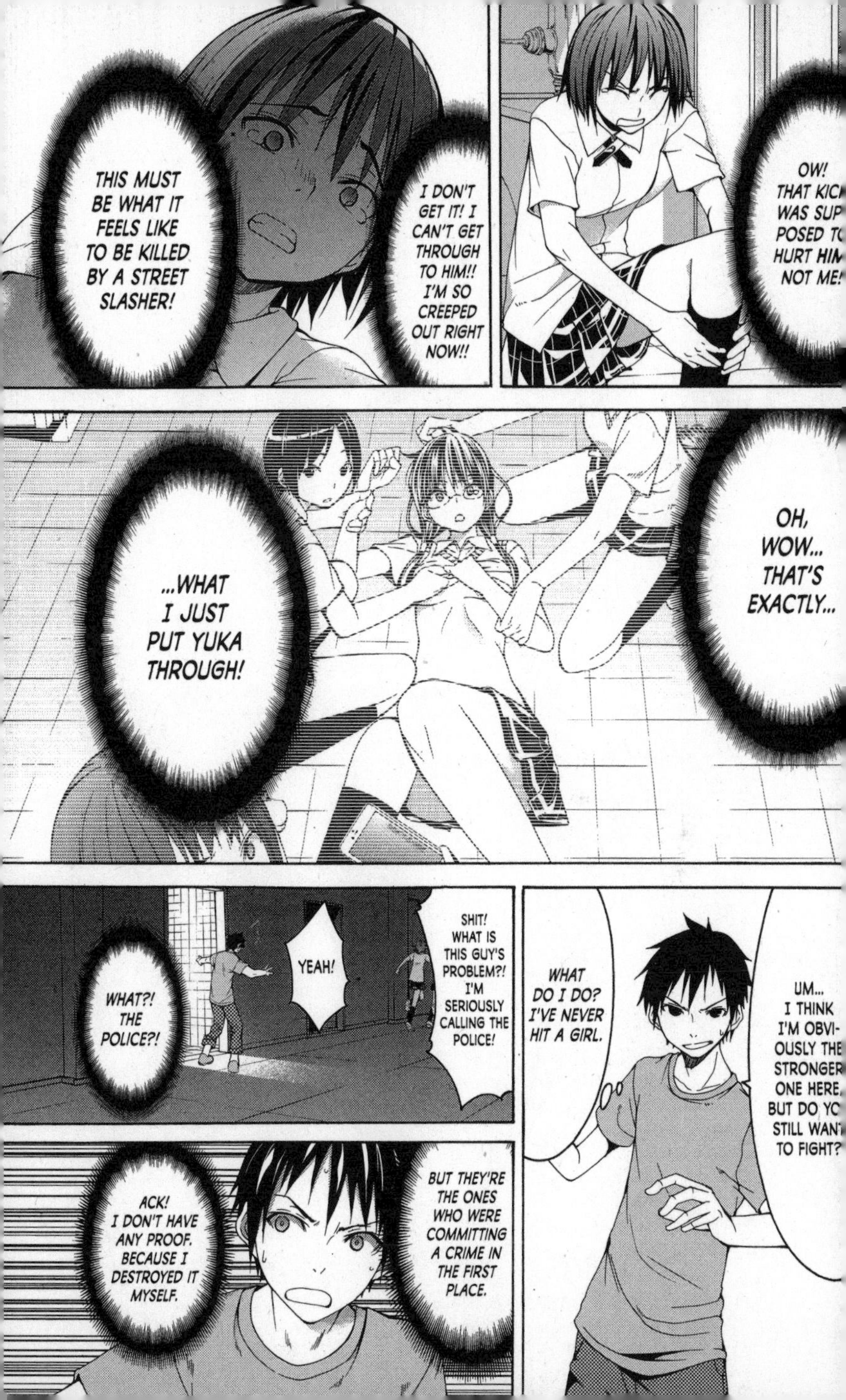

OW! THAT KIC WAS SUP POSED T HURT HIM NOT ME!
I DON'T GET IT! I CAN'T GET THROUGH TO HIM!! I'M SO CREEPED OUT RIGHT NOW!!
THIS MUST BE WHAT IT FEELS LIKE TO BE KILLED BY A STREET SLASHER!
OH, WOW... THAT'S EXACTLY...
...WHAT I JUST PUT YUKA THROUGH!
UM... I THINK I'M OBVI-OUSLY THE STRONGER ONE HERE, BUT DO YO STILL WANT TO FIGHT?
WHAT DO I DO? I'VE NEVER HIT A GIRL.
SHIT! WHAT IS THIS GUY'S PROBLEM?! I'M SERIOUSLY CALLING THE POLICE!
YEAH!
WHAT?! THE POLICE?!
BUT THEY'RE THE ONES WHO WERE COMMITTING A CRIME IN THE FIRST PLACE.
ACK! I DON'T HAVE ANY PROOF. BECAUSE I DESTROYED IT MYSELF.

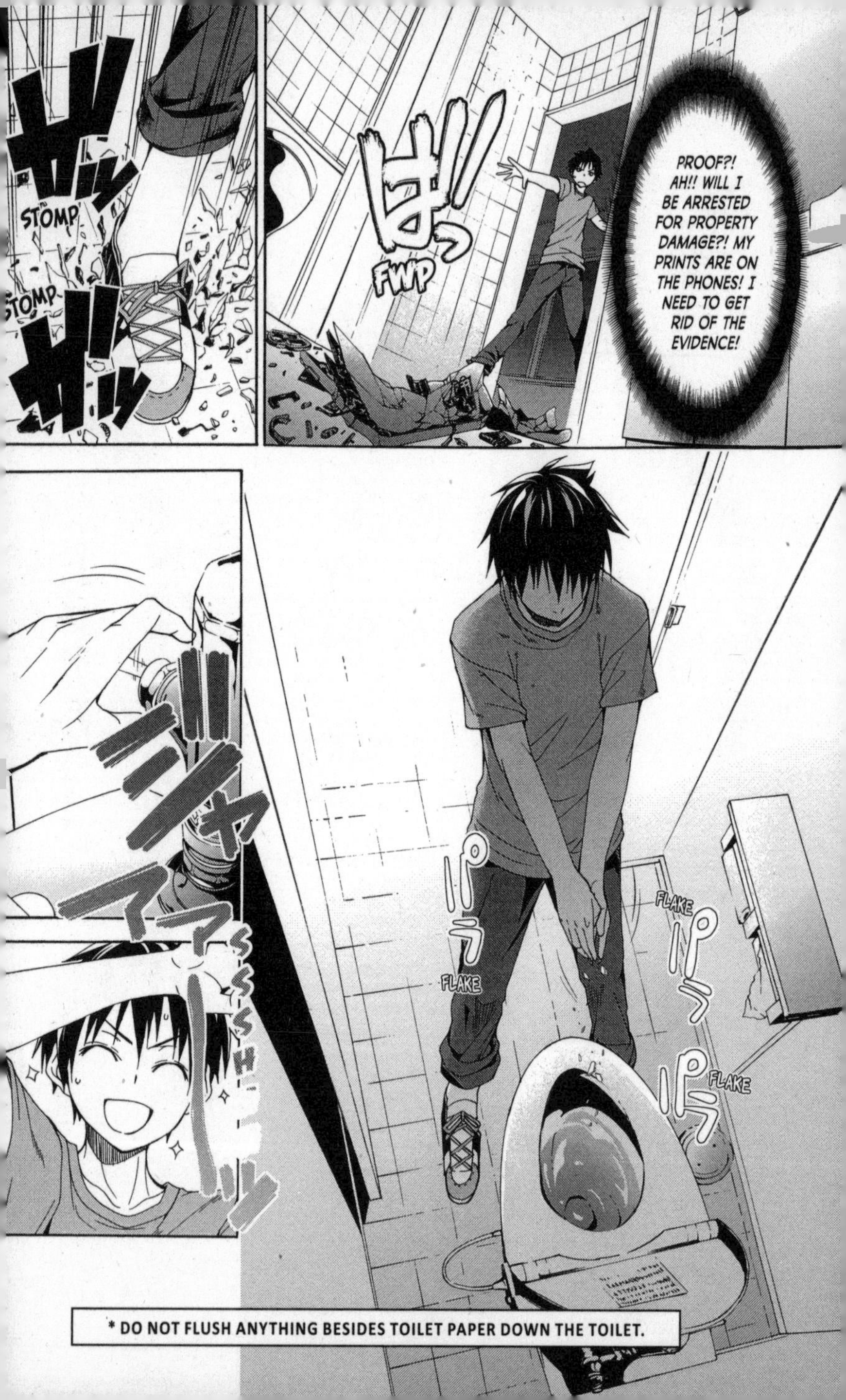
PROOF?! AH!! WILL I BE ARRESTED FOR PROPERTY DAMAGE?! MY PRINTS ARE ON THE PHONES! I NEED TO GET RID OF THE EVIDENCE!
FWP
STOMP
STOMP
FLAKE
FLAKE
FLAKE
SSSSHH
* DO NOT FLUSH ANYTHING BESIDES TOILET PAPER DOWN THE TOILET.

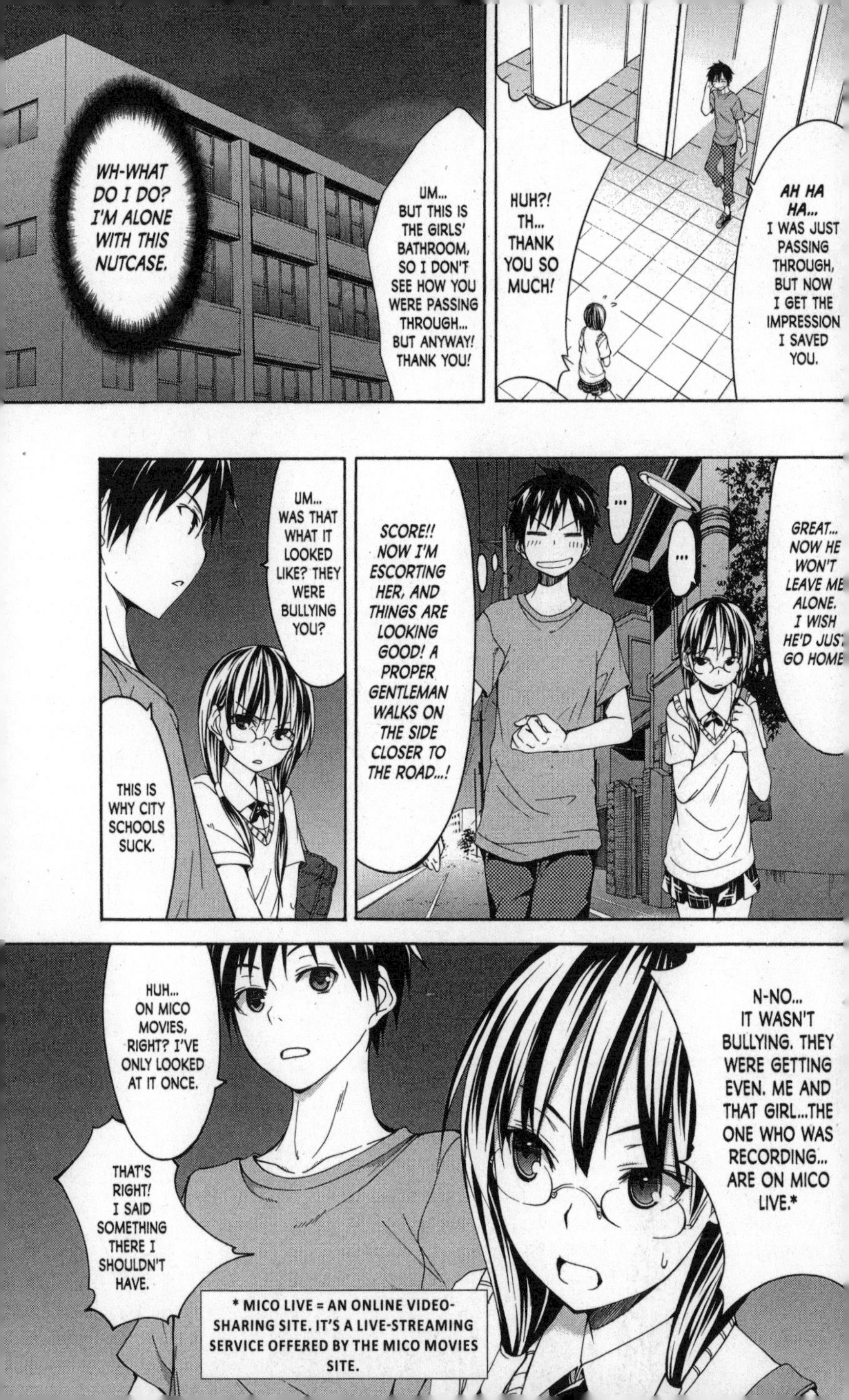
AH HA HA... I WAS JUST PASSING THROUGH, BUT NOW I GET THE IMPRESSION I SAVED YOU.
HUH?! TH... THANK YOU SO MUCH!
UM... BUT THIS IS THE GIRLS' BATHROOM, SO I DON'T SEE HOW YOU WERE PASSING THROUGH... BUT ANYWAY! THANK YOU!
WH-WHAT DO I DO? I'M ALONE WITH THIS NUTCASE.
GREAT... NOW HE WON'T LEAVE ME ALONE. I WISH HE'D JUST GO HOME
...
...
SCORE!! NOW I'M ESCORTING HER, AND THINGS ARE LOOKING GOOD! A PROPER GENTLEMAN WALKS ON THE SIDE CLOSER TO THE ROAD...!
UM... WAS THAT WHAT IT LOOKED LIKE? THEY WERE BULLYING YOU?
THIS IS WHY CITY SCHOOLS SUCK.
N-NO... IT WASN'T BULLYING. THEY WERE GETTING EVEN. ME AND THAT GIRL...THE ONE WHO WAS RECORDING... ARE ON MICO LIVE.*
HUH... ON MICO MOVIES, RIGHT? I'VE ONLY LOOKED AT IT ONCE.
THAT'S RIGHT! I SAID SOMETHING THERE I SHOULDN'T HAVE.

* MICO LIVE = AN ONLINE VIDEO-SHARING SITE. IT'S A LIVE-STREAMING SERVICE OFFERED BY THE MICO MOVIES SITE.

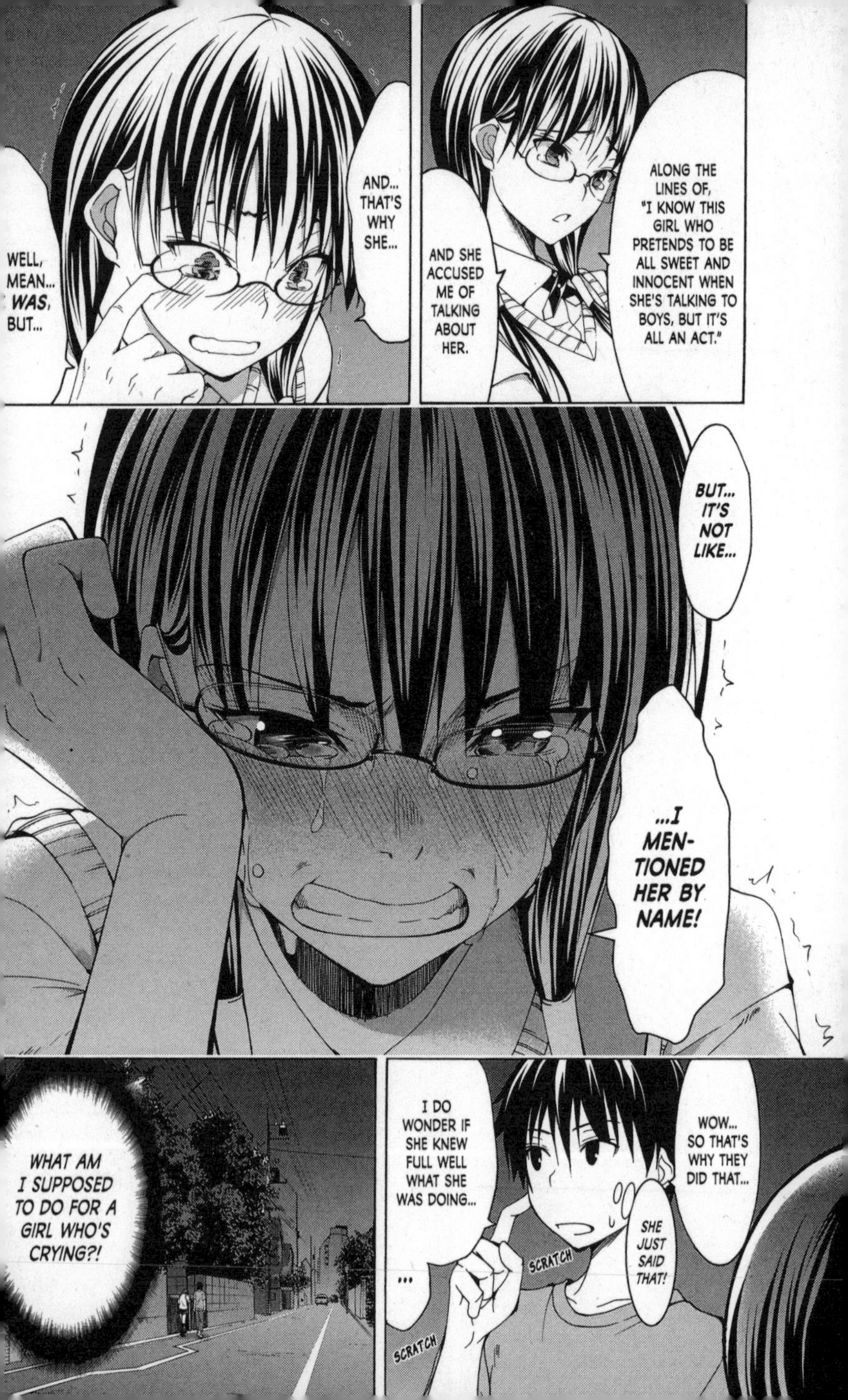
ALONG THE LINES OF, "I KNOW THIS GIRL WHO PRETENDS TO BE ALL SWEET AND INNOCENT WHEN SHE'S TALKING TO BOYS, BUT IT'S ALL AN ACT."
AND SHE ACCUSED ME OF TALKING ABOUT HER.
AND... THAT'S WHY SHE...
WELL, MEAN... WAS, BUT...
BUT... IT'S NOT LIKE...
...I MENTIONED HER BY NAME!
WOW... SO THAT'S WHY THEY DID THAT...
SHE JUST SAID THAT!
I DO WONDER IF SHE KNEW FULL WELL WHAT SHE WAS DOING...
SCRATCH
...
SCRATCH
WHAT AM I SUPPOSED TO DO FOR A GIRL WHO'S CRYING?!

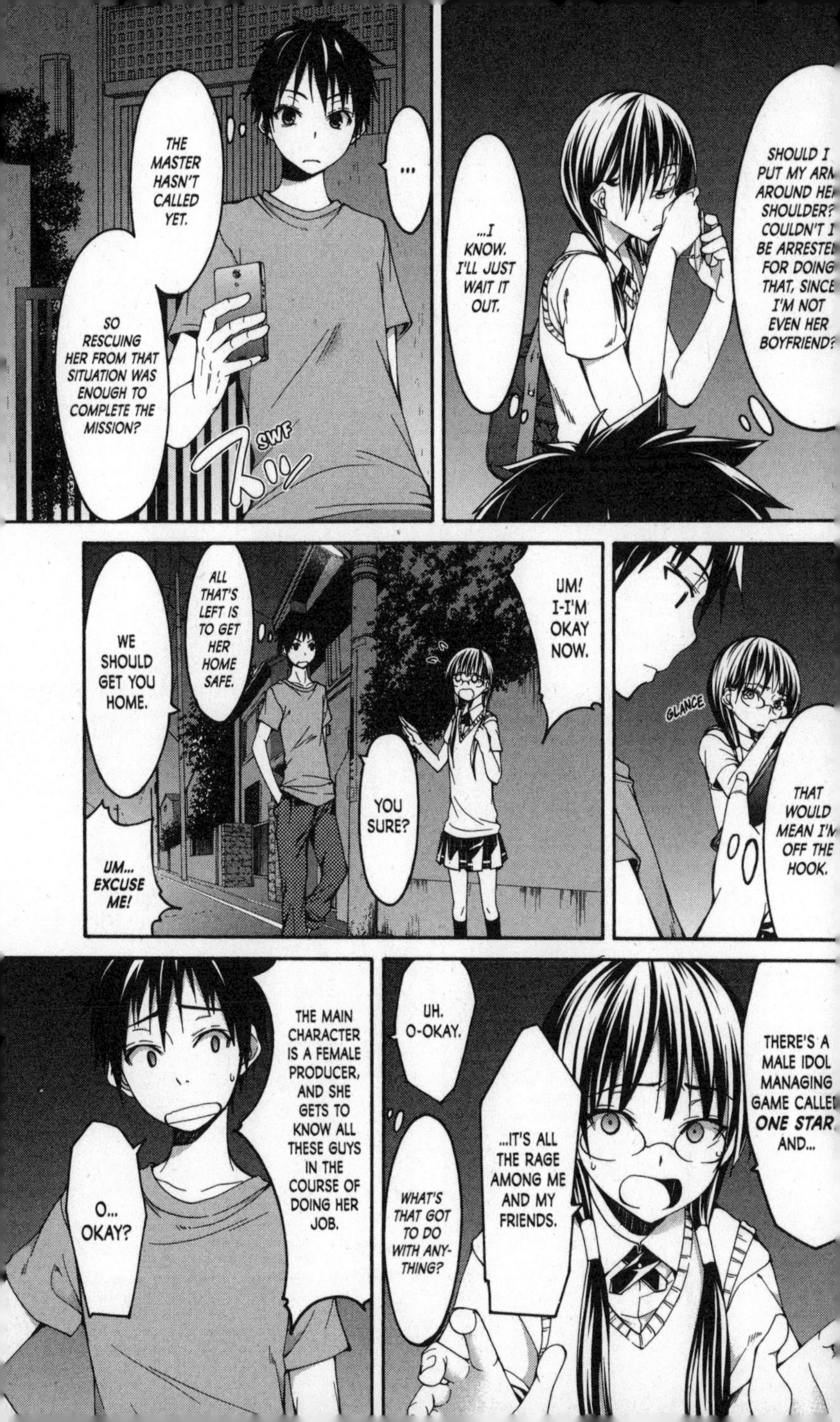
SHOULD I PUT MY ARM AROUND HER SHOULDER? COULDN'T I BE ARRESTED FOR DOING THAT, SINCE I'M NOT EVEN HER BOYFRIEND?
...I KNOW. I'LL JUST WAIT IT OUT.
...
THE MASTER HASN'T CALLED YET.
SO RESCUING HER FROM THAT SITUATION WAS ENOUGH TO COMPLETE THE MISSION?
SWF
UM! I-I'M OKAY NOW.
GLANCE
THAT WOULD MEAN I'M OFF THE HOOK.
ALL THAT'S LEFT IS TO GET HER HOME SAFE.
WE SHOULD GET YOU HOME.
YOU SURE?
UM... EXCUSE ME!
THERE'S A MALE IDOL MANAGING GAME CALLED *ONE STAR*, AND...
UH. O-OKAY.
...IT'S ALL THE RAGE AMONG ME AND MY FRIENDS.
WHAT'S THAT GOT TO DO WITH ANY-THING?
THE MAIN CHARACTER IS A FEMALE PRODUCER, AND SHE GETS TO KNOW ALL THESE GUYS IN THE COURSE OF DOING HER JOB.
O... OKAY?

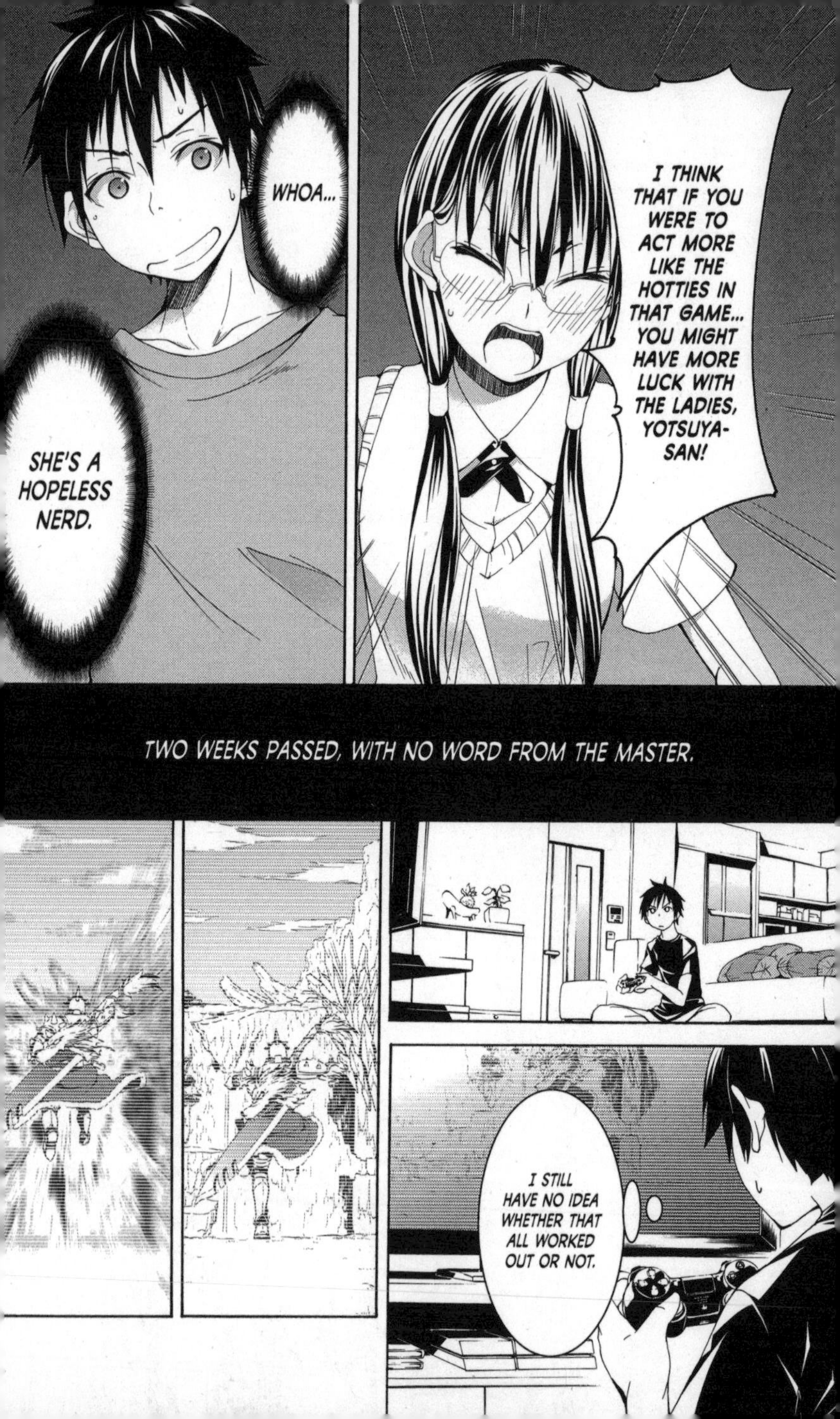
I THINK THAT IF YOU WERE TO ACT MORE LIKE THE HOTTIES IN THAT GAME... YOU MIGHT HAVE MORE LUCK WITH THE LADIES, YOTSUYA-SAN!
WHOA...
SHE'S A HOPELESS NERD.
TWO WEEKS PASSED, WITH NO WORD FROM THE MASTER.
I STILL HAVE NO IDEA WHETHER THAT ALL WORKED OUT OR NOT.

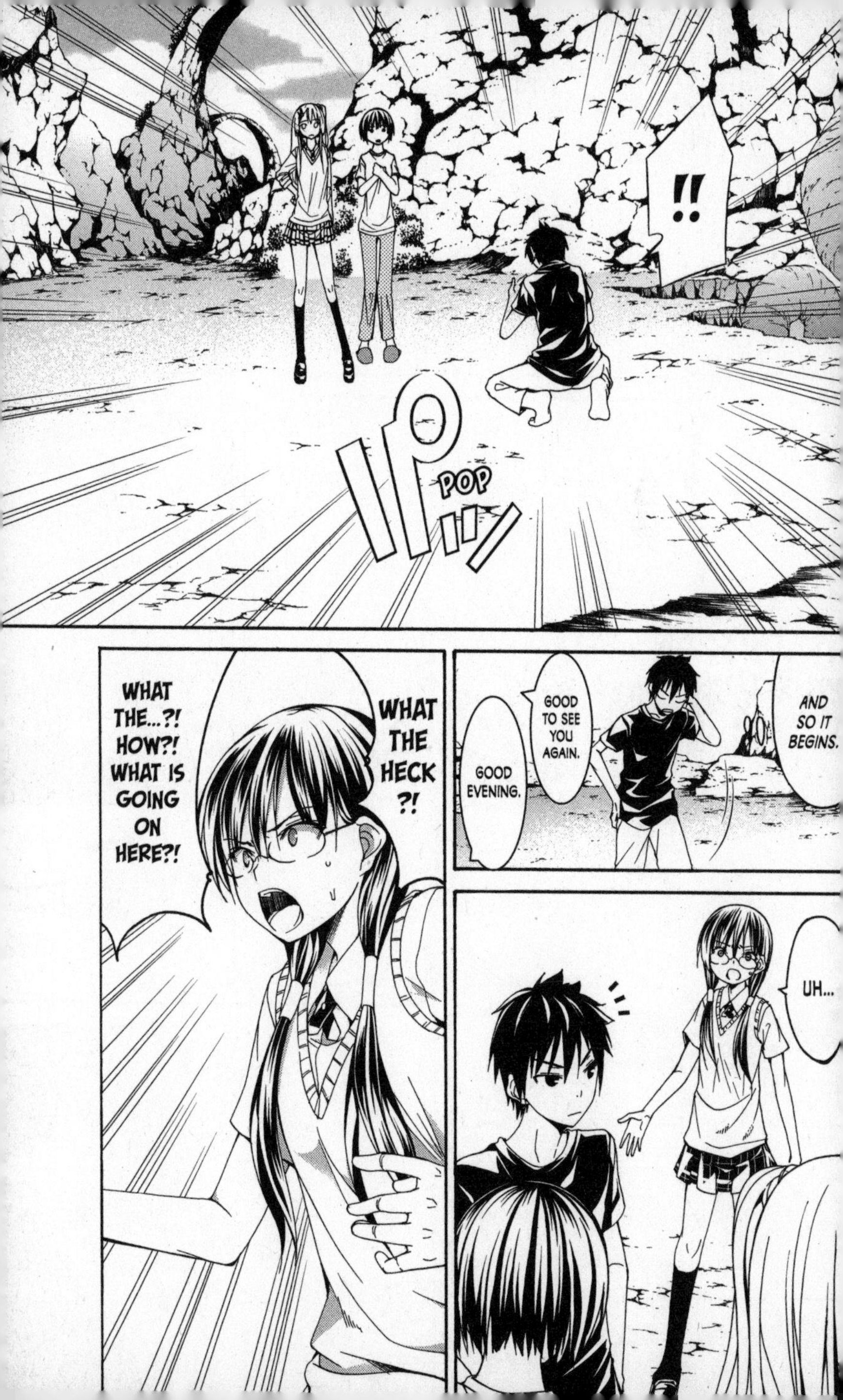
!!
POP
AND SO IT BEGINS.
GOOD TO SEE YOU AGAIN.
GOOD EVENING.
UH...
WHAT THE HECK?!
WHAT THE...?! HOW?! WHAT IS GOING ON HERE?!

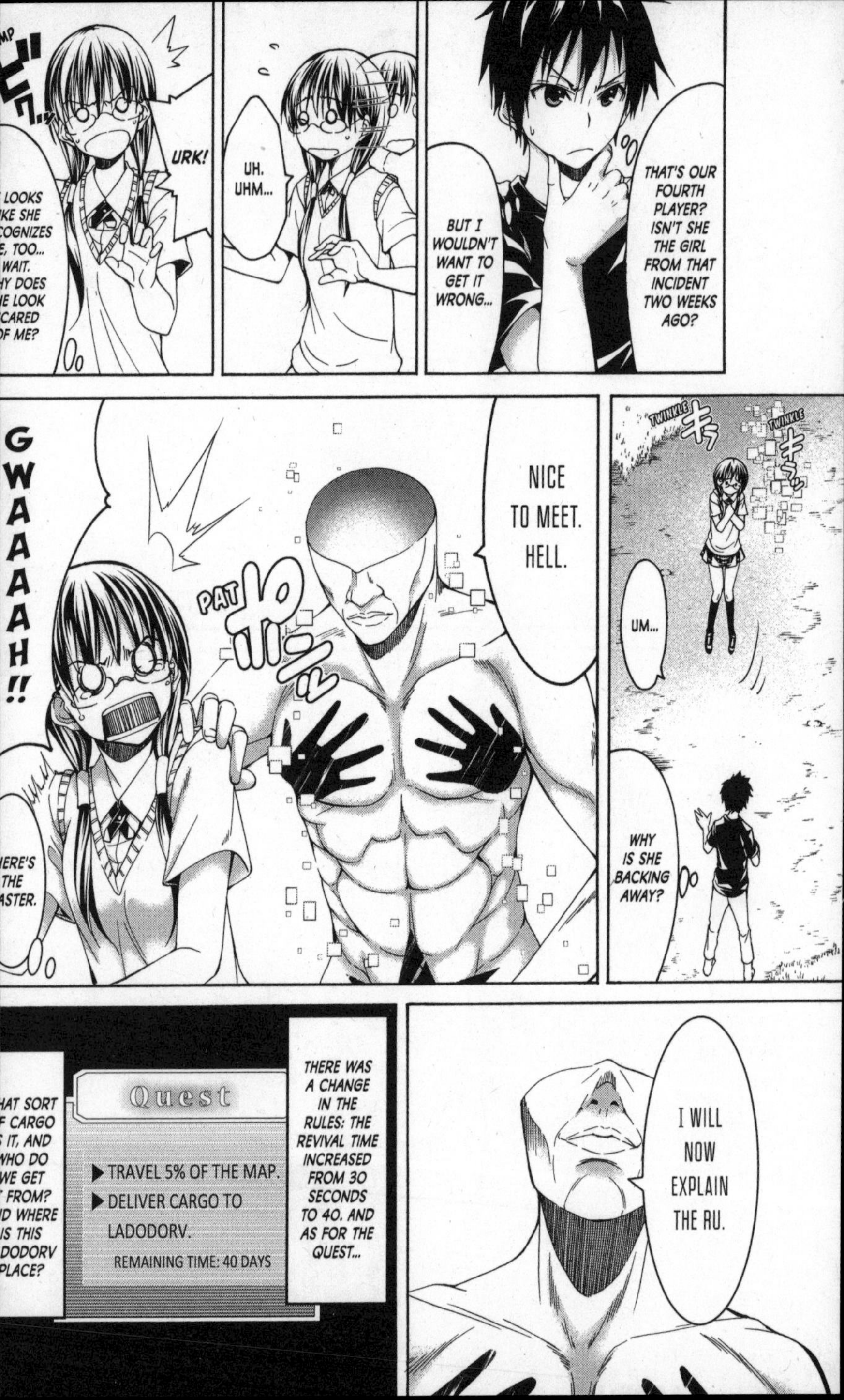
THAT'S OUR FOURTH PLAYER? ISN'T SHE THE GIRL FROM THAT INCIDENT TWO WEEKS AGO?
BUT I WOULDN'T WANT TO GET IT WRONG...
UH. UHM...
MP
URK!
LOOKS KE SHE COGNIZES E, TOO... WAIT. HY DOES HE LOOK CARED F ME?
TWINKLE
TWINKLE
UM...
WHY IS SHE BACKING AWAY?
NICE TO MEET. HELL.
PAT
GWAAAAAAH!!
ERE'S THE ASTER.
I WILL NOW EXPLAIN THE RU.
THERE WAS A CHANGE IN THE RULES: THE REVIVAL TIME INCREASED FROM 30 SECONDS TO 40. AND AS FOR THE QUEST...
Quest
▶TRAVEL 5% OF THE MAP.
▶DELIVER CARGO TO LADODORV.
REMAINING TIME: 40 DAYS
HAT SORT F CARGO S IT, AND HO DO WE GET T FROM? D WHERE IS THIS DODORV PLACE?

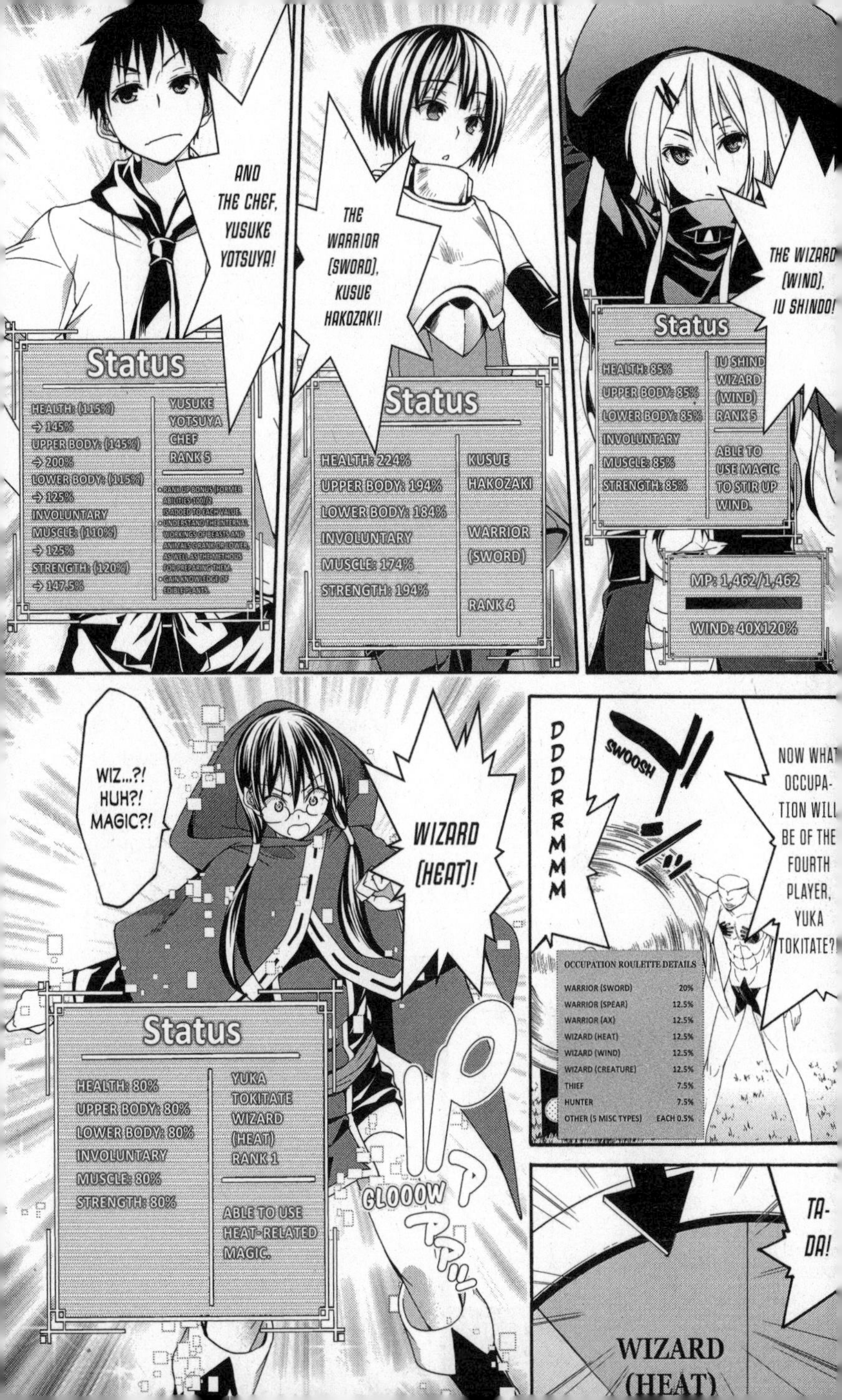
THE WIZARD (WIND), IU SHINDO!
Status
HEALTH: 85%
UPPER BODY: 85%
LOWER BODY: 85%
INVOLUNTARY MUSCLE: 85%
STRENGTH: 85%
IU SHIND
WIZARD (WIND)
RANK 5
ABLE TO USE MAGIC TO STIR UP WIND.
MP: 1,462/1,462
WIND: 40X120%
THE WARRIOR (SWORD), KUSUE HAKOZAKI!
Status
HEALTH: 224%
UPPER BODY: 194%
LOWER BODY: 184%
INVOLUNTARY MUSCLE: 174%
STRENGTH: 194%
KUSUE HAKOZAKI
WARRIOR (SWORD)
RANK 4
AND THE CHEF, YUSUKE YOTSUYA!
Status
HEALTH: (115%) → 145%
UPPER BODY: (145%) → 200%
LOWER BODY: (115%) → 125%
INVOLUNTARY MUSCLE: (110%) → 125%
STRENGTH: (120%) → 147.5%
YUSUKE YOTSUYA
CHEF
RANK 5
• RANK UP BONUS (FORMER ABILITIES-100)/2 IS ADDED TO EACH VALUE.
• UNDERSTAND THE INTERNAL WORKINGS OF BEASTS AND ANIMALS C RANK OR LOWER, AS WELL AS THE METHODS FOR PREPARING THEM.
• GAIN KNOWLEDGE OF EDIBLE PLANTS.
NOW WHAT OCCUPATION WILL BE OF THE FOURTH PLAYER, YUKA TOKITATE?
SWOOSH
DDDRRMMM
OCCUPATION ROULETTE DETAILS
WARRIOR (SWORD) 20%
WARRIOR (SPEAR) 12.5%
WARRIOR (AX) 12.5%
WIZARD (HEAT) 12.5%
WIZARD (WIND) 12.5%
WIZARD (CREATURE) 12.5%
THIEF 7.5%
HUNTER 7.5%
OTHER (5 MISC TYPES) EACH 0.5%
TA-DA!
WIZARD (HEAT)
WIZARD (HEAT)!
WIZ...?! HUH?! MAGIC?!
GLOOOW
PP
Status
HEALTH: 80%
UPPER BODY: 80%
LOWER BODY: 80%
INVOLUNTARY MUSCLE: 80%
STRENGTH: 80%
YUKA TOKITATE
WIZARD (HEAT)
RANK 1
ABLE TO USE HEAT-RELATED MAGIC.

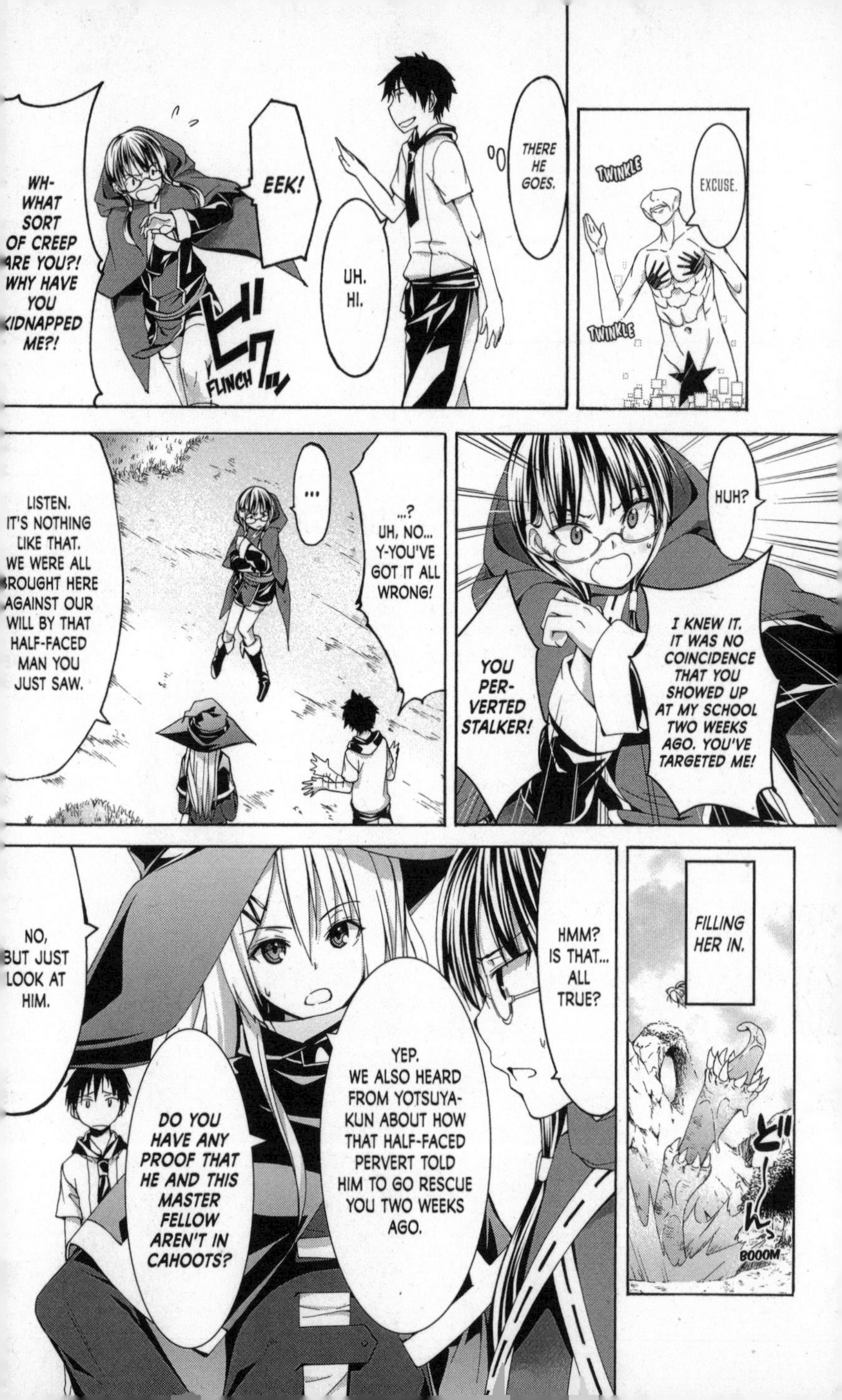
TWINKLE
EXCUSE.
TWINKLE
THERE HE GOES.
EEK!
UH. HI.
WH- WHAT SORT OF CREEP ARE YOU?! WHY HAVE YOU KIDNAPPED ME?!
FLINCH
HUH?
I KNEW IT. IT WAS NO COINCIDENCE THAT YOU SHOWED UP AT MY SCHOOL TWO WEEKS AGO. YOU'VE TARGETED ME!
YOU PER- VERTED STALKER!
...
...? UH, NO... Y-YOU'VE GOT IT ALL WRONG!
LISTEN. IT'S NOTHING LIKE THAT. WE WERE ALL BROUGHT HERE AGAINST OUR WILL BY THAT HALF-FACED MAN YOU JUST SAW.
FILLING HER IN.
BOOOM
HMM? IS THAT... ALL TRUE?
YEP. WE ALSO HEARD FROM YOTSUYA-KUN ABOUT HOW THAT HALF-FACED PERVERT TOLD HIM TO GO RESCUE YOU TWO WEEKS AGO.
NO, BUT JUST LOOK AT HIM.
DO YOU HAVE ANY PROOF THAT HE AND THIS MASTER FELLOW AREN'T IN CAHOOTS?

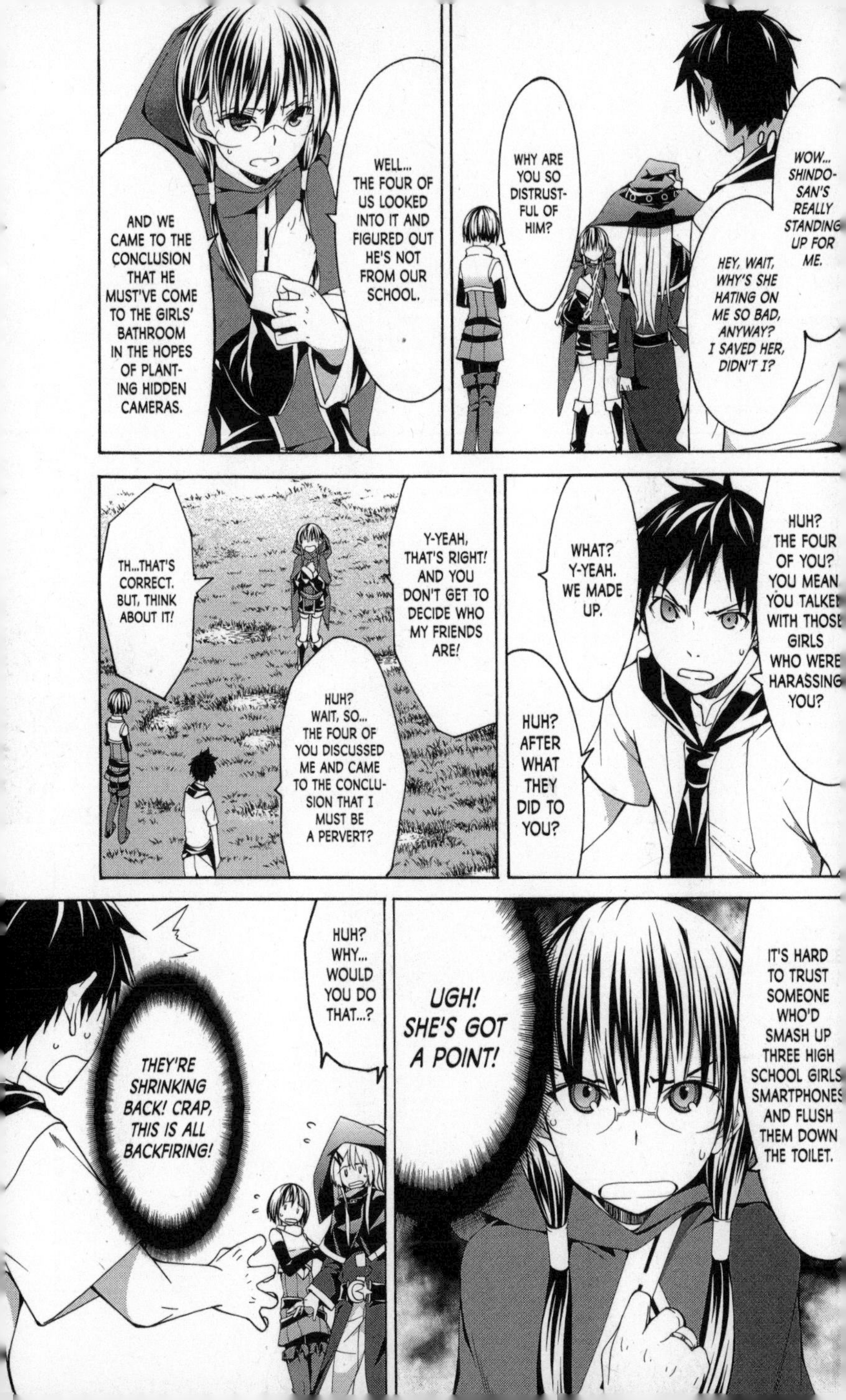
WOW... SHINDO-SAN'S REALLY STANDING UP FOR ME.
HEY, WAIT, WHY'S SHE HATING ON ME SO BAD, ANYWAY? I SAVED HER, DIDN'T I?
WHY ARE YOU SO DISTRUST-FUL OF HIM?
WELL... THE FOUR OF US LOOKED INTO IT AND FIGURED OUT HE'S NOT FROM OUR SCHOOL.
AND WE CAME TO THE CONCLUSION THAT HE MUST'VE COME TO THE GIRLS' BATHROOM IN THE HOPES OF PLANT-ING HIDDEN CAMERAS.
HUH? THE FOUR OF YOU? YOU MEAN YOU TALKED WITH THOSE GIRLS WHO WERE HARASSING YOU?
WHAT? Y-YEAH. WE MADE UP.
HUH? AFTER WHAT THEY DID TO YOU?
Y-YEAH, THAT'S RIGHT! AND YOU DON'T GET TO DECIDE WHO MY FRIENDS ARE!
TH...THAT'S CORRECT. BUT, THINK ABOUT IT!
HUH? WAIT, SO... THE FOUR OF YOU DISCUSSED ME AND CAME TO THE CONCLU-SION THAT I MUST BE A PERVERT?
IT'S HARD TO TRUST SOMEONE WHO'D SMASH UP THREE HIGH SCHOOL GIRLS' SMARTPHONES AND FLUSH THEM DOWN THE TOILET.
UGH! SHE'S GOT A POINT!
HUH? WHY... WOULD YOU DO THAT...?
THEY'RE SHRINKING BACK! CRAP, THIS IS ALL BACKFIRING!

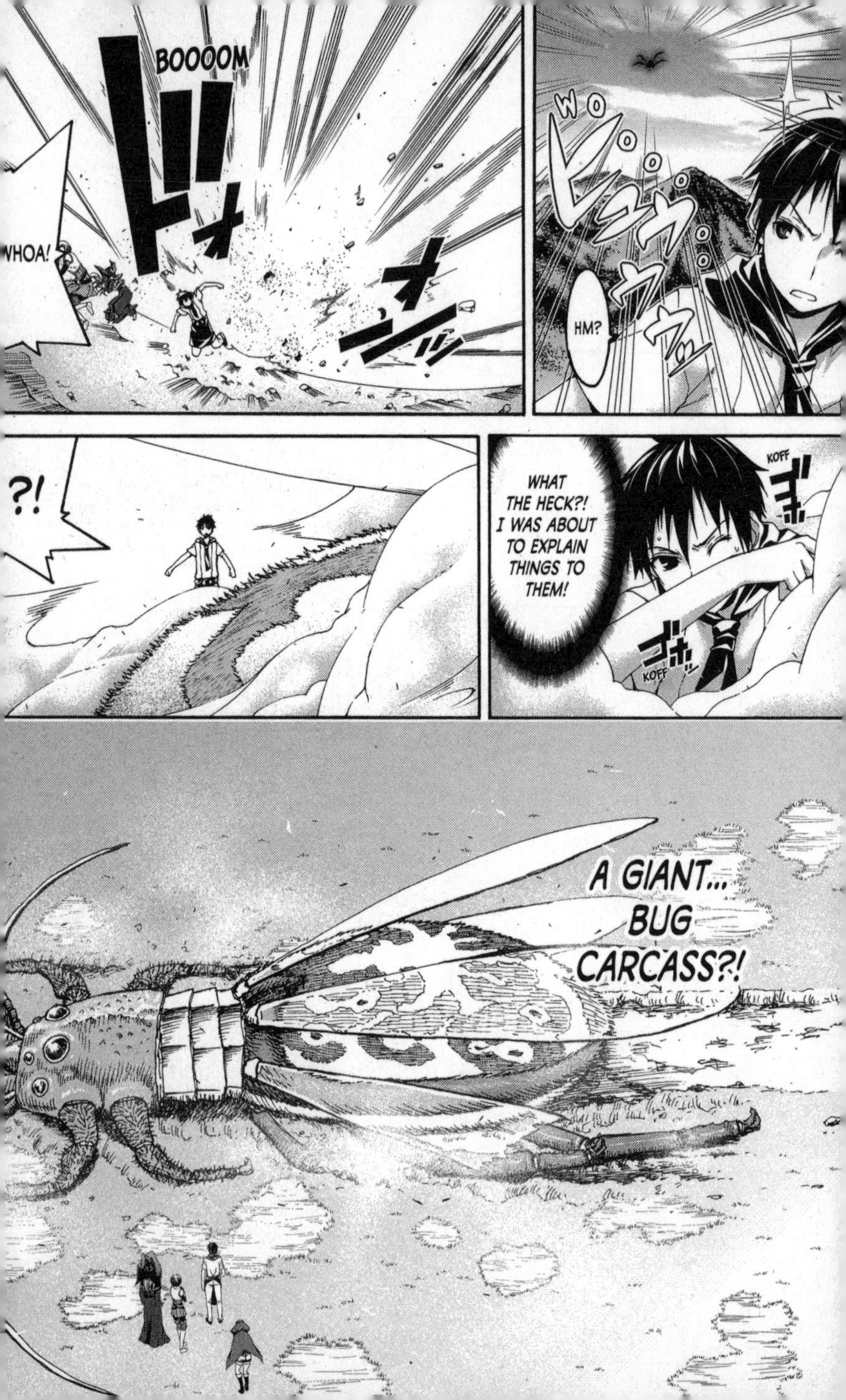
WOOOOO
HM?
BOOOOM
WHOA!
WHAT THE HECK?! I WAS ABOUT TO EXPLAIN THINGS TO THEM!
KOFF
KOFF
?!
A GIANT... BUG CARCASS?!

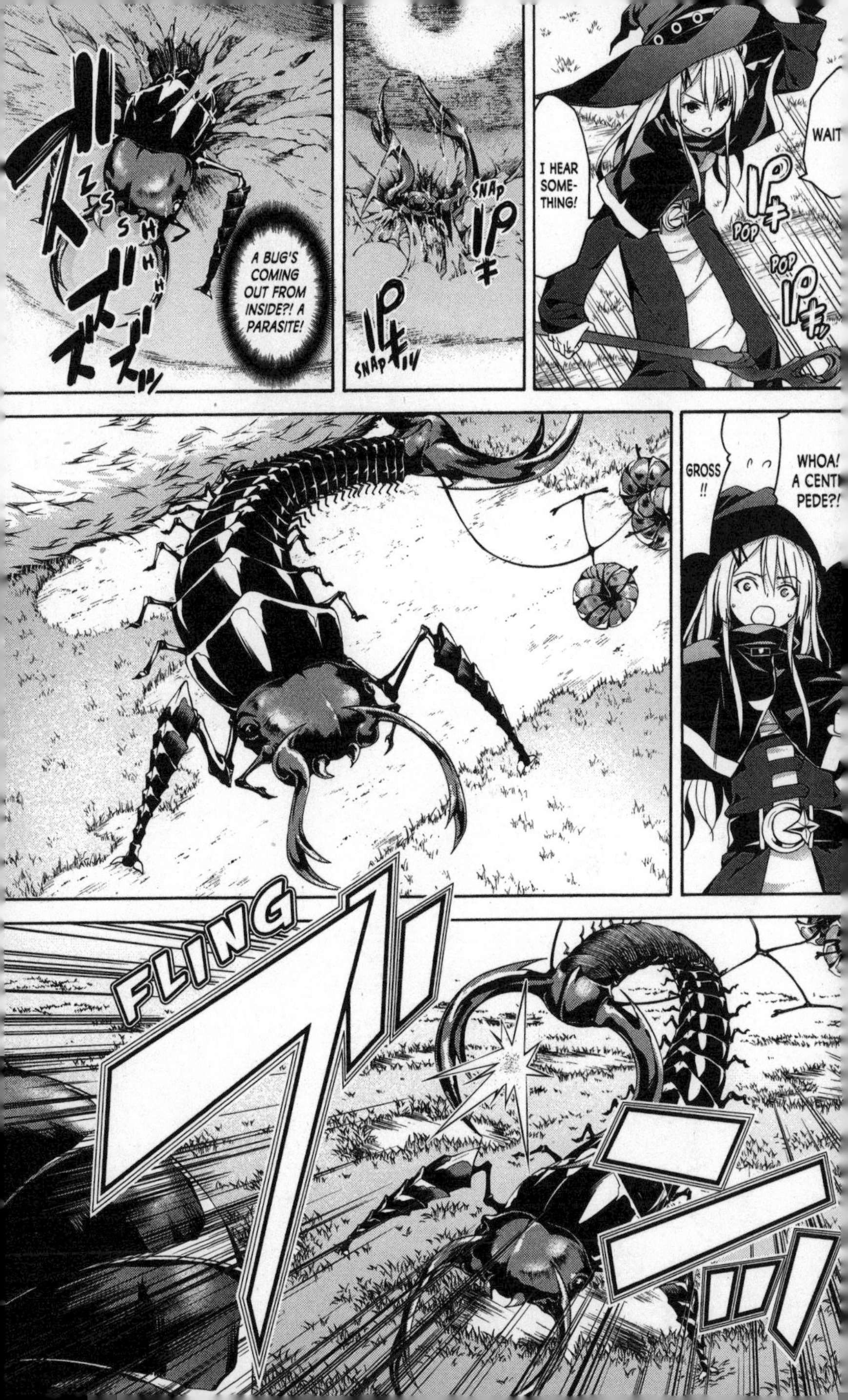

WAIT
I HEAR SOMETHING!
POP
POP
SNAP
SNAP
ZSSHHH
A BUG'S COMING OUT FROM INSIDE?! A PARASITE!
WHOA! A CENTI PEDE?!
GROSS !!
FLING

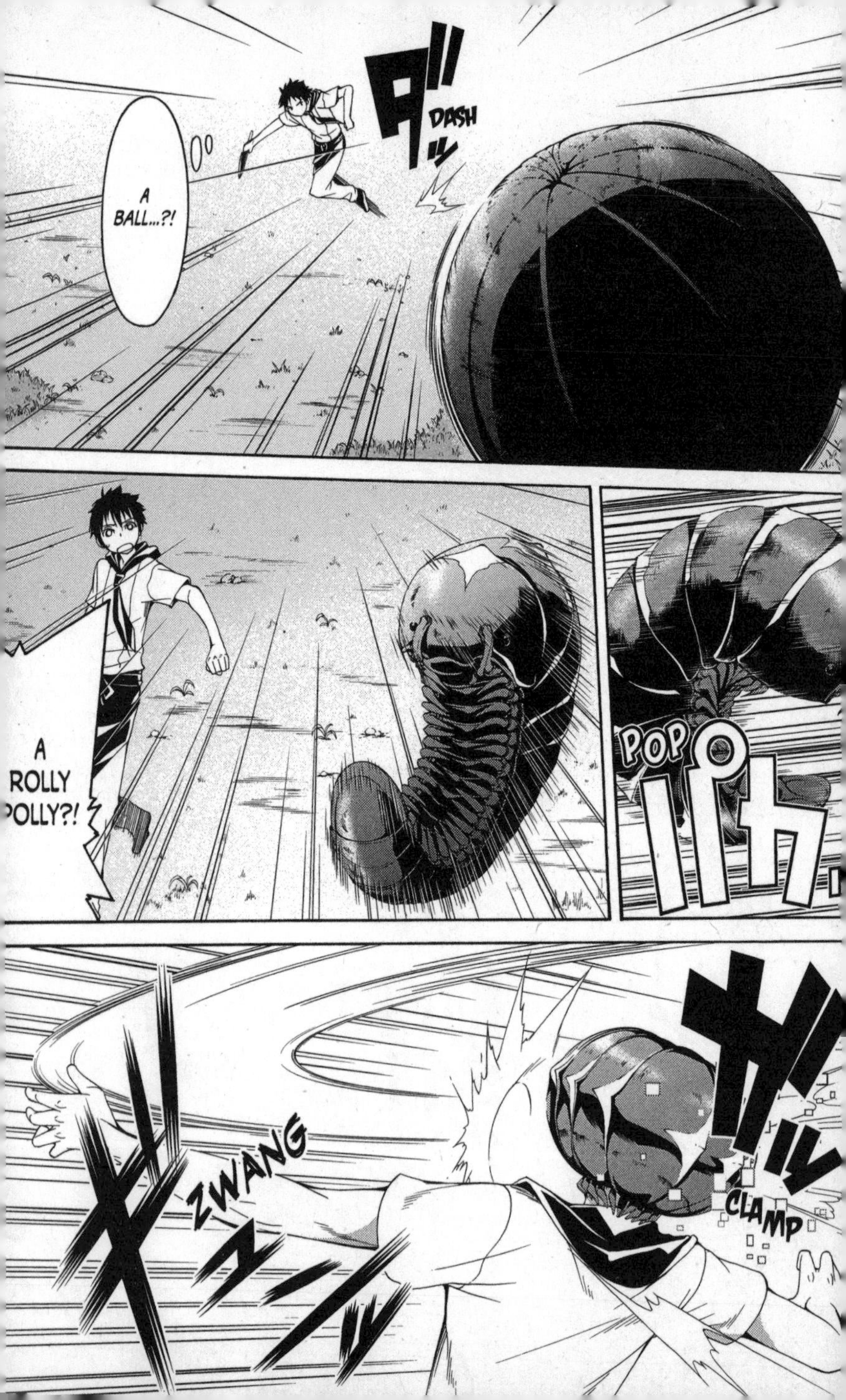
DASH
A BALL...?!
POP
A ROLLY POLLY?!
CLAMP
ZWANG

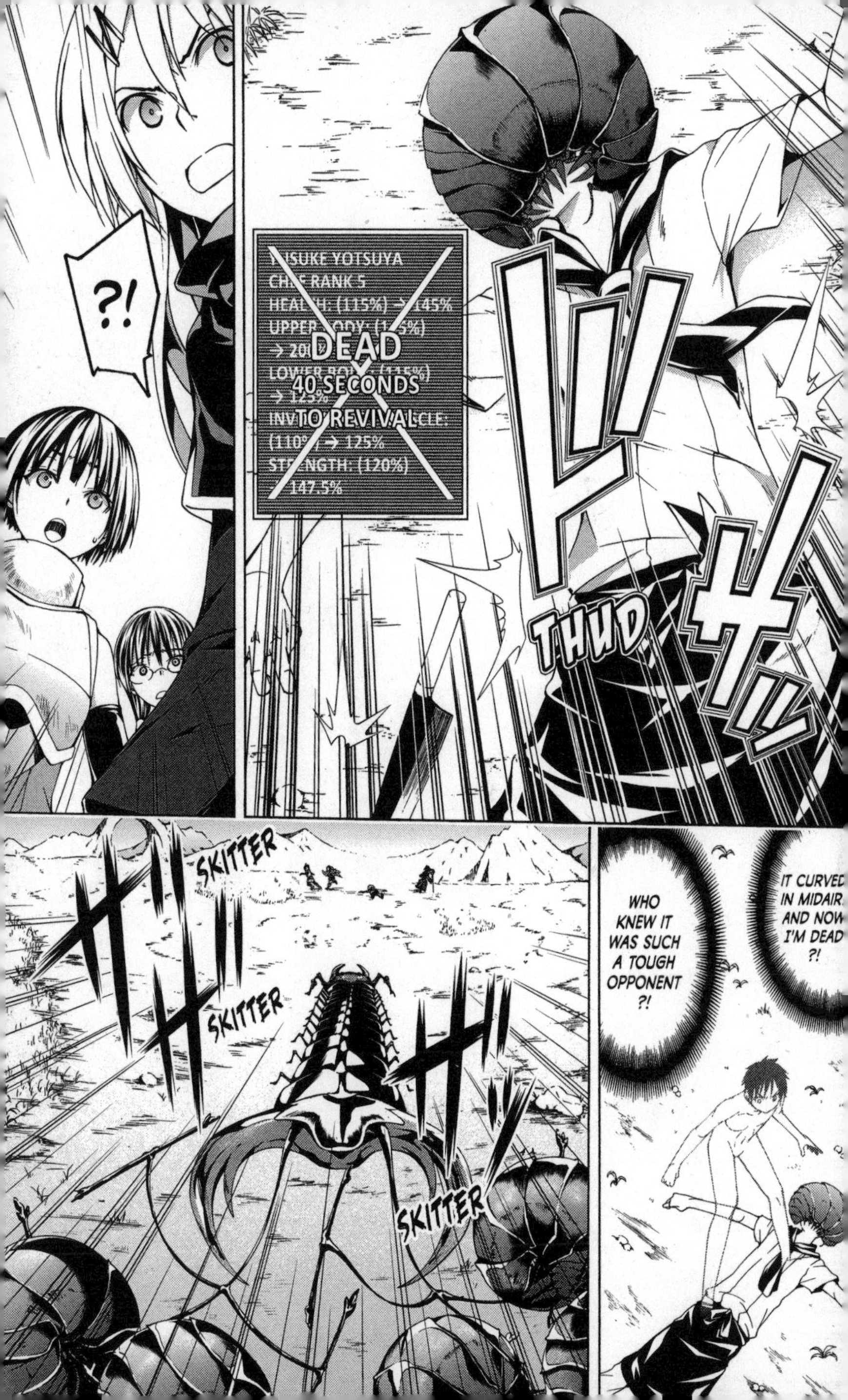
DEAD
40 SECONDS TO REVIVAL
THUD
?!
IT CURVED IN MIDAIR AND NOW I'M DEAD ?!
WHO KNEW IT WAS SUCH A TOUGH OPPONENT ?!
SKITTER
SKITTER
SKITTER

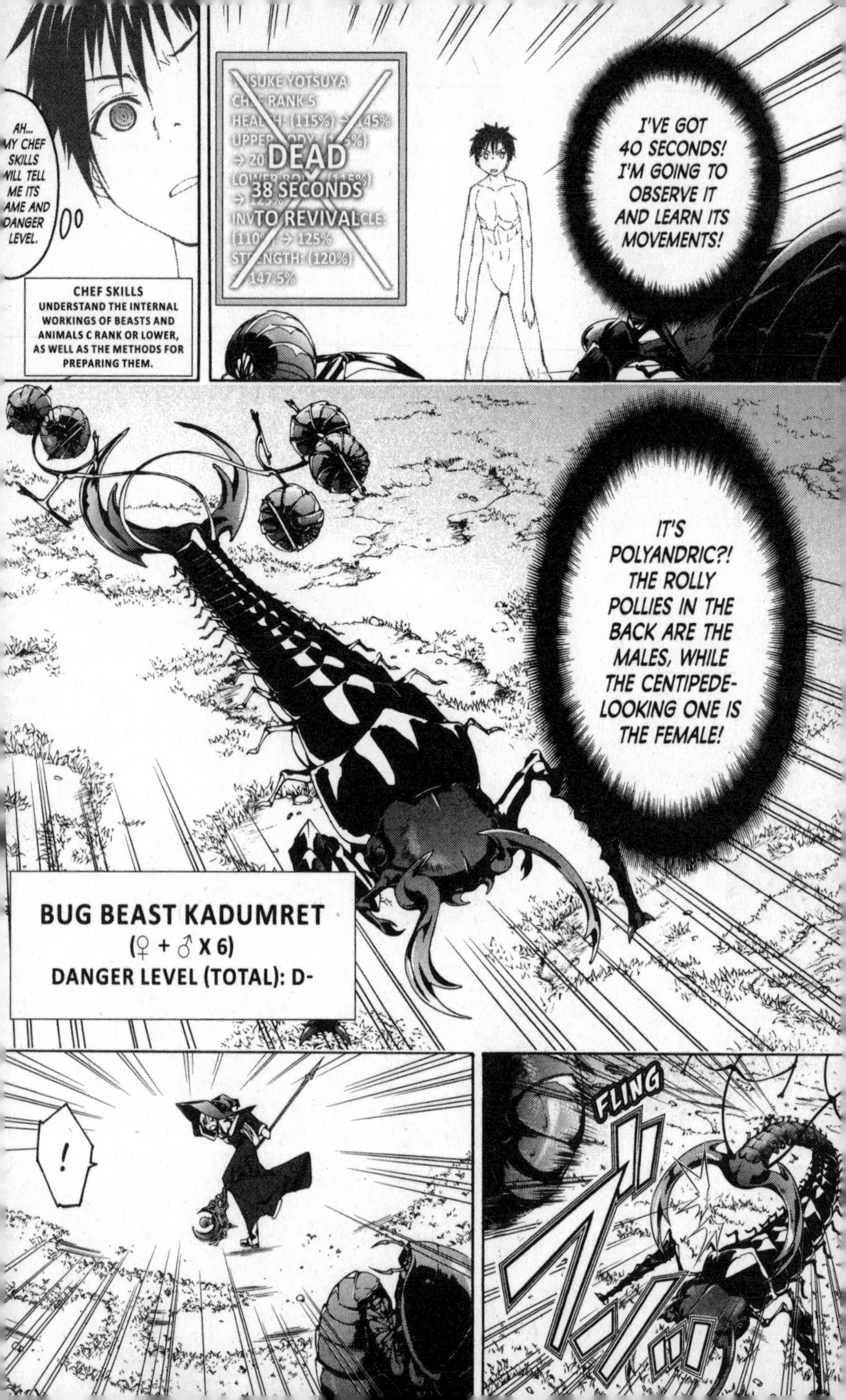

I'VE GOT 40 SECONDS! I'M GOING TO OBSERVE IT AND LEARN ITS MOVEMENTS!
DEAD
38 SECONDS
TO REVIVAL
AH... MY CHEF SKILLS WILL TELL ME ITS AME AND DANGER LEVEL.
CHEF SKILLS
UNDERSTAND THE INTERNAL WORKINGS OF BEASTS AND ANIMALS C RANK OR LOWER, AS WELL AS THE METHODS FOR PREPARING THEM.
IT'S POLYANDRIC?! THE ROLLY POLLIES IN THE BACK ARE THE MALES, WHILE THE CENTIPEDE-LOOKING ONE IS THE FEMALE!
BUG BEAST KADUMRET
(♀ + ♂ X 6)
DANGER LEVEL (TOTAL): D-
FLING
!

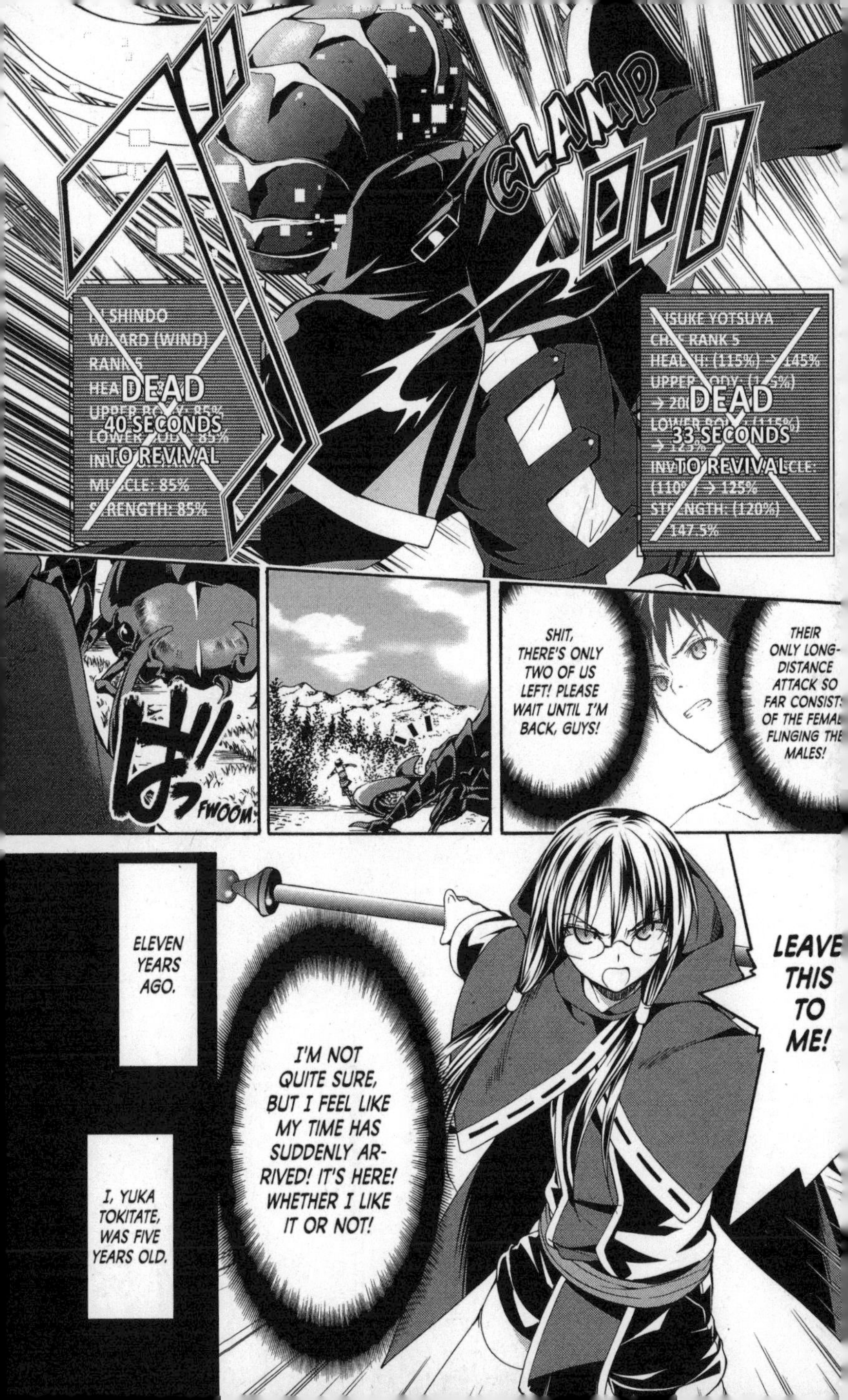
CLAMP
DEAD
33 SECONDS TO REVIVAL
DEAD
40 SECONDS TO REVIVAL
THEIR ONLY LONG-DISTANCE ATTACK SO FAR CONSISTS OF THE FEMAL FLINGING THE MALES!
SHIT, THERE'S ONLY TWO OF US LEFT! PLEASE WAIT UNTIL I'M BACK, GUYS!
FWOOM
LEAVE THIS TO ME!
I'M NOT QUITE SURE, BUT I FEEL LIKE MY TIME HAS SUDDENLY AR-RIVED! IT'S HERE! WHETHER I LIKE IT OR NOT!
ELEVEN YEARS AGO.
I, YUKA TOKITATE, WAS FIVE YEARS OLD.

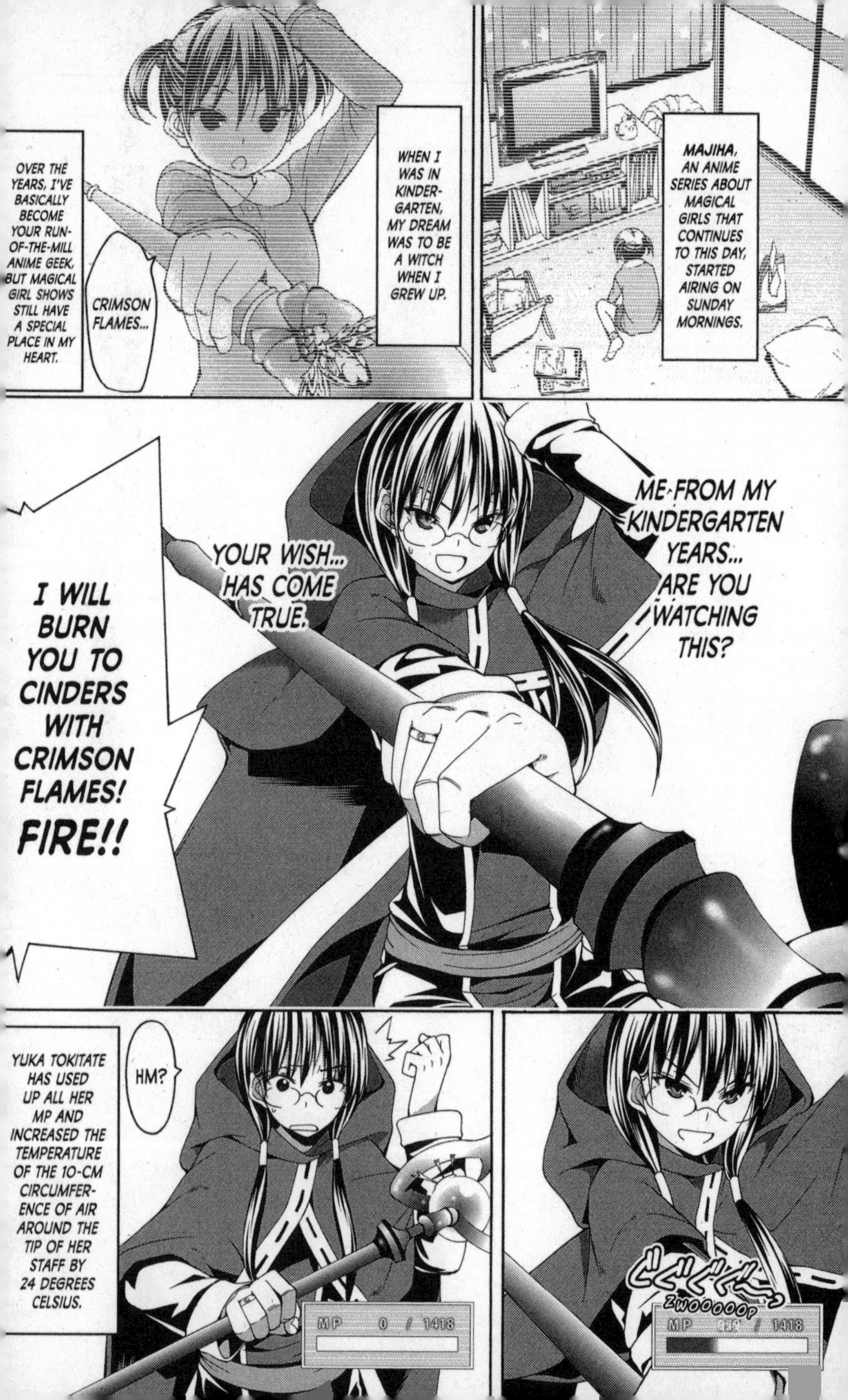
MAJIHA, AN ANIME SERIES ABOUT MAGICAL GIRLS THAT CONTINUES TO THIS DAY, STARTED AIRING ON SUNDAY MORNINGS.
WHEN I WAS IN KINDER-GARTEN, MY DREAM WAS TO BE A WITCH WHEN I GREW UP.
OVER THE YEARS, I'VE BASICALLY BECOME YOUR RUN-OF-THE-MILL ANIME GEEK, BUT MAGICAL GIRL SHOWS STILL HAVE A SPECIAL PLACE IN MY HEART.
CRIMSON FLAMES...
ME FROM MY KINDERGARTEN YEARS... ARE YOU WATCHING THIS?
YOUR WISH... HAS COME TRUE.
I WILL BURN YOU TO CINDERS WITH CRIMSON FLAMES! FIRE!!
ZWOOOOOOP
HM?
YUKA TOKITATE HAS USED UP ALL HER MP AND INCREASED THE TEMPERATURE OF THE 10-CM CIRCUMFER-ENCE OF AIR AROUND THE TIP OF HER STAFF BY 24 DEGREES CELSIUS.
MP 0 / 1418

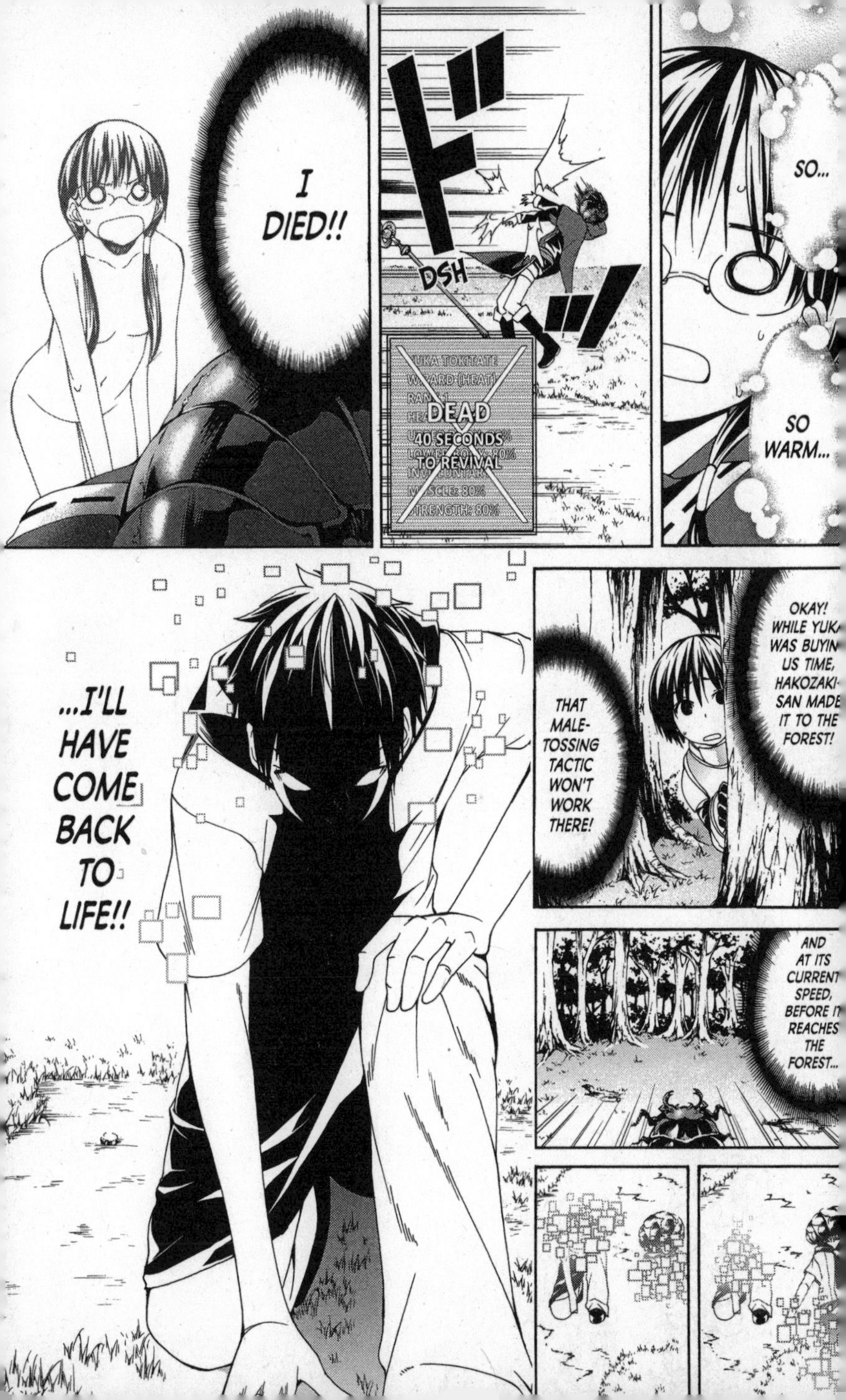
SO...
SO WARM...
ド
ド
DSH
DEAD
40 SECONDS TO REVIVAL
I DIED!!
OKAY! WHILE YUKA WAS BUYIN US TIME, HAKOZAKI-SAN MADE IT TO THE FOREST!
THAT MALE-TOSSING TACTIC WON'T WORK THERE!
AND AT ITS CURRENT SPEED, BEFORE IT REACHES THE FOREST...
...I'LL HAVE COME BACK TO LIFE!!

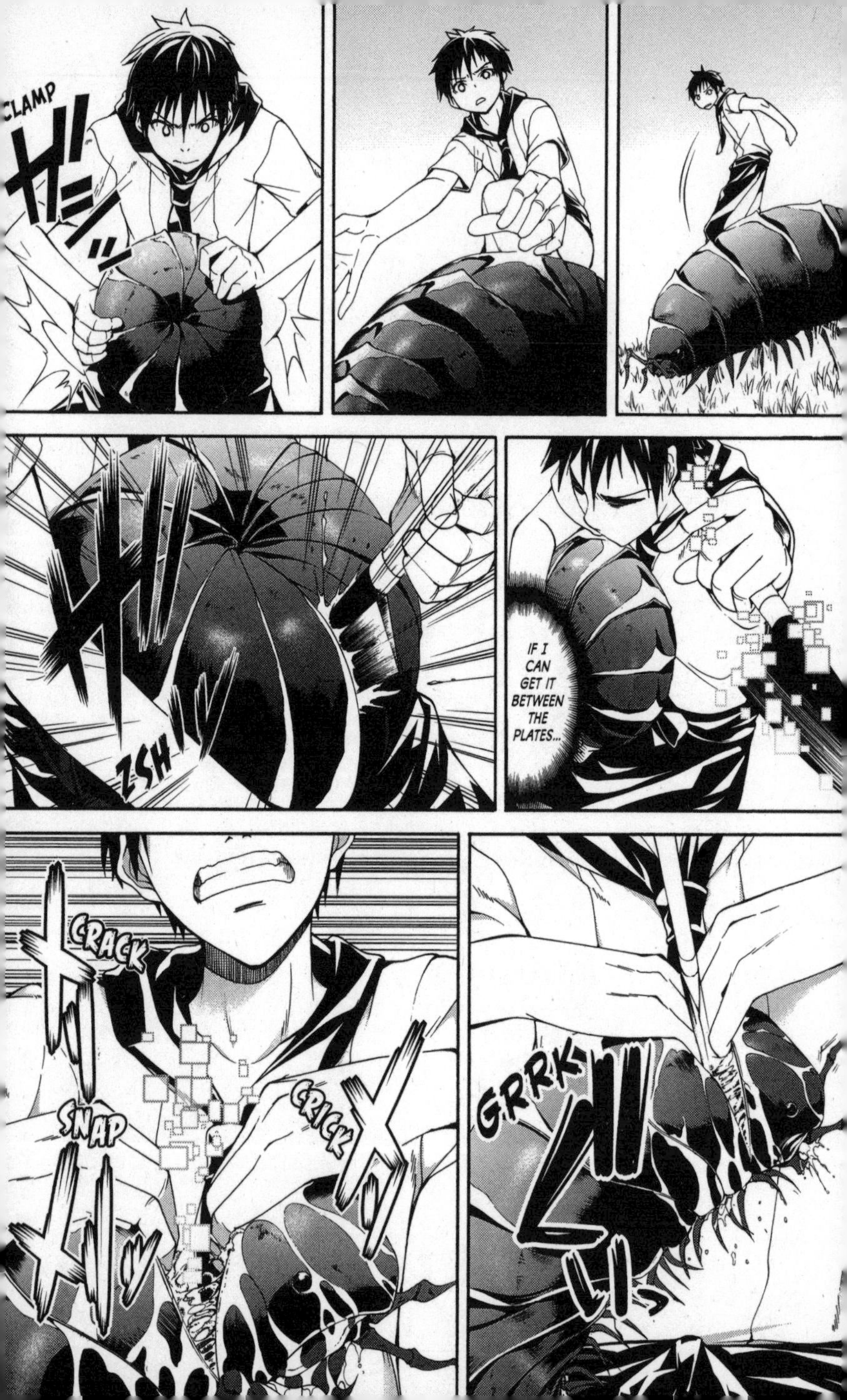
CLAMP
ZSH
IF I CAN GET IT BETWEEN THE PLATES...
GRRK
CRICK
CRACK
SNAP

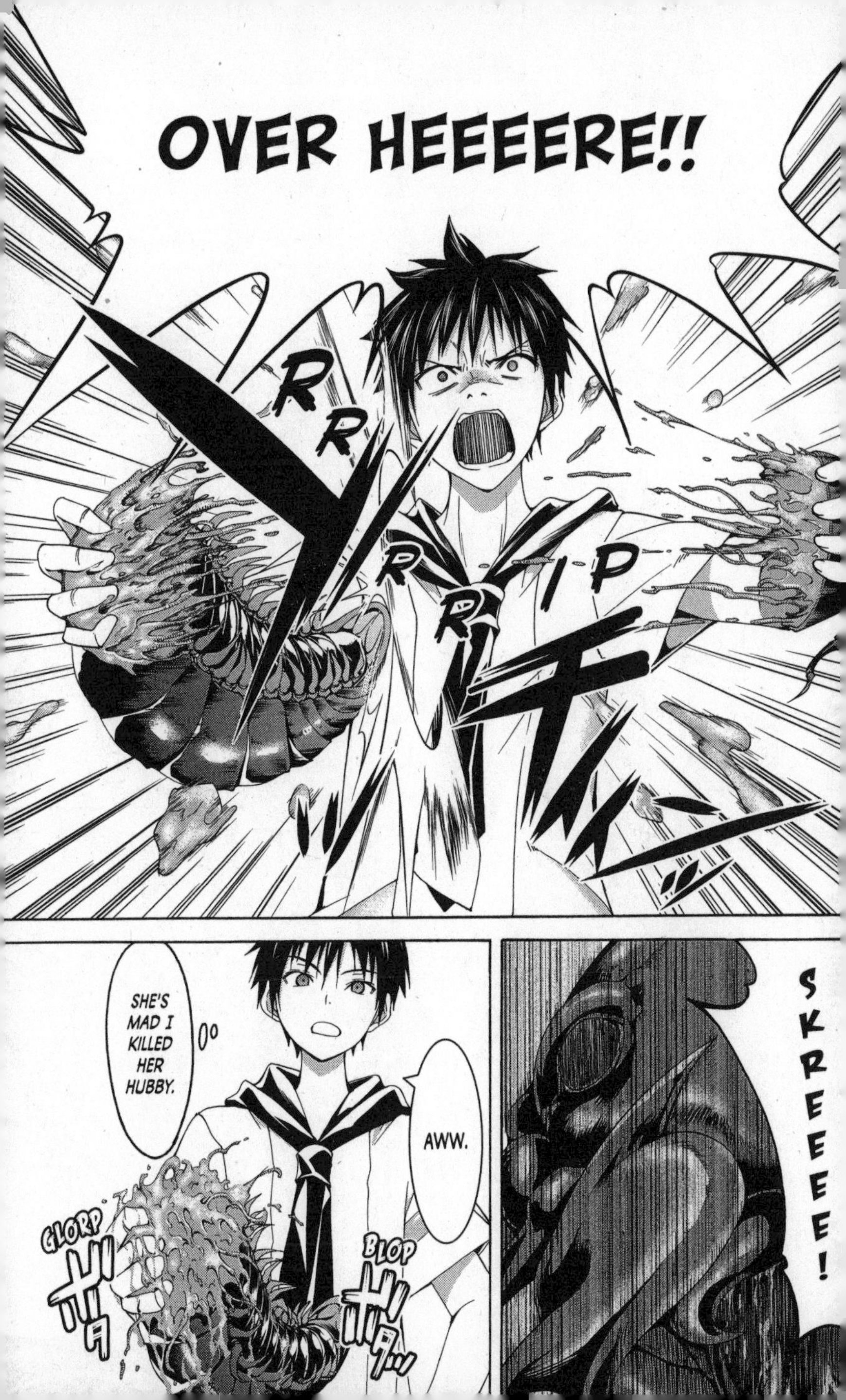
OVER HEEEEERE!!
RRRRIP
SKREEEEE!
AWW.
SHE'S MAD I KILLED HER HUBBY.
BLOP
GLORP

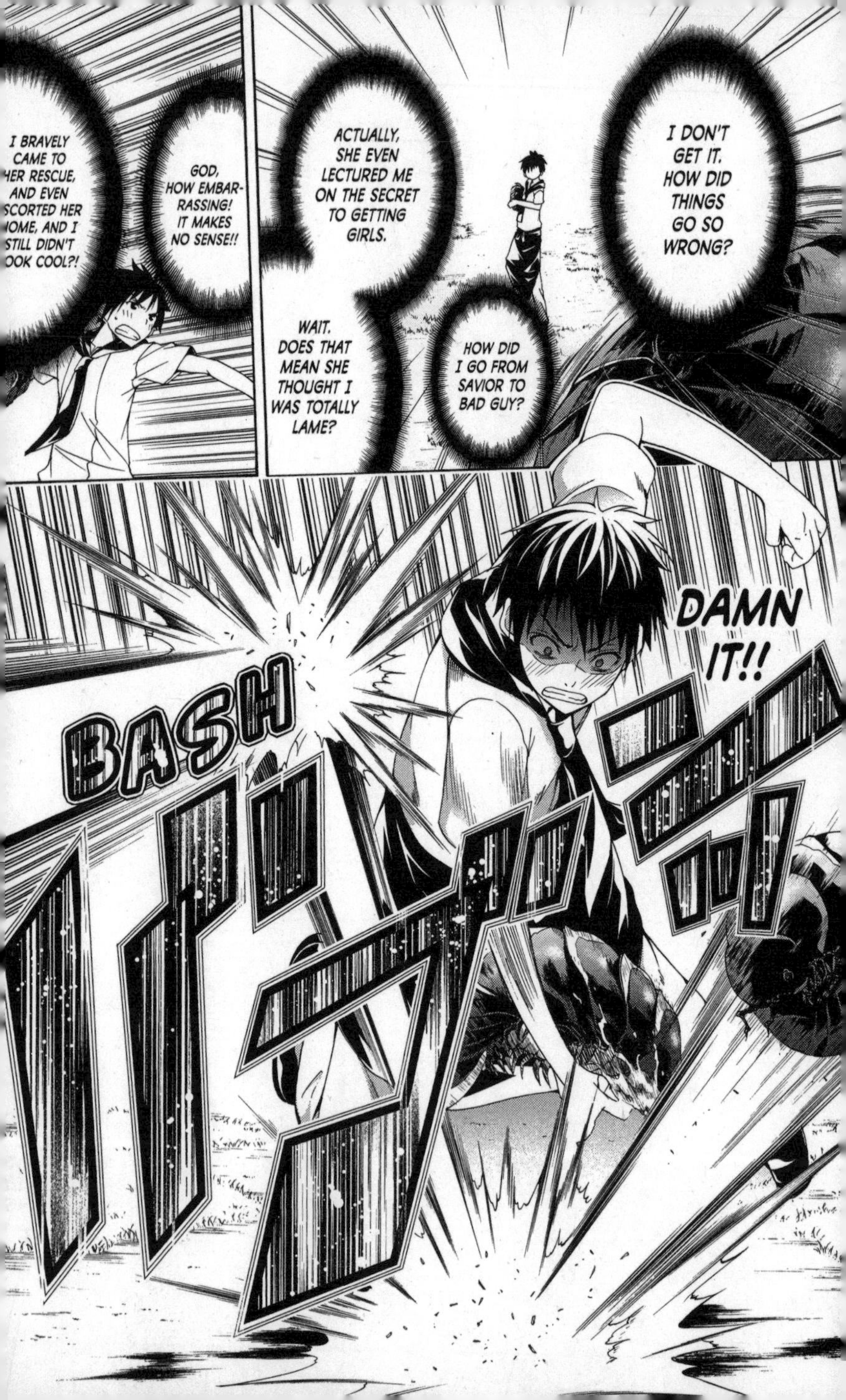
I DON'T GET IT. HOW DID THINGS GO SO WRONG?
ACTUALLY, SHE EVEN LECTURED ME ON THE SECRET TO GETTING GIRLS.
HOW DID I GO FROM SAVIOR TO BAD GUY?
WAIT. DOES THAT MEAN SHE THOUGHT I WAS TOTALLY LAME?
GOD, HOW EMBARRASSING! IT MAKES NO SENSE!!
I BRAVELY CAME TO HER RESCUE, AND EVEN SCORTED HER HOME, AND I STILL DIDN'T OOK COOL?!
DAMN IT!!
BASH

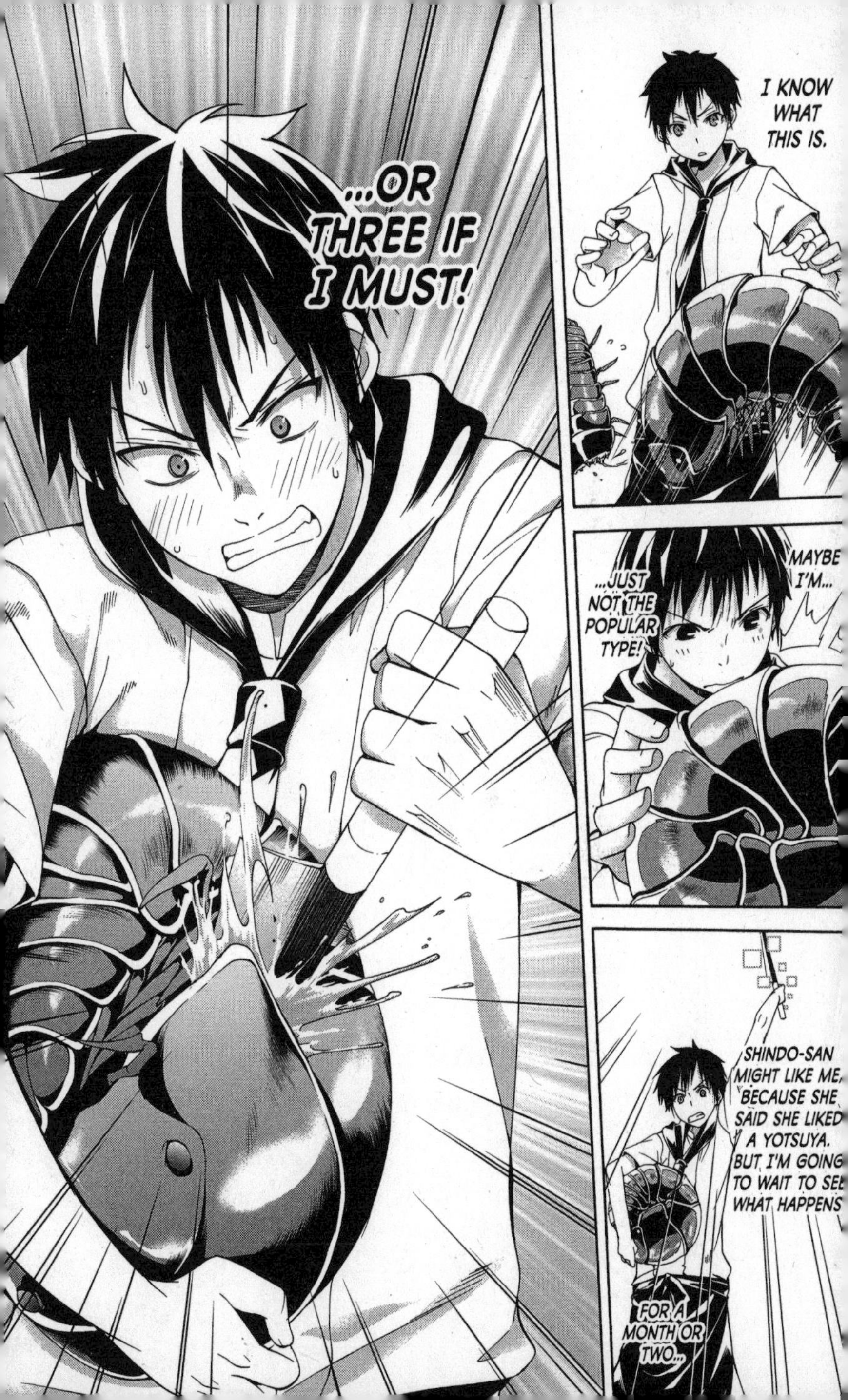
I KNOW WHAT THIS IS.
MAYBE I'M...
...JUST NOT THE POPULAR TYPE!
SHINDO-SAN MIGHT LIKE ME, BECAUSE SHE SAID SHE LIKED A YOTSUYA. BUT I'M GOING TO WAIT TO SEE WHAT HAPPENS
FOR A MONTH OR TWO...
...OR THREE IF I MUST!

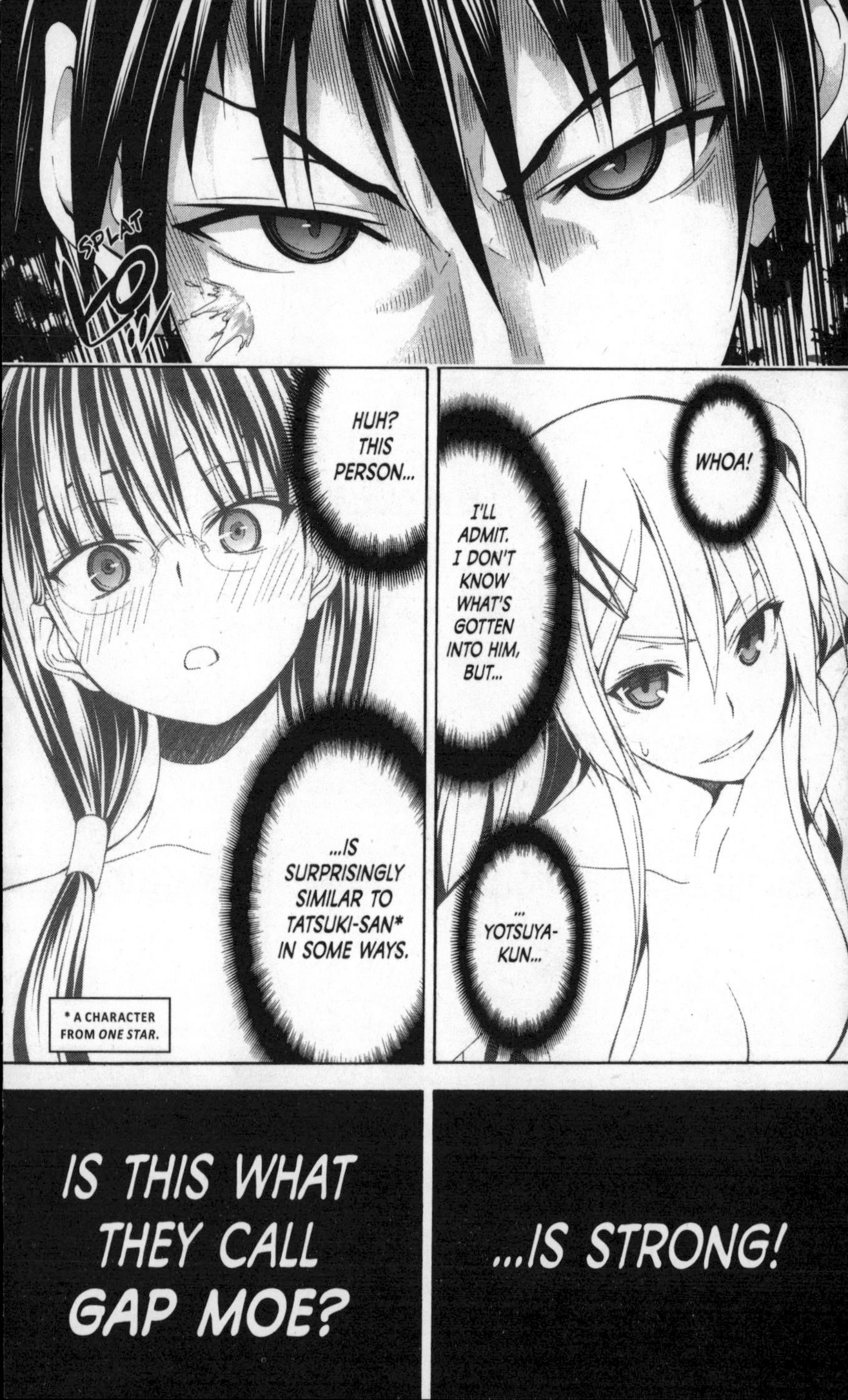
SPLAT
WHOA!
I'LL ADMIT. I DON'T KNOW WHAT'S GOTTEN INTO HIM, BUT...
... YOTSUYA-KUN...
HUH? THIS PERSON...
...IS SURPRISINGLY SIMILAR TO TATSUKI-SAN* IN SOME WAYS.
* A CHARACTER FROM *ONE STAR*.
...IS STRONG!
IS THIS WHAT THEY CALL GAP MOE?

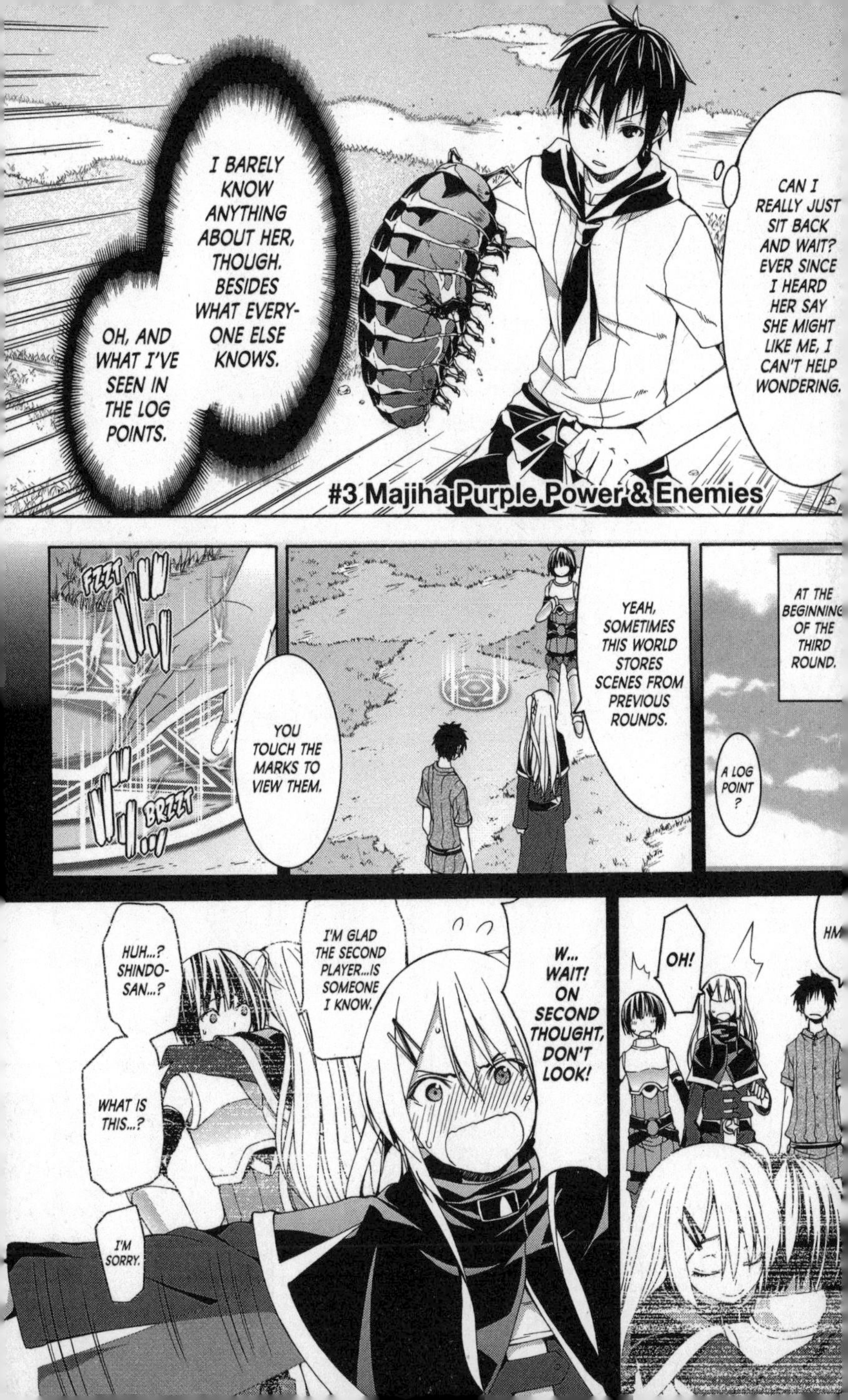
CAN I REALLY JUST SIT BACK AND WAIT? EVER SINCE I HEARD HER SAY SHE MIGHT LIKE ME, I CAN'T HELP WONDERING.
I BARELY KNOW ANYTHING ABOUT HER, THOUGH. BESIDES WHAT EVERY-ONE ELSE KNOWS.
OH, AND WHAT I'VE SEEN IN THE LOG POINTS.
#3 Majiha Purple Power & Enemies
AT THE BEGINNING OF THE THIRD ROUND.
A LOG POINT?
YEAH, SOMETIMES THIS WORLD STORES SCENES FROM PREVIOUS ROUNDS.
YOU TOUCH THE MARKS TO VIEW THEM.
FZZT
BRZZT
HM
OH!
I'M GLAD THE SECOND PLAYER...IS SOMEONE I KNOW.
W... WAIT! ON SECOND THOUGHT, DON'T LOOK!
HUH...? SHINDO-SAN...?
WHAT IS THIS...?
I'M SORRY.

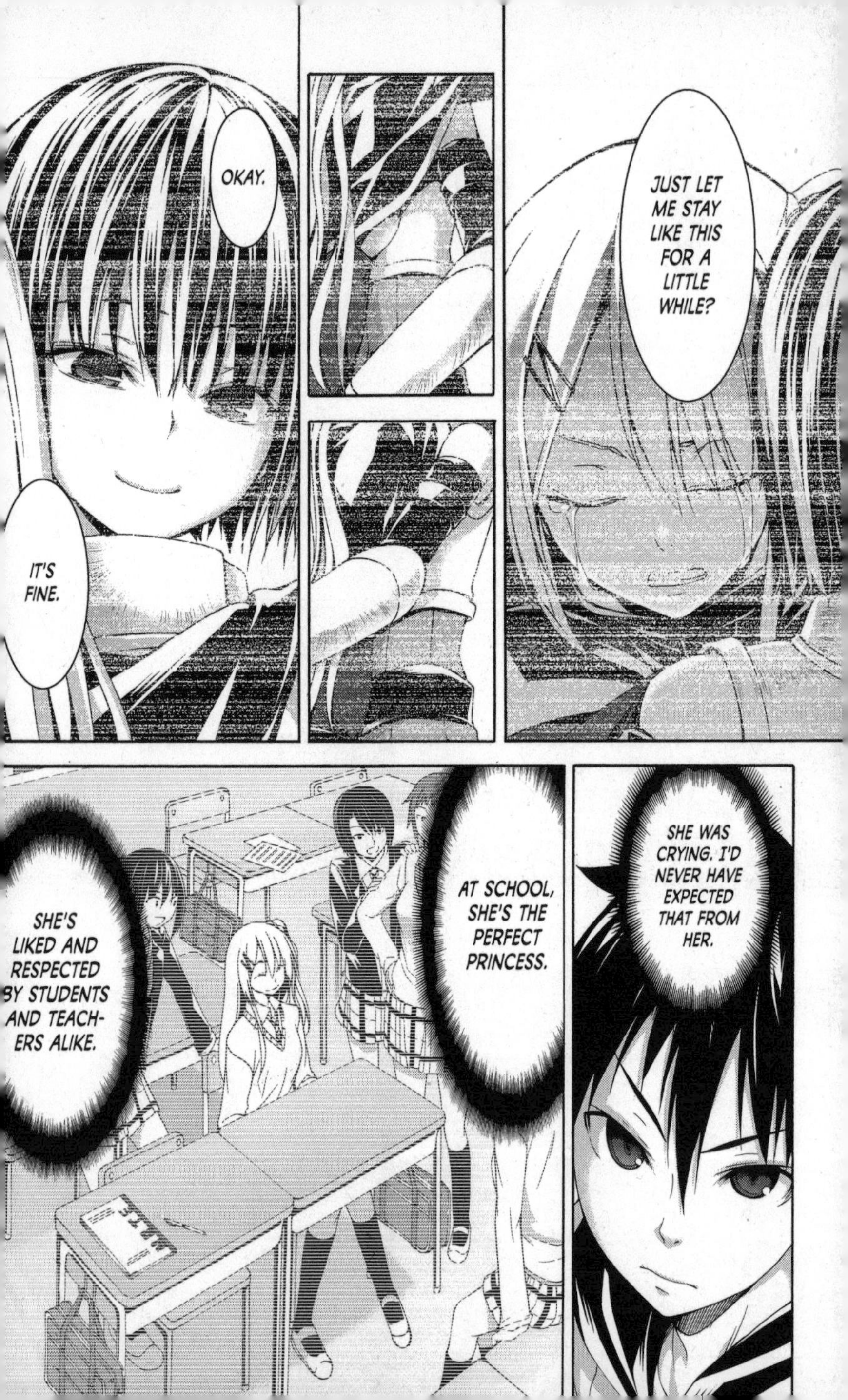
JUST LET ME STAY LIKE THIS FOR A LITTLE WHILE?
OKAY.
IT'S FINE.
SHE WAS CRYING. I'D NEVER HAVE EXPECTED THAT FROM HER.
AT SCHOOL, SHE'S THE PERFECT PRINCESS.
SHE'S LIKED AND RESPECTED BY STUDENTS AND TEACHERS ALIKE.

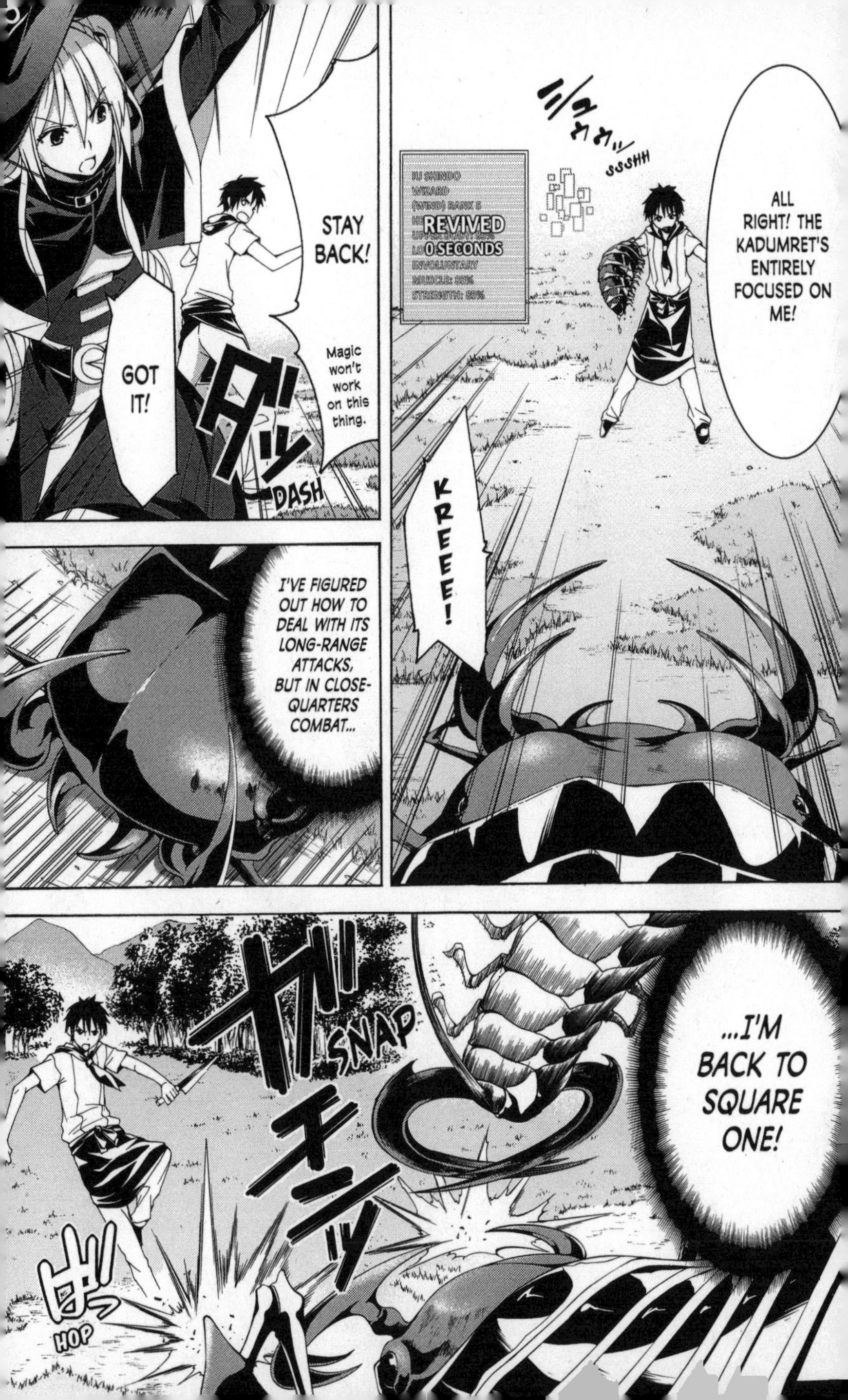

SSSHH
ALL RIGHT! THE KADUMRET'S ENTIRELY FOCUSED ON ME!
IU SHINDO
WIZARD
(WIND) RANK 5
REVIVED
0 SECONDS
INVOLUNTARY
MUSCLE: 85%
STRENGTH: 95%
KREEEE!
STAY BACK!
Magic won't work on this thing.
GOT IT!
DASH
I'VE FIGURED OUT HOW TO DEAL WITH ITS LONG-RANGE ATTACKS, BUT IN CLOSE-QUARTERS COMBAT...
...I'M BACK TO SQUARE ONE!
SNAP
HOP

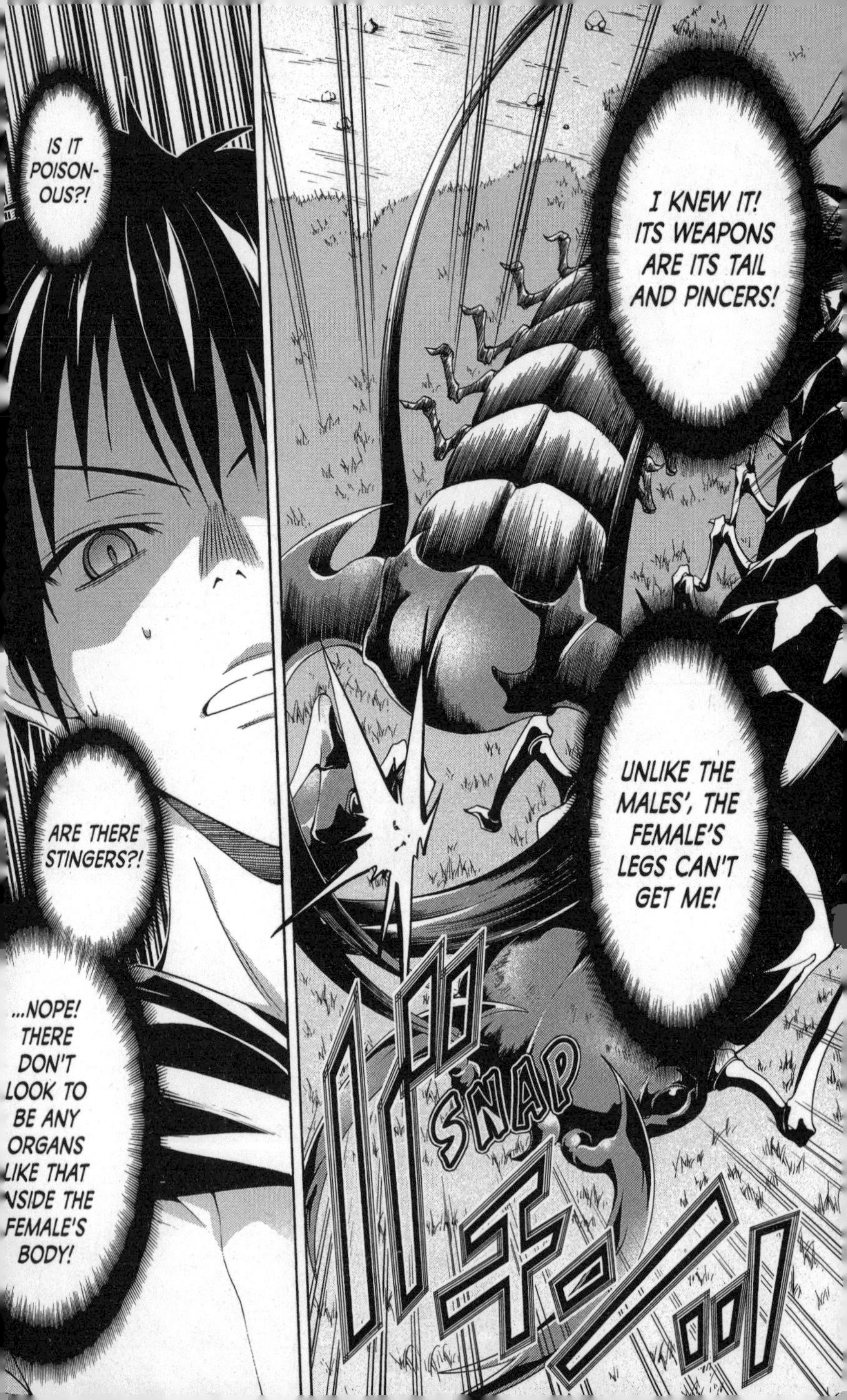
I KNEW IT! ITS WEAPONS ARE ITS TAIL AND PINCERS!
UNLIKE THE MALES', THE FEMALE'S LEGS CAN'T GET ME!
SNAP
IS IT POISON-OUS?!
ARE THERE STINGERS?!
...NOPE! THERE DON'T LOOK TO BE ANY ORGANS LIKE THAT NSIDE THE FEMALE'S BODY!

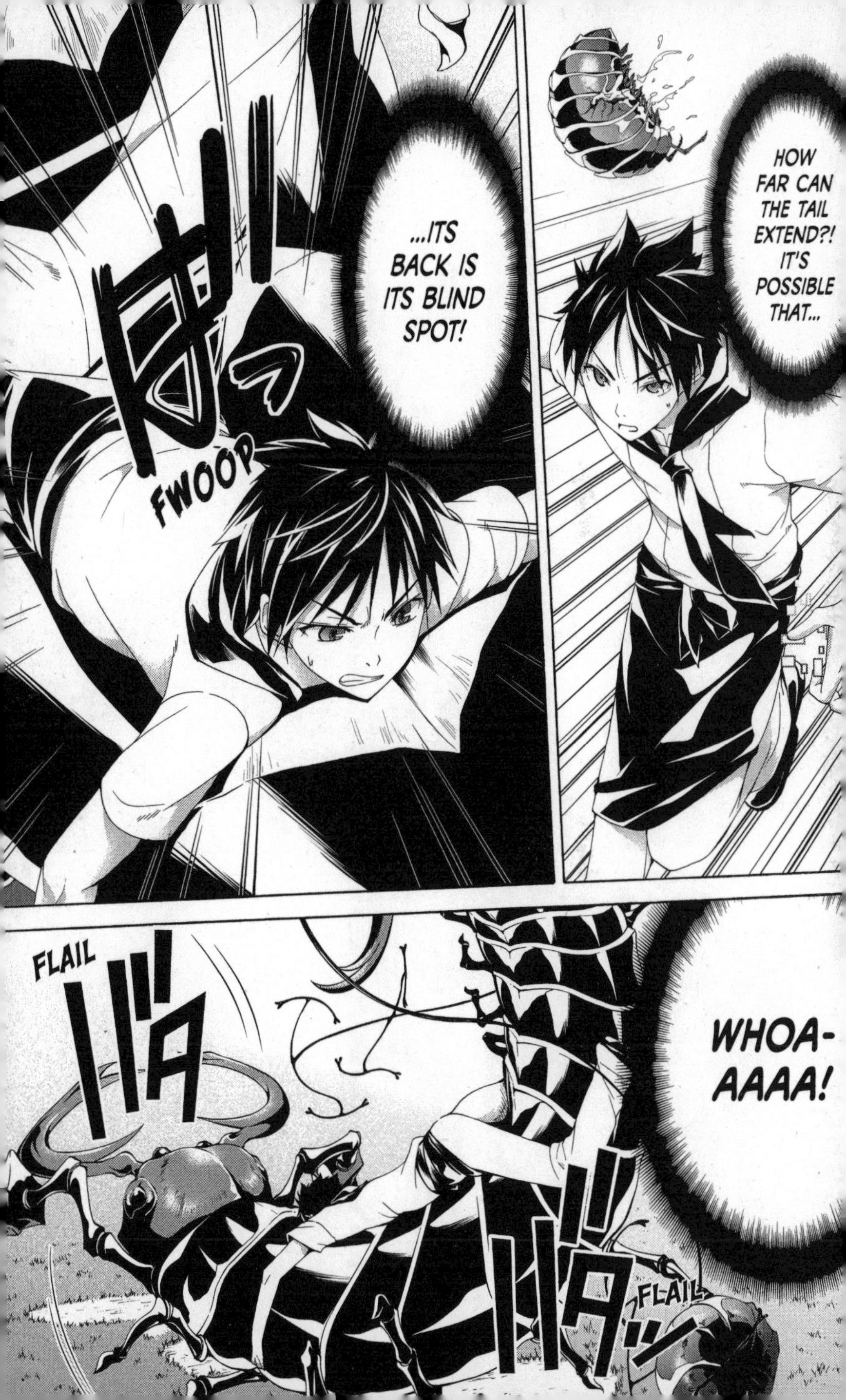
HOW FAR CAN THE TAIL EXTEND?! IT'S POSSIBLE THAT...
...ITS BACK IS ITS BLIND SPOT!
FWOOP
WHOA-AAAA!
FLAIL
FLAIL

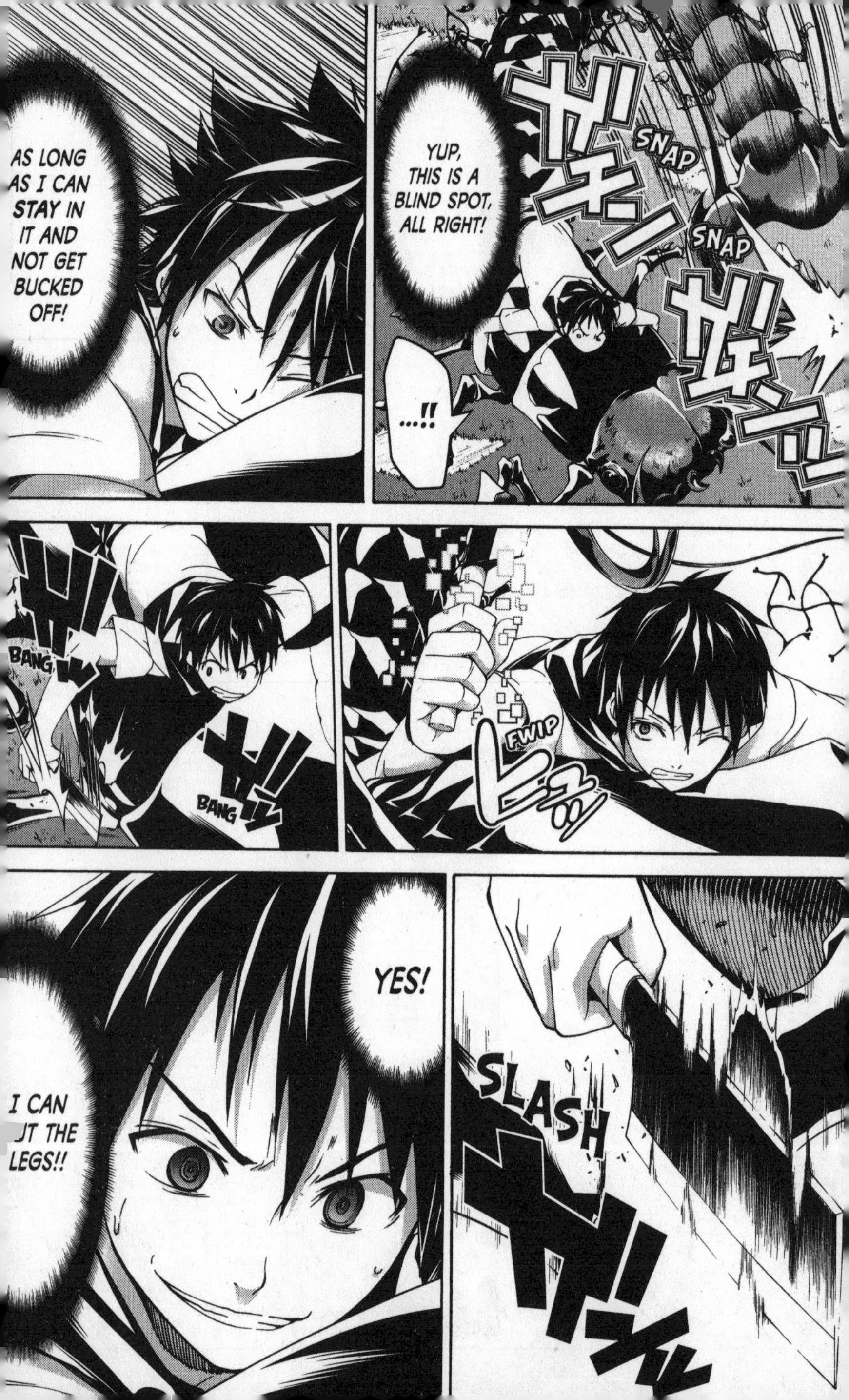
YUP, THIS IS A BLIND SPOT, ALL RIGHT!
SNAP
SNAP
...!!
AS LONG AS I CAN STAY IN IT AND NOT GET BUCKED OFF!
FWIP
BANG
BANG
SLASH
YES!
I CAN JT THE LEGS!!

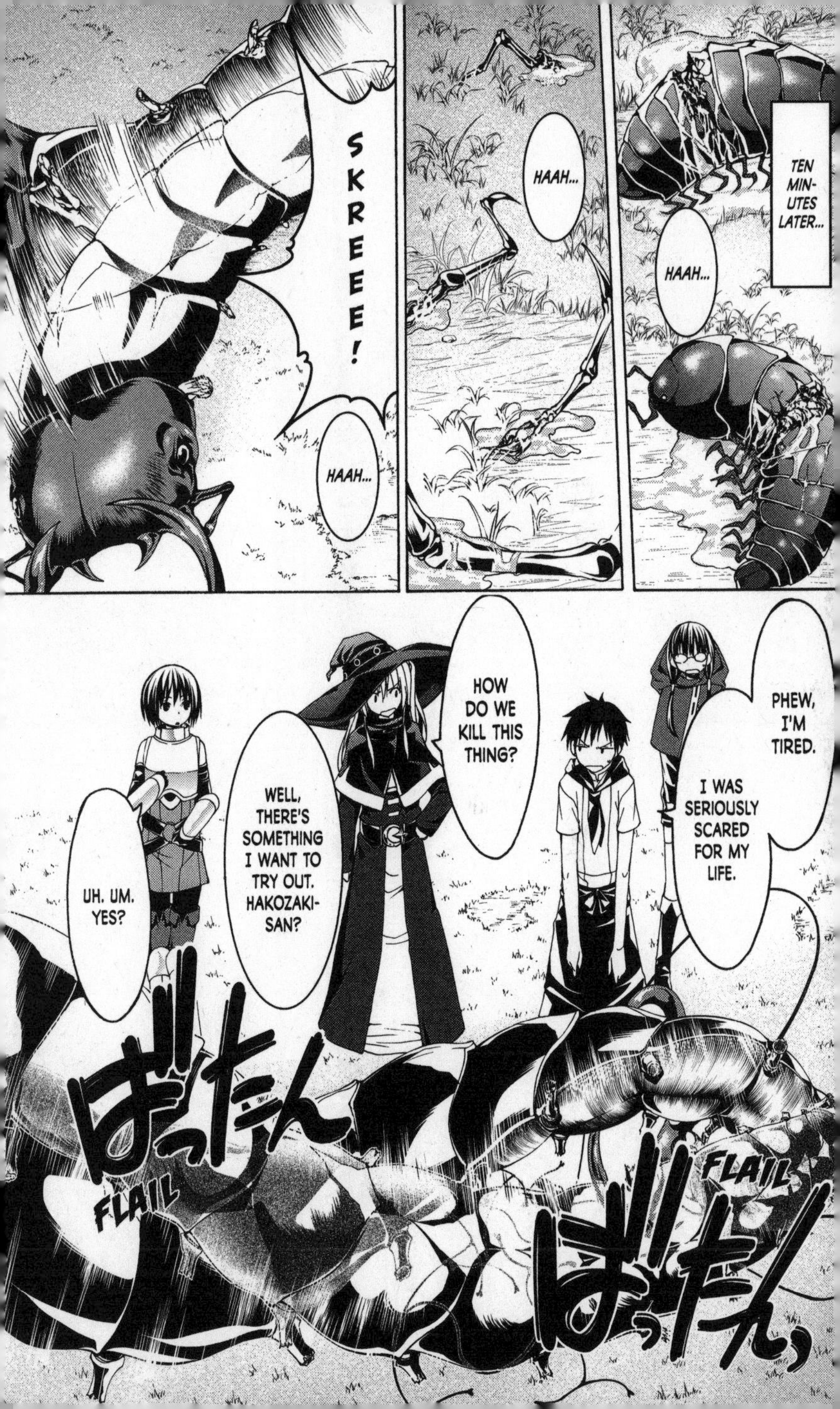
TEN MIN-UTES LATER...
HAAH...
HAAH...
SKREEEE!
HAAH...
PHEW, I'M TIRED.
I WAS SERIOUSLY SCARED FOR MY LIFE.
HOW DO WE KILL THIS THING?
WELL, THERE'S SOMETHING I WANT TO TRY OUT. HAKOZAKI-SAN?
UH. UM. YES?
FLAIL
ばったん
FLAIL
ばったん

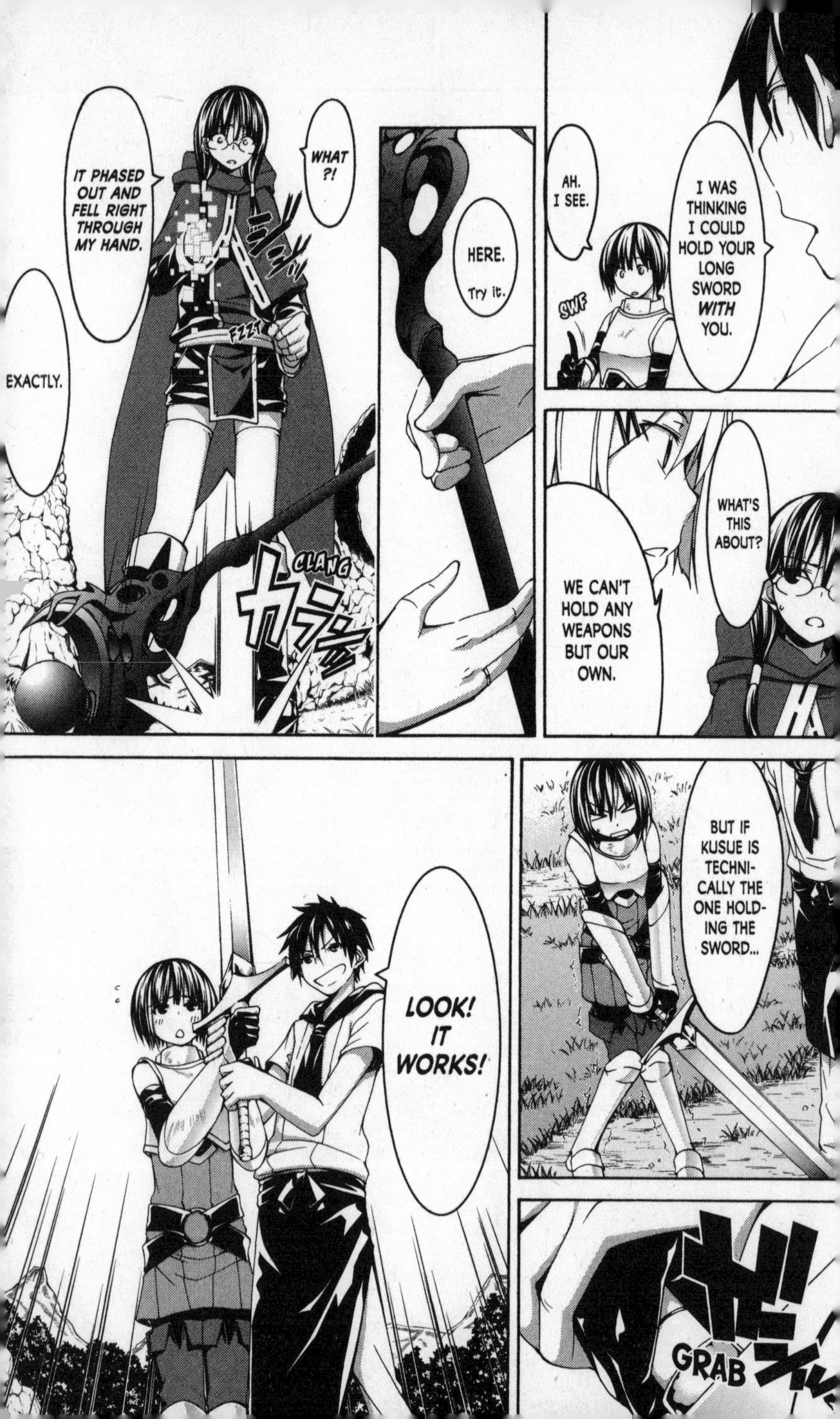
I WAS THINKING I COULD HOLD YOUR LONG SWORD WITH YOU.
AH. I SEE.
SWF
WHAT'S THIS ABOUT?
WE CAN'T HOLD ANY WEAPONS BUT OUR OWN.
HERE.
Try it.
WHAT ?!
IT PHASED OUT AND FELL RIGHT THROUGH MY HAND.
FZZT
EXACTLY.
CLANG
カラン
BUT IF KUSUE IS TECHNI-CALLY THE ONE HOLD-ING THE SWORD...
GRAB
LOOK! IT WORKS!

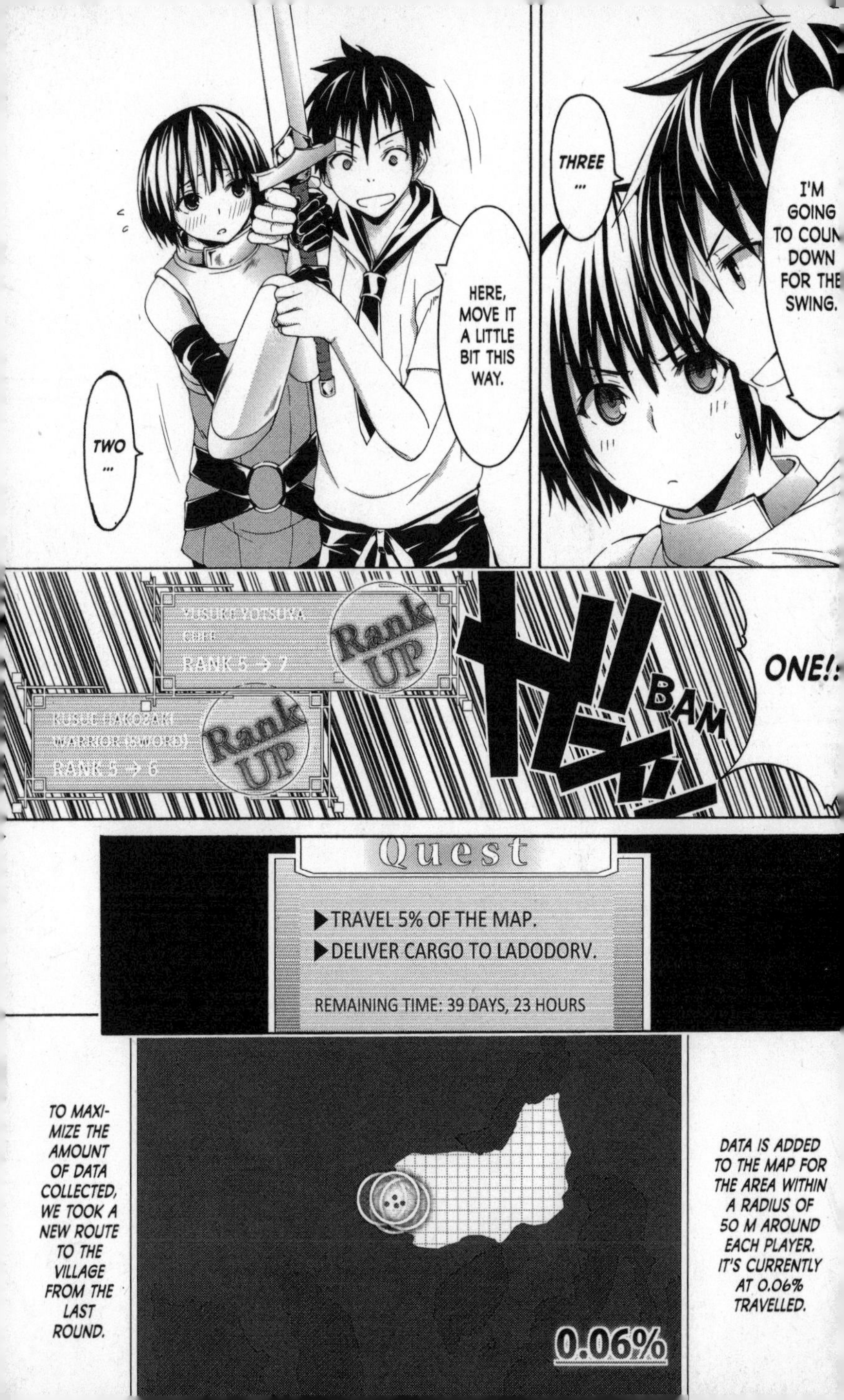
I'M GOING TO COUN DOWN FOR THE SWING.
THREE …
HERE, MOVE IT A LITTLE BIT THIS WAY.
TWO …
ONE!!
BAM
YUSUKE YOTSUYA
CHEF
RANK 5 → 7
Rank UP
KUSUE HAKOZAKI
WARRIOR (SWORD)
RANK 5 → 6
Rank UP
Quest
▶TRAVEL 5% OF THE MAP.
▶DELIVER CARGO TO LADODORV.
REMAINING TIME: 39 DAYS, 23 HOURS
DATA IS ADDED TO THE MAP FOR THE AREA WITHIN A RADIUS OF 50 M AROUND EACH PLAYER. IT'S CURRENTLY AT 0.06% TRAVELLED.
TO MAXIMIZE THE AMOUNT OF DATA COLLECTED, WE TOOK A NEW ROUTE TO THE VILLAGE FROM THE LAST ROUND.
0.06%

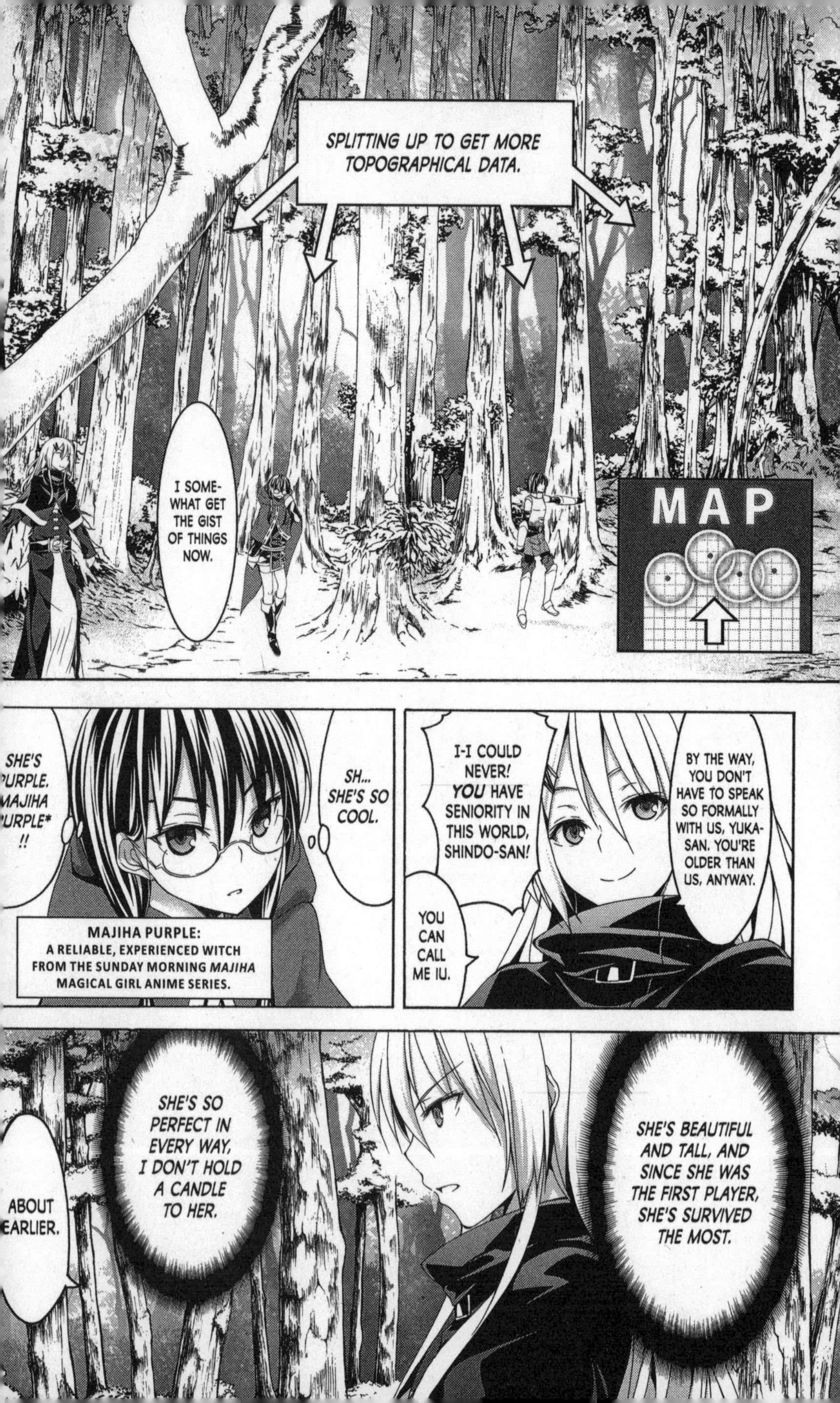
SPLITTING UP TO GET MORE TOPOGRAPHICAL DATA.
MAP
I SOME-WHAT GET THE GIST OF THINGS NOW.
BY THE WAY, YOU DON'T HAVE TO SPEAK SO FORMALLY WITH US, YUKA-SAN. YOU'RE OLDER THAN US, ANYWAY.
YOU CAN CALL ME IU.
I-I COULD NEVER! *YOU* HAVE SENIORITY IN THIS WORLD, SHINDO-SAN!
SH... SHE'S SO COOL.
SHE'S URPLE. MAJIHA URPLE* !!
MAJIHA PURPLE: A RELIABLE, EXPERIENCED WITCH FROM THE SUNDAY MORNING *MAJIHA* MAGICAL GIRL ANIME SERIES.
SHE'S BEAUTIFUL AND TALL, AND SINCE SHE WAS THE FIRST PLAYER, SHE'S SURVIVED THE MOST.
SHE'S SO PERFECT IN EVERY WAY, I DON'T HOLD A CANDLE TO HER.
ABOUT EARLIER.

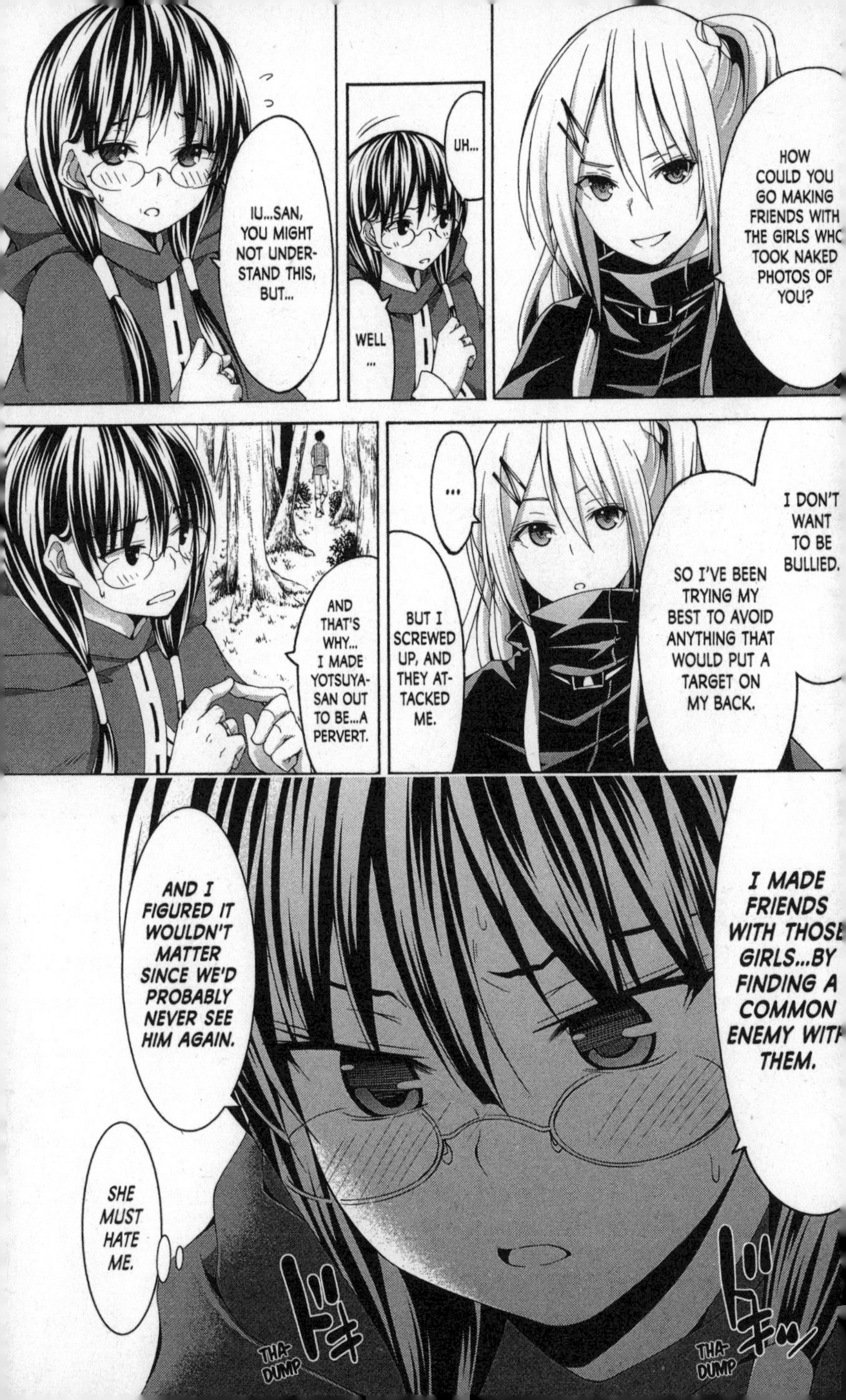
HOW COULD YOU GO MAKING FRIENDS WITH THE GIRLS WHO TOOK NAKED PHOTOS OF YOU?
UH...
WELL ...
IU...SAN, YOU MIGHT NOT UNDER-STAND THIS, BUT...
I DON'T WANT TO BE BULLIED.
SO I'VE BEEN TRYING MY BEST TO AVOID ANYTHING THAT WOULD PUT A TARGET ON MY BACK.
...
BUT I SCREWED UP, AND THEY AT-TACKED ME.
AND THAT'S WHY... I MADE YOTSUYA-SAN OUT TO BE...A PERVERT.
I MADE FRIENDS WITH THOSE GIRLS...BY FINDING A COMMON ENEMY WITH THEM.
AND I FIGURED IT WOULDN'T MATTER SINCE WE'D PROBABLY NEVER SEE HIM AGAIN.
ドキッ
THA-DUMP
ドキ
THA-DUMP
SHE MUST HATE ME.

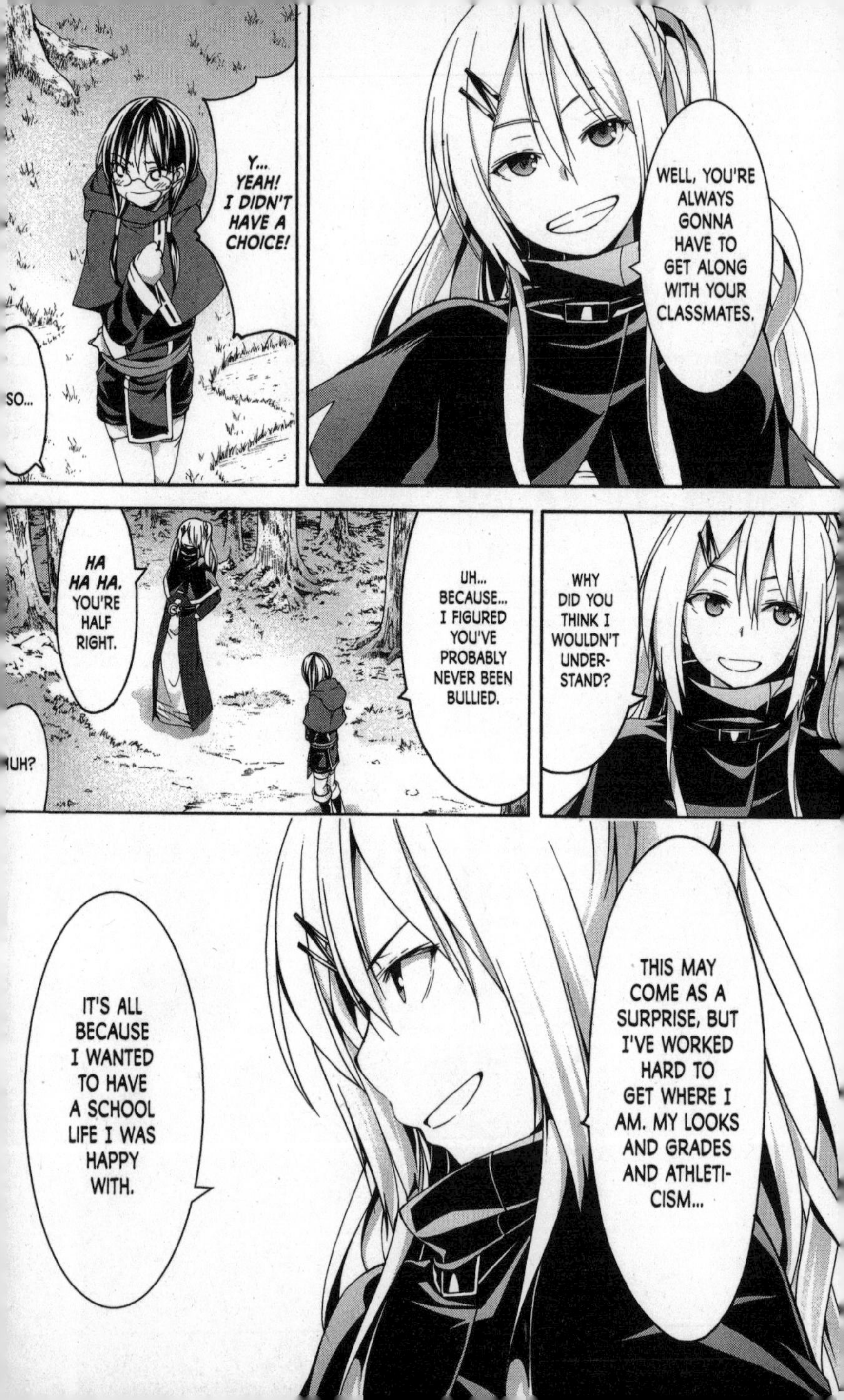
WELL, YOU'RE ALWAYS GONNA HAVE TO GET ALONG WITH YOUR CLASSMATES.
Y... YEAH! I DIDN'T HAVE A CHOICE!
SO...
WHY DID YOU THINK I WOULDN'T UNDER-STAND?
UH... BECAUSE... I FIGURED YOU'VE PROBABLY NEVER BEEN BULLIED.
HA HA HA. YOU'RE HALF RIGHT.
HUH?
THIS MAY COME AS A SURPRISE, BUT I'VE WORKED HARD TO GET WHERE I AM. MY LOOKS AND GRADES AND ATHLETI-CISM...
IT'S ALL BECAUSE I WANTED TO HAVE A SCHOOL LIFE I WAS HAPPY WITH.

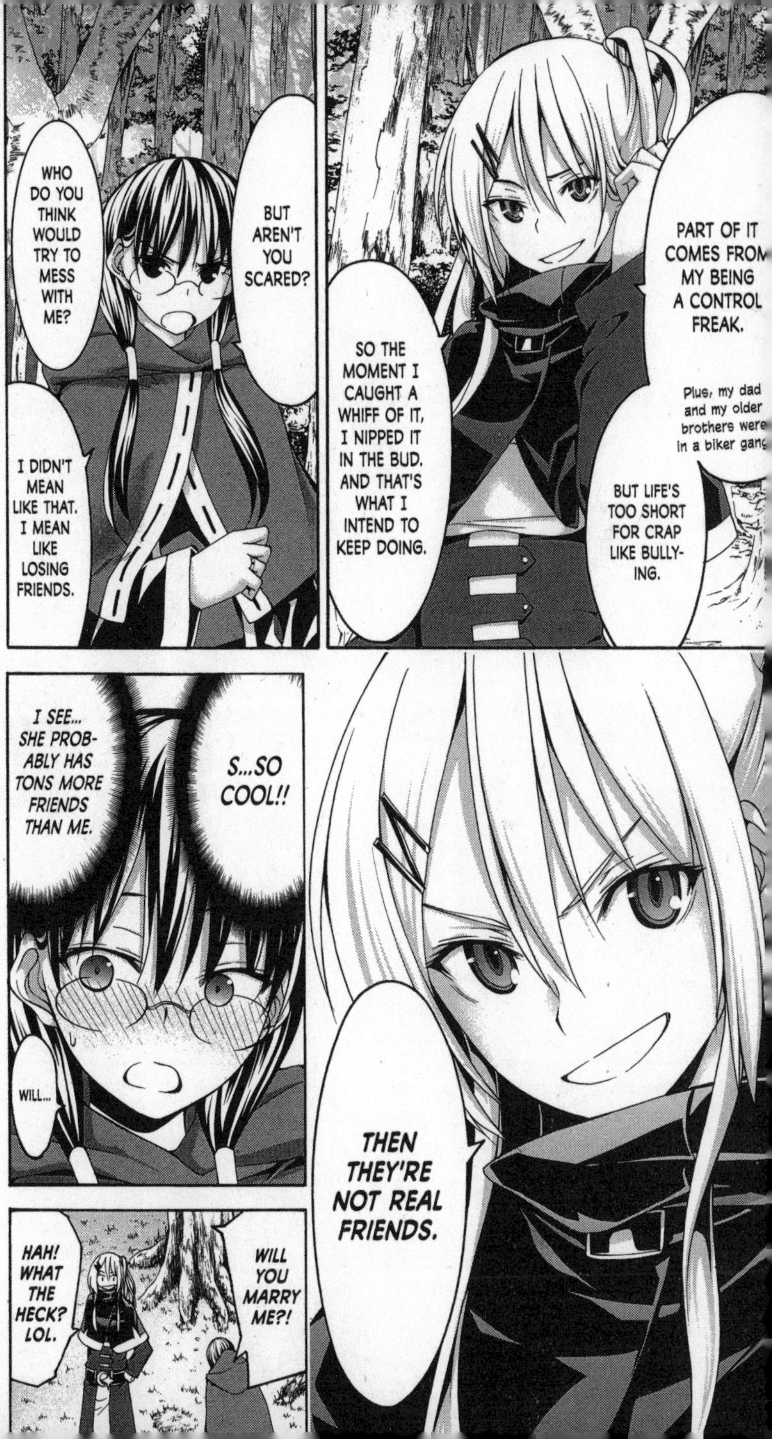
PART OF IT COMES FROM MY BEING A CONTROL FREAK.
Plus, my dad and my older brothers were in a biker gang.
BUT LIFE'S TOO SHORT FOR CRAP LIKE BULLY-ING.
SO THE MOMENT I CAUGHT A WHIFF OF IT, I NIPPED IT IN THE BUD. AND THAT'S WHAT I INTEND TO KEEP DOING.
BUT AREN'T YOU SCARED?
WHO DO YOU THINK WOULD TRY TO MESS WITH ME?
I DIDN'T MEAN LIKE THAT. I MEAN LIKE LOSING FRIENDS.
THEN THEY'RE NOT REAL FRIENDS.
S...SO COOL!!
I SEE... SHE PROBABLY HAS TONS MORE FRIENDS THAN ME.
WILL...
WILL YOU MARRY ME?!
HAH! WHAT THE HECK? LOL.

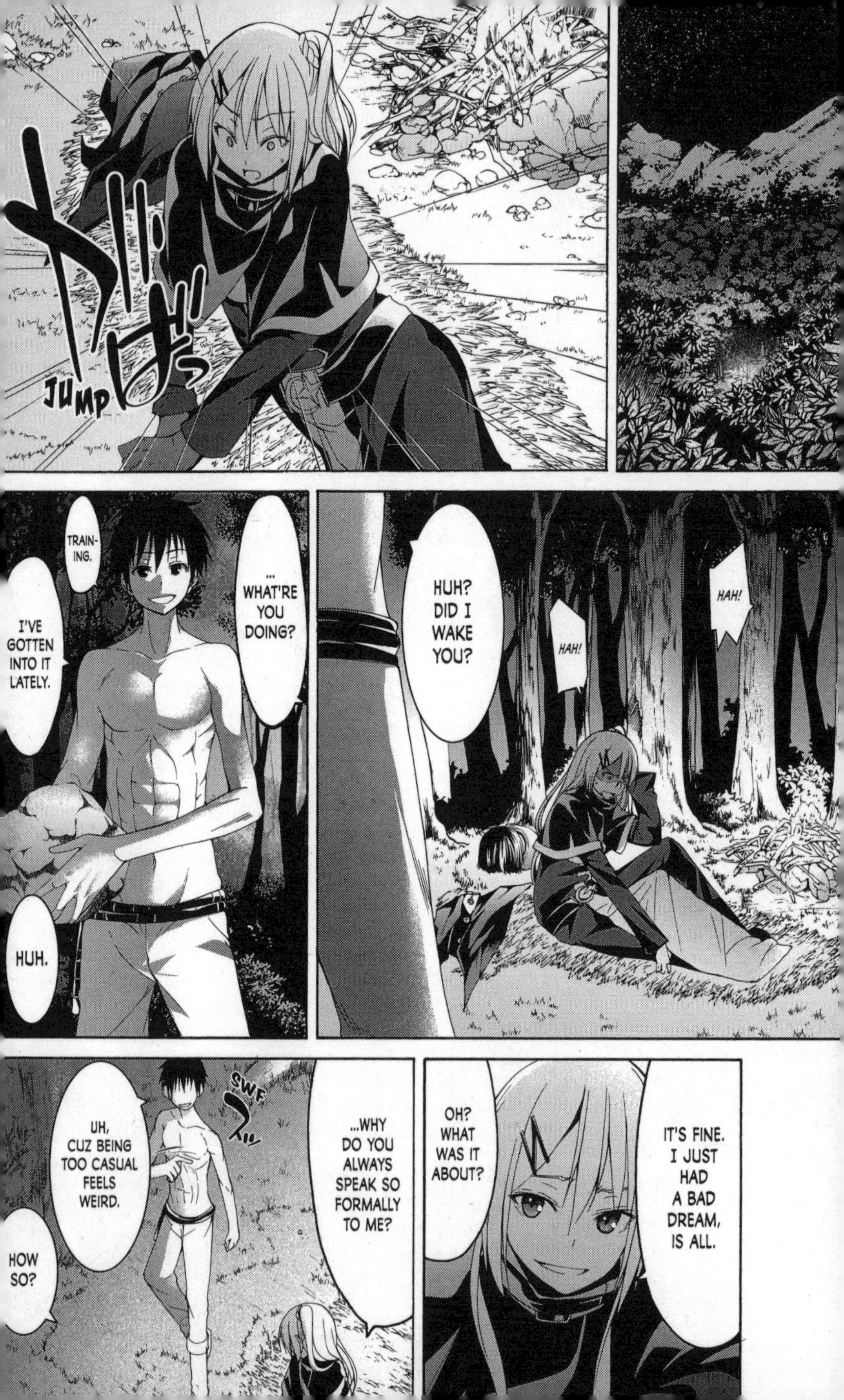

JUMP
HAH!
HAH!
HUH? DID I WAKE YOU?
... WHAT'RE YOU DOING?
TRAIN-ING.
I'VE GOTTEN INTO IT LATELY.
HUH.
IT'S FINE. I JUST HAD A BAD DREAM, IS ALL.
OH? WHAT WAS IT ABOUT?
...WHY DO YOU ALWAYS SPEAK SO FORMALLY TO ME?
SWF
UH, CUZ BEING TOO CASUAL FEELS WEIRD.
HOW SO?

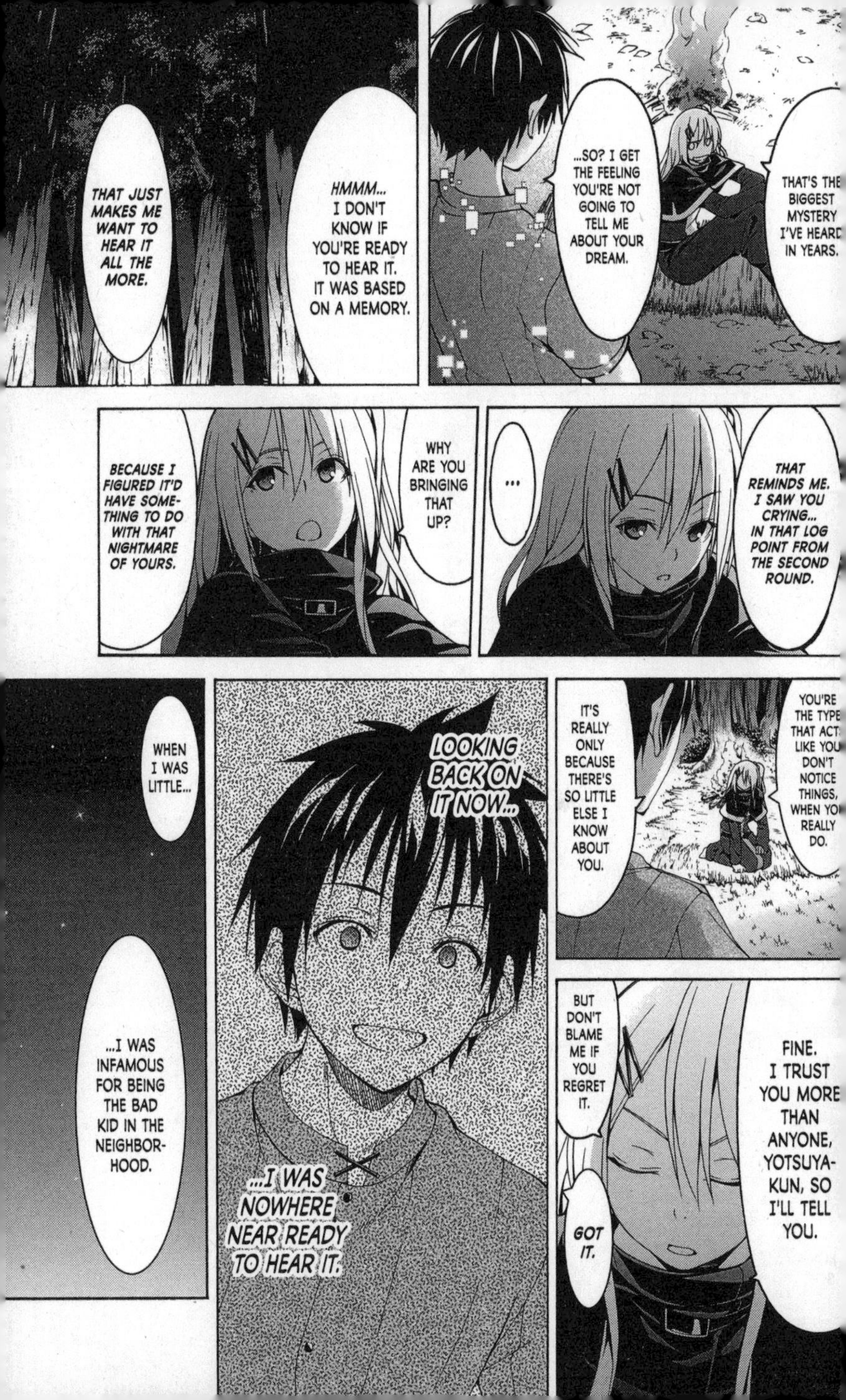
THAT'S THE BIGGEST MYSTERY I'VE HEARD IN YEARS.
...SO? I GET THE FEELING YOU'RE NOT GOING TO TELL ME ABOUT YOUR DREAM.
HMMM... I DON'T KNOW IF YOU'RE READY TO HEAR IT. IT WAS BASED ON A MEMORY.
THAT JUST MAKES ME WANT TO HEAR IT ALL THE MORE.
THAT REMINDS ME. I SAW YOU CRYING... IN THAT LOG POINT FROM THE SECOND ROUND.
...
WHY ARE YOU BRINGING THAT UP?
BECAUSE I FIGURED IT'D HAVE SOME-THING TO DO WITH THAT NIGHTMARE OF YOURS.
YOU'RE THE TYPE THAT ACTS LIKE YOU DON'T NOTICE THINGS, WHEN YOU REALLY DO.
IT'S REALLY ONLY BECAUSE THERE'S SO LITTLE ELSE I KNOW ABOUT YOU.
FINE. I TRUST YOU MORE THAN ANYONE, YOTSUYA-KUN, SO I'LL TELL YOU.
BUT DON'T BLAME ME IF YOU REGRET IT.
GOT IT.
LOOKING BACK ON IT NOW...
...I WAS NOWHERE NEAR READY TO HEAR IT.
WHEN I WAS LITTLE...
...I WAS INFAMOUS FOR BEING THE BAD KID IN THE NEIGHBOR-HOOD.

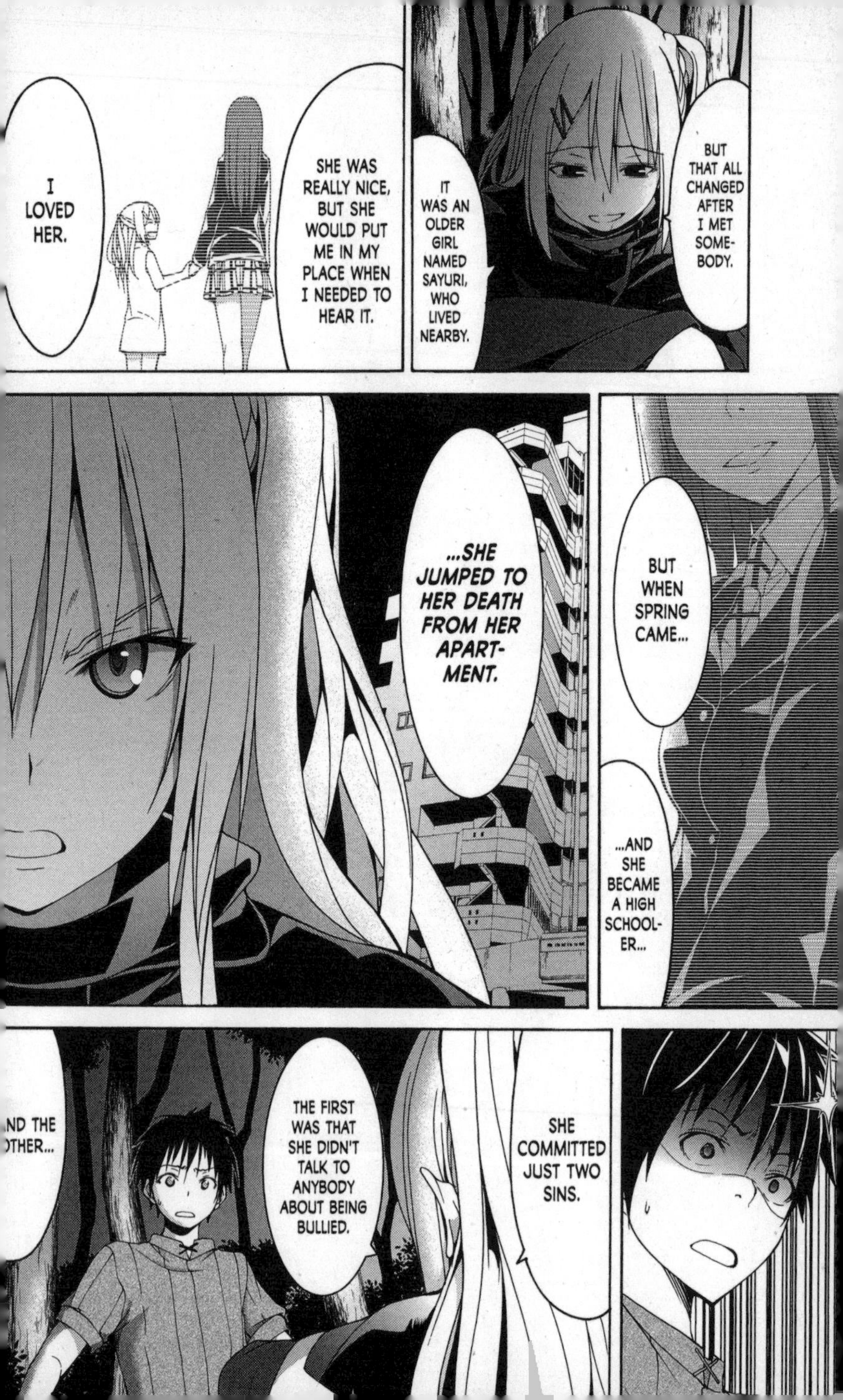
BUT THAT ALL CHANGED AFTER I MET SOMEBODY.
IT WAS AN OLDER GIRL NAMED SAYURI, WHO LIVED NEARBY.
SHE WAS REALLY NICE, BUT SHE WOULD PUT ME IN MY PLACE WHEN I NEEDED TO HEAR IT.
I LOVED HER.
BUT WHEN SPRING CAME...
...AND SHE BECAME A HIGH SCHOOLER...
...SHE JUMPED TO HER DEATH FROM HER APARTMENT.
SHE COMMITTED JUST TWO SINS.
THE FIRST WAS THAT SHE DIDN'T TALK TO ANYBODY ABOUT BEING BULLIED.
ND THE THER...

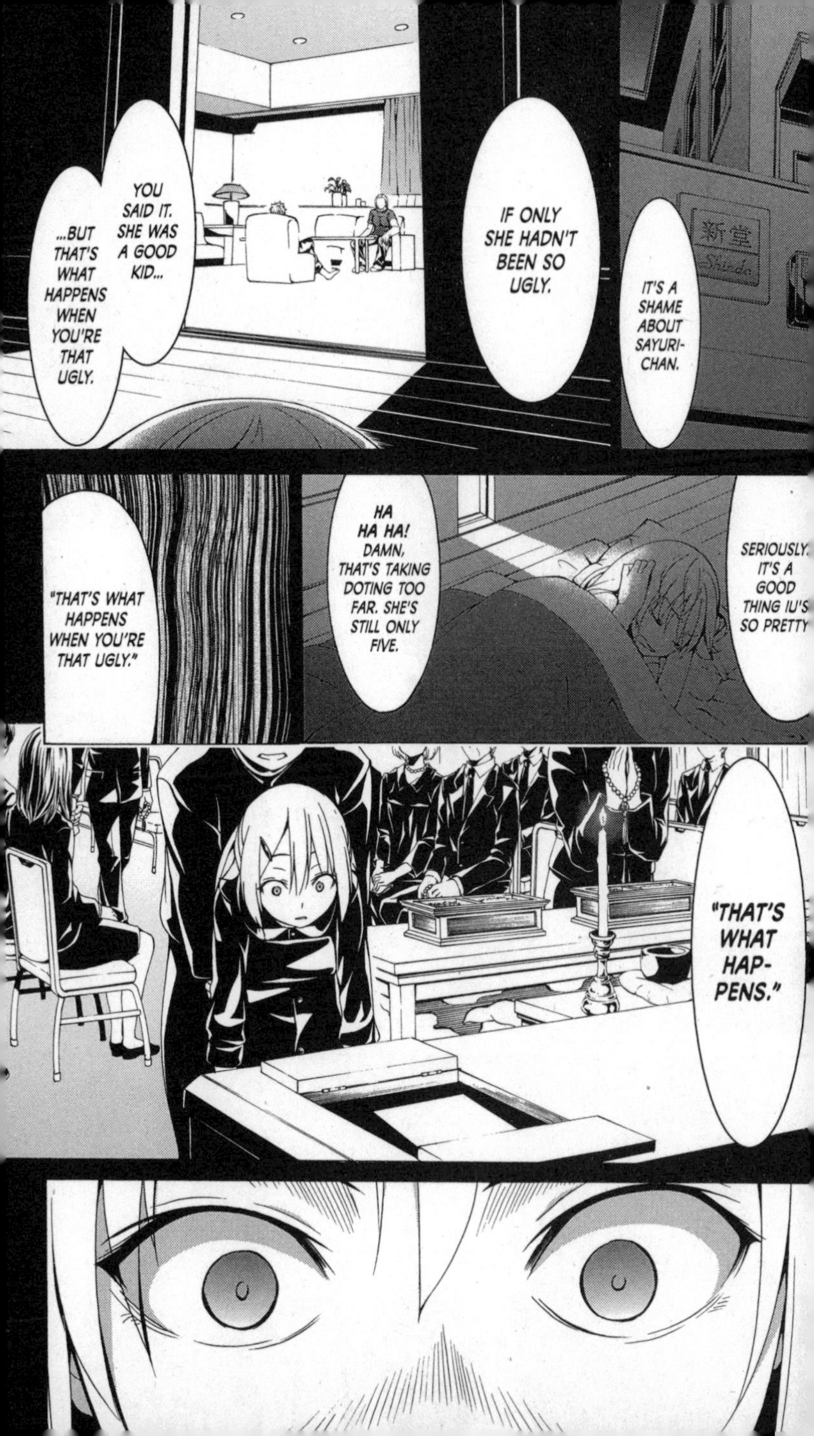
新堂
Shindo
IT'S A SHAME ABOUT SAYURI-CHAN.
IF ONLY SHE HADN'T BEEN SO UGLY.
YOU SAID IT. SHE WAS A GOOD KID...
...BUT THAT'S WHAT HAPPENS WHEN YOU'RE THAT UGLY.
SERIOUSLY. IT'S A GOOD THING IU'S SO PRETTY
HA HA HA! DAMN, THAT'S TAKING DOTING TOO FAR. SHE'S STILL ONLY FIVE.
"THAT'S WHAT HAPPENS WHEN YOU'RE THAT UGLY."
"THAT'S WHAT HAP-PENS."

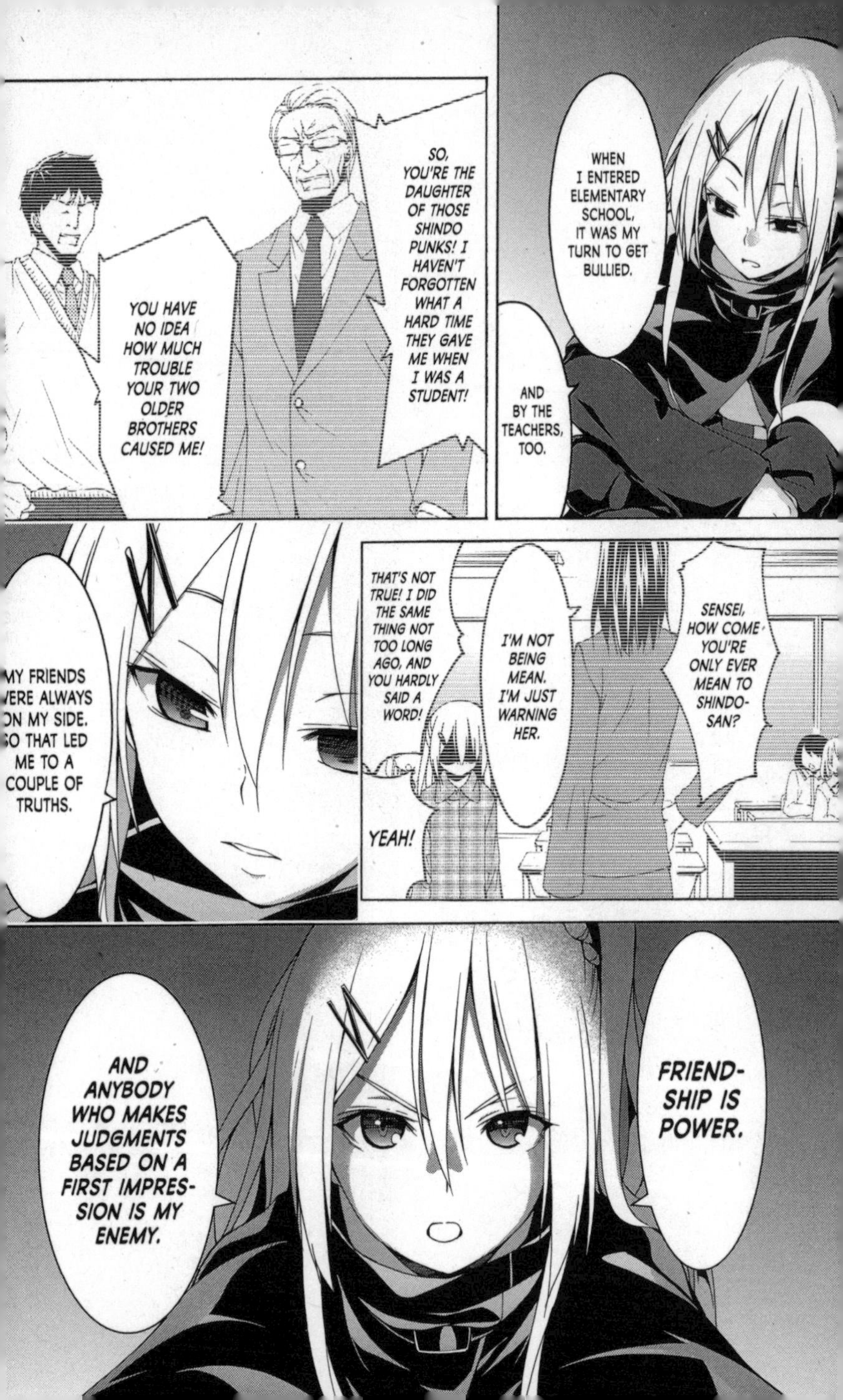
WHEN I ENTERED ELEMENTARY SCHOOL, IT WAS MY TURN TO GET BULLIED.
AND BY THE TEACHERS, TOO.
SO, YOU'RE THE DAUGHTER OF THOSE SHINDO PUNKS! I HAVEN'T FORGOTTEN WHAT A HARD TIME THEY GAVE ME WHEN I WAS A STUDENT!
YOU HAVE NO IDEA HOW MUCH TROUBLE YOUR TWO OLDER BROTHERS CAUSED ME!
SENSEI, HOW COME YOU'RE ONLY EVER MEAN TO SHINDO-SAN?
I'M NOT BEING MEAN. I'M JUST WARNING HER.
THAT'S NOT TRUE! I DID THE SAME THING NOT TOO LONG AGO, AND YOU HARDLY SAID A WORD!
YEAH!
MY FRIENDS WERE ALWAYS ON MY SIDE. SO THAT LED ME TO A COUPLE OF TRUTHS.
FRIEND-SHIP IS POWER.
AND ANYBODY WHO MAKES JUDGMENTS BASED ON A FIRST IMPRES-SION IS MY ENEMY.

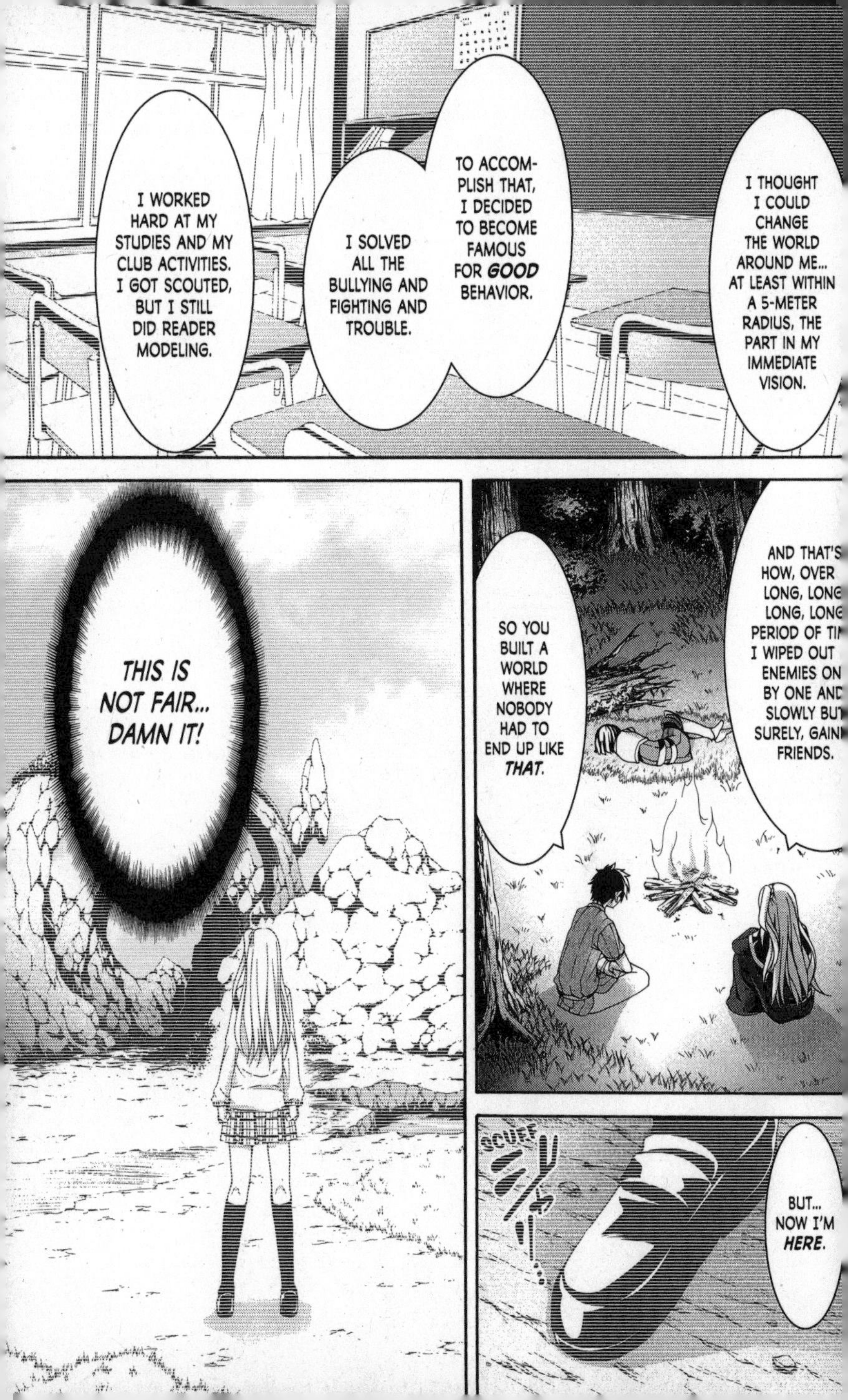
I THOUGHT I COULD CHANGE THE WORLD AROUND ME... AT LEAST WITHIN A 5-METER RADIUS, THE PART IN MY IMMEDIATE VISION.
TO ACCOMPLISH THAT, I DECIDED TO BECOME FAMOUS FOR *GOOD* BEHAVIOR.
I SOLVED ALL THE BULLYING AND FIGHTING AND TROUBLE.
I WORKED HARD AT MY STUDIES AND MY CLUB ACTIVITIES. I GOT SCOUTED, BUT I STILL DID READER MODELING.
AND THAT'S HOW, OVER LONG, LONG LONG, LONG PERIOD OF TI I WIPED OUT ENEMIES ON BY ONE AND SLOWLY BUT SURELY, GAIN FRIENDS.
SO YOU BUILT A WORLD WHERE NOBODY HAD TO END UP LIKE *THAT*.
SCUFF
BUT... NOW I'M *HERE*.
THIS IS NOT FAIR... DAMN IT!

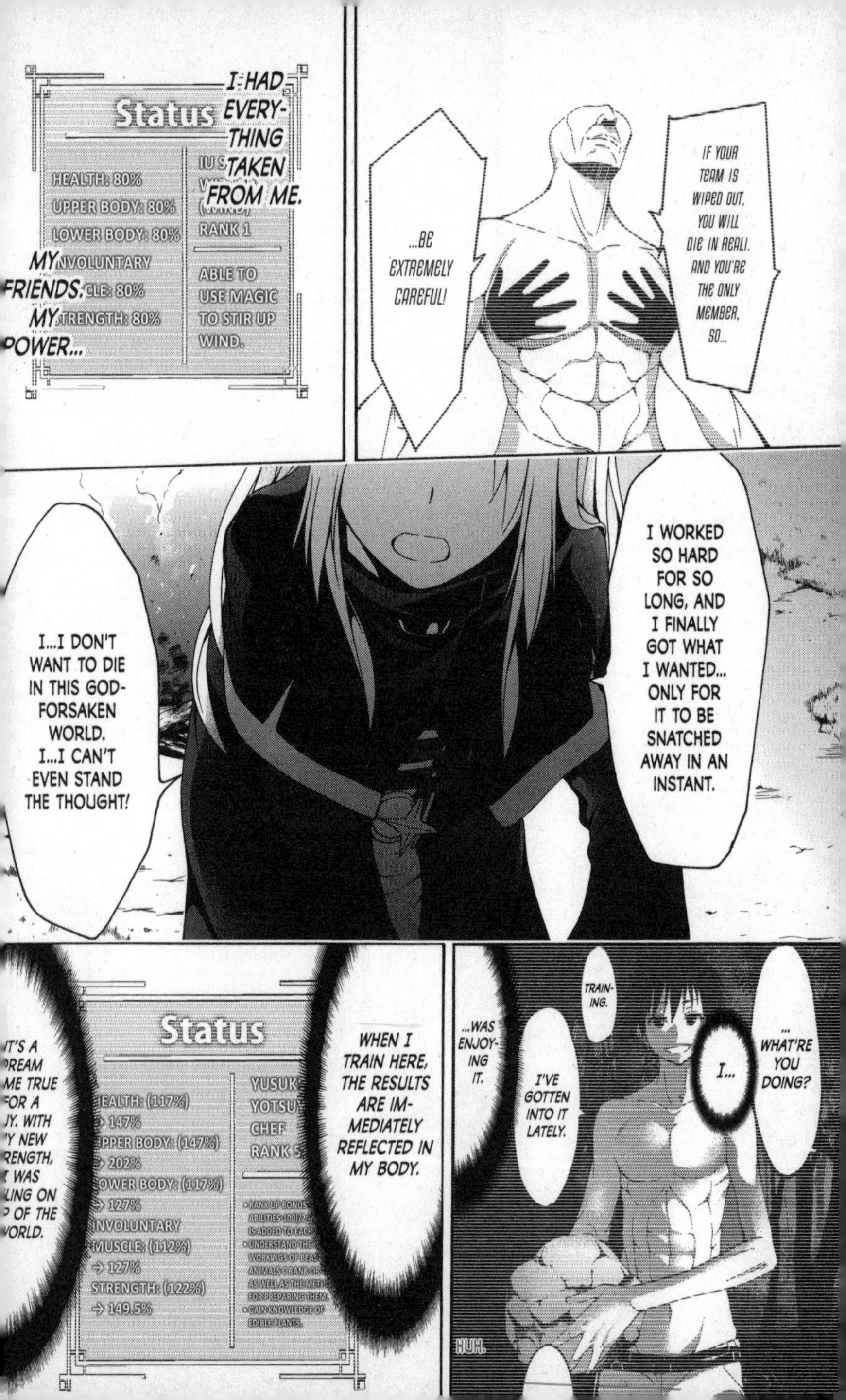
IF YOUR TEAM IS WIPED OUT, YOU WILL DIE IN REALI. AND YOU'RE THE ONLY MEMBER, SO...
...BE EXTREMELY CAREFUL!
I HAD EVERYTHING TAKEN FROM ME.
Status
HEALTH: 80%
UPPER BODY: 80%
LOWER BODY: 80%
NVOLUNTARY
CLE: 80%
TRENGTH: 80%
IU S
W
(WIND)
RANK 1
ABLE TO USE MAGIC TO STIR UP WIND.
MY FRIENDS. MY POWER...
I WORKED SO HARD FOR SO LONG, AND I FINALLY GOT WHAT I WANTED... ONLY FOR IT TO BE SNATCHED AWAY IN AN INSTANT.
I...I DON'T WANT TO DIE IN THIS GOD-FORSAKEN WORLD. I...I CAN'T EVEN STAND THE THOUGHT!
...WHAT'RE YOU DOING?
I...
TRAINING.
...WAS ENJOYING IT.
I'VE GOTTEN INTO IT LATELY.
HUH.
WHEN I TRAIN HERE, THE RESULTS ARE IMMEDIATELY REFLECTED IN MY BODY.
Status
EALTH: (117%)
→ 147%
PPER BODY: (147%)
→ 202%
OWER BODY: (117%)
→ 127%
NVOLUNTARY
MUSCLE: (112%)
→ 127%
STRENGTH: (122%)
→ 149.5%
YUSUK
YOTSU
CHEF
RANK 5
• RANK UP BONUS
ABILITIES 100/2
IS ADDED TO EACH
• UNDERSTAND THE
WORKINGS OF BEAS
ANIMALS CRANK OR
AS WELL AS THE METH
FOR PREPARING THEM.
• GAIN KNOWLEDGE OF EDIBLE PLANTS.
IT'S A
REAM
ME TRUE
FOR A
Y. WITH
Y NEW
RENGTH,
WAS
ING ON
P OF THE
VORLD.

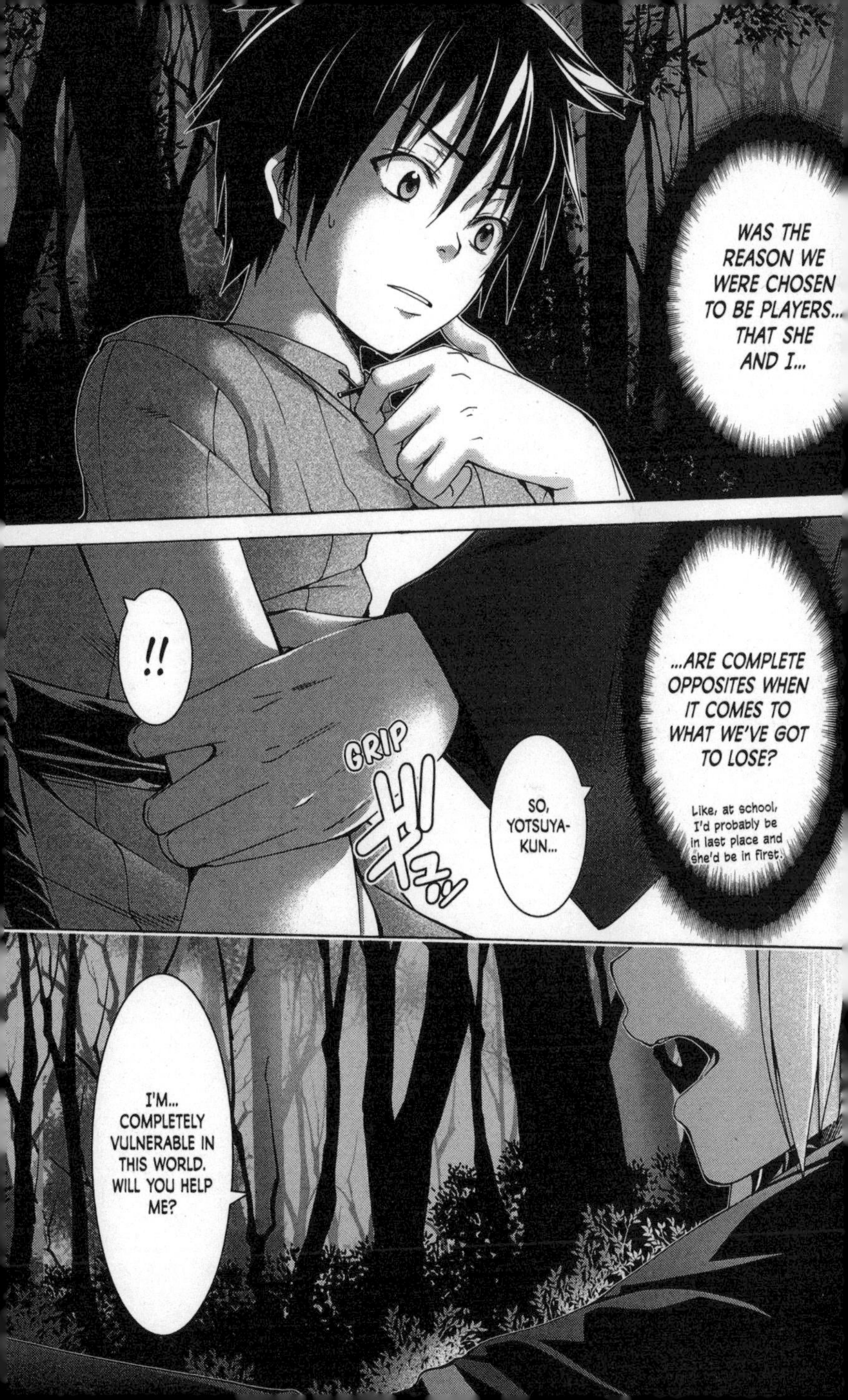
WAS THE REASON WE WERE CHOSEN TO BE PLAYERS... THAT SHE AND I...
...ARE COMPLETE OPPOSITES WHEN IT COMES TO WHAT WE'VE GOT TO LOSE?
Like, at school, I'd probably be in last place and she'd be in first.
SO, YOTSUYA-KUN...
GRIP
!!
I'M... COMPLETELY VULNERABLE IN THIS WORLD. WILL YOU HELP ME?

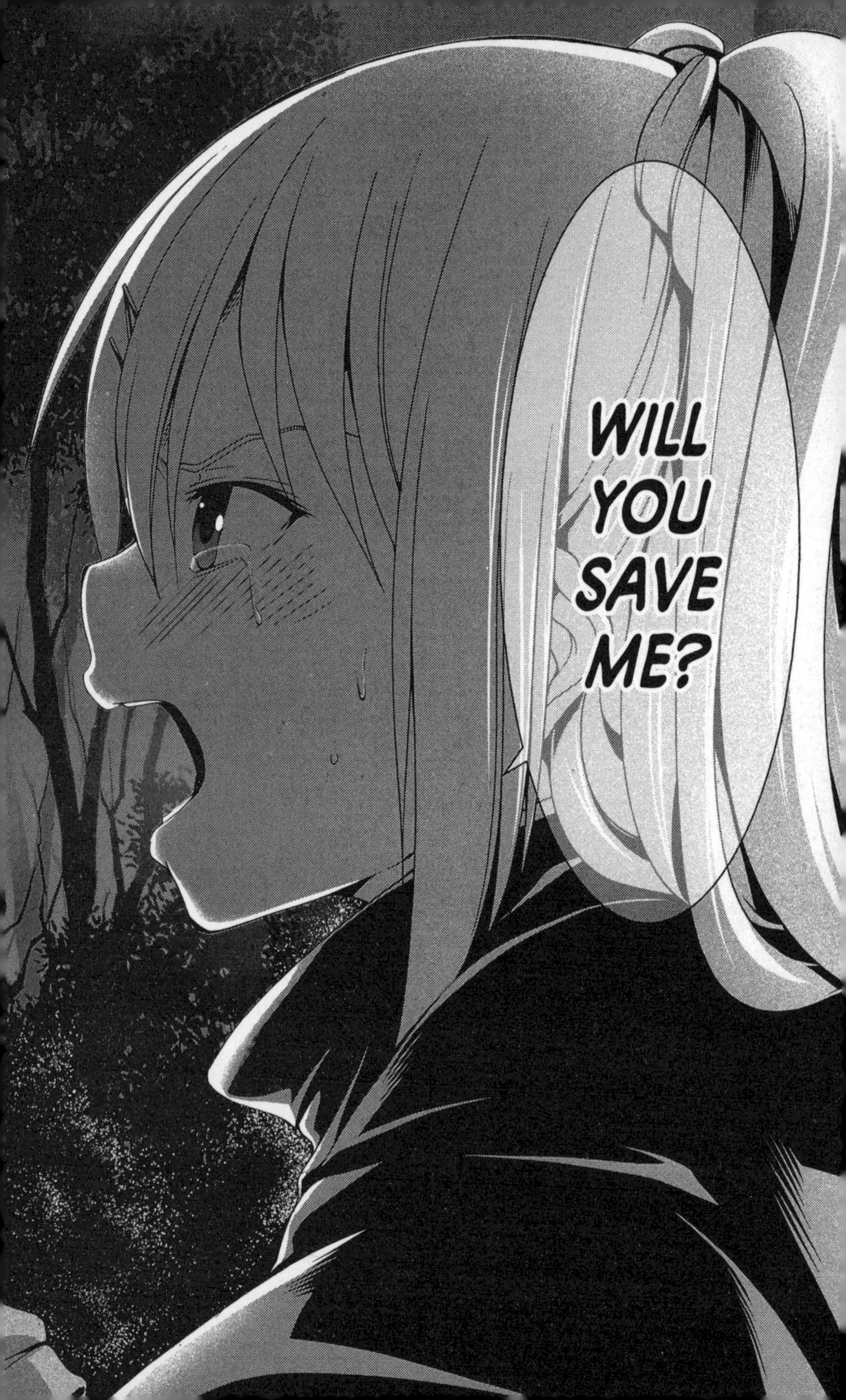
WILL YOU SAVE ME?

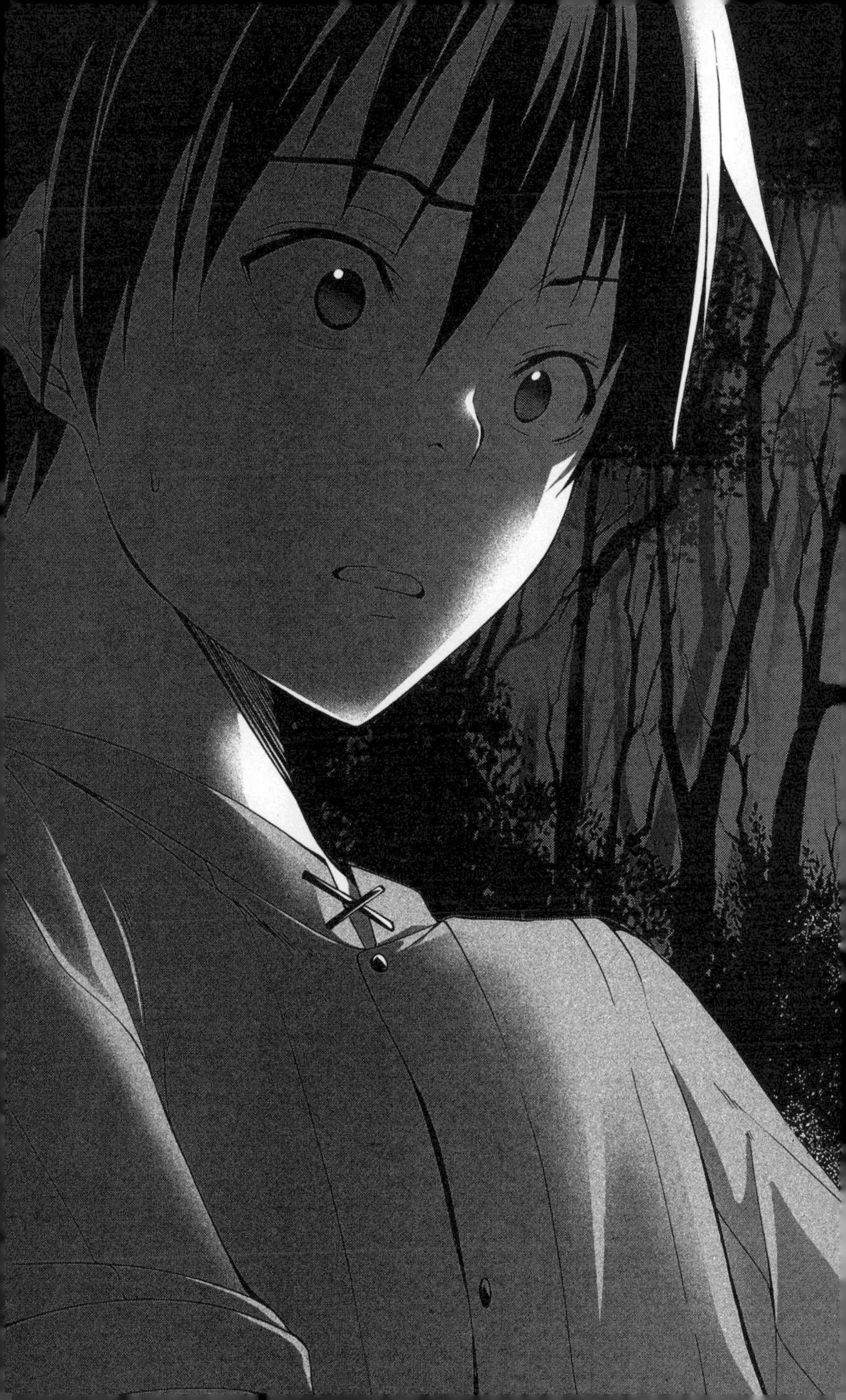

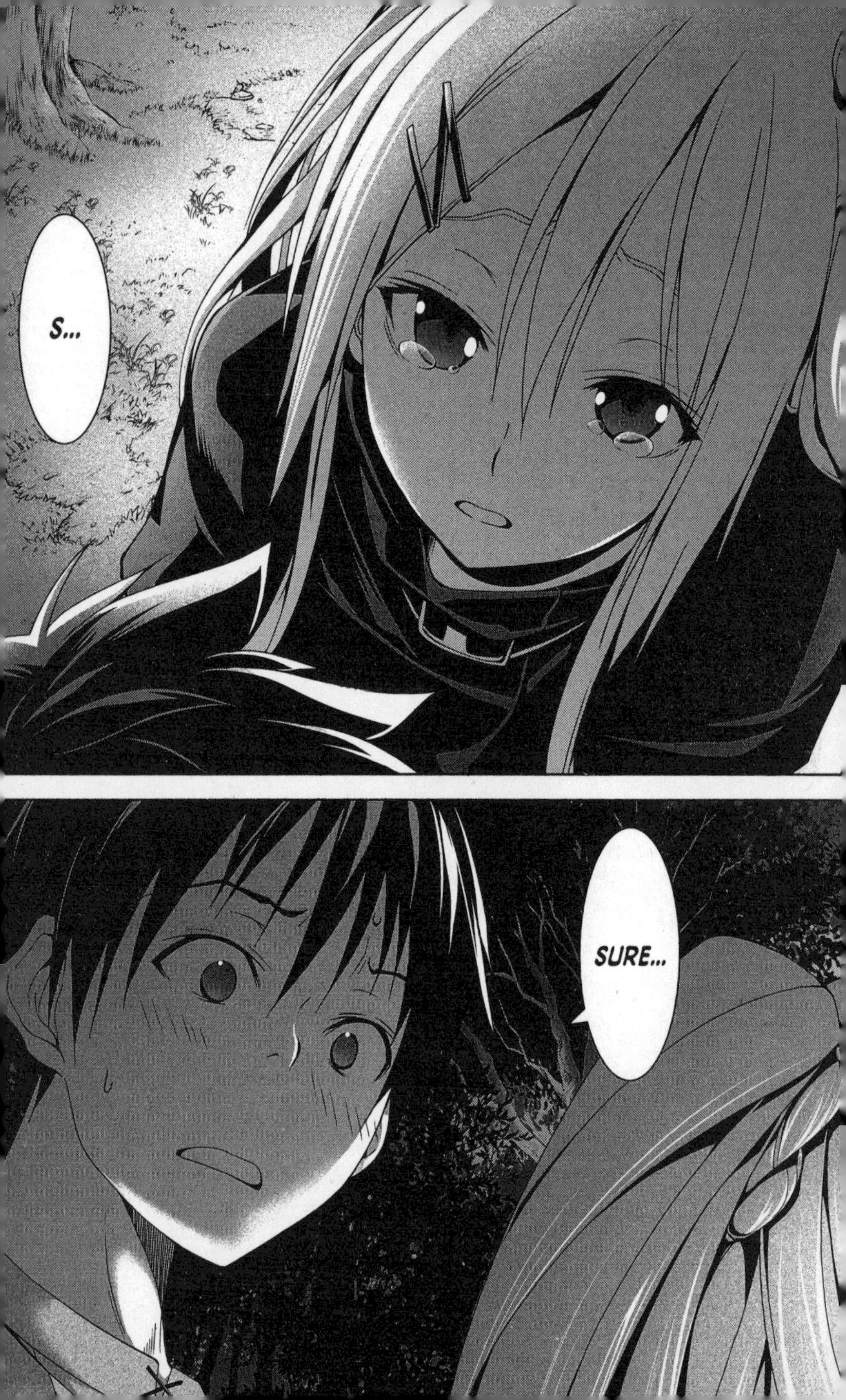
S...
SURE...

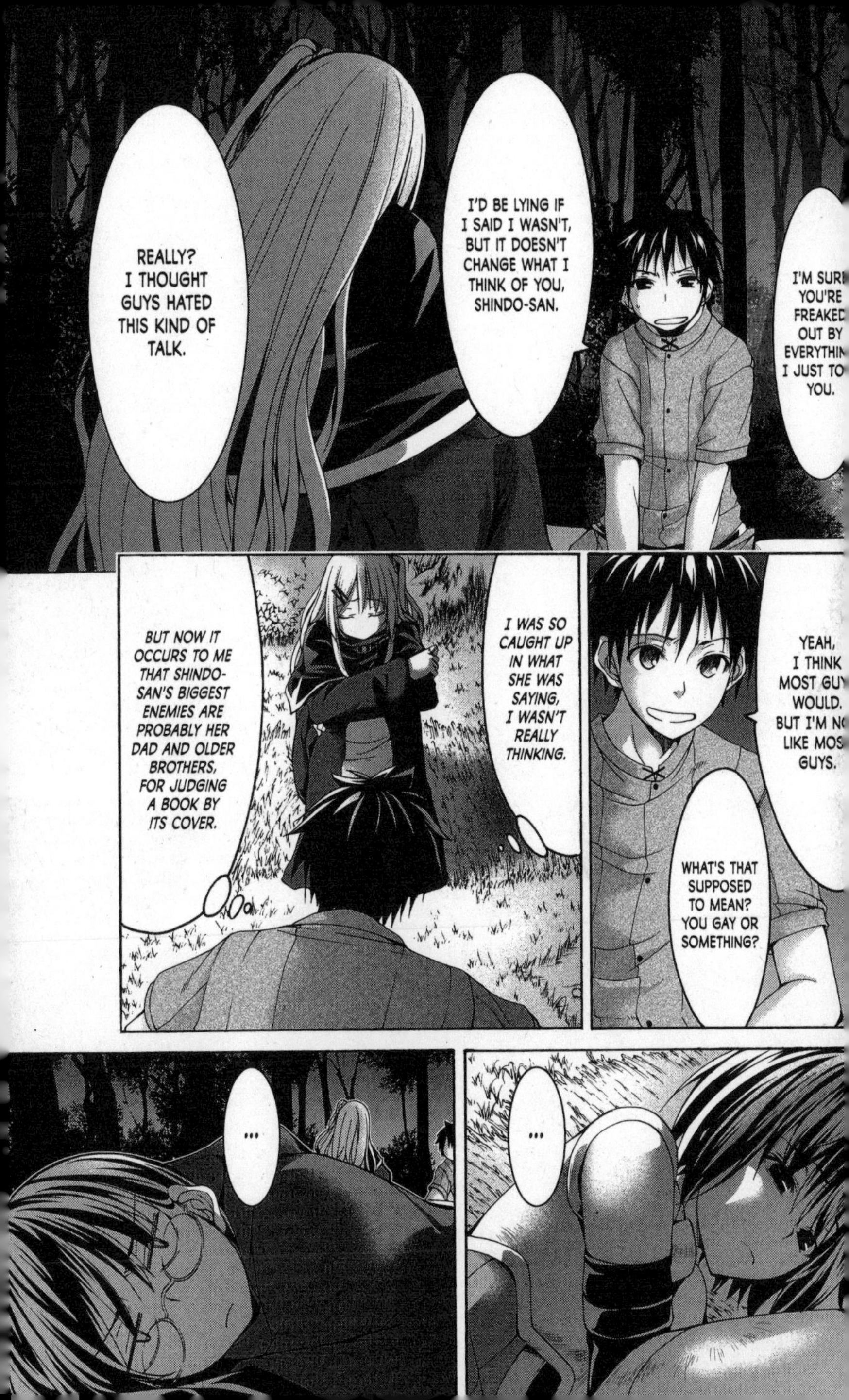
I'M SURI YOU'RE FREAKED OUT BY EVERYTHIN I JUST TO YOU.
I'D BE LYING IF I SAID I WASN'T, BUT IT DOESN'T CHANGE WHAT I THINK OF YOU, SHINDO-SAN.
REALLY? I THOUGHT GUYS HATED THIS KIND OF TALK.
YEAH, I THINK MOST GU WOULD. BUT I'M N LIKE MOS GUYS.
WHAT'S THAT SUPPOSED TO MEAN? YOU GAY OR SOMETHING?
I WAS SO CAUGHT UP IN WHAT SHE WAS SAYING, I WASN'T REALLY THINKING.
BUT NOW IT OCCURS TO ME THAT SHINDO-SAN'S BIGGEST ENEMIES ARE PROBABLY HER DAD AND OLDER BROTHERS, FOR JUDGING A BOOK BY ITS COVER.
...
...

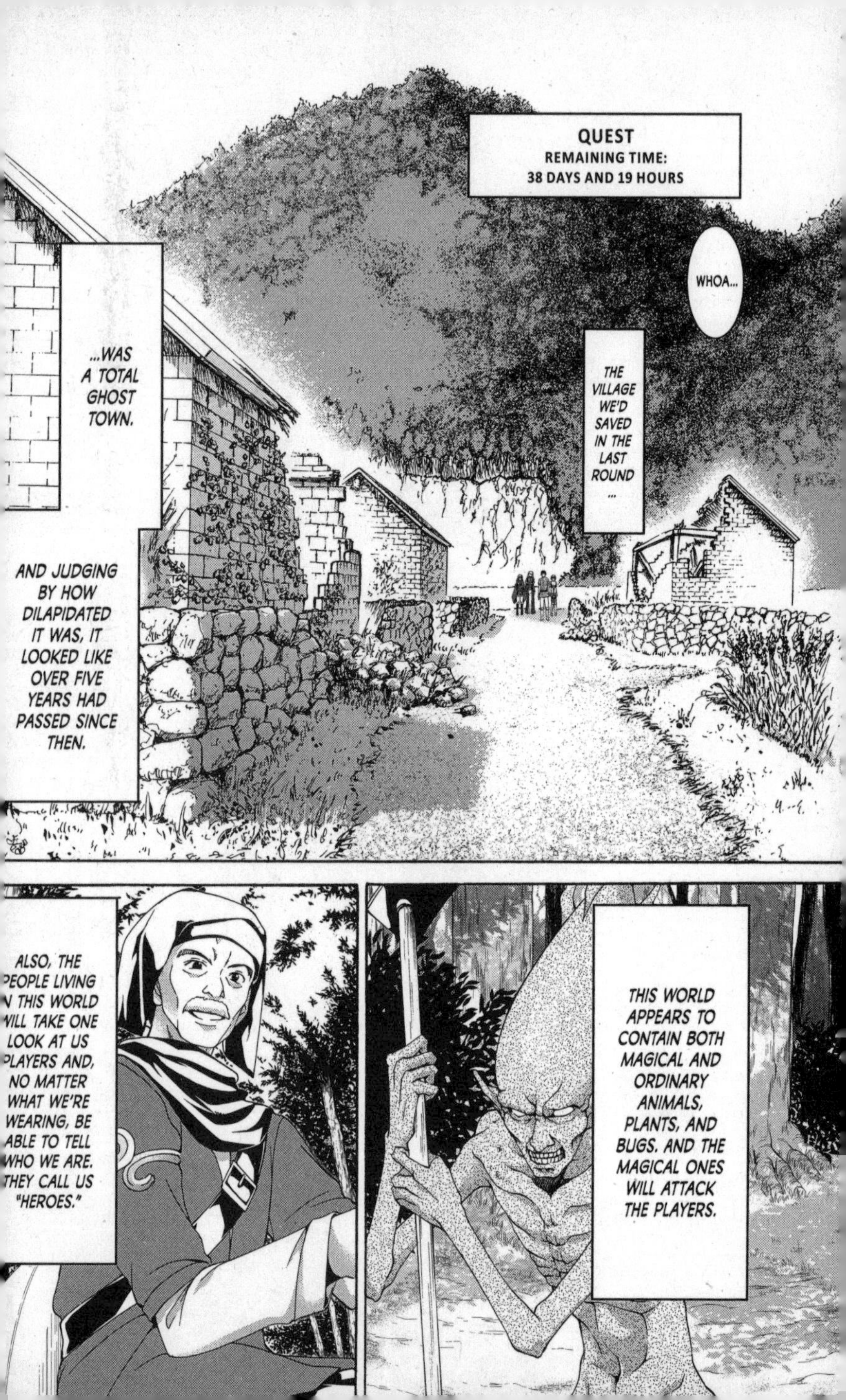
QUEST
REMAINING TIME:
38 DAYS AND 19 HOURS
WHOA...
THE VILLAGE WE'D SAVED IN THE LAST ROUND ...
...WAS A TOTAL GHOST TOWN.
AND JUDGING BY HOW DILAPIDATED IT WAS, IT LOOKED LIKE OVER FIVE YEARS HAD PASSED SINCE THEN.
THIS WORLD APPEARS TO CONTAIN BOTH MAGICAL AND ORDINARY ANIMALS, PLANTS, AND BUGS. AND THE MAGICAL ONES WILL ATTACK THE PLAYERS.
ALSO, THE PEOPLE LIVING IN THIS WORLD WILL TAKE ONE LOOK AT US PLAYERS AND, NO MATTER WHAT WE'RE WEARING, BE ABLE TO TELL WHO WE ARE. THEY CALL US "HEROES."

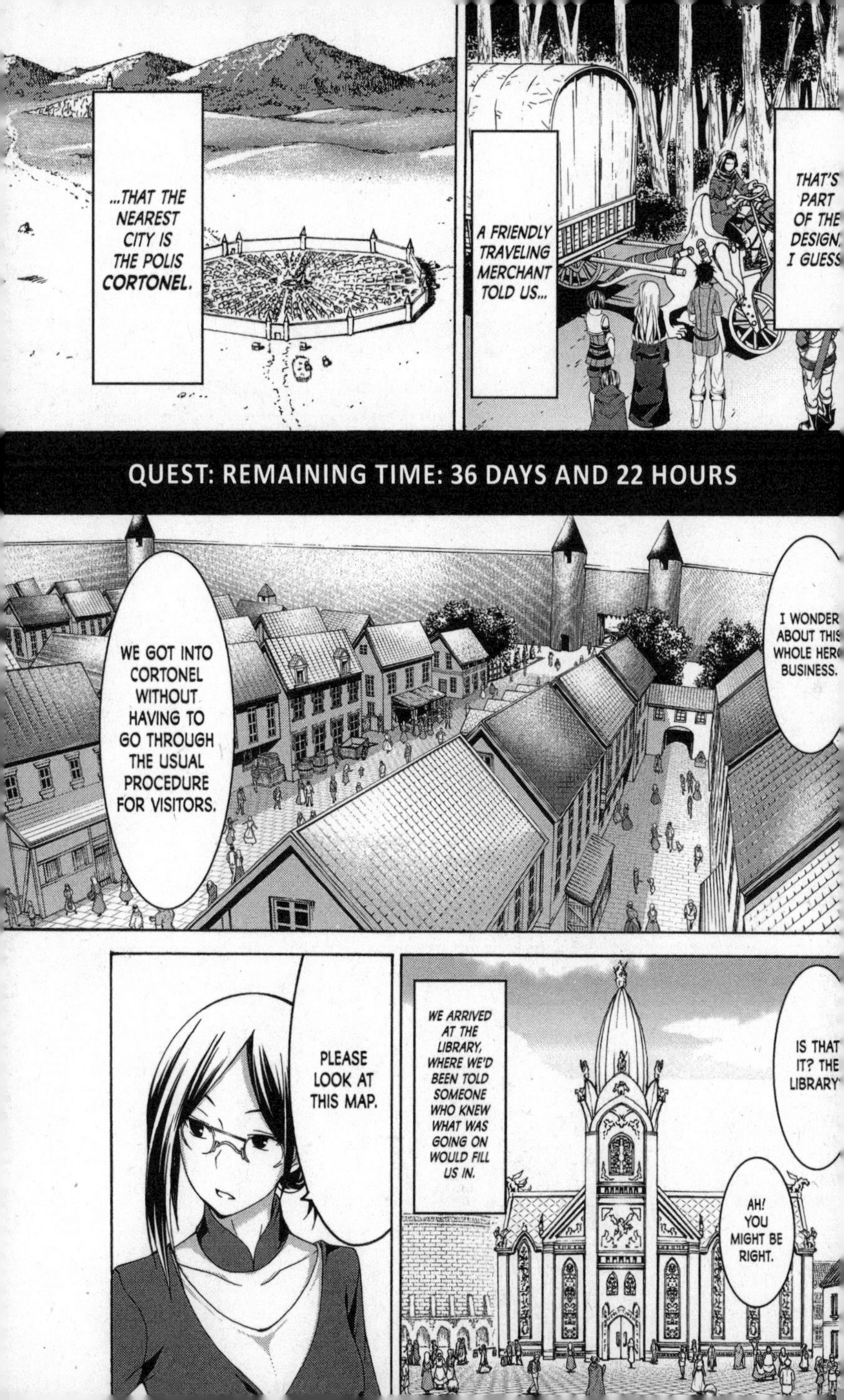
THAT'S PART OF THE DESIGN, I GUESS
A FRIENDLY TRAVELING MERCHANT TOLD US...
...THAT THE NEAREST CITY IS THE POLIS CORTONEL.
QUEST: REMAINING TIME: 36 DAYS AND 22 HOURS
I WONDER ABOUT THIS WHOLE HER BUSINESS.
WE GOT INTO CORTONEL WITHOUT HAVING TO GO THROUGH THE USUAL PROCEDURE FOR VISITORS.
IS THAT IT? THE LIBRARY
WE ARRIVED AT THE LIBRARY, WHERE WE'D BEEN TOLD SOMEONE WHO KNEW WHAT WAS GOING ON WOULD FILL US IN.
AH! YOU MIGHT BE RIGHT.
PLEASE LOOK AT THIS MAP.

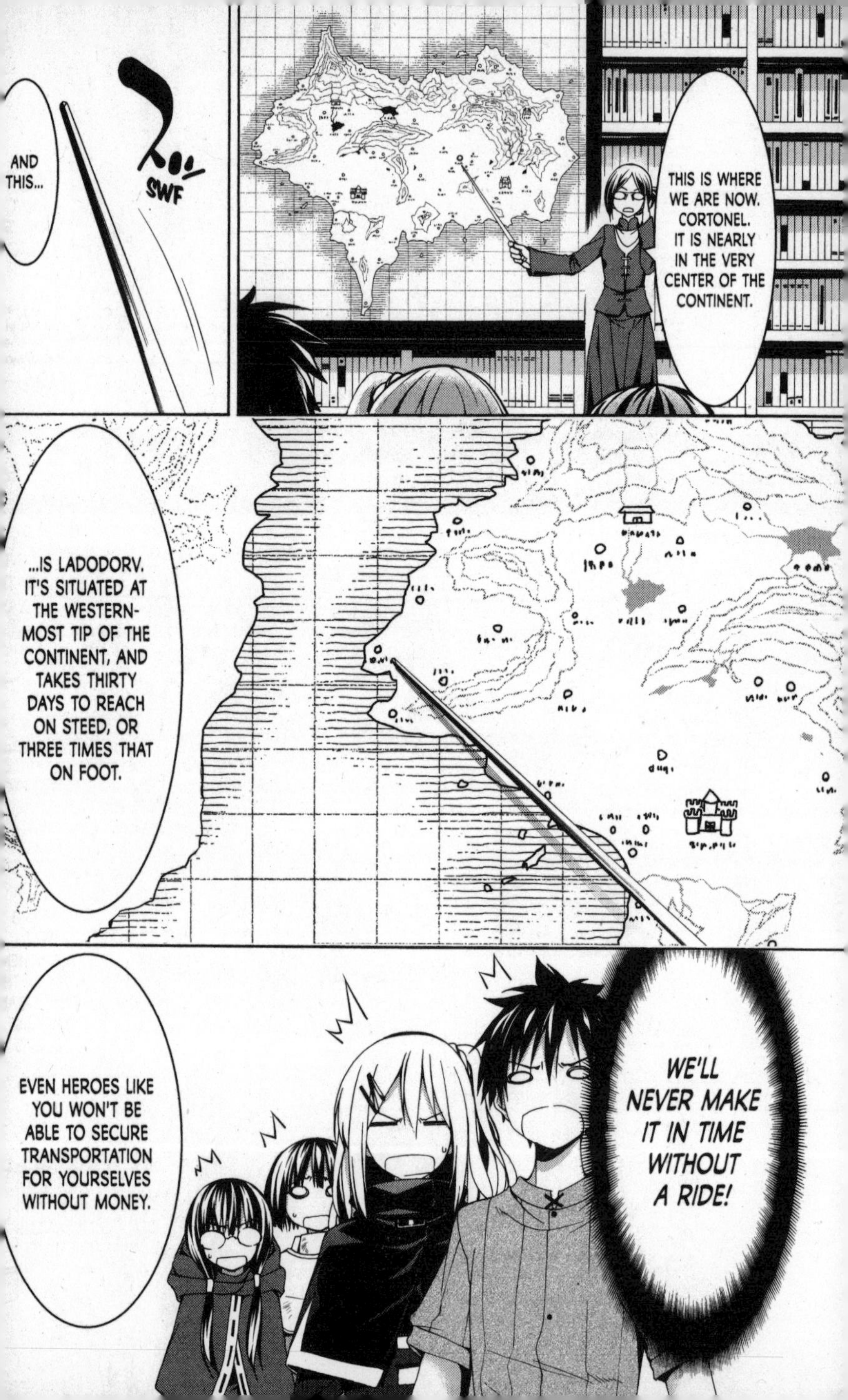
THIS IS WHERE WE ARE NOW. CORTONEL. IT IS NEARLY IN THE VERY CENTER OF THE CONTINENT.
AND THIS...
SWF
...IS LADODORV. IT'S SITUATED AT THE WESTERN-MOST TIP OF THE CONTINENT, AND TAKES THIRTY DAYS TO REACH ON STEED, OR THREE TIMES THAT ON FOOT.
WE'LL NEVER MAKE IT IN TIME WITHOUT A RIDE!
EVEN HEROES LIKE YOU WON'T BE ABLE TO SECURE TRANSPORTATION FOR YOURSELVES WITHOUT MONEY.

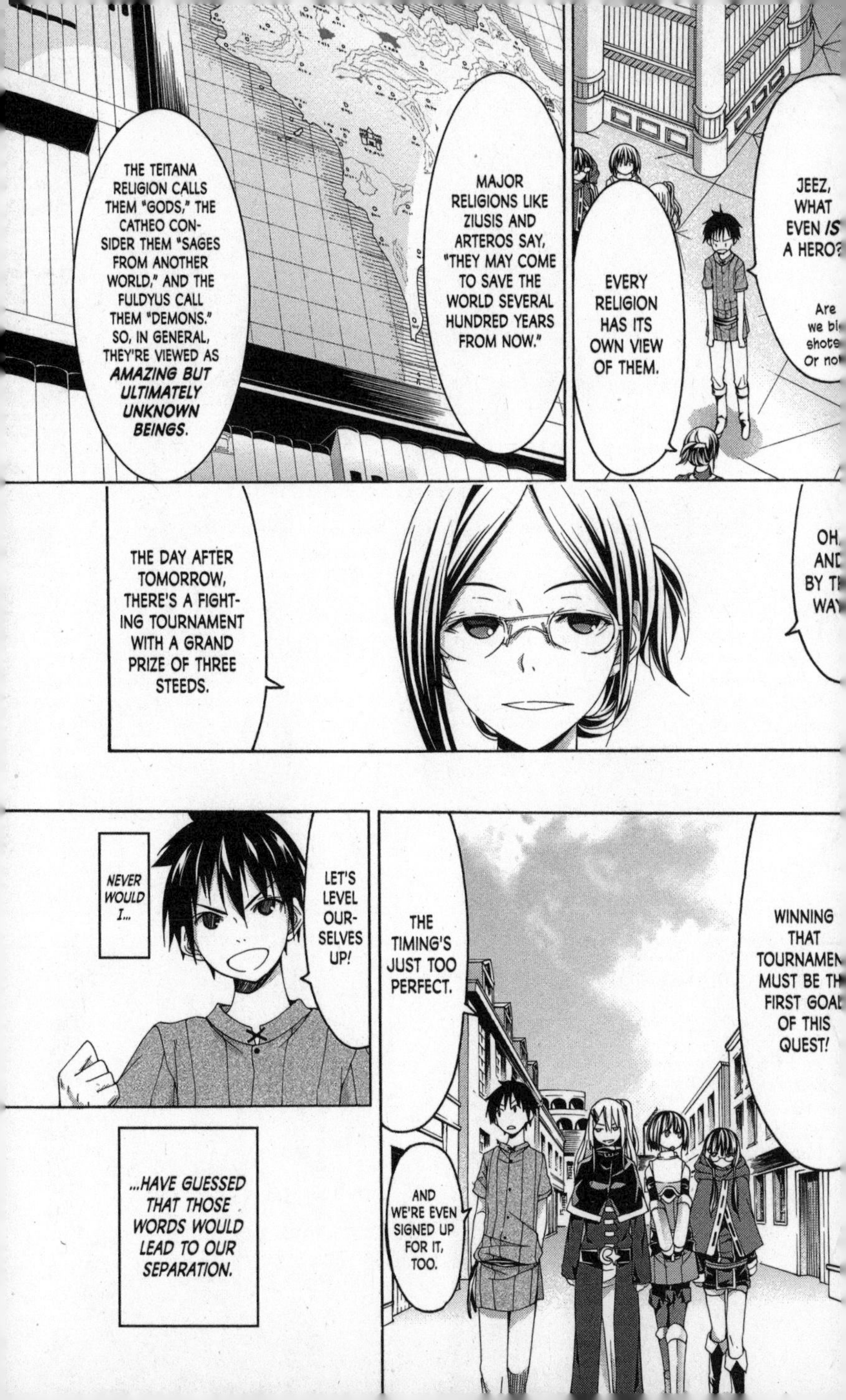

JEEZ, WHAT EVEN IS A HERO?
Are we bi shots Or no
EVERY RELIGION HAS ITS OWN VIEW OF THEM.
MAJOR RELIGIONS LIKE ZIUSIS AND ARTEROS SAY, "THEY MAY COME TO SAVE THE WORLD SEVERAL HUNDRED YEARS FROM NOW."
THE TEITANA RELIGION CALLS THEM "GODS," THE CATHEO CONSIDER THEM "SAGES FROM ANOTHER WORLD," AND THE FULDYUS CALL THEM "DEMONS." SO, IN GENERAL, THEY'RE VIEWED AS ***AMAZING BUT ULTIMATELY UNKNOWN BEINGS***.
OH, AND BY T WAY
THE DAY AFTER TOMORROW, THERE'S A FIGHTING TOURNAMENT WITH A GRAND PRIZE OF THREE STEEDS.
WINNING THAT TOURNAMEN MUST BE TH FIRST GOAL OF THIS QUEST!
THE TIMING'S JUST TOO PERFECT.
AND WE'RE EVEN SIGNED UP FOR IT, TOO.
LET'S LEVEL OURSELVES UP!
NEVER WOULD I...
...HAVE GUESSED THAT THOSE WORDS WOULD LEAD TO OUR SEPARATION.

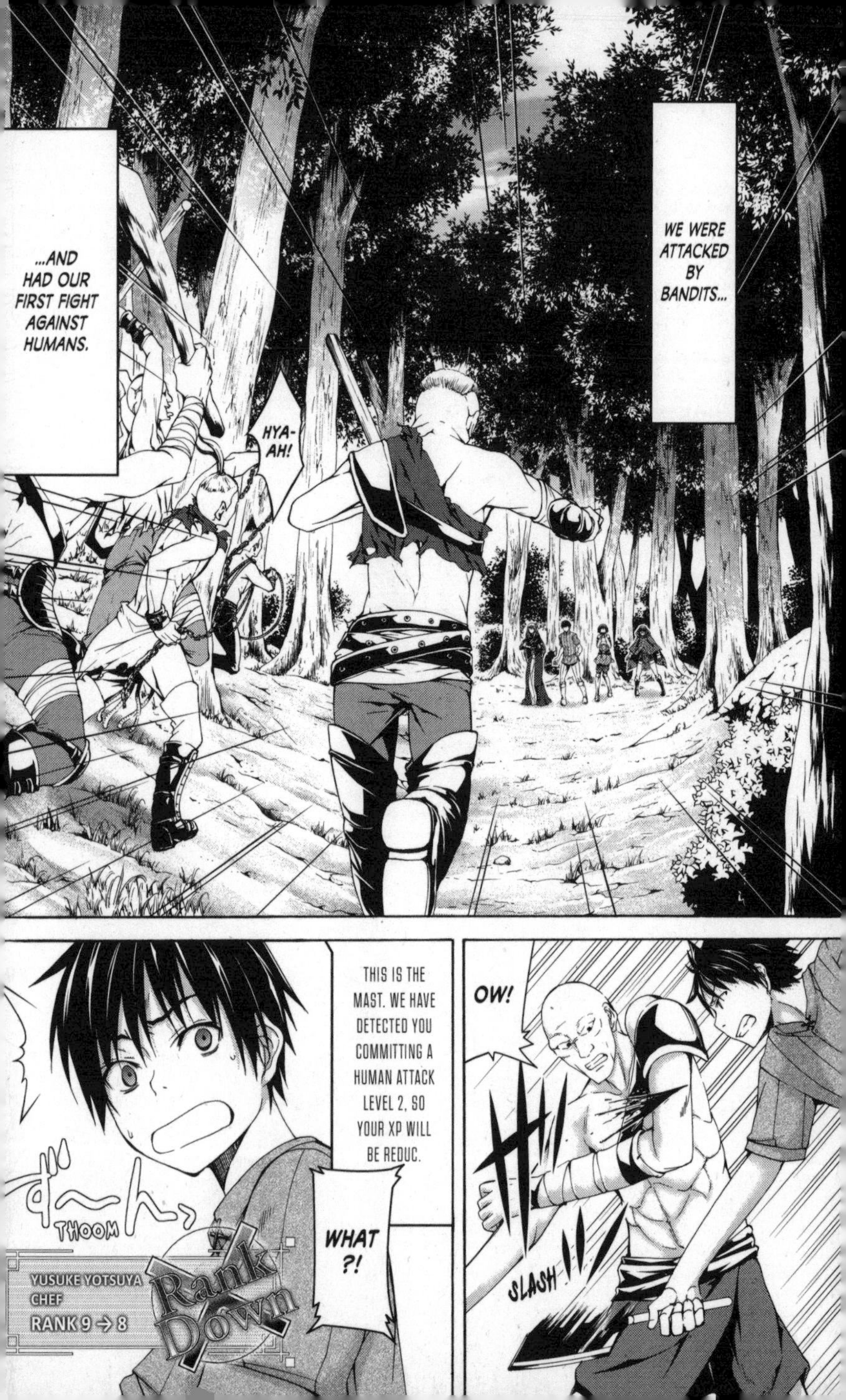
WE WERE ATTACKED BY BANDITS...
...AND HAD OUR FIRST FIGHT AGAINST HUMANS.
HYA-AH!
OW!
SLASH
THIS IS THE MAST. WE HAVE DETECTED YOU COMMITTING A HUMAN ATTACK LEVEL 2, SO YOUR XP WILL BE REDUC.
WHAT ?!
ず〜ん
THOOM
YUSUKE YOTSUYA
CHEF
RANK 9 → 8
Rank Down

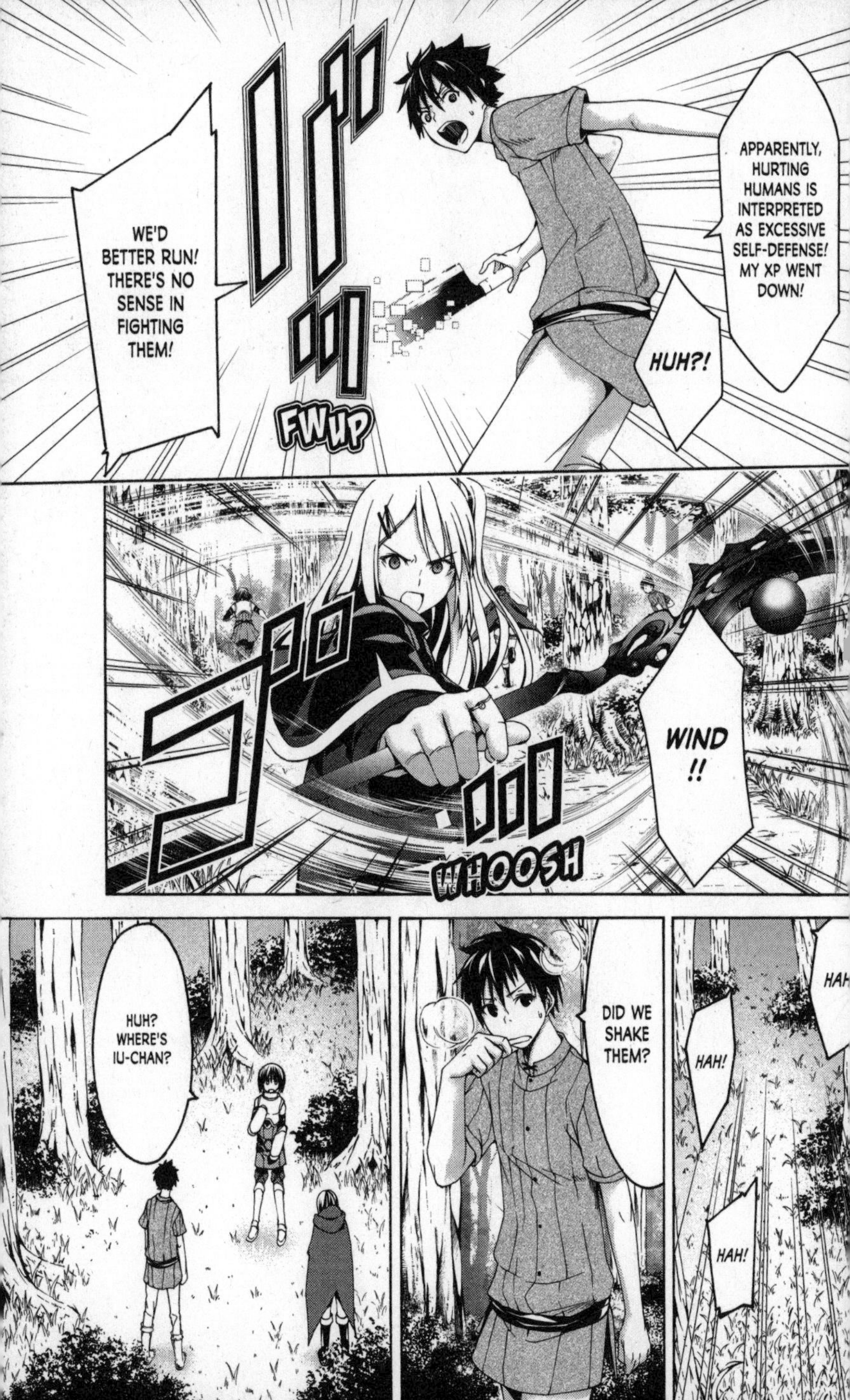
APPARENTLY, HURTING HUMANS IS INTERPRETED AS EXCESSIVE SELF-DEFENSE! MY XP WENT DOWN!
HUH?!
FWUP
WE'D BETTER RUN! THERE'S NO SENSE IN FIGHTING THEM!
WIND!!
WHOOSH
HAH
HAH!
HAH!
DID WE SHAKE THEM?
HUH? WHERE'S IU-CHAN?

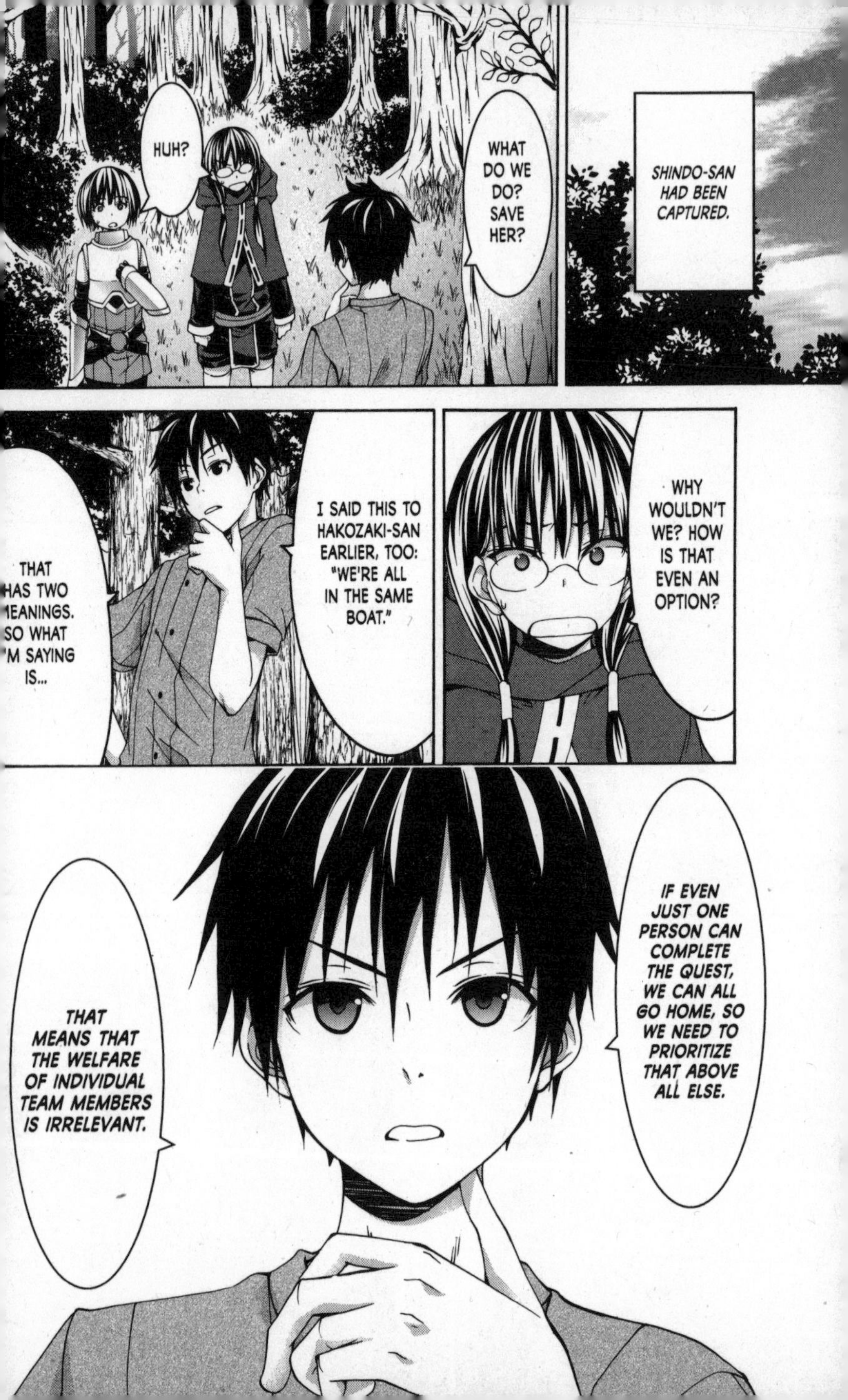
SHINDO-SAN HAD BEEN CAPTURED.
WHAT DO WE DO? SAVE HER?
HUH?
WHY WOULDN'T WE? HOW IS THAT EVEN AN OPTION?
I SAID THIS TO HAKOZAKI-SAN EARLIER, TOO: "WE'RE ALL IN THE SAME BOAT."
THAT HAS TWO MEANINGS. SO WHAT I'M SAYING IS...
IF EVEN JUST ONE PERSON CAN COMPLETE THE QUEST, WE CAN ALL GO HOME, SO WE NEED TO PRIORITIZE THAT ABOVE ALL ELSE.
THAT MEANS THAT THE WELFARE OF INDIVIDUAL TEAM MEMBERS IS IRRELEVANT.

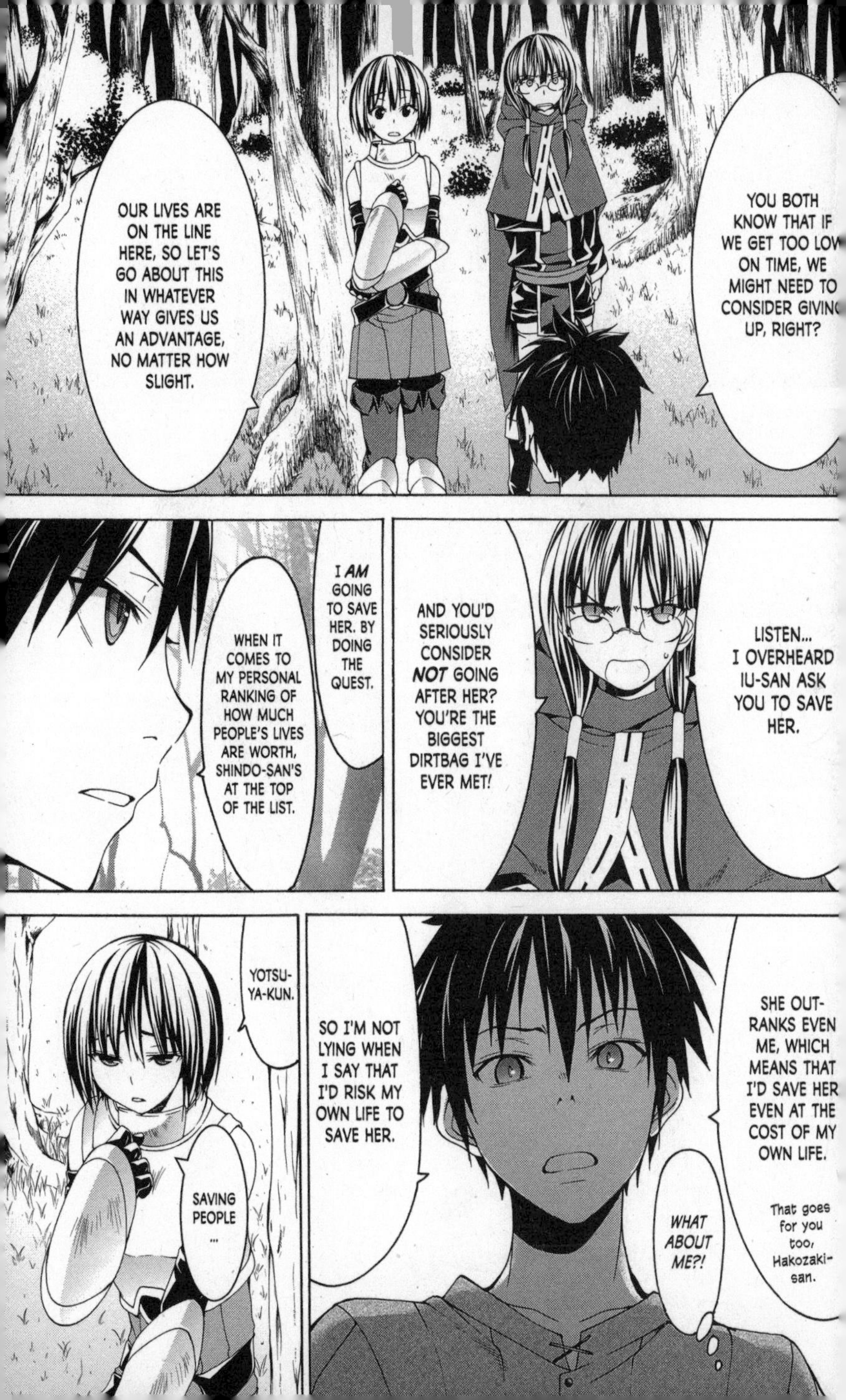
YOU BOTH KNOW THAT IF WE GET TOO LOW ON TIME, WE MIGHT NEED TO CONSIDER GIVING UP, RIGHT?
OUR LIVES ARE ON THE LINE HERE, SO LET'S GO ABOUT THIS IN WHATEVER WAY GIVES US AN ADVANTAGE, NO MATTER HOW SLIGHT.
LISTEN... I OVERHEARD IU-SAN ASK YOU TO SAVE HER.
AND YOU'D SERIOUSLY CONSIDER *NOT* GOING AFTER HER? YOU'RE THE BIGGEST DIRTBAG I'VE EVER MET!
I *AM* GOING TO SAVE HER. BY DOING THE QUEST.
WHEN IT COMES TO MY PERSONAL RANKING OF HOW MUCH PEOPLE'S LIVES ARE WORTH, SHINDO-SAN'S AT THE TOP OF THE LIST.
SHE OUT-RANKS EVEN ME, WHICH MEANS THAT I'D SAVE HER EVEN AT THE COST OF MY OWN LIFE.
That goes for you too, Hakozaki-san.
WHAT ABOUT ME?!
SO I'M NOT LYING WHEN I SAY THAT I'D RISK MY OWN LIFE TO SAVE HER.
YOTSU-YA-KUN.
SAVING PEOPLE ...

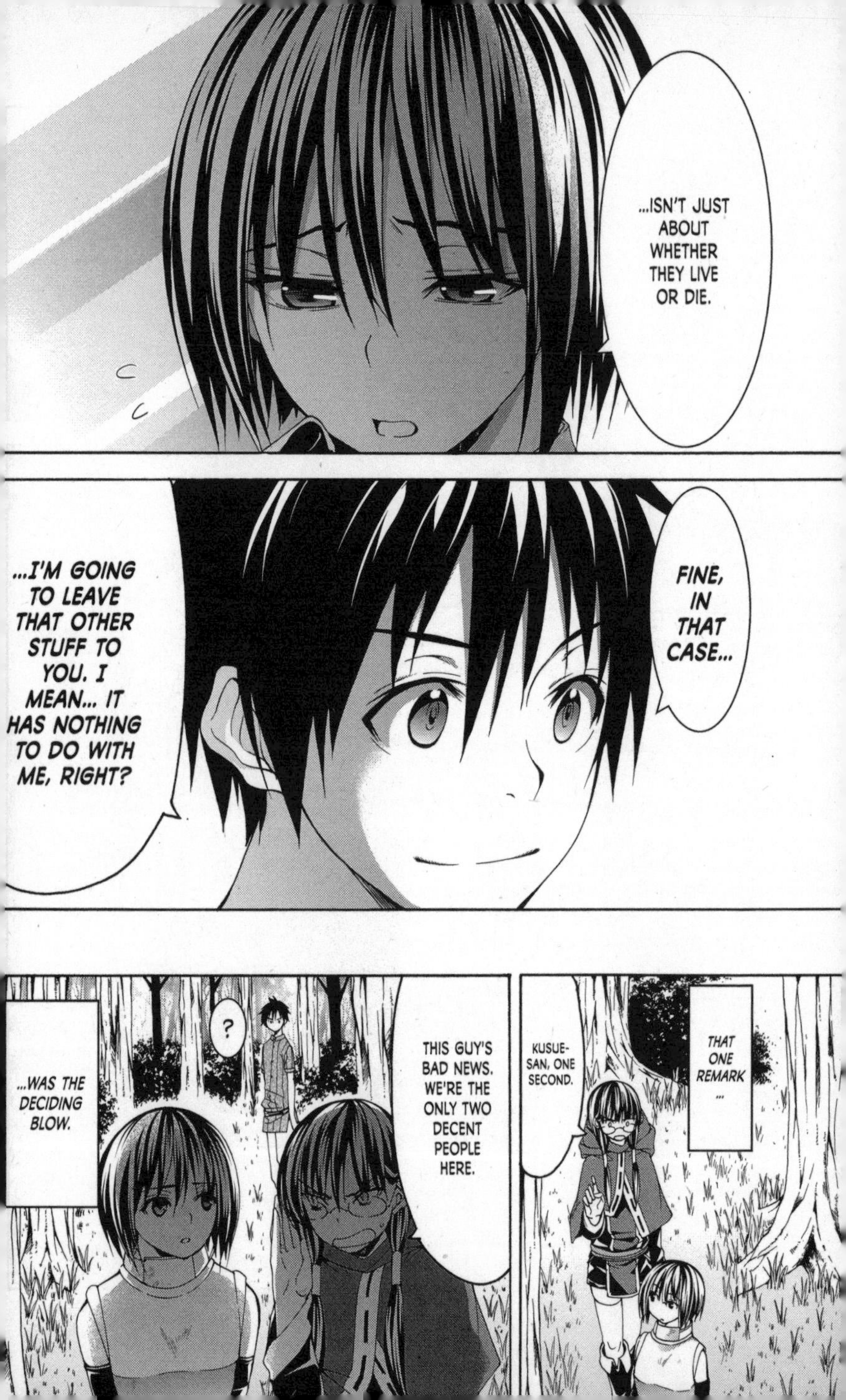
...ISN'T JUST ABOUT WHETHER THEY LIVE OR DIE.
FINE, IN THAT CASE...
...I'M GOING TO LEAVE THAT OTHER STUFF TO YOU. I MEAN... IT HAS NOTHING TO DO WITH ME, RIGHT?
THAT ONE REMARK ...
KUSUE-SAN, ONE SECOND.
THIS GUY'S BAD NEWS. WE'RE THE ONLY TWO DECENT PEOPLE HERE.
?
...WAS THE DECIDING BLOW.

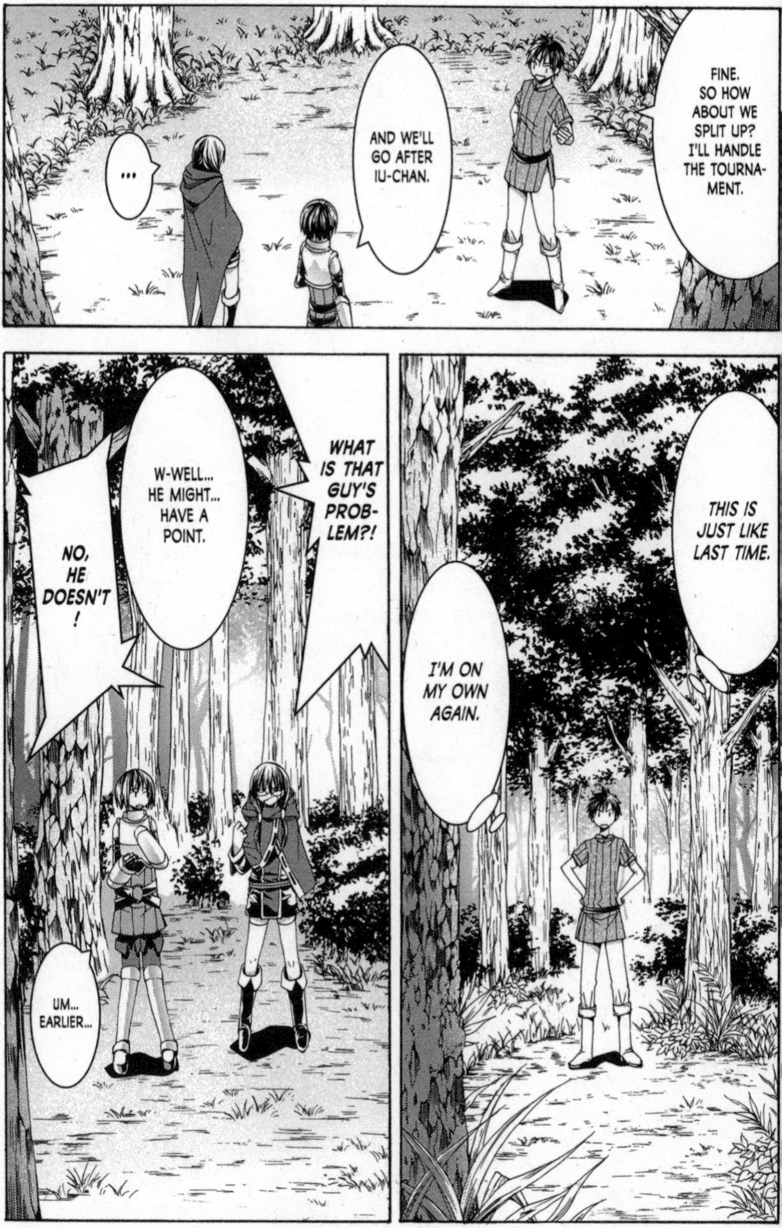
FINE. SO HOW ABOUT WE SPLIT UP? I'LL HANDLE THE TOURNAMENT.
AND WE'LL GO AFTER IU-CHAN.
...
THIS IS JUST LIKE LAST TIME.
I'M ON MY OWN AGAIN.
WHAT IS THAT GUY'S PROBLEM?!
W-WELL... HE MIGHT... HAVE A POINT.
NO, HE DOESN'T!
UM... EARLIER...

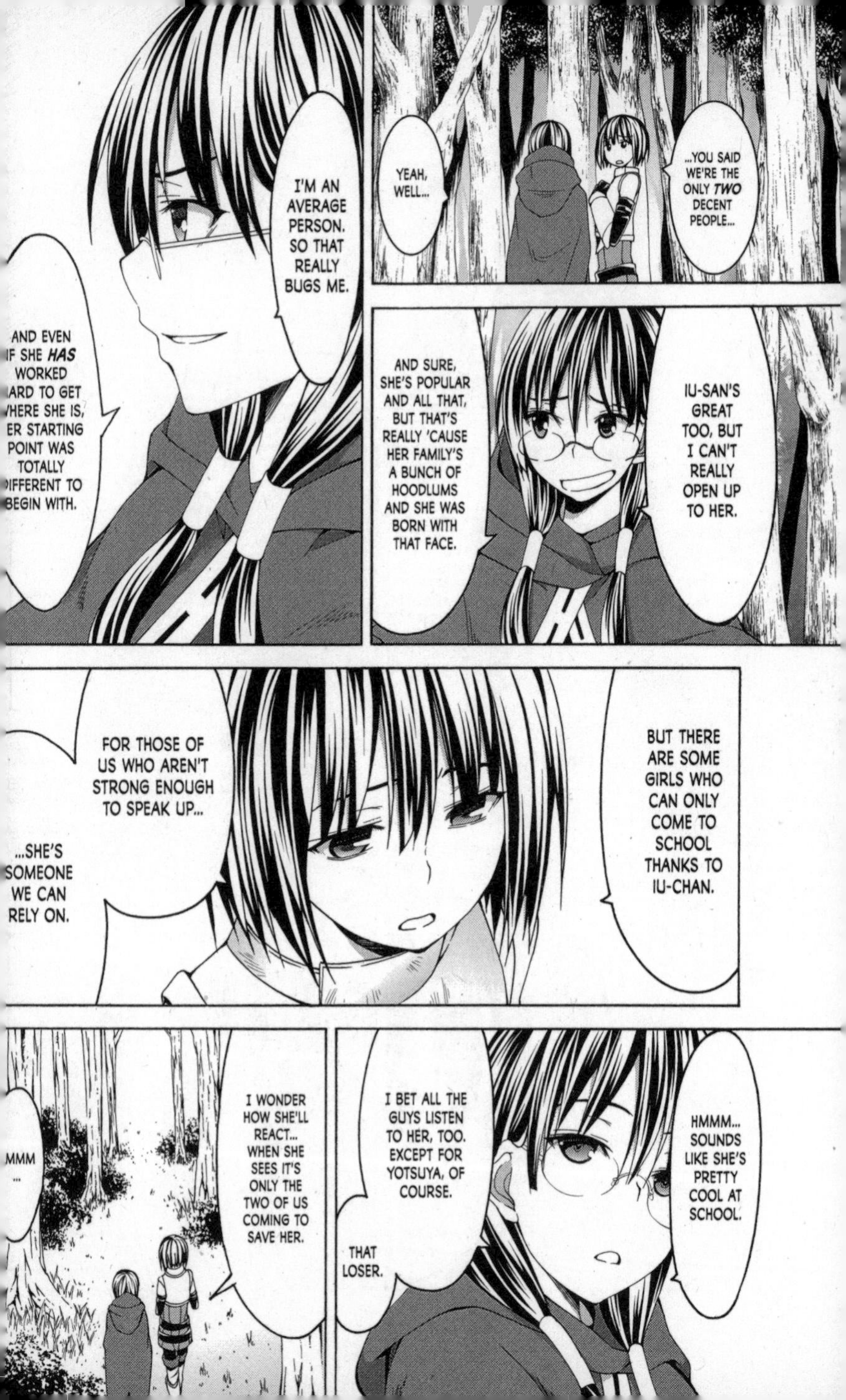
...YOU SAID WE'RE THE ONLY *TWO* DECENT PEOPLE...
YEAH, WELL...
IU-SAN'S GREAT TOO, BUT I CAN'T REALLY OPEN UP TO HER.
AND SURE, SHE'S POPULAR AND ALL THAT, BUT THAT'S REALLY 'CAUSE HER FAMILY'S A BUNCH OF HOODLUMS AND SHE WAS BORN WITH THAT FACE.
I'M AN AVERAGE PERSON. SO THAT REALLY BUGS ME.
AND EVEN IF SHE *HAS* WORKED ARD TO GET HERE SHE IS, ER STARTING POINT WAS TOTALLY IFFERENT TO BEGIN WITH.
BUT THERE ARE SOME GIRLS WHO CAN ONLY COME TO SCHOOL THANKS TO IU-CHAN.
FOR THOSE OF US WHO AREN'T STRONG ENOUGH TO SPEAK UP...
...SHE'S SOMEONE WE CAN RELY ON.
HMMM... SOUNDS LIKE SHE'S PRETTY COOL AT SCHOOL.
I BET ALL THE GUYS LISTEN TO HER, TOO. EXCEPT FOR YOTSUYA, OF COURSE.
THAT LOSER.
I WONDER HOW SHE'LL REACT... WHEN SHE SEES IT'S ONLY THE TWO OF US COMING TO SAVE HER.
MMM ...

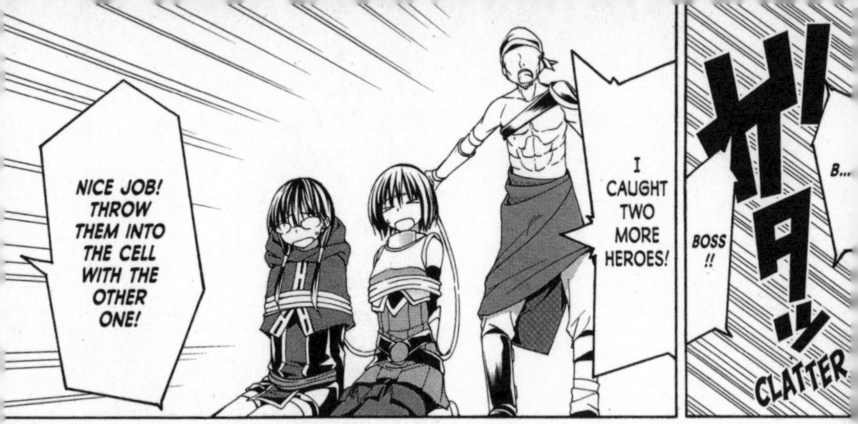
CLATTER
B...
BOSS !!
I CAUGHT TWO MORE HEROES!
NICE JOB! THROW THEM INTO THE CELL WITH THE OTHER ONE!

QUEST: REMAINING TIME: 35 DAYS AND 3 HOURS

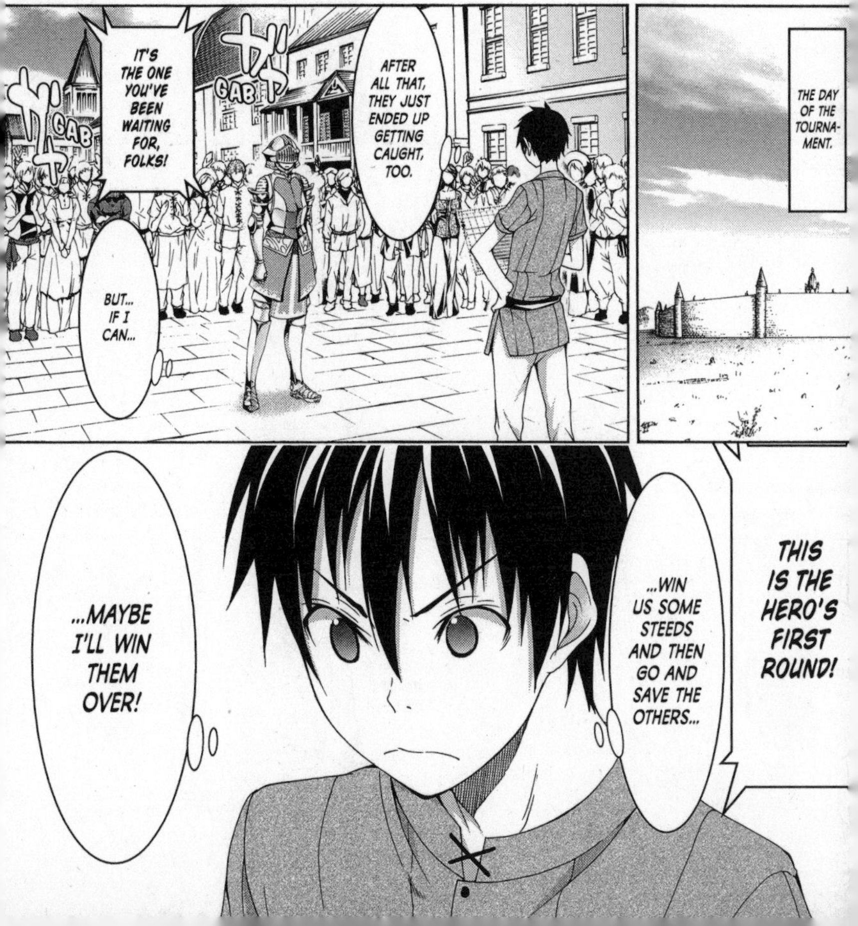
THE DAY OF THE TOURNA-MENT.
AFTER ALL THAT, THEY JUST ENDED UP GETTING CAUGHT, TOO.
IT'S THE ONE YOU'VE BEEN WAITING FOR, FOLKS!
GAB
GAB
BUT... IF I CAN...
THIS IS THE HERO'S FIRST ROUND!
...WIN US SOME STEEDS AND THEN GO AND SAVE THE OTHERS...
...MAYBE I'LL WIN THEM OVER!

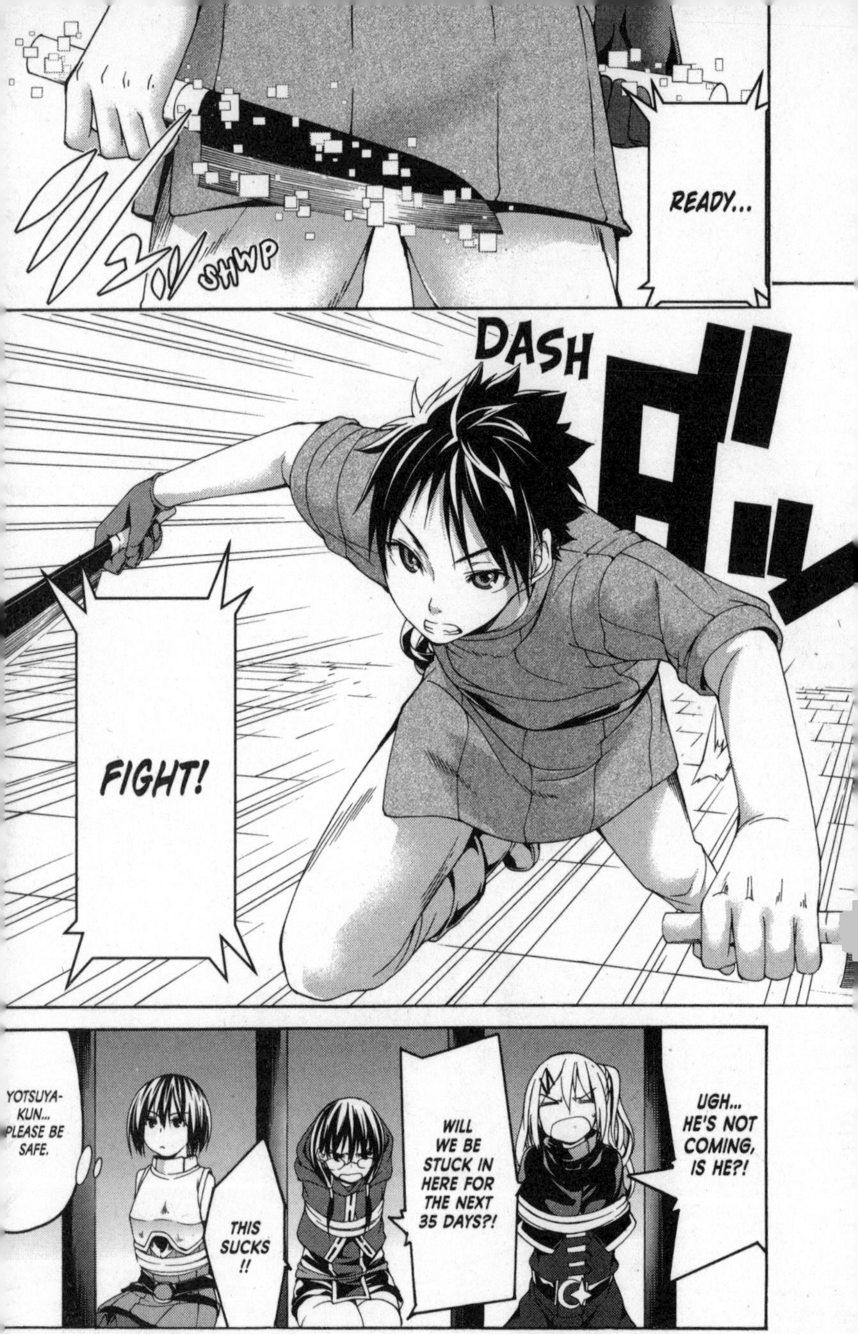
READY...
SHWP
DASH
FIGHT!
UGH... HE'S NOT COMING, IS HE?!
WILL WE BE STUCK IN HERE FOR THE NEXT 35 DAYS?!
THIS SUCKS !!
YOTSUYA-KUN... PLEASE BE SAFE.

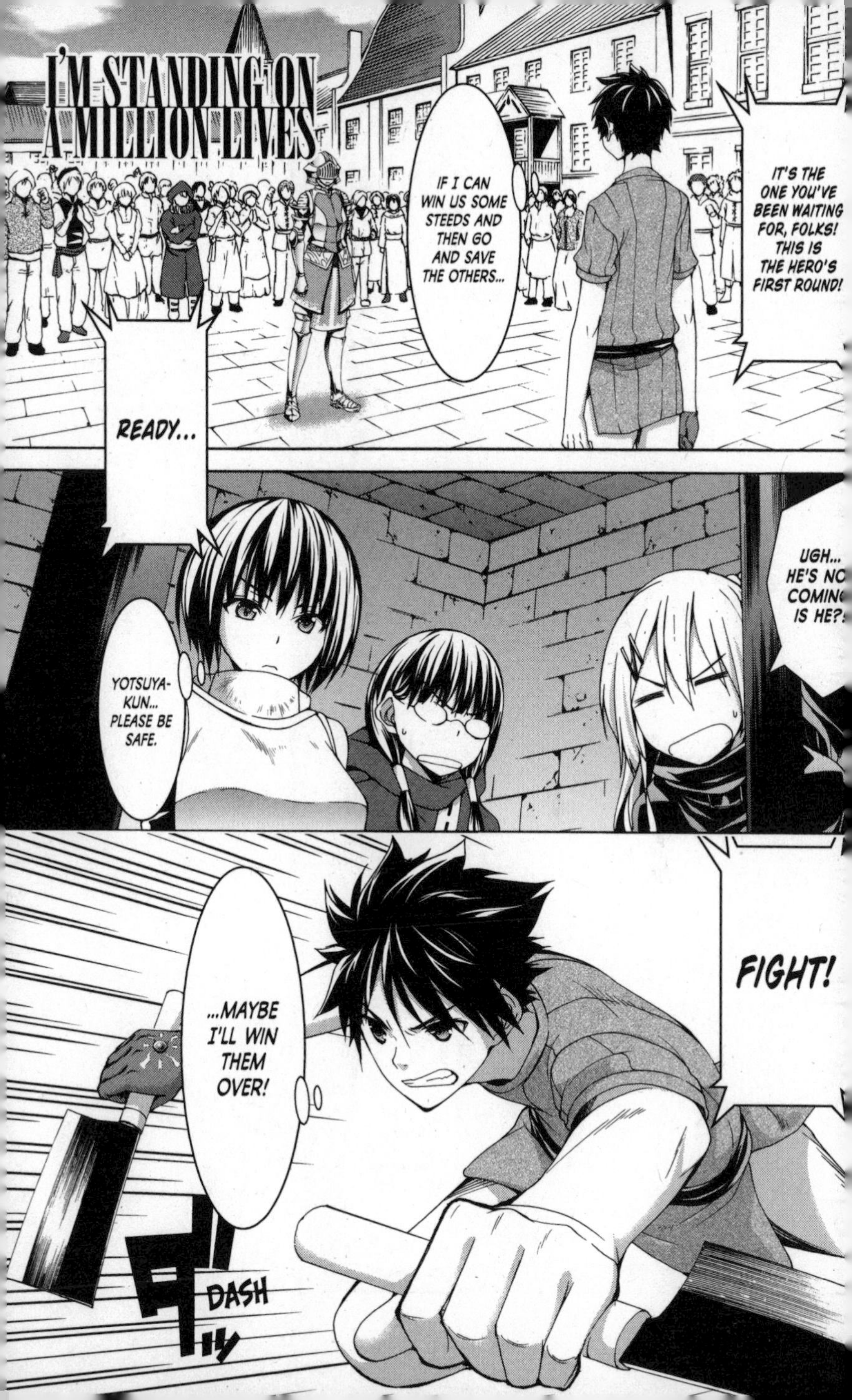
I'M STANDING ON A MILLION LIVES
IT'S THE ONE YOU'VE BEEN WAITING FOR, FOLKS! THIS IS THE HERO'S FIRST ROUND!
IF I CAN WIN US SOME STEEDS AND THEN GO AND SAVE THE OTHERS...
READY...
UGH... HE'S NO COMING IS HE?
YOTSUYA-KUN... PLEASE BE SAFE.
FIGHT!
...MAYBE I'LL WIN THEM OVER!
DASH

#4 Carver Girl & Way of the Knight

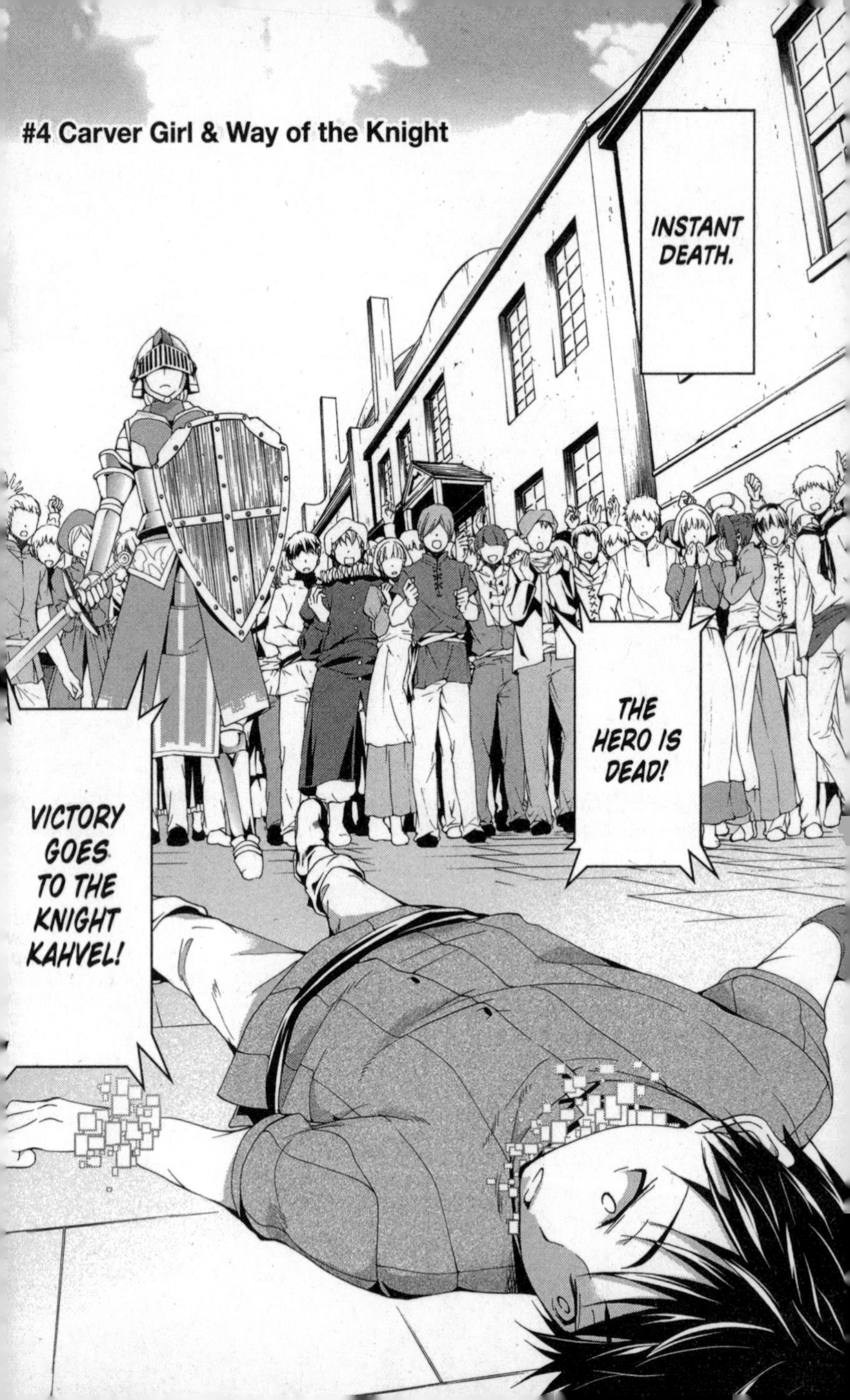
INSTANT DEATH.
THE HERO IS DEAD!
VICTORY GOES TO THE KNIGHT KAHVEL!

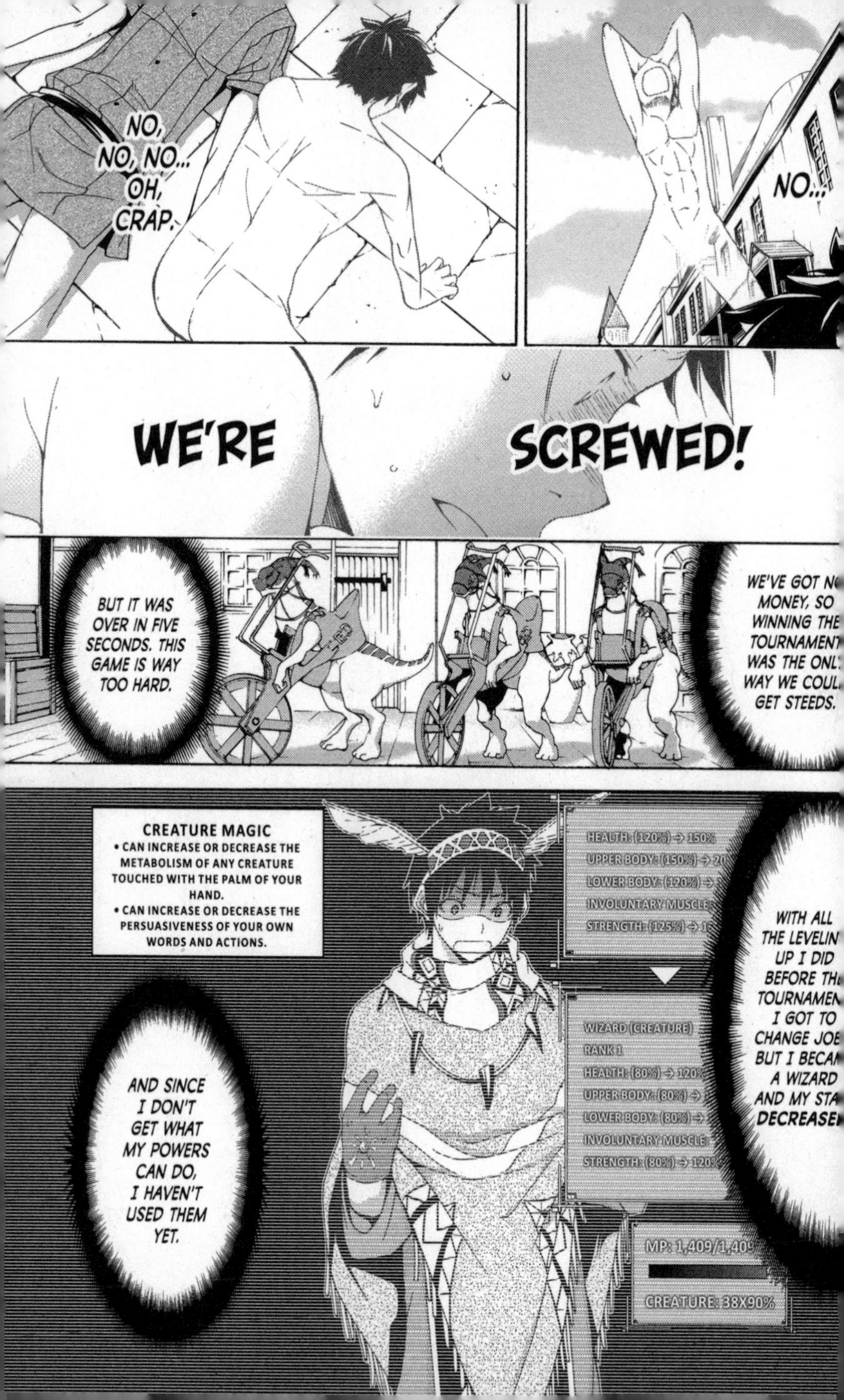
NO...
NO, NO, NO... OH, CRAP.
WE'RE SCREWED!
WE'VE GOT N MONEY, SO WINNING THE TOURNAMENT WAS THE ONL WAY WE COUL GET STEEDS.
BUT IT WAS OVER IN FIVE SECONDS. THIS GAME IS WAY TOO HARD.
WITH ALL THE LEVELIN UP I DID BEFORE TH TOURNAMEN I GOT TO CHANGE JOB BUT I BECA A WIZARD AND MY STA DECREASE
HEALTH: (120%) → 150%
UPPER BODY: (150%) → 20
LOWER BODY: (120%) →
INVOLUNTARY MUSCLE:
STRENGTH: (125%) → 1
WIZARD (CREATURE)
RANK 1
HEALTH: (80%) → 120%
UPPER BODY: (80%) →
LOWER BODY: (80%) →
INVOLUNTARY MUSCLE:
STRENGTH: (80%) → 120%
MP: 1,409/1,40
CREATURE: 38X90%
CREATURE MAGIC
• CAN INCREASE OR DECREASE THE METABOLISM OF ANY CREATURE TOUCHED WITH THE PALM OF YOUR HAND.
• CAN INCREASE OR DECREASE THE PERSUASIVENESS OF YOUR OWN WORDS AND ACTIONS.
AND SINCE I DON'T GET WHAT MY POWERS CAN DO, I HAVEN'T USED THEM YET.

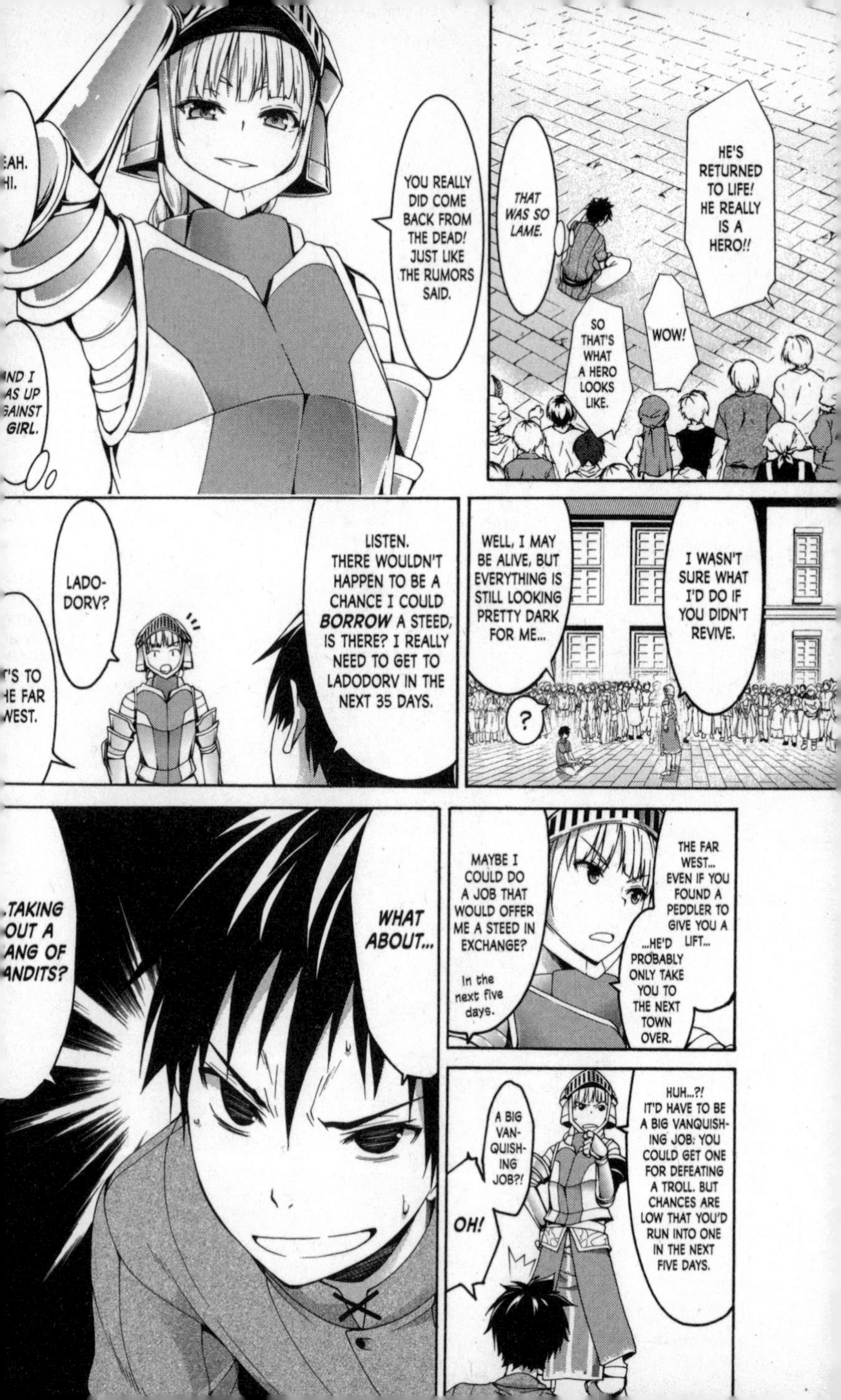

HE'S RETURNED TO LIFE! HE REALLY IS A HERO!!
WOW!
SO THAT'S WHAT A HERO LOOKS LIKE.
THAT WAS SO LAME.
YOU REALLY DID COME BACK FROM THE DEAD! JUST LIKE THE RUMORS SAID.
EAH. HI.
ND I AS UP GAINST GIRL.
I WASN'T SURE WHAT I'D DO IF YOU DIDN'T REVIVE.
WELL, I MAY BE ALIVE, BUT EVERYTHING IS STILL LOOKING PRETTY DARK FOR ME...
?
LISTEN. THERE WOULDN'T HAPPEN TO BE A CHANCE I COULD *BORROW* A STEED, IS THERE? I REALLY NEED TO GET TO LADODORV IN THE NEXT 35 DAYS.
LADO-DORV?
'S TO HE FAR WEST.
THE FAR WEST... EVEN IF YOU FOUND A PEDDLER TO GIVE YOU A LIFT... ...HE'D PROBABLY ONLY TAKE YOU TO THE NEXT TOWN OVER.
MAYBE I COULD DO A JOB THAT WOULD OFFER ME A STEED IN EXCHANGE?
In the next five days.
HUH...?! IT'D HAVE TO BE A BIG VANQUISHING JOB. YOU COULD GET ONE FOR DEFEATING A TROLL. BUT CHANCES ARE LOW THAT YOU'D RUN INTO ONE IN THE NEXT FIVE DAYS.
A BIG VAN-QUISH-ING JOB?!
OH!
WHAT ABOUT...
.TAKING OUT A ANG OF ANDITS?

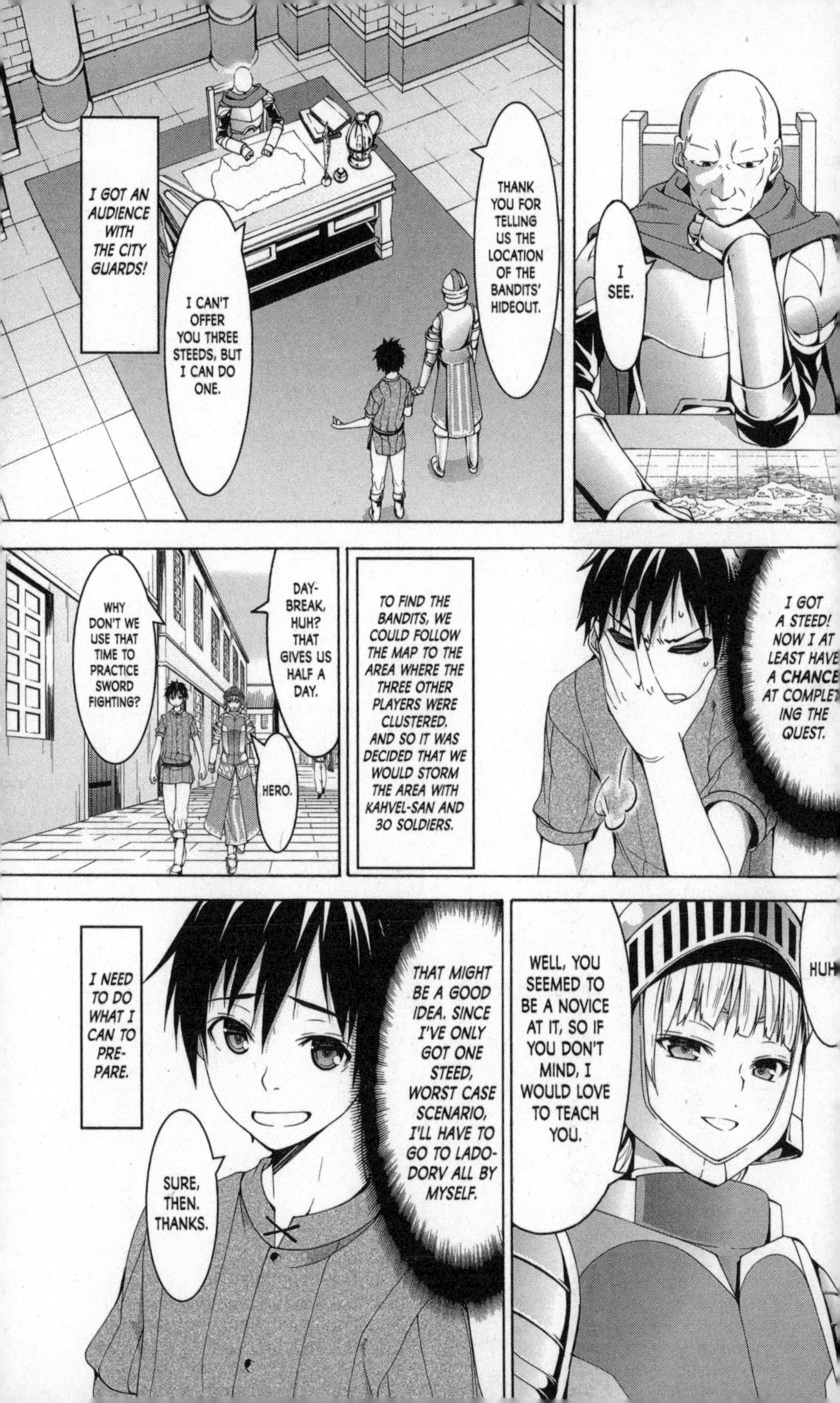
I SEE.
THANK YOU FOR TELLING US THE LOCATION OF THE BANDITS' HIDEOUT.
I CAN'T OFFER YOU THREE STEEDS, BUT I CAN DO ONE.
I GOT AN AUDIENCE WITH THE CITY GUARDS!
I GOT A STEED! NOW I AT LEAST HAVE A CHANCE AT COMPLET ING THE QUEST.
TO FIND THE BANDITS, WE COULD FOLLOW THE MAP TO THE AREA WHERE THE THREE OTHER PLAYERS WERE CLUSTERED. AND SO IT WAS DECIDED THAT WE WOULD STORM THE AREA WITH KAHVEL-SAN AND 30 SOLDIERS.
DAY-BREAK, HUH? THAT GIVES US HALF A DAY.
HERO.
WHY DON'T WE USE THAT TIME TO PRACTICE SWORD FIGHTING?
HUH
WELL, YOU SEEMED TO BE A NOVICE AT IT, SO IF YOU DON'T MIND, I WOULD LOVE TO TEACH YOU.
THAT MIGHT BE A GOOD IDEA. SINCE I'VE ONLY GOT ONE STEED, WORST CASE SCENARIO, I'LL HAVE TO GO TO LADO-DORV ALL BY MYSELF.
I NEED TO DO WHAT I CAN TO PRE-PARE.
SURE, THEN. THANKS.

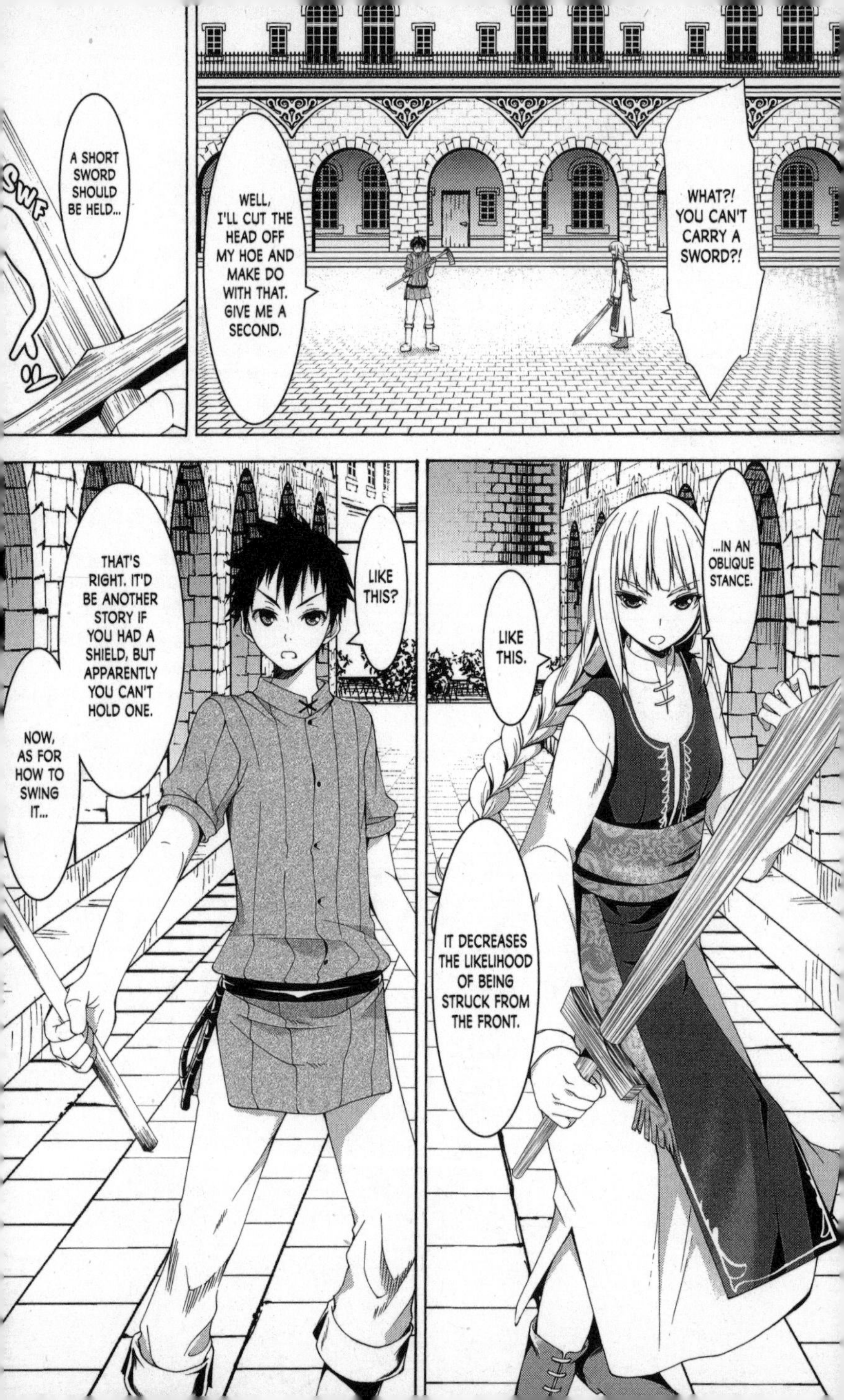
WHAT?! YOU CAN'T CARRY A SWORD?!
WELL, I'LL CUT THE HEAD OFF MY HOE AND MAKE DO WITH THAT. GIVE ME A SECOND.
SWF
A SHORT SWORD SHOULD BE HELD...
...IN AN OBLIQUE STANCE.
LIKE THIS.
IT DECREASES THE LIKELIHOOD OF BEING STRUCK FROM THE FRONT.
LIKE THIS?
THAT'S RIGHT. IT'D BE ANOTHER STORY IF YOU HAD A SHIELD, BUT APPARENTLY YOU CAN'T HOLD ONE.
NOW, AS FOR HOW TO SWING IT...

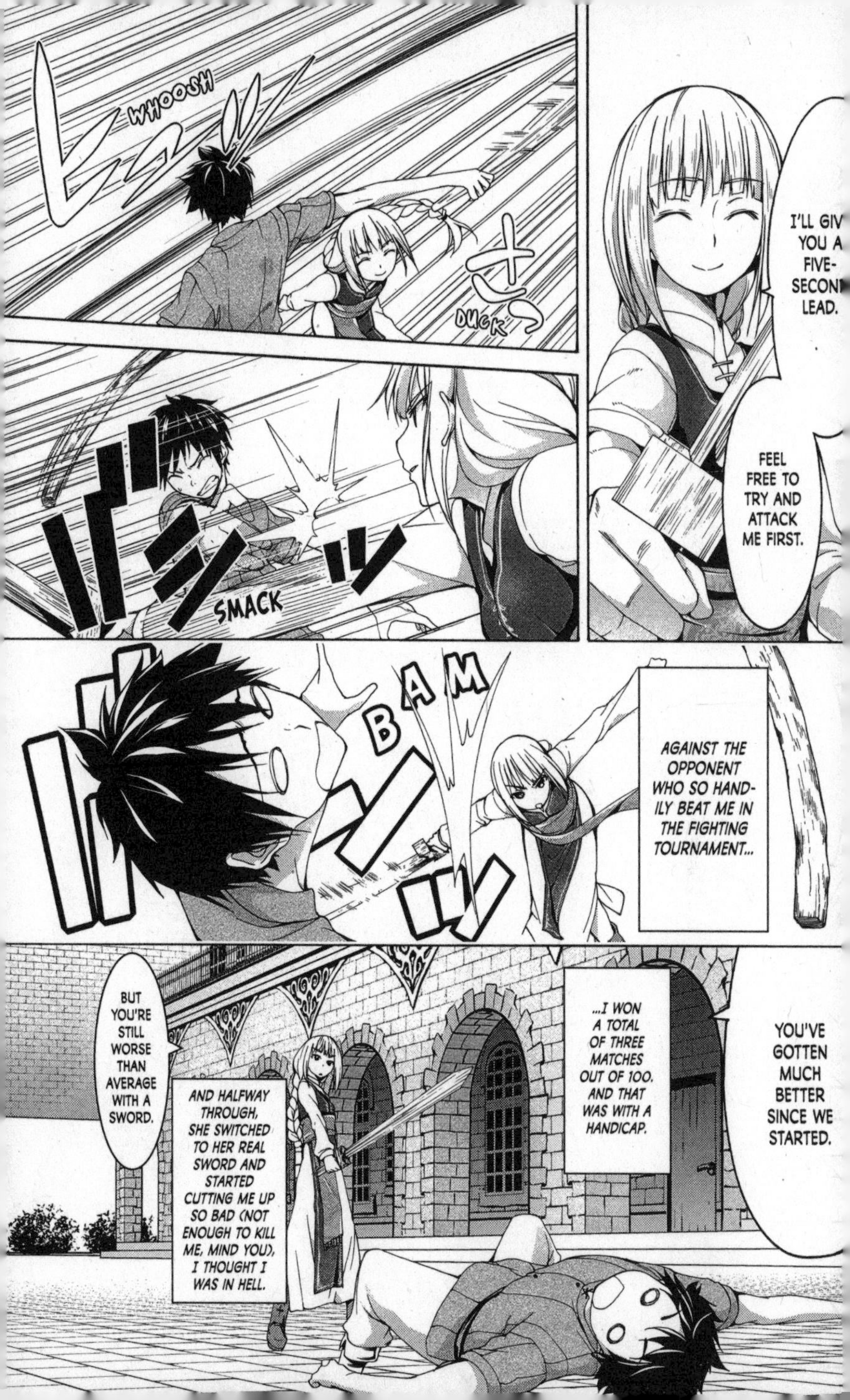
I'LL GIV YOU A FIVE-SECON LEAD.
FEEL FREE TO TRY AND ATTACK ME FIRST.
WHOOSH
DUCK
SMACK
AGAINST THE OPPONENT WHO SO HANDILY BEAT ME IN THE FIGHTING TOURNAMENT...
BAM
YOU'VE GOTTEN MUCH BETTER SINCE WE STARTED.
...I WON A TOTAL OF THREE MATCHES OUT OF 100. AND THAT WAS WITH A HANDICAP.
BUT YOU'RE STILL WORSE THAN AVERAGE WITH A SWORD.
AND HALFWAY THROUGH, SHE SWITCHED TO HER REAL SWORD AND STARTED CUTTING ME UP SO BAD (NOT ENOUGH TO KILL ME, MIND YOU), I THOUGHT I WAS IN HELL.

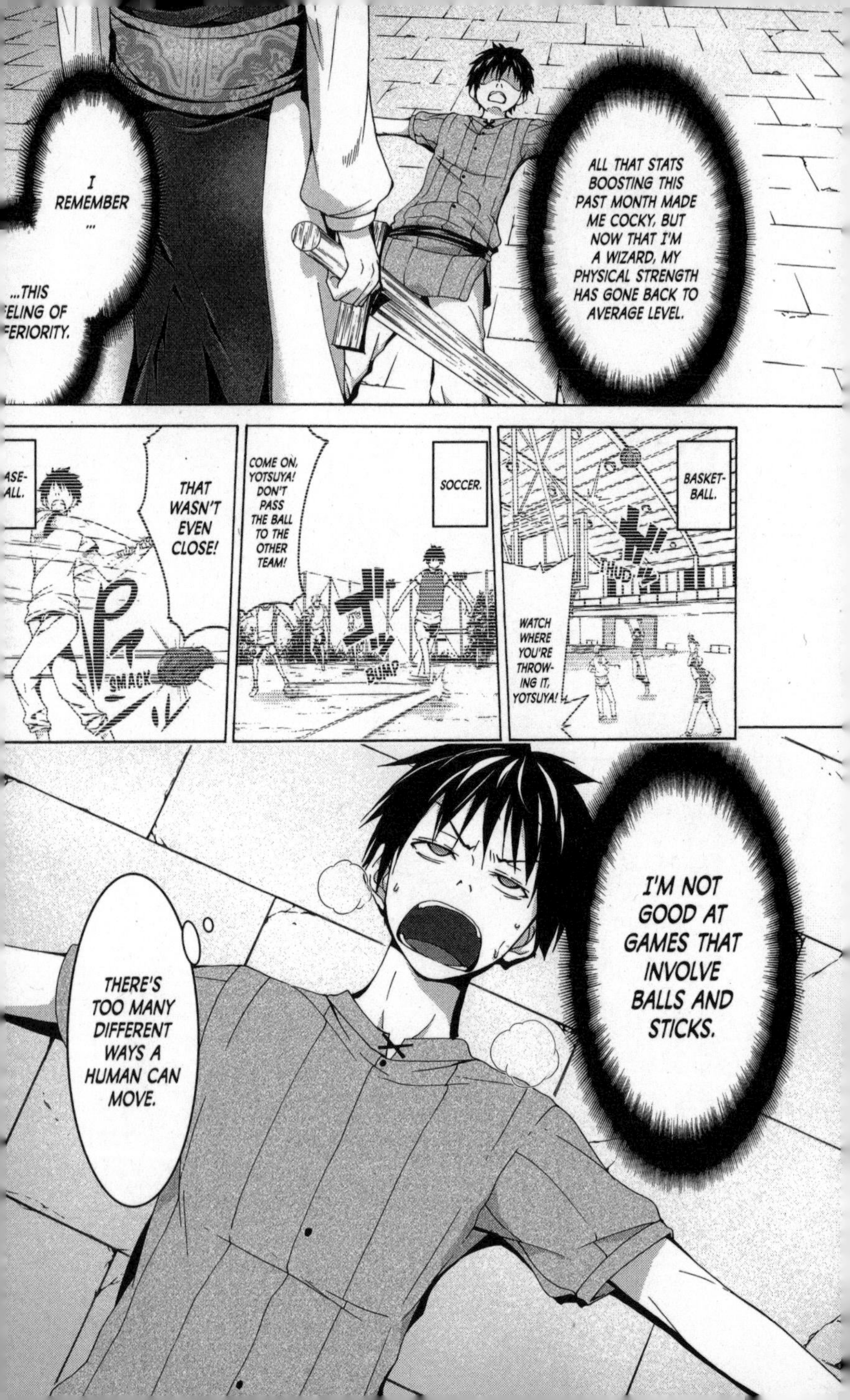
ALL THAT STATS BOOSTING THIS PAST MONTH MADE ME COCKY, BUT NOW THAT I'M A WIZARD, MY PHYSICAL STRENGTH HAS GONE BACK TO AVERAGE LEVEL.
I REMEMBER ...
...THIS ELING OF FERIORITY.
BASKET-BALL.
THUD
WATCH WHERE YOU'RE THROWING IT, YOTSUYA!
SOCCER.
COME ON, YOTSUYA! DON'T PASS THE BALL TO THE OTHER TEAM!
BUMP
ASE-ALL.
THAT WASN'T EVEN CLOSE!
SMACK
I'M NOT GOOD AT GAMES THAT INVOLVE BALLS AND STICKS.
THERE'S TOO MANY DIFFERENT WAYS A HUMAN CAN MOVE.

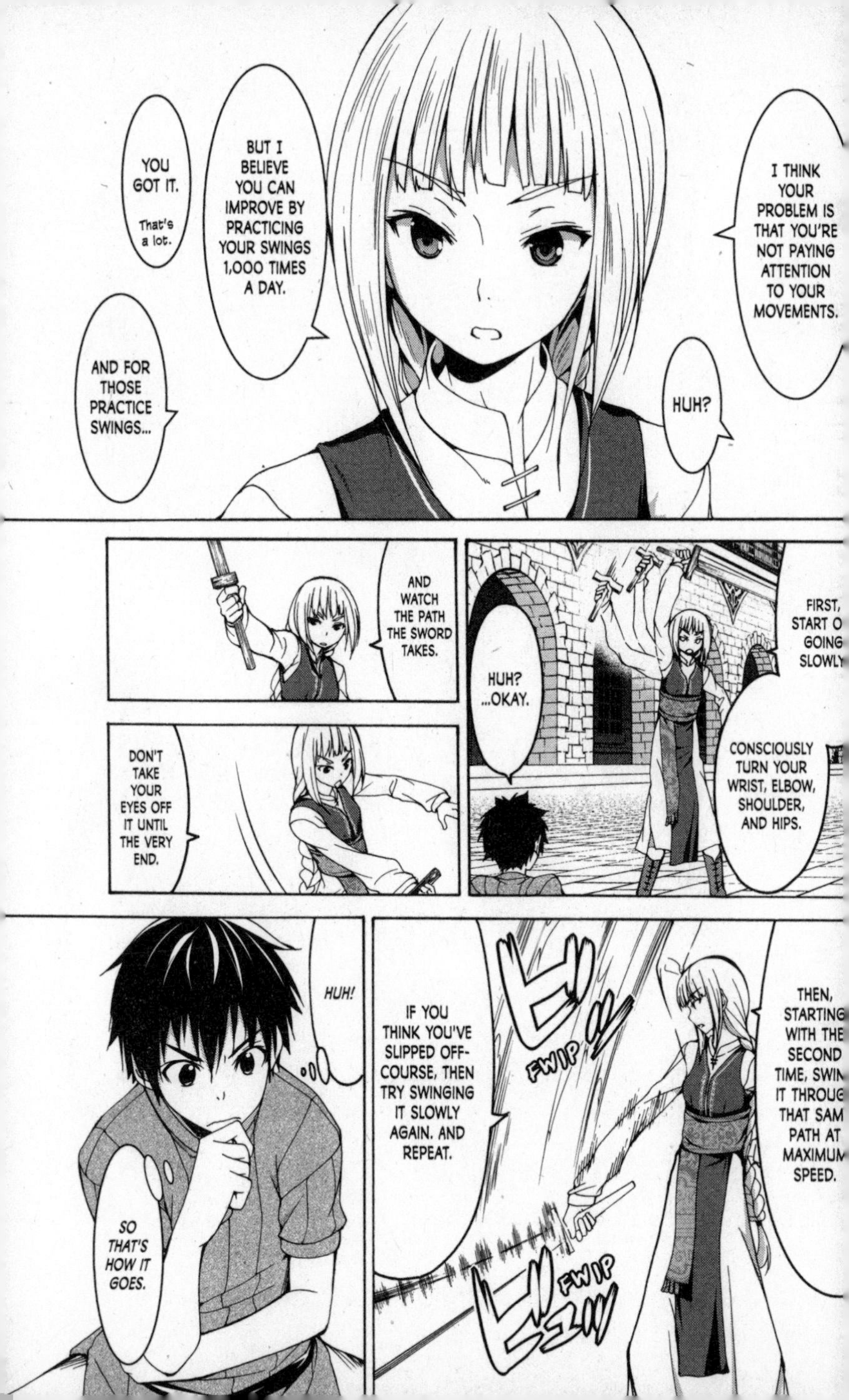

I THINK YOUR PROBLEM IS THAT YOU'RE NOT PAYING ATTENTION TO YOUR MOVEMENTS.
HUH?
BUT I BELIEVE YOU CAN IMPROVE BY PRACTICING YOUR SWINGS 1,000 TIMES A DAY.
YOU GOT IT.
That's a lot.
AND FOR THOSE PRACTICE SWINGS...
FIRST, START O GOING SLOWLY
CONSCIOUSLY TURN YOUR WRIST, ELBOW, SHOULDER, AND HIPS.
HUH? ...OKAY.
AND WATCH THE PATH THE SWORD TAKES.
DON'T TAKE YOUR EYES OFF IT UNTIL THE VERY END.
THEN, STARTING WITH THE SECOND TIME, SWIN IT THROUG THAT SAM PATH AT MAXIMUM SPEED.
FWIP
FWIP
IF YOU THINK YOU'VE SLIPPED OFF-COURSE, THEN TRY SWINGING IT SLOWLY AGAIN. AND REPEAT.
HUH!
SO THAT'S HOW IT GOES.

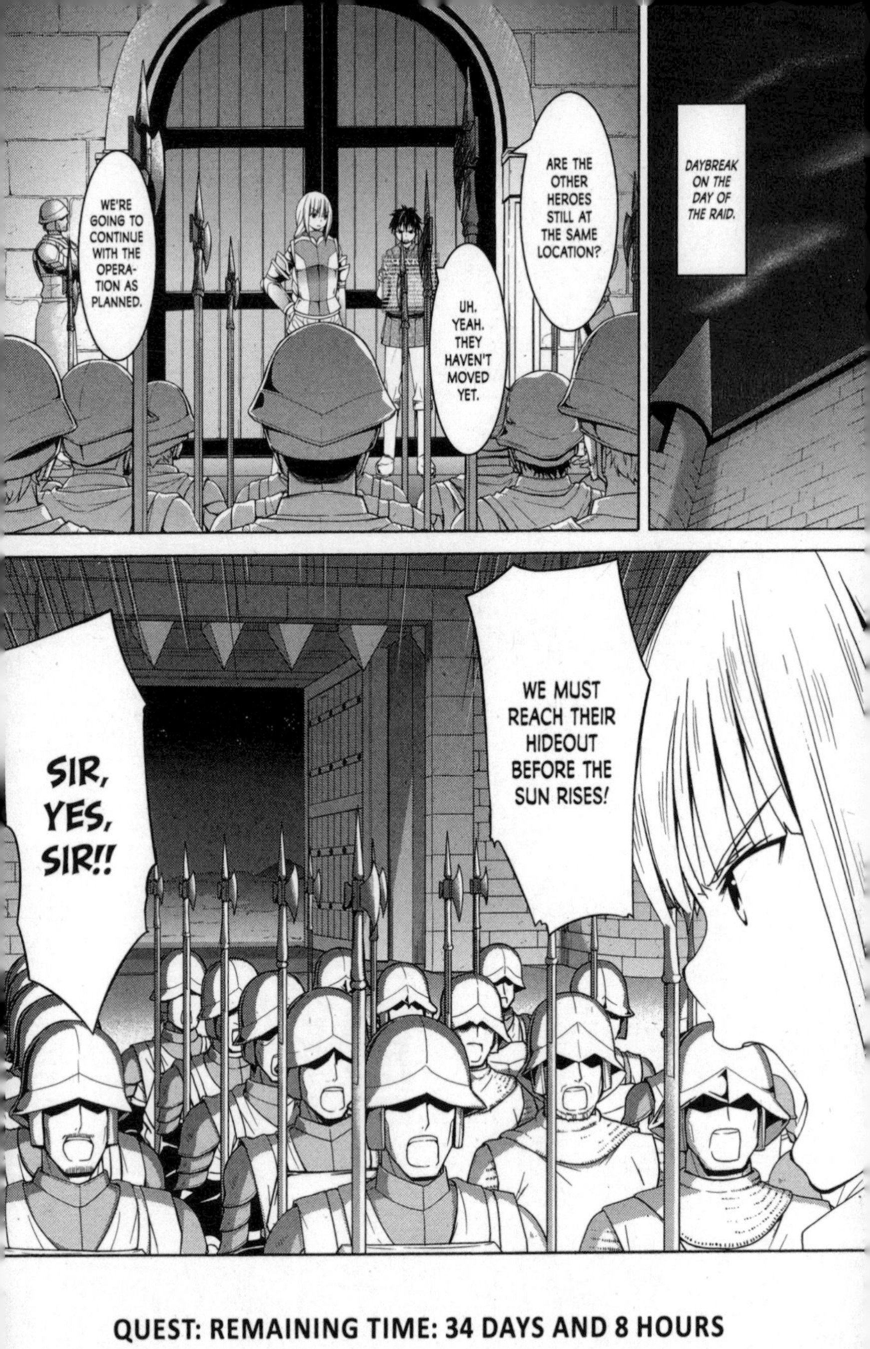
DAYBREAK ON THE DAY OF THE RAID.
ARE THE OTHER HEROES STILL AT THE SAME LOCATION?
UH. YEAH. THEY HAVEN'T MOVED YET.
WE'RE GOING TO CONTINUE WITH THE OPERA-TION AS PLANNED.
WE MUST REACH THEIR HIDEOUT BEFORE THE SUN RISES!
SIR, YES, SIR!!

QUEST: REMAINING TIME: 34 DAYS AND 8 HOURS

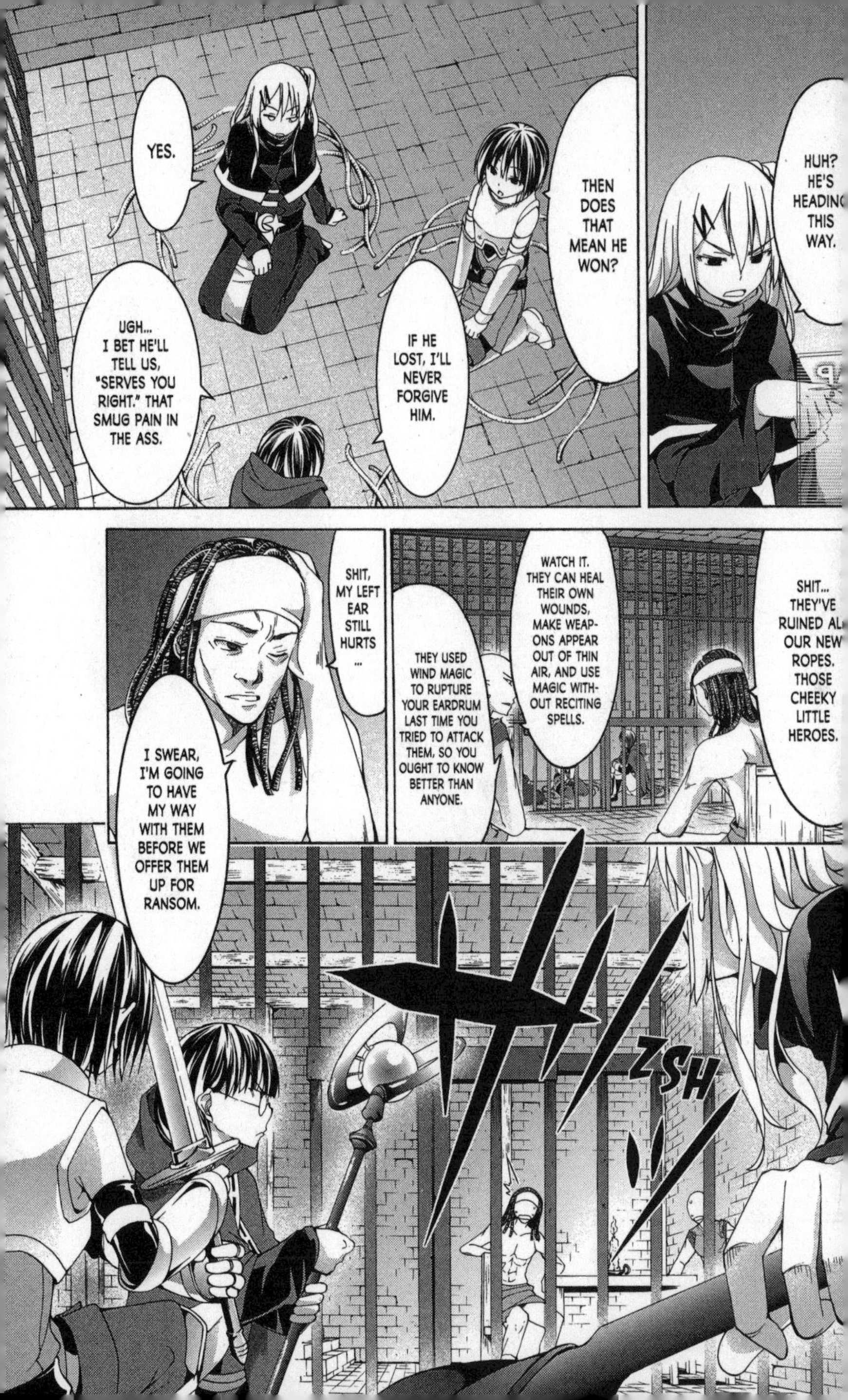
HUH? HE'S HEADIN THIS WAY.
THEN DOES THAT MEAN HE WON?
YES.
IF HE LOST, I'LL NEVER FORGIVE HIM.
UGH... I BET HE'LL TELL US, "SERVES YOU RIGHT." THAT SMUG PAIN IN THE ASS.
SHIT... THEY'VE RUINED AL OUR NEW ROPES. THOSE CHEEKY LITTLE HEROES.
WATCH IT. THEY CAN HEAL THEIR OWN WOUNDS, MAKE WEAP-ONS APPEAR OUT OF THIN AIR, AND USE MAGIC WITH-OUT RECITING SPELLS.
THEY USED WIND MAGIC TO RUPTURE YOUR EARDRUM LAST TIME YOU TRIED TO ATTACK THEM, SO YOU OUGHT TO KNOW BETTER THAN ANYONE.
SHIT, MY LEFT EAR STILL HURTS ...
I SWEAR, I'M GOING TO HAVE MY WAY WITH THEM BEFORE WE OFFER THEM UP FOR RANSOM.
ZSH

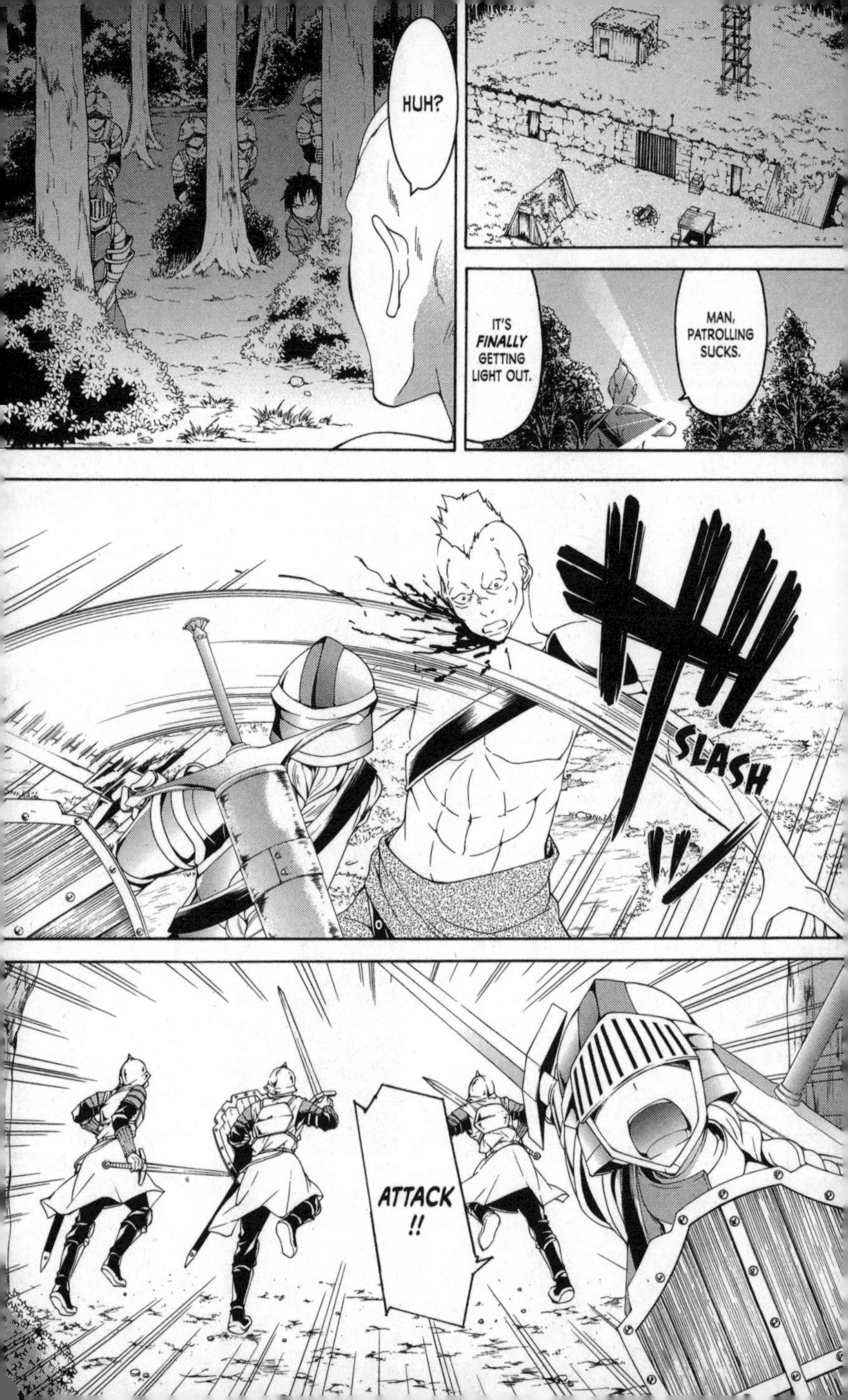
MAN, PATROLLING SUCKS.
IT'S *FINALLY* GETTING LIGHT OUT.
HUH?
SLASH
ATTACK!!

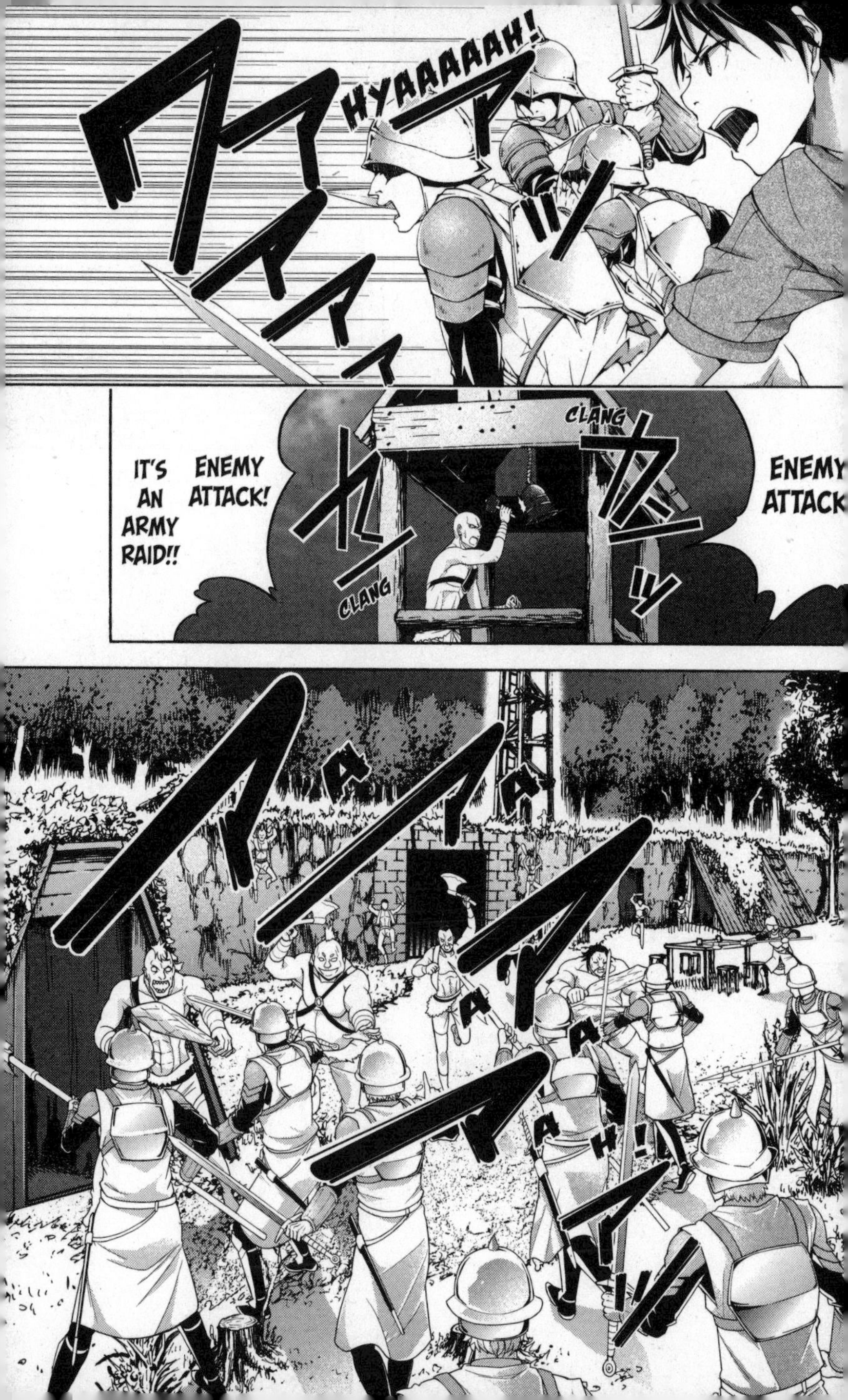
HYAAAAAH!
CLANG
ENEMY ATTACK
CLANG
ENEMY ATTACK!
IT'S AN ARMY RAID!!
AAAAAH!

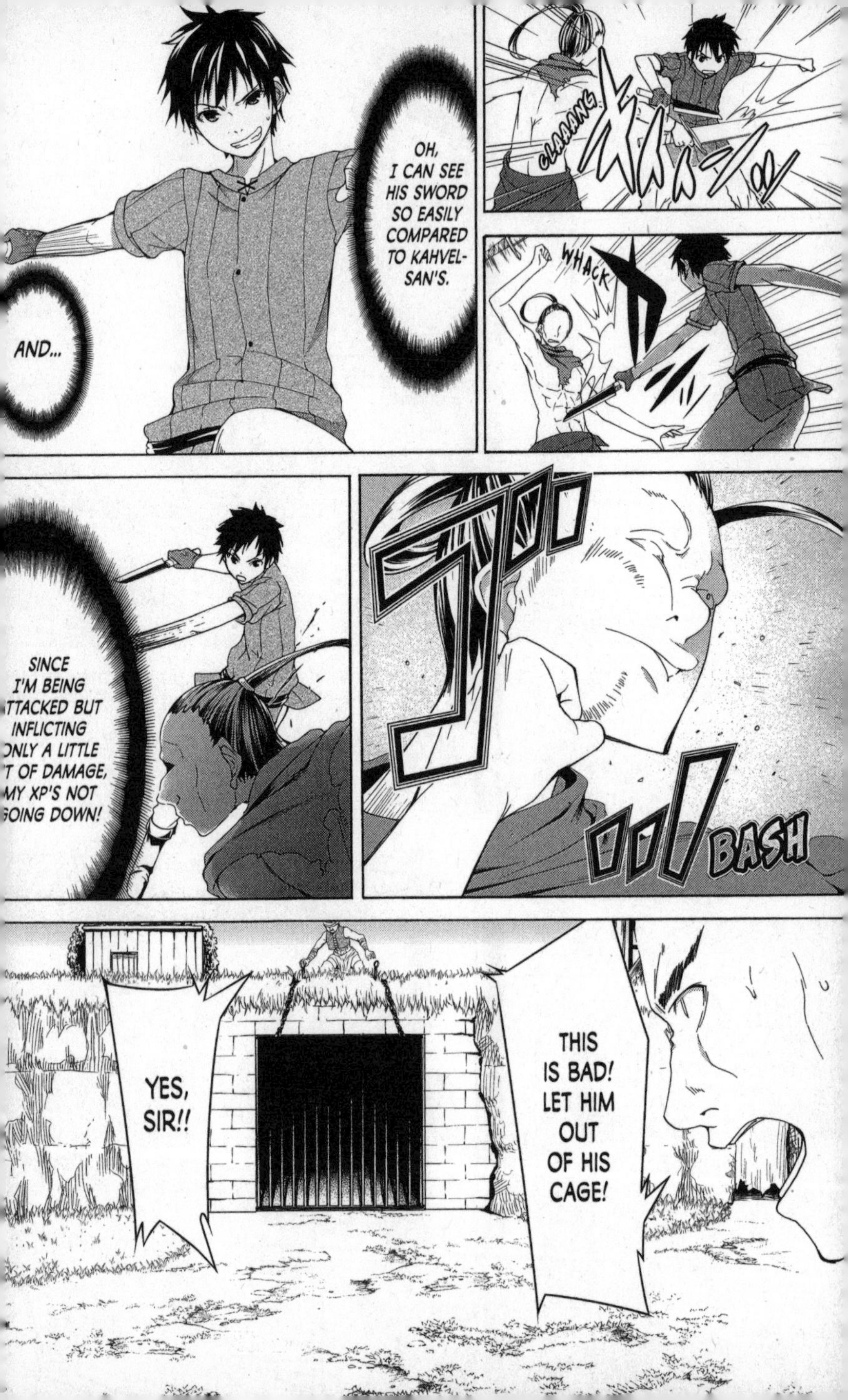
CLAAANG
WHACK
OH, I CAN SEE HIS SWORD SO EASILY COMPARED TO KAHVEL-SAN'S.
AND...
BASH
SINCE I'M BEING TTACKED BUT INFLICTING ONLY A LITTLE T OF DAMAGE, MY XP'S NOT GOING DOWN!
THIS IS BAD! LET HIM OUT OF HIS CAGE!
YES, SIR!!

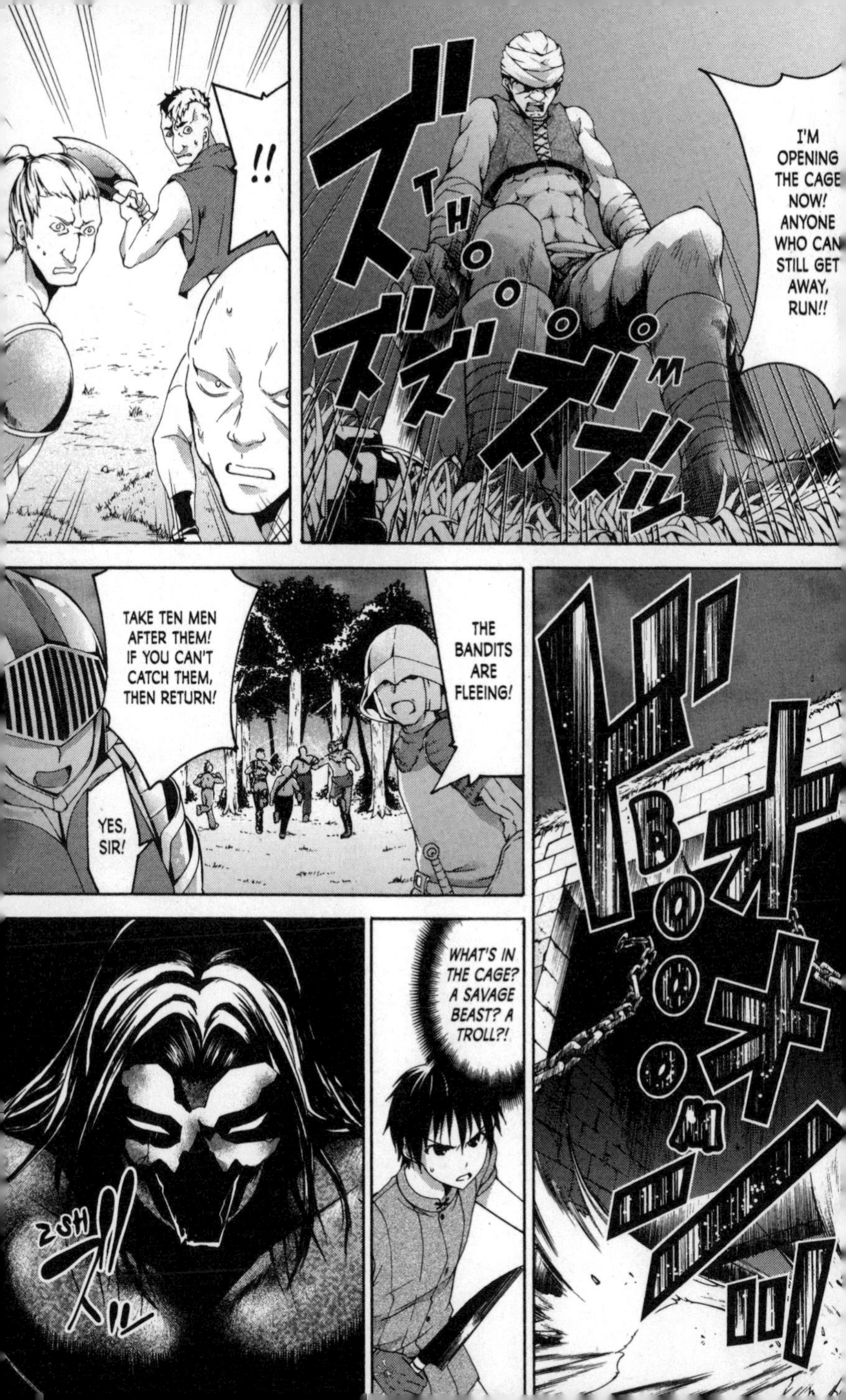
THOOOOM
I'M OPENING THE CAGE NOW! ANYONE WHO CAN STILL GET AWAY, RUN!!
!!
BOOOOM
THE BANDITS ARE FLEEING!
TAKE TEN MEN AFTER THEM! IF YOU CAN'T CATCH THEM, THEN RETURN!
YES, SIR!
WHAT'S IN THE CAGE? A SAVAGE BEAST? A TROLL?!
ZSH

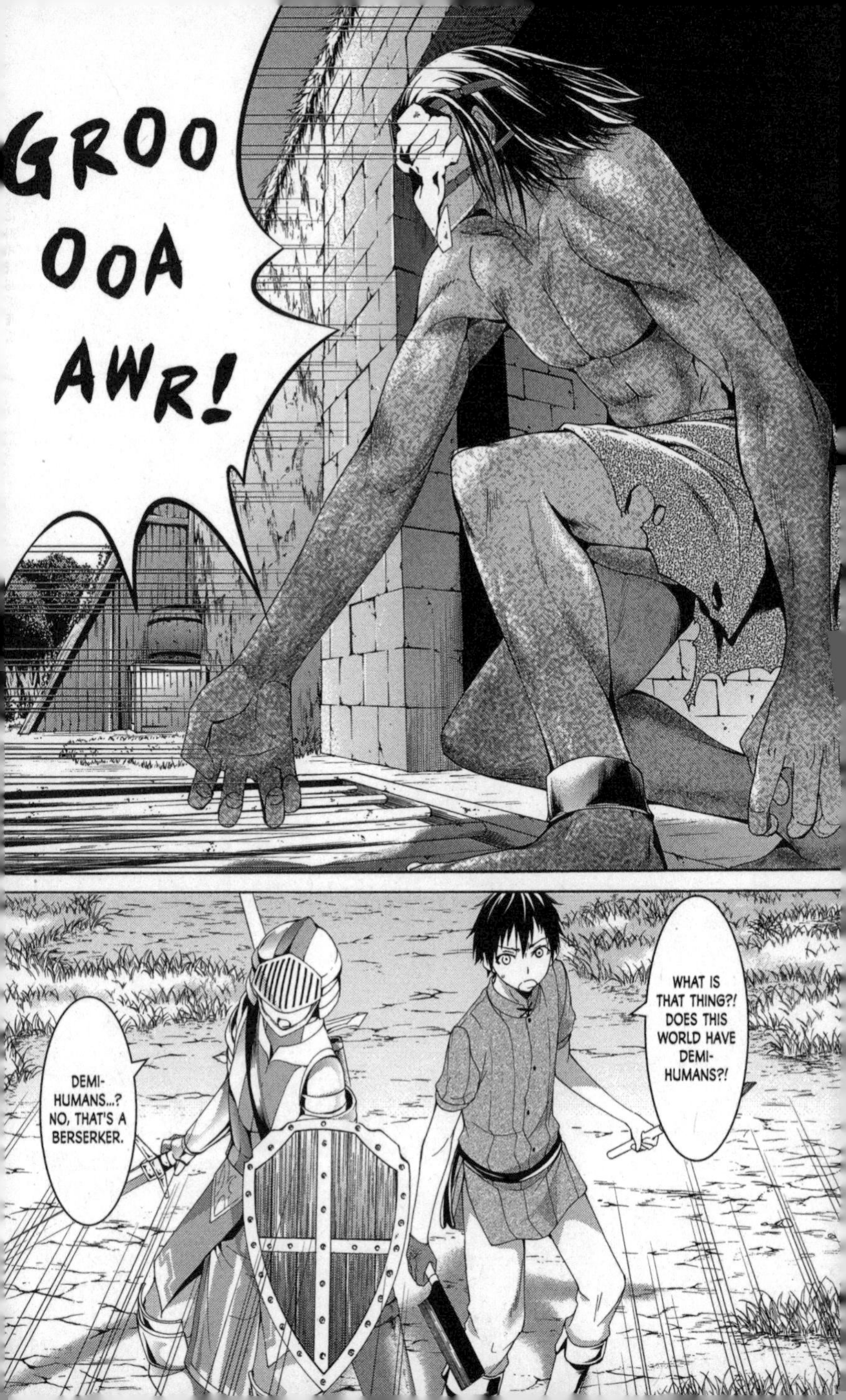
GROOOOAAWR!
WHAT IS THAT THING?! DOES THIS WORLD HAVE DEMI-HUMANS?!
DEMI-HUMANS...? NO, THAT'S A BERSERKER.

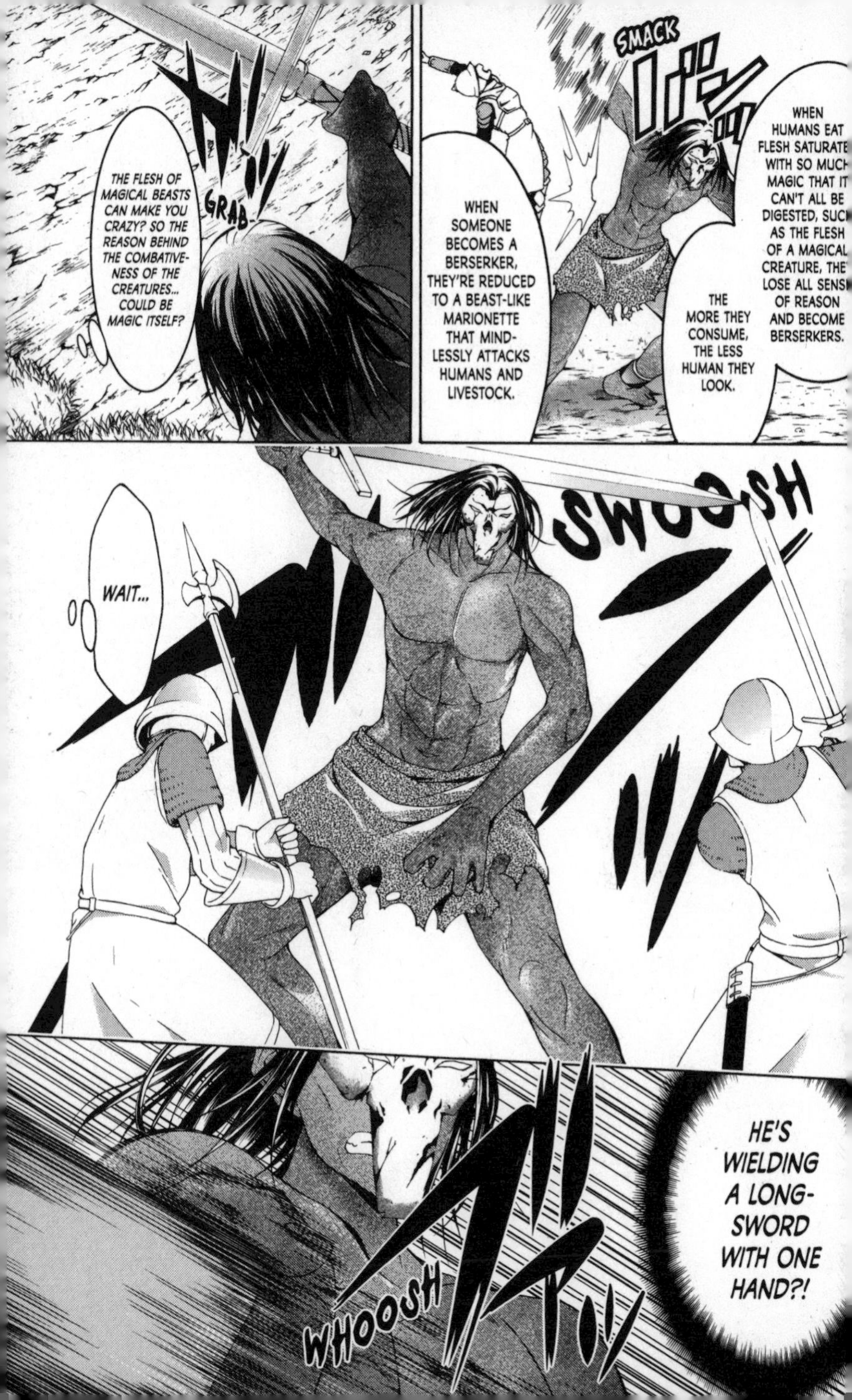
SMACK
WHEN HUMANS EAT FLESH SATURATE WITH SO MUCH MAGIC THAT IT CAN'T ALL BE DIGESTED, SUC AS THE FLESH OF A MAGICAL CREATURE, THE LOSE ALL SENS OF REASON AND BECOME BERSERKERS.
THE MORE THEY CONSUME, THE LESS HUMAN THEY LOOK.
WHEN SOMEONE BECOMES A BERSERKER, THEY'RE REDUCED TO A BEAST-LIKE MARIONETTE THAT MIND-LESSLY ATTACKS HUMANS AND LIVESTOCK.
GRAB
THE FLESH OF MAGICAL BEASTS CAN MAKE YOU CRAZY? SO THE REASON BEHIND THE COMBATIVE-NESS OF THE CREATURES... COULD BE MAGIC ITSELF?
SWOOSH
WAIT...
HE'S WIELDING A LONG-SWORD WITH ONE HAND?!
WHOOSH

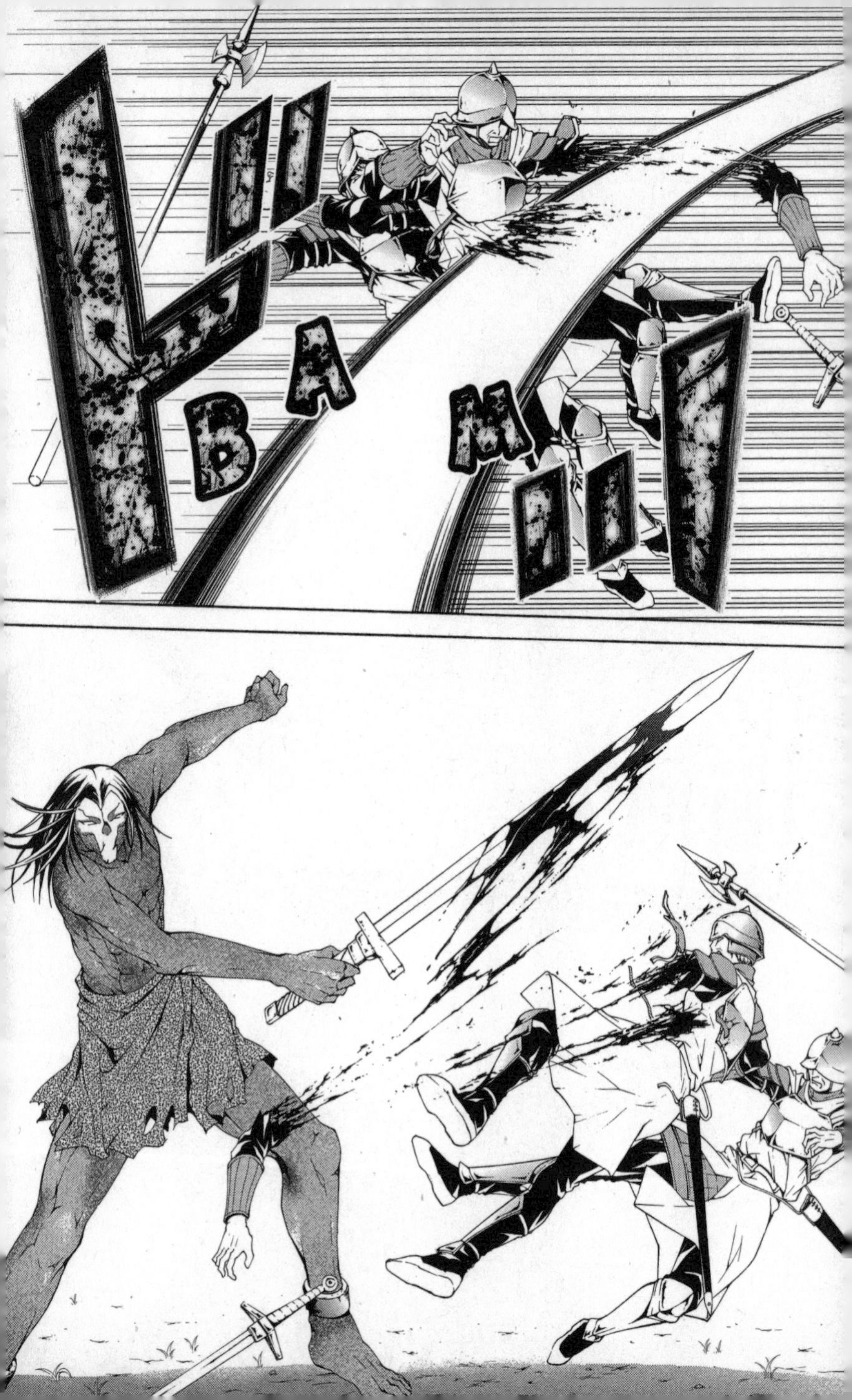
BAM!!

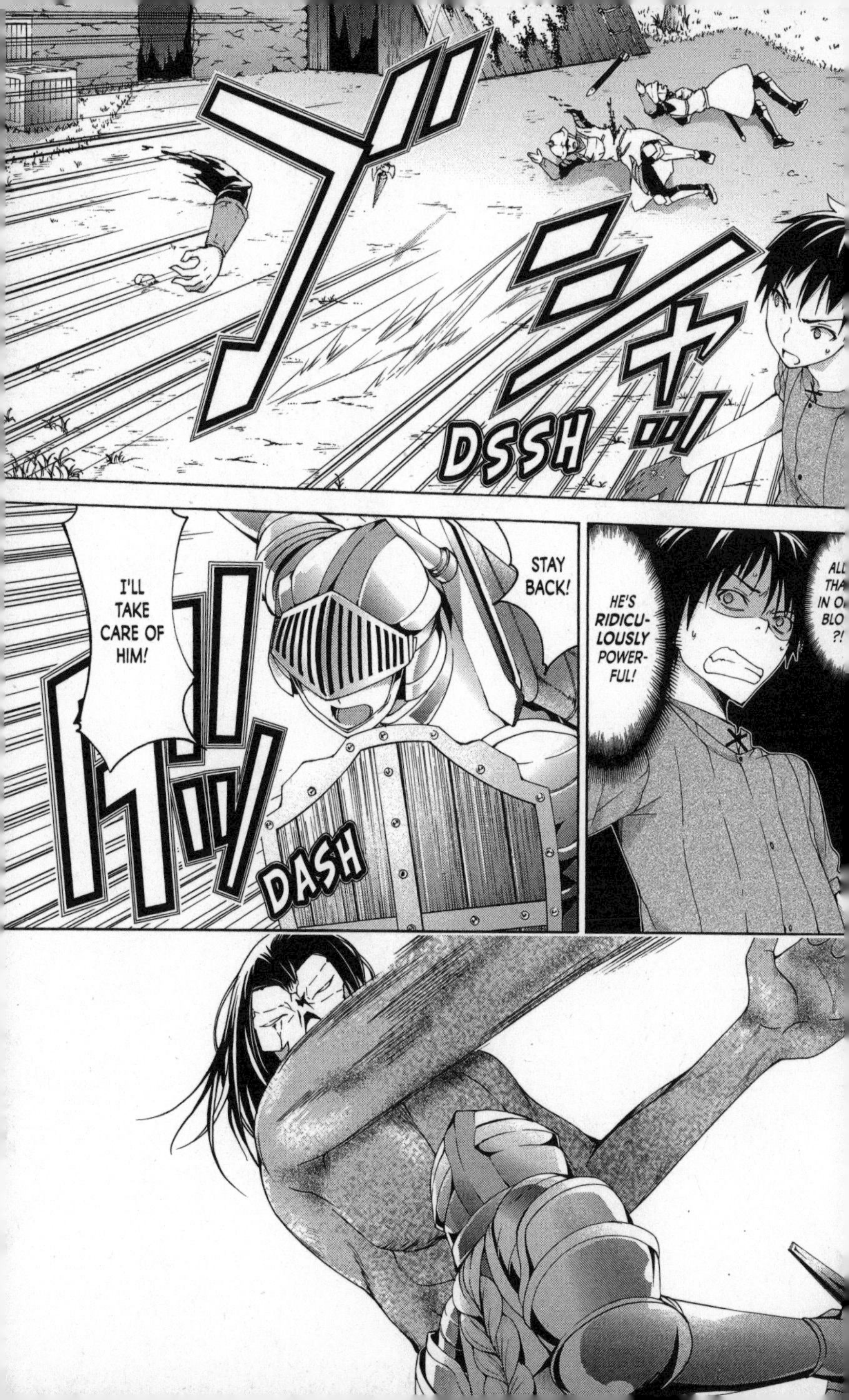
DSSH
HE'S RIDICULOUSLY POWERFUL!
STAY BACK!
I'LL TAKE CARE OF HIM!
DASH

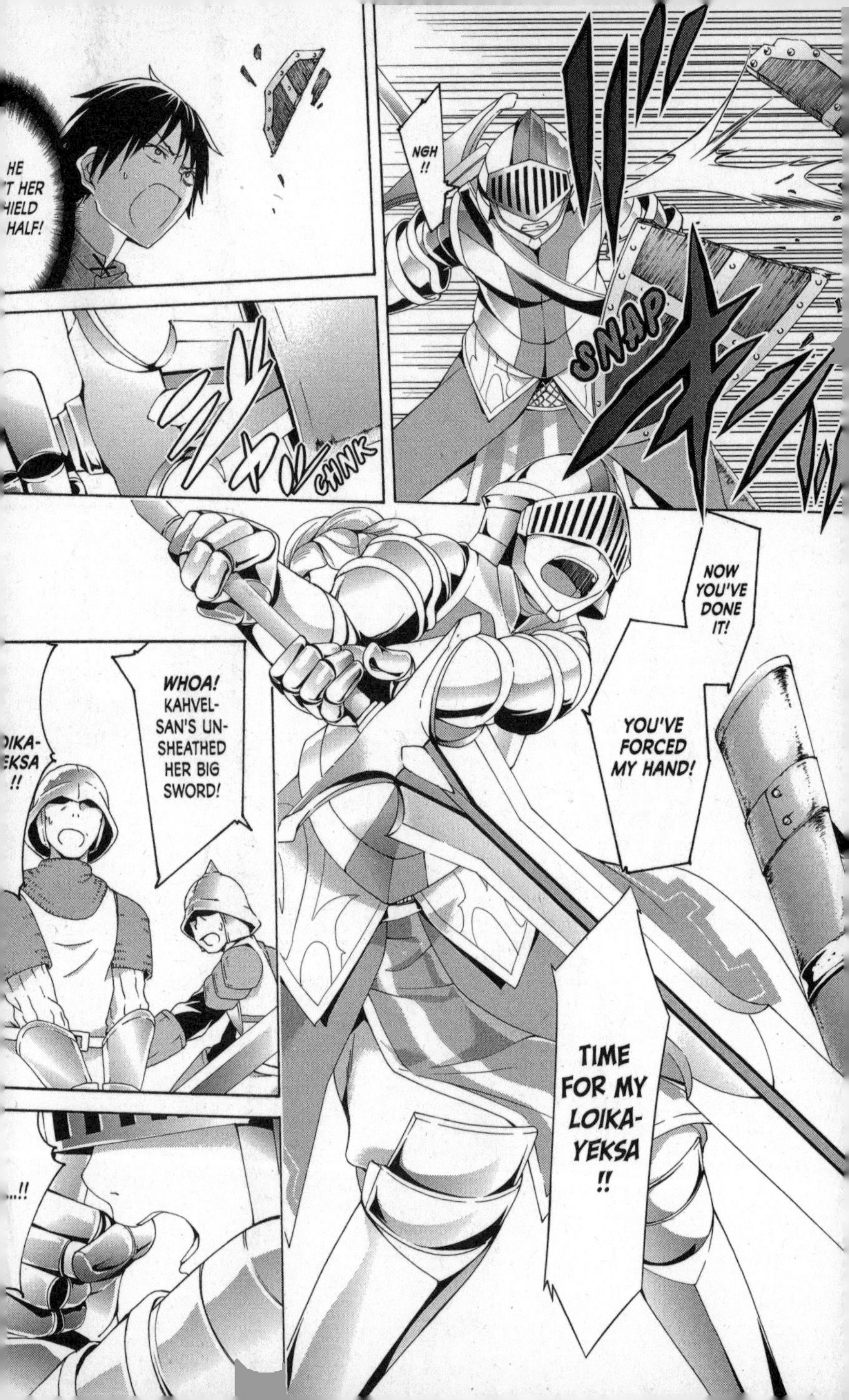
NGH !!
SNAP
HE 'T HER HIELD HALF!
CHINK
NOW YOU'VE DONE IT!
YOU'VE FORCED MY HAND!
TIME FOR MY LOIKA-YEKSA !!
WHOA! KAHVEL-SAN'S UN-SHEATHED HER BIG SWORD!
OIKA-EKSA !!
...!!

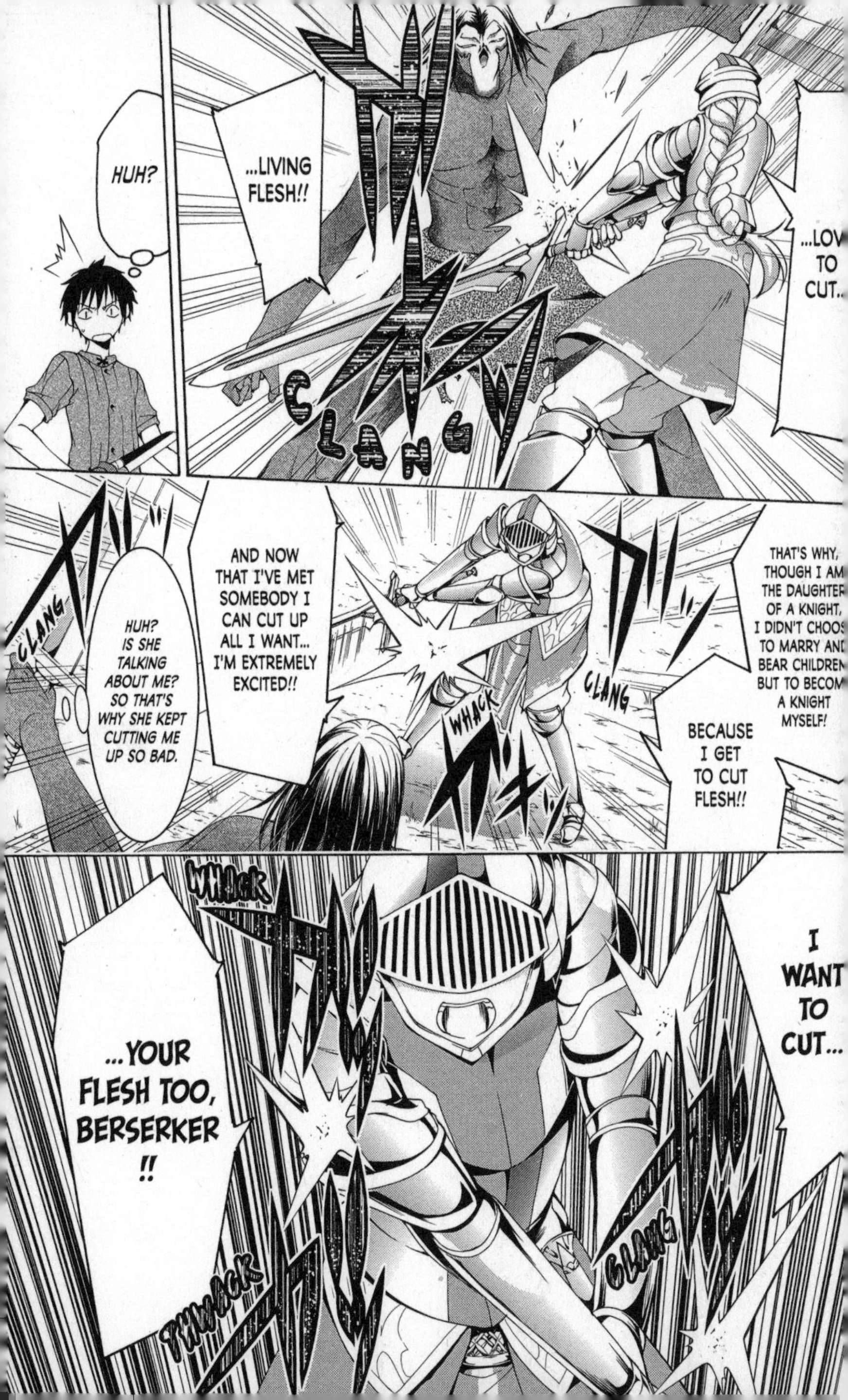
...LOV TO CUT..
...LIVING FLESH!!
HUH?
CLANG
THAT'S WHY, THOUGH I AM THE DAUGHTER OF A KNIGHT, I DIDN'T CHOOS TO MARRY AND BEAR CHILDREN BUT TO BECOM A KNIGHT MYSELF!
BECAUSE I GET TO CUT FLESH!!
CLANG
WHACK
AND NOW THAT I'VE MET SOMEBODY I CAN CUT UP ALL I WANT... I'M EXTREMELY EXCITED!!
HUH? IS SHE TALKING ABOUT ME? SO THAT'S WHY SHE KEPT CUTTING ME UP SO BAD.
CLANG
I WANT TO CUT...
...YOUR FLESH TOO, BERSERKER!!
WHACK
CLANG
THWACK

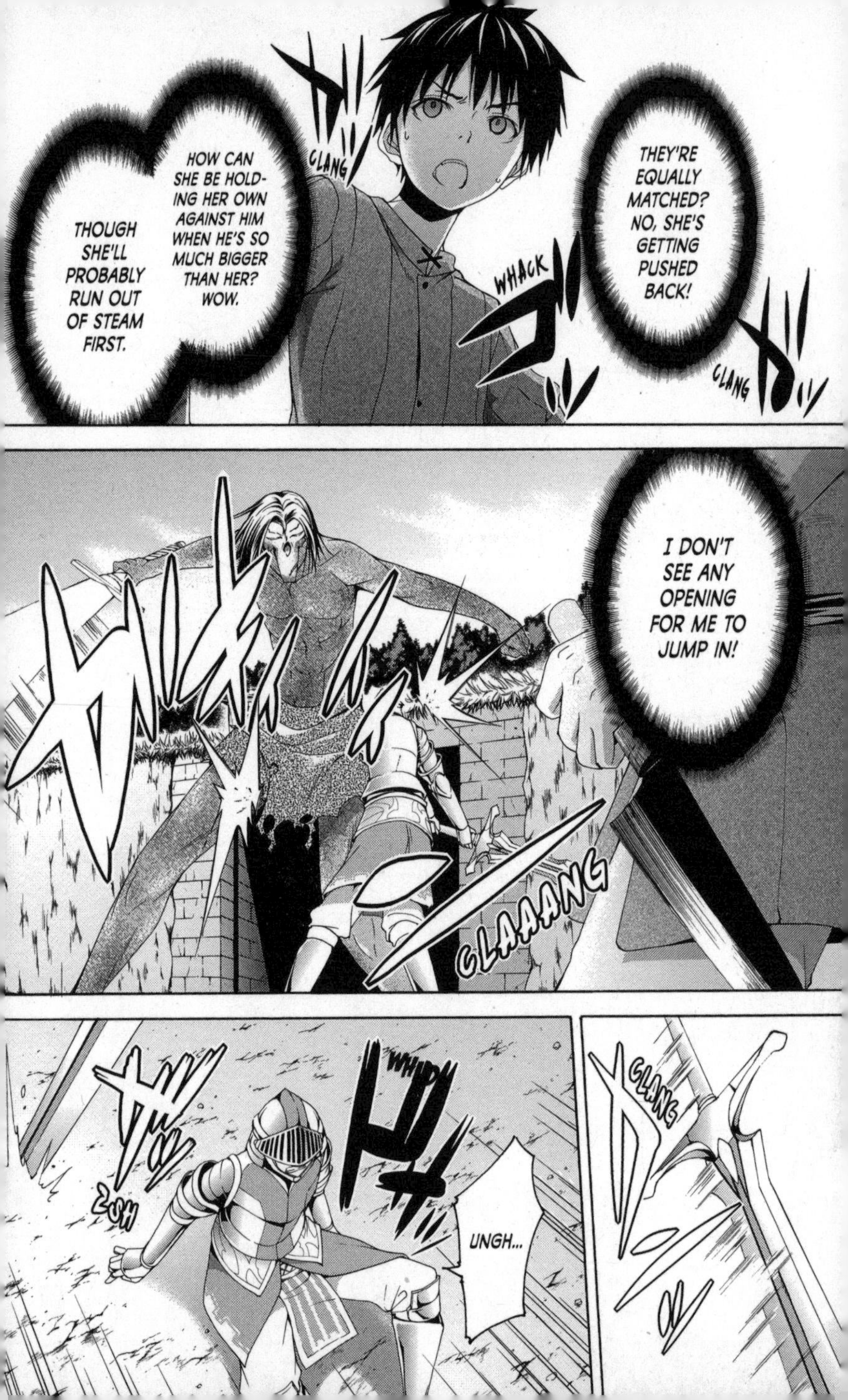
THEY'RE EQUALLY MATCHED? NO, SHE'S GETTING PUSHED BACK!
CLANG
WHACK
CLANG
HOW CAN SHE BE HOLD-ING HER OWN AGAINST HIM WHEN HE'S SO MUCH BIGGER THAN HER? WOW.
THOUGH SHE'LL PROBABLY RUN OUT OF STEAM FIRST.
I DON'T SEE ANY OPENING FOR ME TO JUMP IN!
CLAAANG
CLANG
WHIP
UNGH...
ZSH

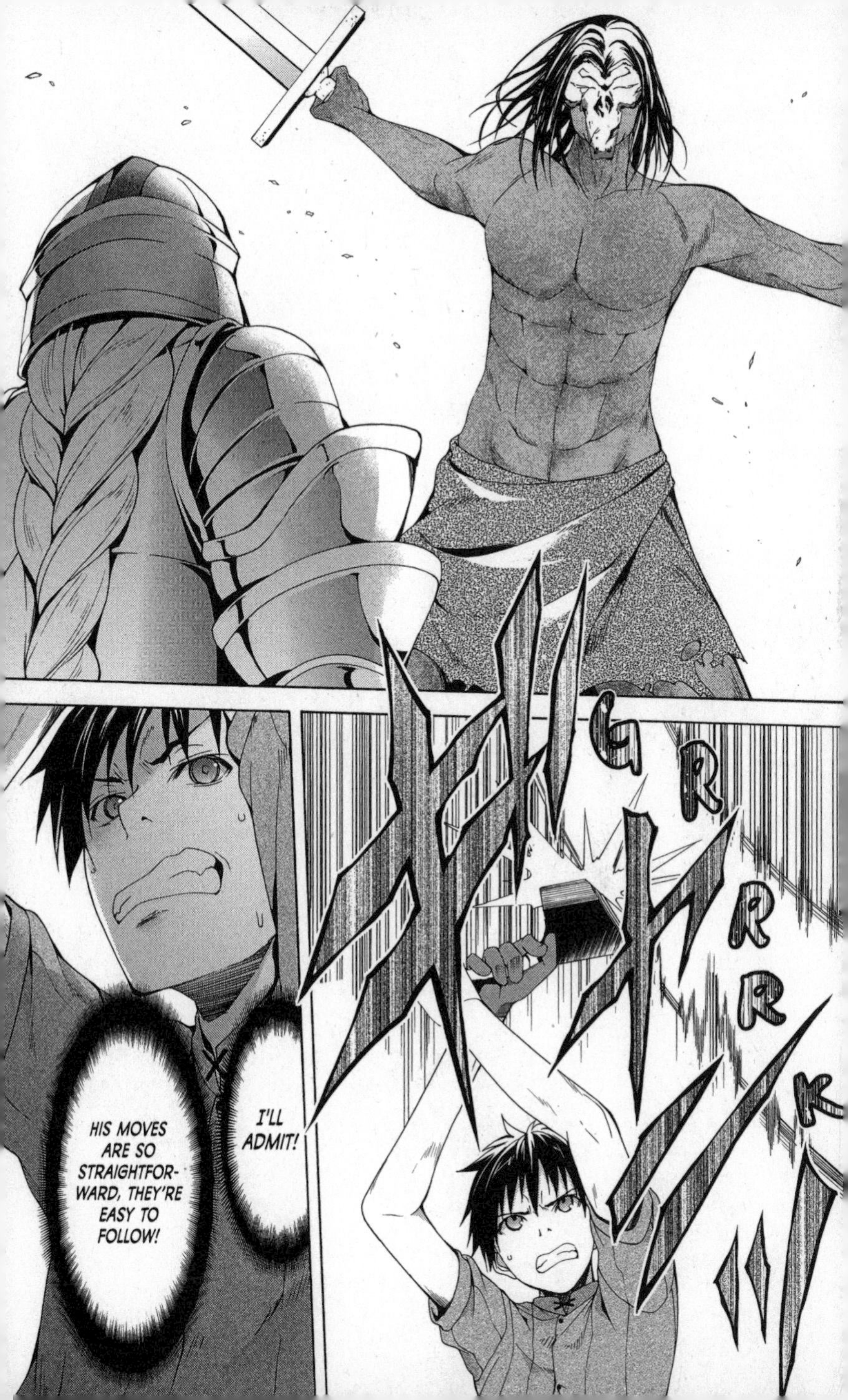
GRRRRK
I'LL ADMIT!
HIS MOVES ARE SO STRAIGHTFOR-WARD, THEY'RE EASY TO FOLLOW!

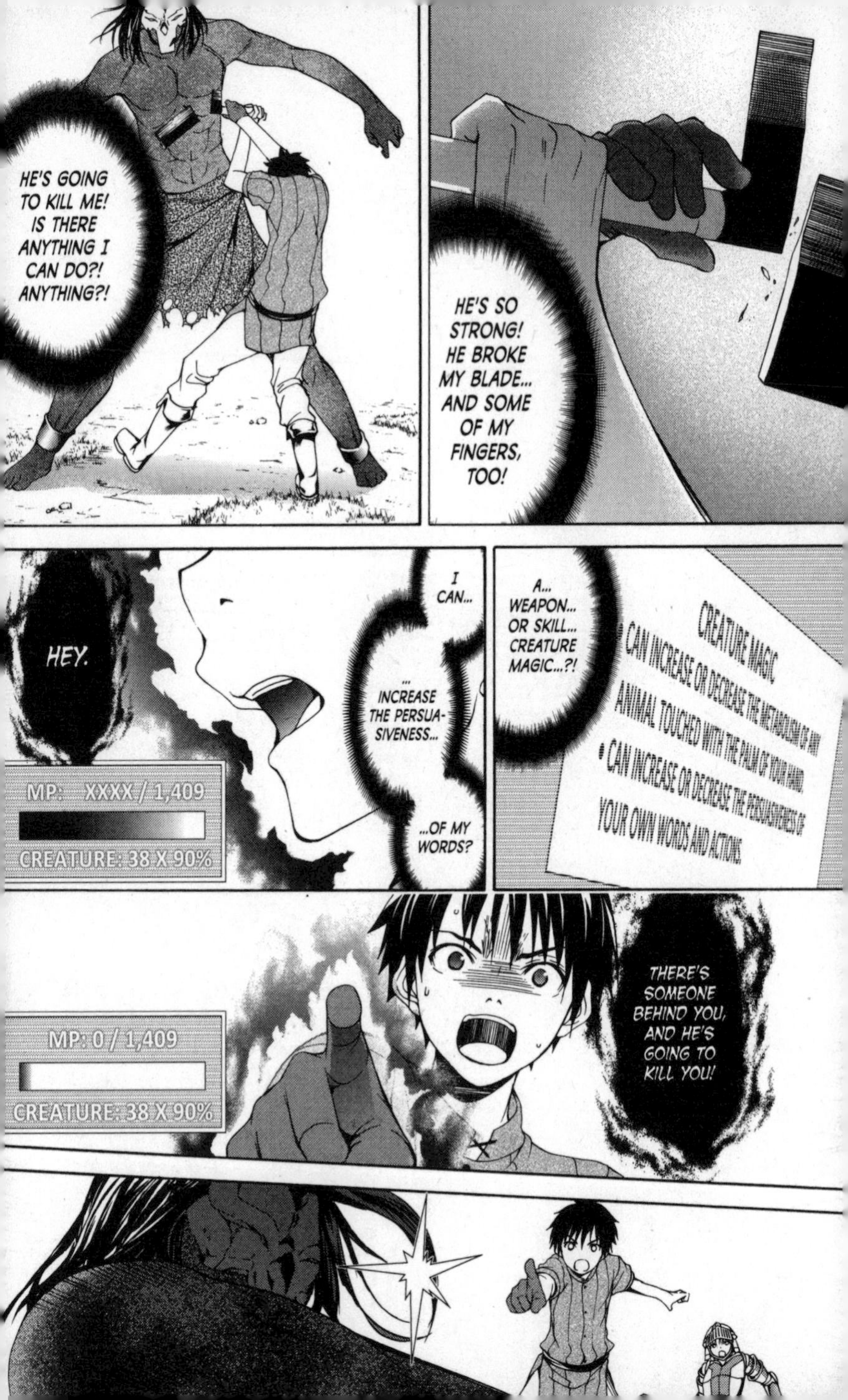
HE'S SO STRONG! HE BROKE MY BLADE... AND SOME OF MY FINGERS, TOO!
HE'S GOING TO KILL ME! IS THERE ANYTHING I CAN DO?! ANYTHING?!
A... WEAPON... OR SKILL... CREATURE MAGIC...?!
CREATURE MAGIC
• CAN INCREASE OR DECREASE THE METABOLISM OF ANY ANIMAL TOUCHED WITH THE PALM OF YOUR HAND
• CAN INCREASE OR DECREASE THE PERSUASIVENESS OF YOUR OWN WORDS AND ACTIONS
I CAN...
...INCREASE THE PERSUA-SIVENESS...
...OF MY WORDS?
HEY.
MP: XXXX / 1,409
CREATURE: 38 X 90%
THERE'S SOMEONE BEHIND YOU, AND HE'S GOING TO KILL YOU!
MP: 0 / 1,409
CREATURE: 38 X 90%

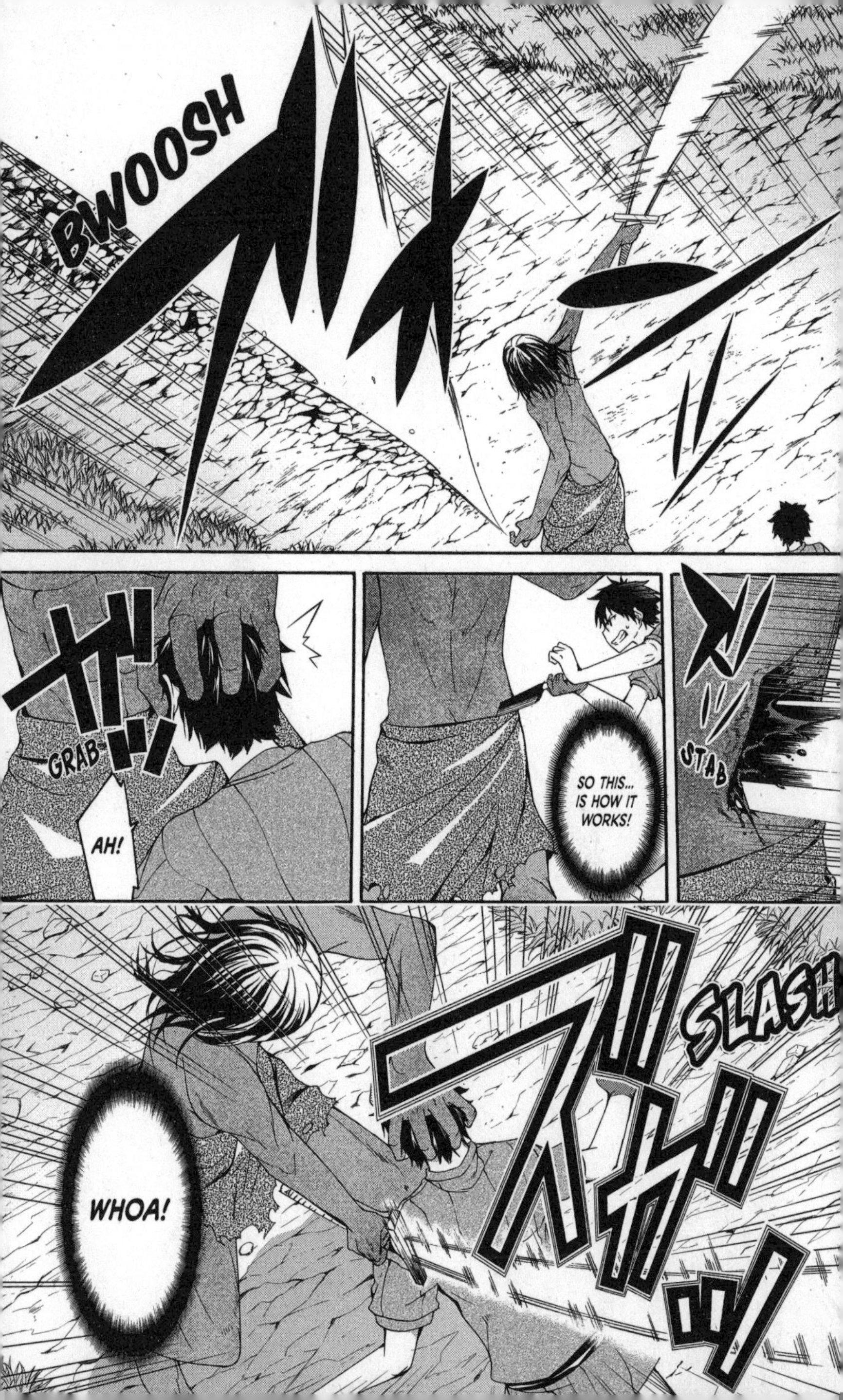
BWOOSH
STAB
SO THIS... IS HOW IT WORKS!
GRAB
AH!
SLASH
WHOA!

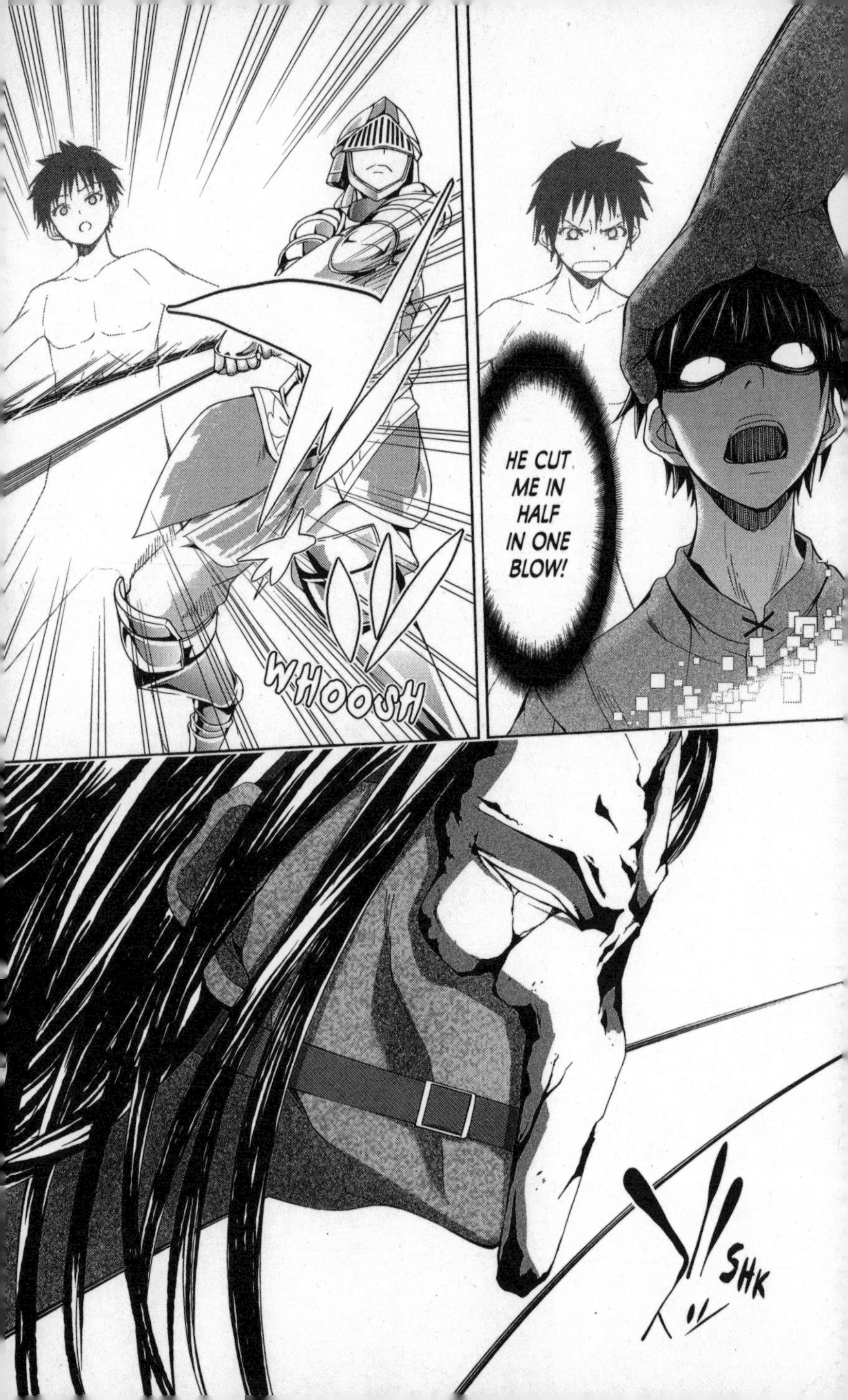
HE CUT ME IN HALF IN ONE BLOW!
WHOOSH
SHK

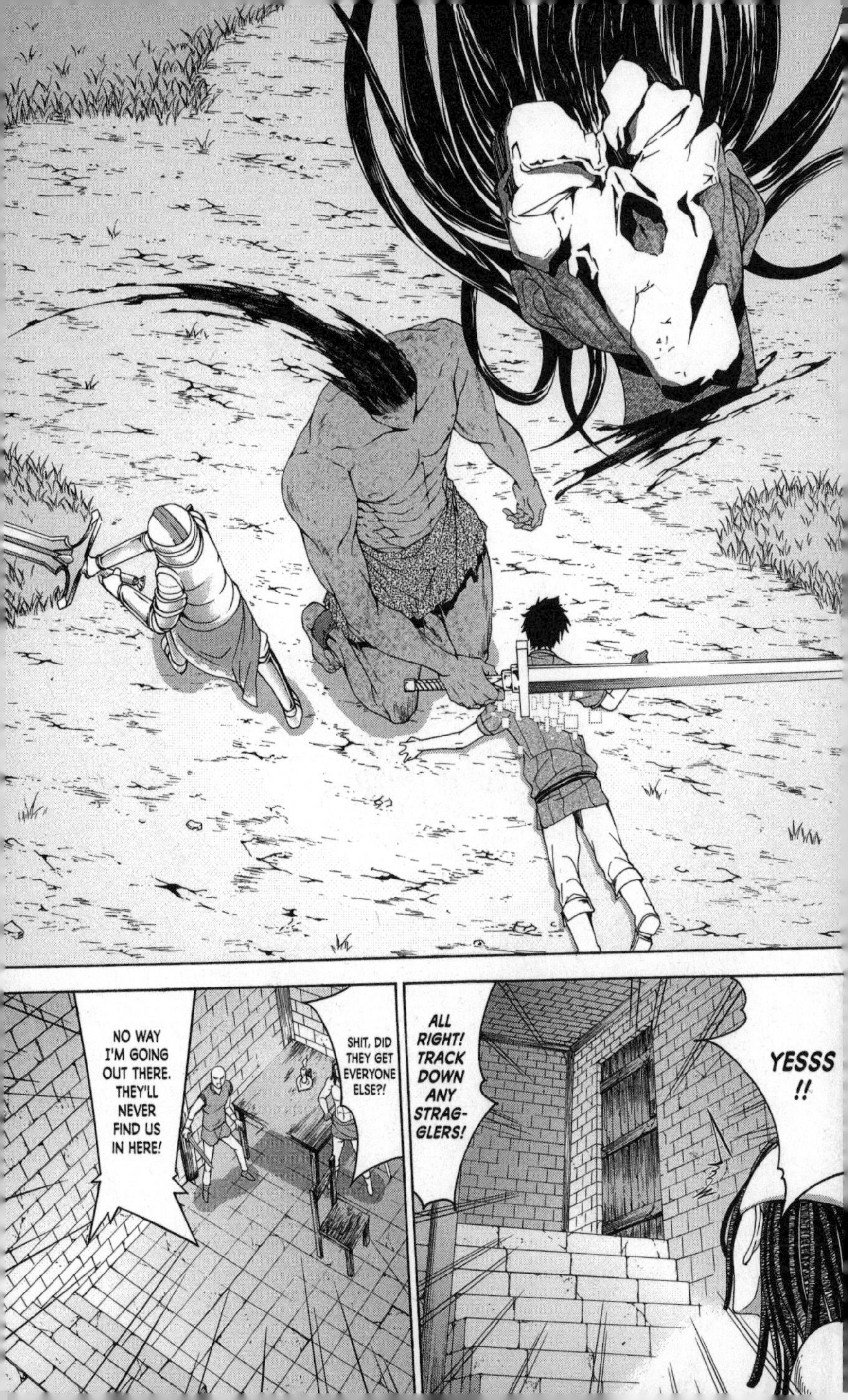
YESSS !!
ALL RIGHT! TRACK DOWN ANY STRAG-GLERS!
SHIT, DID THEY GET EVERYONE ELSE?!
NO WAY I'M GOING OUT THERE. THEY'LL NEVER FIND US IN HERE!

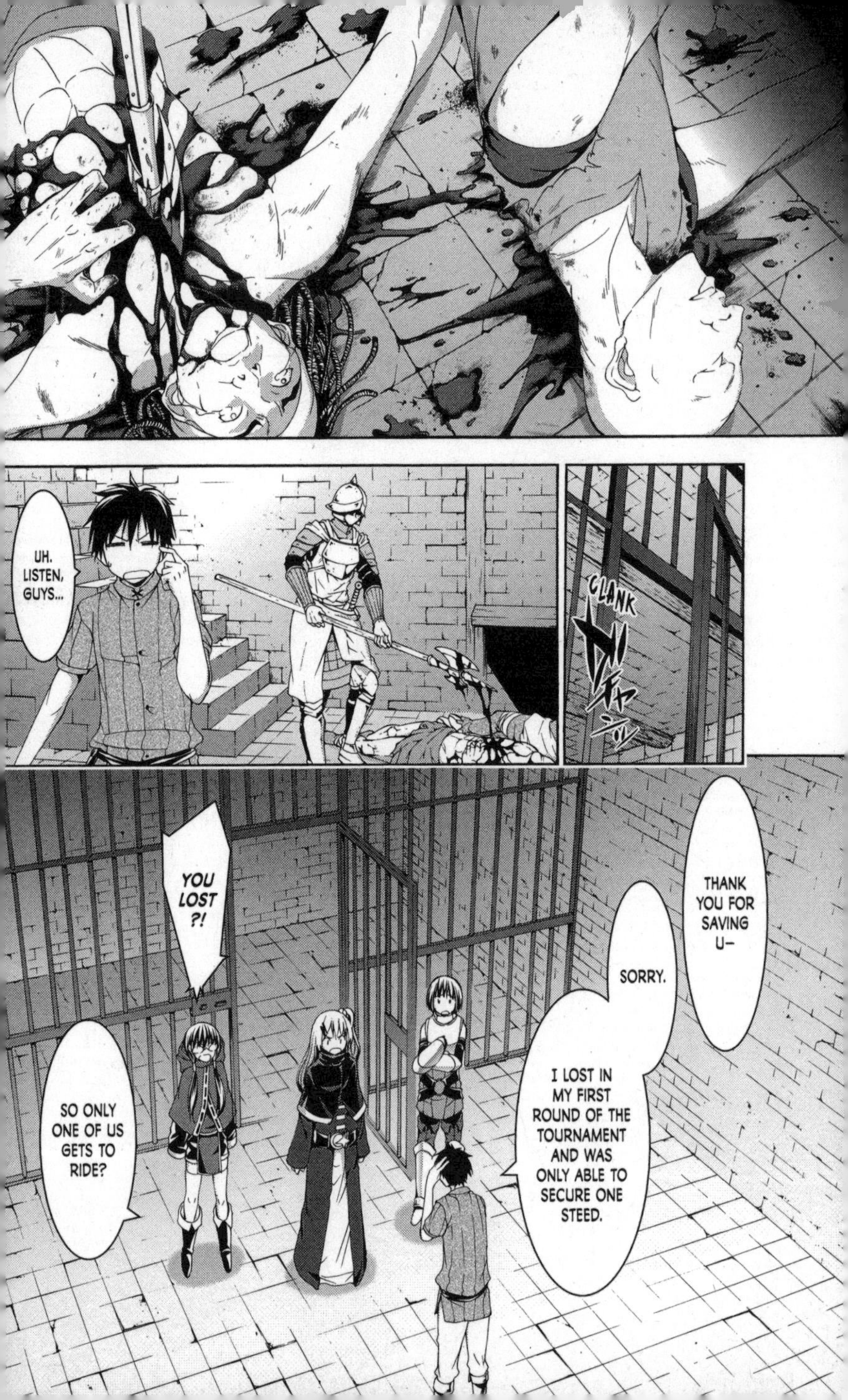
CLANK
UH. LISTEN, GUYS...
THANK YOU FOR SAVING U—
SORRY.
I LOST IN MY FIRST ROUND OF THE TOURNAMENT AND WAS ONLY ABLE TO SECURE ONE STEED.
YOU LOST?!
SO ONLY ONE OF US GETS TO RIDE?

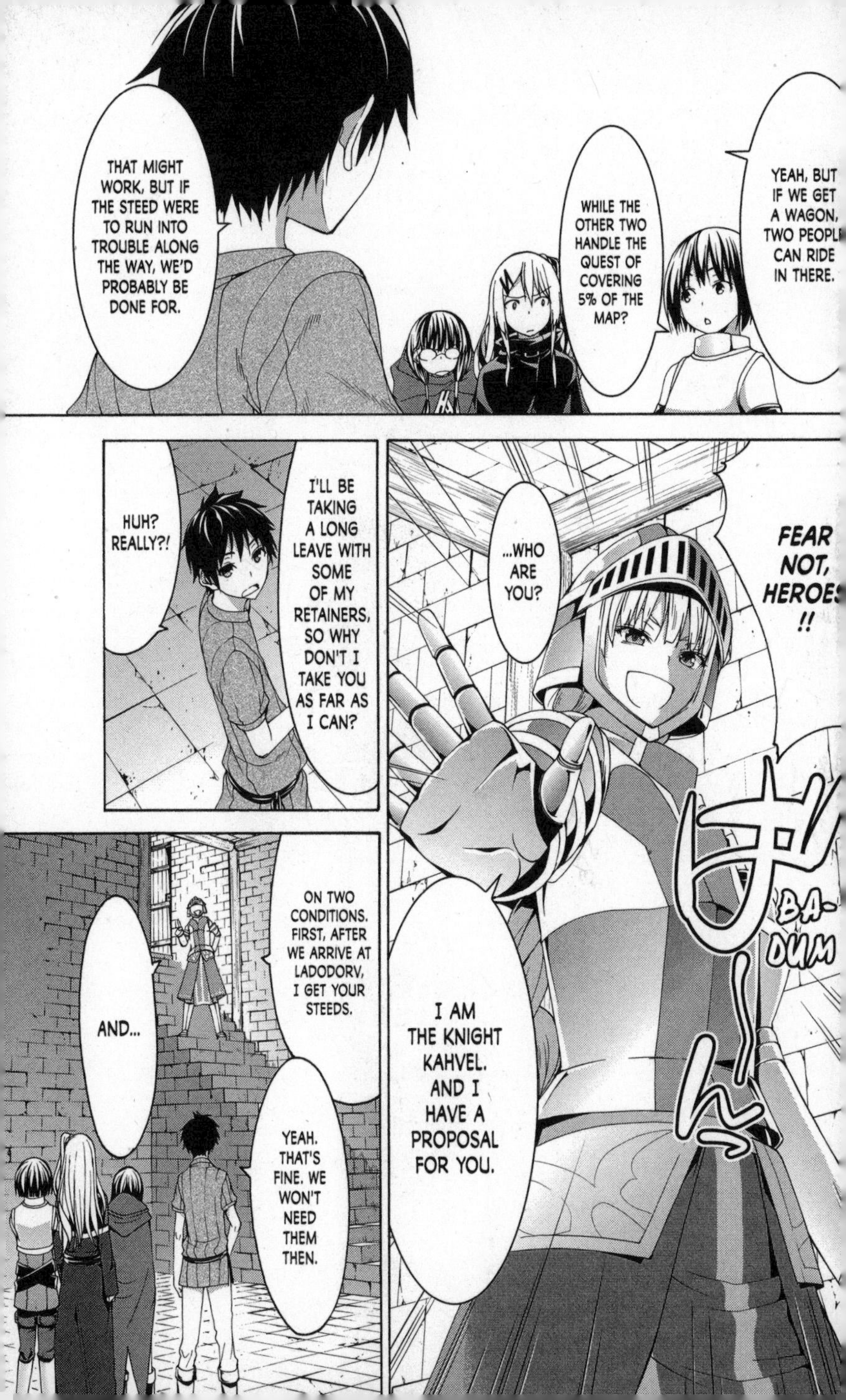
YEAH, BUT IF WE GET A WAGON, TWO PEOPL CAN RIDE IN THERE.
WHILE THE OTHER TWO HANDLE THE QUEST OF COVERING 5% OF THE MAP?
THAT MIGHT WORK, BUT IF THE STEED WERE TO RUN INTO TROUBLE ALONG THE WAY, WE'D PROBABLY BE DONE FOR.
FEAR NOT, HEROES !!
...WHO ARE YOU?
BA-DUM
I AM THE KNIGHT KAHVEL. AND I HAVE A PROPOSAL FOR YOU.
I'LL BE TAKING A LONG LEAVE WITH SOME OF MY RETAINERS, SO WHY DON'T I TAKE YOU AS FAR AS I CAN?
HUH? REALLY?!
ON TWO CONDITIONS. FIRST, AFTER WE ARRIVE AT LADODORV, I GET YOUR STEEDS.
AND...
YEAH. THAT'S FINE. WE WON'T NEED THEM THEN.

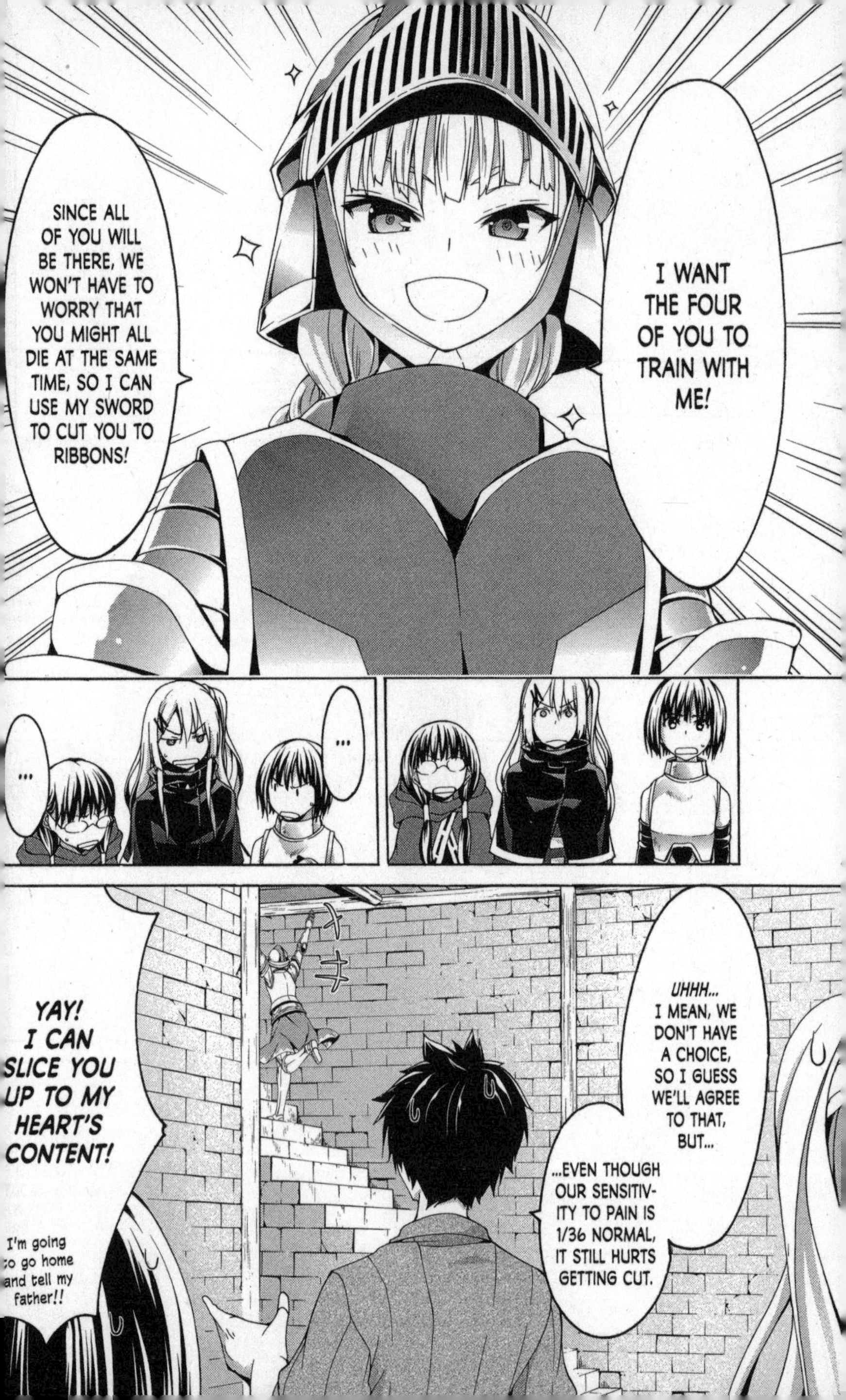
I WANT THE FOUR OF YOU TO TRAIN WITH ME!
SINCE ALL OF YOU WILL BE THERE, WE WON'T HAVE TO WORRY THAT YOU MIGHT ALL DIE AT THE SAME TIME, SO I CAN USE MY SWORD TO CUT YOU TO RIBBONS!
...
...
UHHH... I MEAN, WE DON'T HAVE A CHOICE, SO I GUESS WE'LL AGREE TO THAT, BUT...
...EVEN THOUGH OUR SENSITIVITY TO PAIN IS 1/36 NORMAL, IT STILL HURTS GETTING CUT.
YAY! I CAN SLICE YOU UP TO MY HEART'S CONTENT!
I'm going o go home and tell my father!!

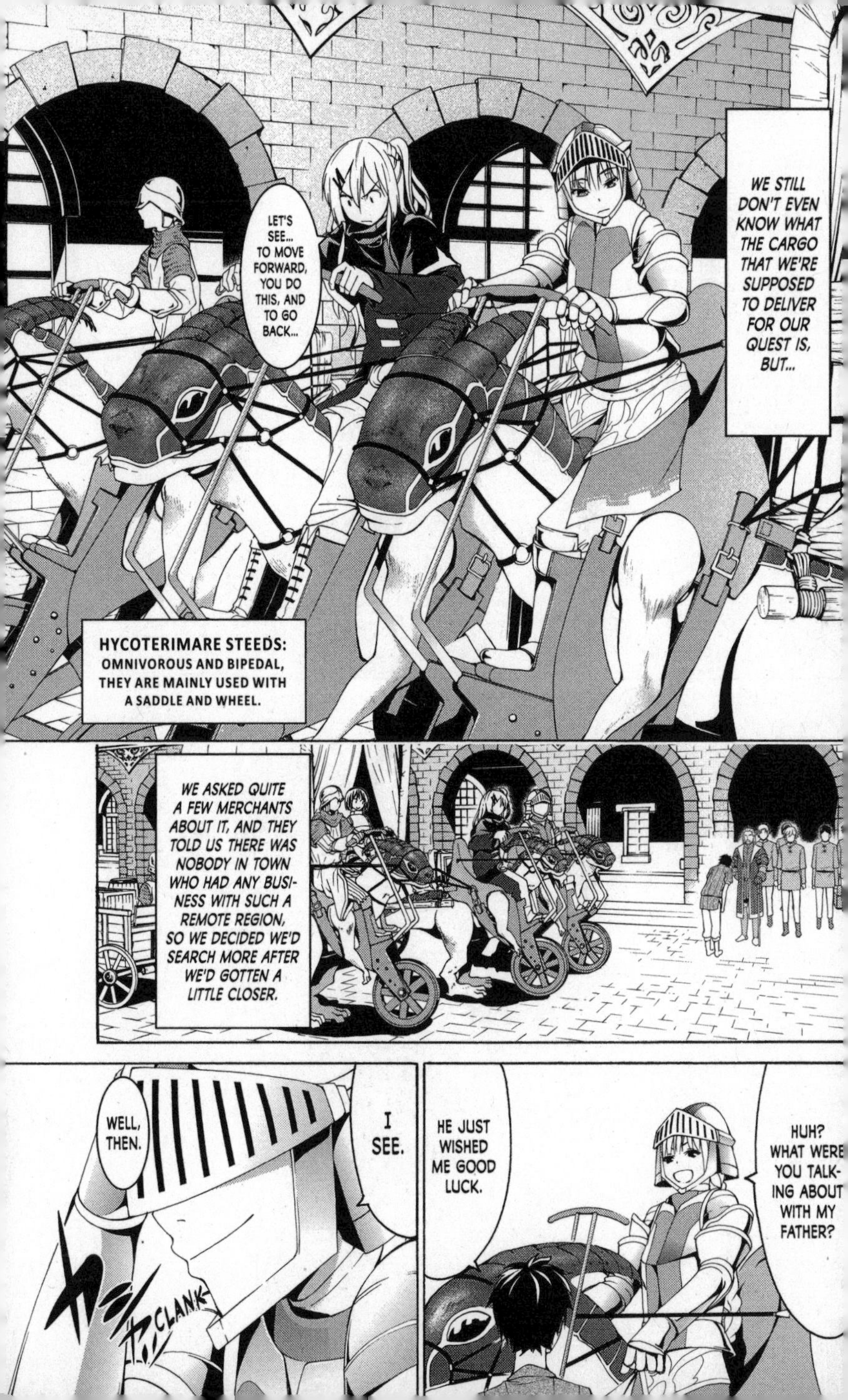
WE STILL DON'T EVEN KNOW WHAT THE CARGO THAT WE'RE SUPPOSED TO DELIVER FOR OUR QUEST IS, BUT...
LET'S SEE... TO MOVE FORWARD, YOU DO THIS, AND TO GO BACK...
HYCOTERIMARE STEEDS: OMNIVOROUS AND BIPEDAL, THEY ARE MAINLY USED WITH A SADDLE AND WHEEL.
WE ASKED QUITE A FEW MERCHANTS ABOUT IT, AND THEY TOLD US THERE WAS NOBODY IN TOWN WHO HAD ANY BUSINESS WITH SUCH A REMOTE REGION, SO WE DECIDED WE'D SEARCH MORE AFTER WE'D GOTTEN A LITTLE CLOSER.
HUH? WHAT WERE YOU TALKING ABOUT WITH MY FATHER?
HE JUST WISHED ME GOOD LUCK.
I SEE.
WELL, THEN.
CLANK

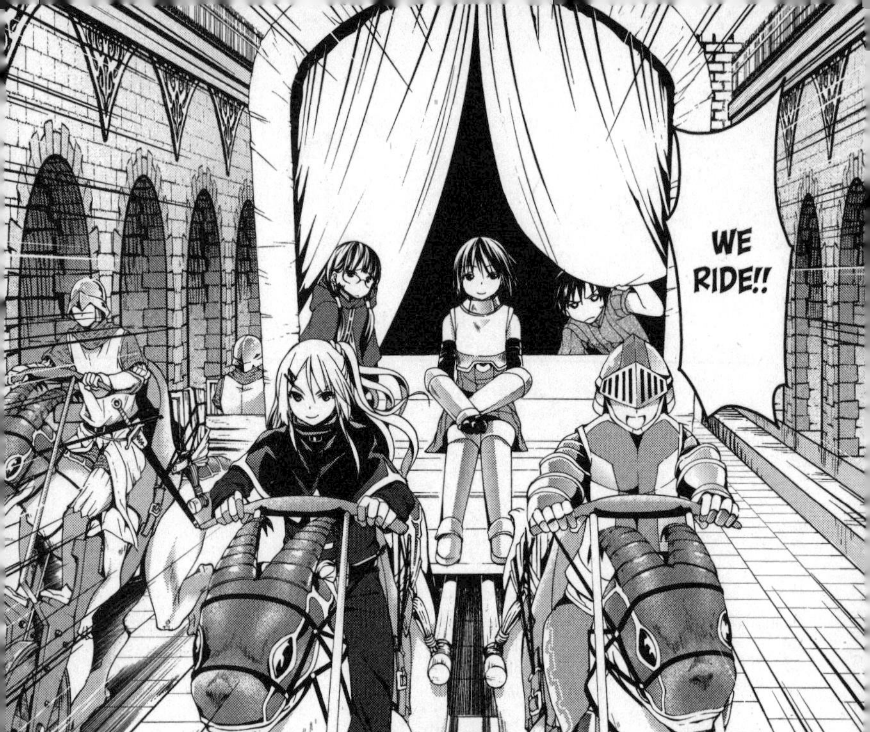
WE RIDE!!

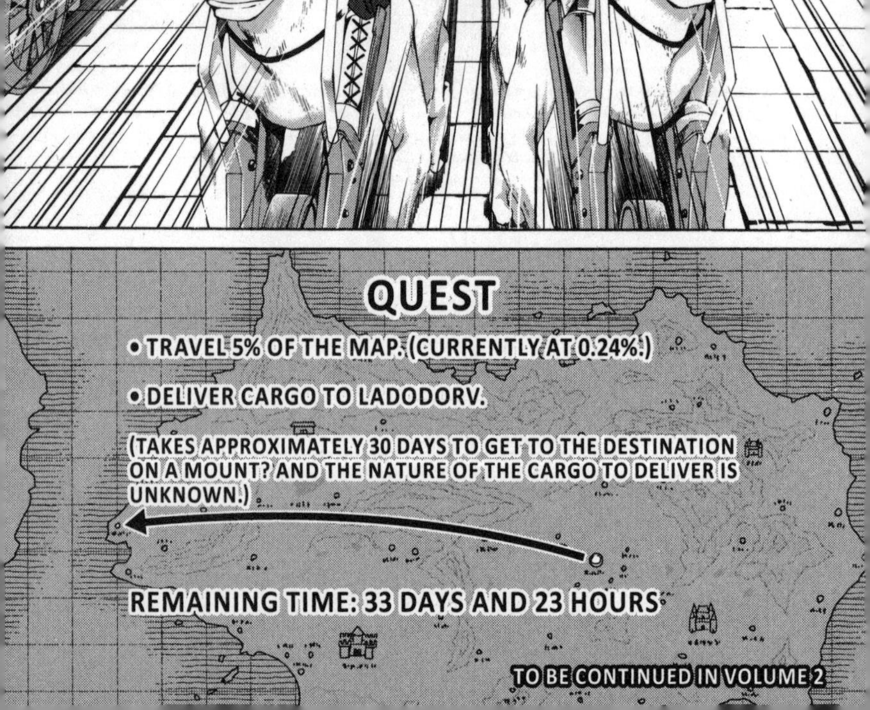
QUEST
• TRAVEL 5% OF THE MAP. (CURRENTLY AT 0.24%.)
• DELIVER CARGO TO LADODORV.
(TAKES APPROXIMATELY 30 DAYS TO GET TO THE DESTINATION ON A MOUNT? AND THE NATURE OF THE CARGO TO DELIVER IS UNKNOWN.)
REMAINING TIME: 33 DAYS AND 23 HOURS
TO BE CONTINUED IN VOLUME 2

This is my first serialization ever, so I'm making your acquaintance for the first time. It's nice to meet you all! My name is Yamakawa, and I am the writer of this story.

I'd say we've been incorporating a lot of current events into this manga, in figurative ways, so from volume 2 onwards, I plan on devoting this corner of the book to going over that. Maybe not so much offering detailed explanations as giving you some brief notes, though.

There are two kinds of elements in manga: universal elements and current elements. Works with comparatively more of the former include *Phoenix*, *Doraemon*, *Crayon Shin-chan*, *Pokemon*, stories without contemporary figures in them in the historical, science fiction, and fantasy genres, and so on. As for current elements, those can be broken down into two categories: physical and mental. The physical elements are generally modern conveniences. For example, I'm sure everyone's heard of how the advent of cell phones has made romantic dramas harder to pull off. In the same vein, detective and cop shows aren't able to rely on the same tricks anymore, what with the emergence of cell phones, smartphones, PCs, the Internet, GPS, ubiquitous security cameras, and faster means of transportation.

We can see a pattern where something that seemed universal at the time of its creation ended up becoming dated due to modern conveniences. As for the mental elements, I refer to writing based on values shared by modern-day Japanese people. This applies to the majority of works that would be classified as contemporary, though almost all works possess both universal and current elements. The ratio simply differs between one work and the next.

Among the titles listed above, the ratio of universal elements to current ones isn't 100/0, it's simply above 50/50. For example, *Astro Boy* is a sci-fi that doesn't feature the people of its time, but since its image of the future was created back in 1952, it feels less futuristic to us modern-day people.

You may recall that I specified that only those historical, sci-fi, and fantasy series without contemporary figures in them would be more universal. Well, in the vision of the future that *Astro Boy* presents, you can imagine that Professor Ochanomizu has the mentality of a Japanese man from 1952. If that mentality doesn't resonate with the reader due to generational changes, then that portion is dated, while other aspects of the work remain universal. Let's say that in *Astro Boy*, the ratio of universal to current elements is 70/30.

Phoenix and *Doraemon* would both have a ratio of around 90/10. Even in the contemporary category, the ratio tends to be around 50/50. For example, right now in 2016, how you incorporate the March 11, 2011 earthquake off the Pacific coast of Tohoku, Japan into a work would vastly change that ratio. Whether or not you include the earthquake in a story is not what matters. It's whether your characters share the same losses, learn the same lessons, and have the same fears. For example, the movie *Shin Godzilla* (aka *Godzilla Resurgence*), which came out in 2016, used the monster as a metaphor for an earthquake, posing the question, "How should a government react to such a catastrophe?" Let's say here that it's got a 30/70 ratio.

And right now in 2016, in the Kanto region (Tokyo and several of its surrounding prefectures), when people say "disastrous earthquake," they're referring to the one from March 11th. That's because the Kumamoto earthquakes from earlier this year didn't shock the psyches of the Kanto people the same way the 2011 one did, with its proximity, high death toll, resulting tsunami, and nuclear power plant accident. If we were back in 1923, people would surely think of the Great Kanto Earthquake, and it's easy to imagine that in the future, there will be yet more earthquakes to overwrite the old ones. Having that one word, "earthquake," automatically point to the March 11th one is an element that would make a work dated.

So you see how there can be a clear divide in the reading experience when it comes to stories that are more universal versus ones that are more current. One has to wonder whether a given work will resonate with future or overseas readers in the same way as contemporary readers. You could even say that a work can have an expiration date of sorts.

Of course, works with more universal elements in them will have a longer shelf life. But those with more current elements in them can resonate more easily with contemporary Japanese readers, because the characters are living in modern-day Japan just like they are. It's that kind of resonance I felt when reading *Lucifer and the Biscuit Hammer* when I was around 20, which is why I still consider it the second-best manga I've ever read.

So I'm going to do my best to reach the quality of *Lucifer and the Biscuit Hammer*, or even surpass it. And now, I will write the conclusion to what turned out to be a very long opening remark:

I am aiming for this manga to be about 30/70.

The end.
That was a really short conclusion (LOL)

August 2016

"This manga is super weird."

It was about two years ago that I heard those words. It was my editor, handing me the script to this story and wanting me to read it in the *Shonen Magazine* editorial department.

And it turned out to be true. This story really is a weird one. I don't mean that in a bad way, though. When it comes to manga, and this editor in particular, "weird" can be the highest of compliments.

In any case, it's not that it's refreshing and that the hero is really likable. In fact, it's unlikely you'll be able to sympathize with him. And the heroines are super realistic and true to life. In what is nowadays probably the most popular genre—the ol' students being transported into another world story—these could very well be lethal points against it.

But you cannot help turning the page to see what happens next.

When enjoying manga, novels, or video games, there are times when we find ourselves thinking the same things Yotsuya does:

"I'm abandoning this cute girl, ethical choices be damned!"

"Screw that. I'm just going to carry out the mission and be done with it!"

I believe that mysterious charm of the protagonist, Yusuke Yotsuya, is one of the things that makes this manga fun to read.

I've never drawn a manga of this type before, but I am going to give it my all.

Akinari Nao

GAME MAST'S NOTES FROM TRANSLATE

GAP MOE

A CHARACTER WHO'S APPEALING BECAUSE THEY ACT SURPRISINGLY (DUE TO THE GAP BETWEEN EXPECTATIONS AND THEIR ACTIONS).

IS THIS WHAT THEY CALL GAP MOE?

LOIKA-YEKSA

A NAME DERIVED FROM ESTONIAN WORDS FOR "EIGHT" AND "CUT," BASED ON THE JAPANESE TERM *YATSUZAKI*, MEANING TO CUT TO PIECES (LITERALLY, "CUT INTO EIGHTHS").

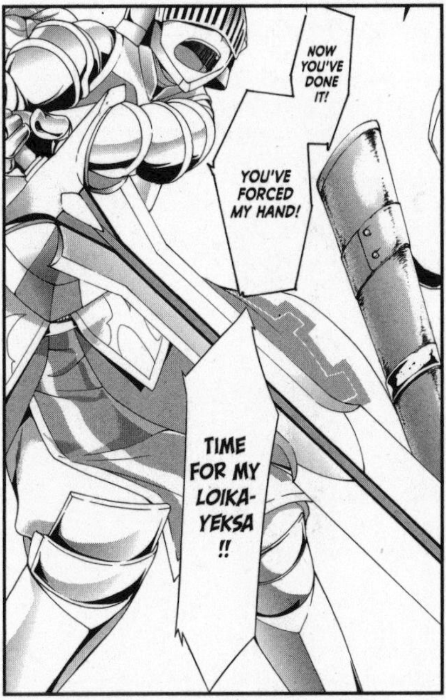
NOW YOU'VE DONE IT!
YOU'VE FORCED MY HAND!
TIME FOR MY LOIKA-YEKSA !!

I'm Standing on a Million Lives volume 1 is a work of fiction. Names, characters, places, and incidents are the products of the author's imagination or are used fictitiously. Any resemblance to actual events, locales, or persons, living or dead, is entirely coincidental.

A Kodansha Comics Trade Paperback Original
I'm Standing on a Million Lives volume 1 copyright © 2016 Naoki Yamakawa/Akinari Nao
English translation copyright © 2019 Naoki Yamakawa/Akinari Nao

All rights reserved.

Published in the United States by Kodansha Comics, an imprint of
Kodansha USA Publishing, LLC, New York.

Publication rights for this English edition arranged through
Kodansha Ltd, Tokyo.

First published in Japan in 2016 by Kodansha Ltd., Tokyo.

ISBN 978-1-63236-821-8

Printed in the United States of America.

www.kodanshacomics.com

9 8 7 6 5 4 3 2 1
Translation: Christine Dashiell
Lettering: Thea Willis
Editing: Erin Subramanian, Ben Applegate, and Tiff Ferentini
Kodansha Comics edition cover design by Phil Balsman